Camping and Tramping
in Australia's national parks

CAMPING AND TRAMPING
IN AUSTRALIA'S NATIONAL PARKS

Keren Flavell

RANDOM HOUSE AUSTRALIA

Random House Australia Pty Ltd
20 Alfred Street, Milsons Point, NSW 2061
http://www.randomhouse.com.au

Sydney New York Toronto
London Auckland Johannesburg

First published 1994, second edition published 1999.
This edition published 2002.

Copyright © Keren Flavell 1994, 1999, 2002.

All rights reserved. No part of this publication may be reproduced, stored in a retrieval system, or transmitted in any form or by any means, electronic, mechanical, photocopying, recording or otherwise, without the prior written permission of the publisher.

National Library of Australia
Cataloguing-in-Publication Entry

Flavell, Keren.
  Camping and tramping in Australia's national parks.

  [Updated and Rev ed.].
  Includes index.
  ISBN 1 74051 131 X.

  1. Campsites, facilities, etc. – Australia. 2. Trails –
  Australia – Guidebooks. 3. Australia – Guidebooks.
  I. Title.

919.4047

Maps by Theo Chiotis. State maps by Anna Warren
Typeset by Asset Typesetting Pty Ltd, Moruya, New South Wales
Printed and bound by Griffin Press, Netley, South Australia

10 9 8 7 6 5 4

Disclaimer: Every effort has been made to ensure information provided in this book was correct at time of publication. Neither the author nor the publisher accepts any liability for difficulties of any kind arising as a result of any opinion, advice, recommendation, representation or information expressly or implicitly published in or relating to this publication notwithstanding any negligence, default or lack of care.

Contents

KEY TO MAPS	VI	**WESTERN AUSTRALIA**	**203**
		The Kimberley	206
INTRODUCTION	VII	The Pilbara	210
		The Gascoyne	219
VICTORIA	**1**	The Midwest	220
Southwest and Coast	3	Swan Region	223
The Mallee	15	Central Forest	226
Around Melbourne	21	Southern Forest	229
Northeast and Alps	26	South Coast	234
Gippsland and the Far East	38		
		SOUTH AUSTRALIA	**245**
AUSTRALIAN CAPITAL		Far West	248
TERRITORY	**55**	Eyre Peninsula	249
		Far North	250
NEW SOUTH WALES	**59**	North	255
Alpine	63	Yorke Peninsula	256
Southeast	64	Fleurieu Peninsula	259
Central	77	The Murraylands	261
New England and		Southeast	261
Escarpment Forests	97		
North Coast and Hinterland	105	**TASMANIA**	**265**
West	115	Northeast	268
Far West	121	Southeast	271
		Southwest	277
QUEENSLAND	**127**	West	282
Southwest	130	Northwest	285
Southeast	140		
Central Coast	152	**INFORMATION AND**	
North	155	**BOOKING CENTRES**	**289**
Far North	162		
Inland	171	**DIARY OF EVENTS**	
		AND HOLIDAYS	**303**
NORTHERN TERRITORY	**177**		
The Centre	179	**INDEX**	**309**
Katherine Region	189		
The Top End	199		

Key to Maps

Aboriginal art

Boat ramp

Camping area

Caravan park

Drinking water

Fireplace

First aid

Historic site

Information

Lookout

Parking

Petrol station

Picnic area

Ranger station

Refreshments

Roads
   Sealed road
   Unsealed road
   4WD track
   Track

Showers

Telephone

Toilets

Walking track

INTRODUCTION

Few people would disagree that Australia's national parks and state forests contain the most exciting range of natural features and wildlife in the country: from deserts to waterfalls and rugged gorges; mangroves to alpine wildflowers; bush stone curlews to yellow-footed wallabies.

In Australia we can see the landscape in its natural form, occupied and maintained by Aboriginal people for thousands of years. This is the drawcard for tourists in much the same way as are the cathedrals and palaces which attract tourists to Europe.

Before this guide was written I found it a costly and time-consuming exercise to access information about national parks and state forests throughout Australia. That was nearly ten years ago, and with the evolution of the internet it is now much easier to access park information from each of the environment and heritage departments. Web site and email addresses for the relevant parks service are located at the beginning of each chapter.

This revised edition also includes a new Aboriginal history section to help people find out more about the traditional owners for each area. Read the full description later in this Introduction.

In the seven years since *Camping and Tramping* first hit the shelves it has been reprinted three times and has sold over 12,000 copies, proving its success in helping vehicle-based travellers enjoy getting out into the natural spaces.

If you want to embark on more serious hiking, this book will guide you to the parks, but you will need to contact the park offices for the more detailed information you'll require to hike safely.

Although I have included around 300 national parks, state forests and historical sites, there will still be some omissions. The criteria for inclusion are, loosely, that there are some facilities for staying in the park, recognised walking tracks or other recreation opportunities, and access is not too difficult, or restricted. Many of the parks established as flora and fauna sanctuaries, or for the preservation of a particular environment, have not been included. Likewise, not all the established camping spots are listed here. Those that are included have been hand-picked from the many hundreds out there.

I do talk about caravan parks and resorts, but I prefer to camp in national park and state forest areas. There are usually picnic tables and fireplaces to make your stay more comfortable. The fees are quite inexpensive, and the low-key system of payment is often through a self-registration station, or directly to the ranger — invariably a valuable source of information on all aspects of the park. Campsites are often spaced well apart, so that even if you are staying in the national park during the holiday seasons, the peak-use time, you can still find a peaceful environment.

There are often walks from the campsite, nearby swimming holes to explore and other sights and attractions to see before you get back in the car. And because you're camping in the bush, you're likely to be visited by the local birds and animals.

The delicate nature of the protected species and areas of landscape deserves our respect. In particular, please recognise the immense value of Aboriginal sites and assist in their preservation by not touching rock paintings or disturbing historic features such as middens or canoe trees. Obey the park regulations which are set up to protect them, and follow commonsense rules to minimise the impact of your visit.

- Pets — There is a strict rule banning pets in national parks throughout Australia. The main reason for the rule is the harmful effect pets can have on the flora and fauna in the area; they can also be a nuisance to other travellers.
- Firearms — These are also banned from national parks.
- Washing — It is important not to allow any detergents or soaps near a water system. Even small amounts can pollute streams and rivers, affecting creatures and plants downstream. Sand can be a good alternative to using detergents, but take it away from the water's edge to use it.
- Toilet training — When camping where no facilities are provided, whether it be in national parks or otherwise, please respect the environment and other campers. It is very unpleasant finding piles of toilet paper while searching for firewood. Human faeces break down very quickly; paper does not. Dig a shallow hole and burn the paper. In fire danger season bury the lot or take the paper out with you.
- Food scraps — Some argue that food scraps are natural and can provide food for animals or decompose to help the soil. However, it is unlikely that the scraps you throw out will be part of the local food chain. Burying scraps can encourage animals to dig them up, contributing to erosion, and they may become dependent on an artificial food source. Also, scraps such as orange peel and onion skins take a long time to decompose, creating an eye-sore for others.
- Firewood — The lack of dead and fallen timber in several parks has meant camp-fires are no longer allowed. With high park use it is to be expected that readily accessible wood will run out. Please conserve the wood supply by being mindful of the amount you use and try to collect wood outside the park wherever possible. It is a good idea to check other sites (unoccupied, of course) for left-over wood before rummaging through the surrounding bush.
- Fishing — Normal regulations apply unless there are signs saying otherwise.

HOW TO USE THE BOOK

Travelling around Australia gives you the great advantage of being able to follow the warm weather. Some areas are more dramatic in the wet season (for example Jim Jim Falls in Kakadu), but travel tends to be more comfortable and enjoyable in fine weather. Seasons can be hard to predict at times. In general, the cooler months of April to October are good for spending in the central and northern regions, and the warmer months in the south. *Camping and Tramping* has been written with a bias toward travelling in an anti-clockwise direction.

Wherever necessary I have included the distances and directions from each approach so that whichever way you're travelling, you'll be able to follow the text.

The book is divided into states and territories, beginning with Victoria and ending with Tasmania. At the start of each state or territory there are some handy tips and information — such as the name of the national parks service — to make your visit a little easier.

I have grouped the parks together under the commonly used regional names. For additional information it is best to call the district office or ranger station nearest the park, and contact numbers for these are found in the text, or in the full listing at the back of the book.

Most national parks offices have a good relationship with the local tourist bureaux. The bureaux are often easier to find so you might be wise to inquire with them first or check if they have the national park brochure you want.

Most of the park entries are divided into sections to make the information easy to find.

Location and access gives a run-down on where the park is, how to get there, and the road conditions. This brief guide should be used in conjunction with your road map.

In most cases where the park is off-road, people towing caravans will need to find out the latest road conditions to ensure it is passable. Some roads can become corrugated very quickly and may not leave you a 'plate-to-eat-off' if you are not prepared.

Camping and facilities covers what is available for camping or picnicking, so you can plan where to stay the night or stop for lunch.

The prices included are to give you a rough guide only and were correct at the time of printing. Private operators generally raise prices 10 per cent each year. In most cases, national parks are cheaper than caravan parks, although where private operators manage the camping ground within national parks, this isn't always the case.

Increasingly fees are being charged for entrance to parks. This is often in high-use parks or those located near cities. The fees are collected to implement special conservation measures needed to reduce the environmental impact on the area.

Walks and attractions describes the walking trails and sights in the park so that you can decide which walks suit your level of fitness, interests and time limits.

Here are the basic guidelines which I have used to grade the walks reviewed.

Easy — Well-cleared, even paths. Comfortable for all age groups and fitness levels.

Moderate — Involves some negotiation of slopes, uneven surfaces and distances. Requires a fair level of fitness.

Hard — High level of fitness and agility. May involve climbing and strenuous hiking.

These gradings, and the times given, are a rough guide only, and are based on average fitness levels. Often national park signs give times which a reasonably fit person will halve. They do this to ensure that slower walkers allow enough time to complete the walk safely.

If the track is relatively flat and easy most people will walk one kilometre in 15 minutes. In variable and challenging conditions, such as the alpine areas of Tasmania, the times given are a more accurate guide than this formula. Again, however, these times are dependent on conditions such as weather and the ability of the walker.

I have given only a one way (o/w) distance when I am indicating that it is best used in one direction only. Often it will be in places where it is possible to arrange a vehicle pick-up at the other end, or where the walk can be combined with a ferry ride or the like.

The *On the way* section allows me to suggest a place or particular routes you might want to include on your way from one park to the next.

There are also segments throughout the book describing conservation issues, significant plants or wildlife, which I hope will contribute to your enjoyment of the places you choose to visit. It is quite probable that you will stay in areas which are integral to the survival of one or other species, and understanding a little about them will help you to lessen your impact on their environment.

At the back of the book you'll find a diary of events and school holidays to help when planning your holiday. National park camping grounds are very popular during school holidays and long weekends. Often it will mean you will not get a site unless you have booked in advance. You can assume that the parks in Victoria, Tasmania and NSW, and those near cities in other states and the territories, will be busy in holiday periods. If the park is particularly busy during the holidays, I have tried to say this in the entry for the park.

ABORIGINAL HISTORY

Camping and Tramping has been updated to include a brief section on Aboriginal heritage for many of the parks. Appreciating the Australian environment is incomplete without recognising the spiritual and cultural connection to the land by Aboriginal people.

BRIEF HISTORY

At the time of European settlement the total Indigenous population was between 300,000 and 500,000, a number which had stabilised after at least 40,000 years of virtually uninterrupted occupation.

There were around 250 languages spoken with 600 to 700 dialects.

A sophisticated system of marriage, language and ritual exchanges bind several family groups, or clans, of 30–80 people to make a tribe. These tribes are diverse from one another, so Aboriginal Australia should not be seen as one entity, but rather as a collection of Indigenous tribes, each with their own beliefs and culture.

PARK MANAGEMENT

There is a growing trend for Aboriginal people to manage national parks and heritage sites in Australia. Traditional custodians inherit the responsibility to care for the spiritual, environmental and cultural well-being of the land; this law is called 'Caring for Country'. This presents an opportunity that can benefit both Indigenous communities and the wider society.

ABORIGINAL COMMUNITIES AND TRAVEL PERMITS

Approximately 18% of Australia is now recognised as Aboriginal land. To travel on this land you require a transit or entry permit. Transit permits are for passing through and entry permits are for longer stays. Most places requiring travel permits are in northern and central Australia and some parts of WA and SA. Check with local Aboriginal land councils, national park offices or regional police stations. Permits take time to process and visitors are advised to allow a month for this.

CULTURAL RESPECT

It is a privilege to be able to visit some of the Aboriginal sacred sites and places throughout Australia. Travellers must be very careful not to take, touch or damage any relic of Indigenous culture. To do so will threaten the future of the artefacts and jeopardise visitation rights to these places for generations to come.

Care must be taken not to raise dust in the area close to an artwork.

Living culture must also be respected. Traditions such as 'sorry business' (community wide mortuary rites) require areas to be closed for some time. Please respect the privacy of Aboriginal people and their customs.

SACRED SITES

Sacred sites relate to dreaming sites, ceremonial places or burial grounds. Many sites have been damaged by erosion, vandalism and other disturbances. Laws protect these places and heavy penalties relate to any mistreatment of sites. Most sites are not included in this book due to their cultural significance and the fact they cannot be visited for spiritual or preservation reasons.

CULTURAL OWNERSHIP

Information about Aboriginal cultural heritage is the property of Aboriginal people. It is a living culture that must be acknowledged, recognised and respected. This book attempts to stimulate interest and understanding in Aboriginal heritage by encouraging national park visitors to learn more about Indigenous history and culture. I recommend that you read books written by Aboriginal people or take tours run by Aboriginal people — taking an accredited Indigenous tour is the best way to respectfully travel in a significant place and find out the cultural heritage.

SPELLING

Aboriginal names and words are often based on interpretations of the spoken word. As a result there are often several ways that these words have been recorded. There is no 'right' way to spell Aboriginal words. In most cases the spelling of language groups appearing in this book have been matched with the names used on the AIATSIS Language Group Map — available from AIATSIS (phone: (02) 6249 7310) and many other information centres and map shops.

TOTEMS

Where possible the totems for each region have been noted. Totems, which are generally inherited patrilineally over centuries, signify a sacred symbol for Aboriginal people. A totem signifies a special kinship and prevents the person from hunting and killing their totem. There can be several totems that relate to an individual, including a totem for the nation, tribe, family group and self. Totems are the link between dreamtime and the present. Totems join people to the nature around them and represent the relationship between people, creatures and the land they share.

FURTHER REFERENCE

The information included in *Camping and Tramping* is designed to give the national parks visitor a brief introduction to Aboriginal history of the area. Please explore further from other sources (listed below) in order to appreciate the extraordinary nature of Indigenous culture and people.

Travelling Aboriginal Australia — Discovery and Reconciliation, Paul Kaufman, Hyland House, 2000

Burnum Burnum's Australia, Burnum Burnum, Angus and Robertson, 1988

Aboriginal Australia and the Torres Strait Islands — Guide to Indigenous Australia, Lonely Planet, 2001

The Riches of Ancient Australia, Josephine Flood, UQP, 1990

OTHER RESOURCES:
Aboriginal Tourism Australia (ATA) is the peak Indigenous tourism body. Visit their website at http://www.ataust.org.au

AUTHOR'S NOTE
I would like to say sorry to all Aboriginal and Torres Strait Islander people alive today, and to all generations since invasion. I am appalled by the way you were forced from your land, beaten or killed, maimed with disease and addiction, robbed of your children and are still discriminated against. I hope that despite the horrific past we can work towards a fair system that recognises and respects Aboriginal ways from the past and present.

ROAD ASSISTANCE

Most places suitable for the reasonably adventurous types can be reached by conventional vehicles. If you are going to attempt a 4WD track in dry weather, find out the current conditions, how often it is used, tell someone where you are going and when you expect to be back. Always ensure you have ample drinking water, food and spare car equipment in case you run into trouble. Getting bogged may not only be embarrassing; it can be life threatening if you're in a remote area.

Getting lost is one of the hazards of exploring Australia's national parks. Even with clear instructions and detailed maps on my lap I have still managed to lose my way. Signs get knocked down — or worse, point the wrong way — roads change and maps are inaccurate. You may not be able to avoid getting lost, but there are a few steps you can take which will reduce the likelihood, or help if you need to rediscover your whereabouts.

- Carry a detailed area map. Often state maps cover such a large area that they cannot show details of the back roads you may be using. If you're a member of one of the car clubs, like the RACV or NRMA, you will be able to get detailed road maps from them.
- If you have any doubts about the directions you are following, stop and ask someone, or contact the district office and ask for confirmation.
- Allow enough time before nightfall to find the place you're looking for. Check to see if there's a suitable alternative destination a little closer in case your journey takes longer than planned.
- When travelling through remote areas, always carry ample fuel, water and food.
- If you do get lost in a remote area, stay with your vehicle. It is easier for rescuers to spot a vehicle than a person.

Four-wheel drive travellers who want to further explore regions such as Cape York, the Kimberley region and the remote inland areas, need to contact the relevant national parks offices before setting off. There are also special guide books you can consult, such as those written by Ron and Viv Moon.

Facilities for disabled visitors are available at some national parks. Most of the parks with these services are located near cities and cater primarily for day users. National park brochures, available from the park offices, show where wheelchair access has been installed.

Whether you are off on a short holiday, or a year-long trip, you are bound to discover your own special camping spots, and your favourite national park. If you want to share them with others, please write to the publisher so we can include them in the next edition of *Camping and Tramping*. In any case, I wish you well on your journey. It has the promise to be wonderful.

ACKNOWLEDGEMENTS

Thanks to all the national parks officers who have assisted with the initial research and then up-dating of this guidebook. There are too many to thank individually but their generous assistance is greatly appreciated.

Thanks to all the elders, land council members and Aboriginal rangers who gave their time answering my enquiries. In particular Brian Mansell from the Tasmanian Aboriginal Land Council for his work, and Cecil Keed from ATSIC. Thanks to David Watts, Aboriginal Heritage Manager, for his initial advice. Thanks to the staff at the Information Centre at The Rocks in Sydney and the Aboriginal Affairs library in Melbourne.

Thanks to Joski Tibbets for his contributions to the floral profiles and Jane Calder for her initial encouragement to write this book; also to Judy Reizes, from the Manly Environment Centre, for her inspiration and energy.

I would like to thank my partner J.D. Mittmann for his help and love. Thanks to my family for their ongoing support and care, despite my absences.

Thanks to my publisher, Jeanne Ryckmans, and editor, Roberta Ivers.

VICTORIA

1. Lower Glenelg NP, see p3
2. Discovery Bay CP, see p5
3. Mt Richmond NP, see p7
4. Mt Eccles NP, see p7
5. Grampians NP, see p10
6. Port Campbell NP, see p12
7. Otway NP, see p13
8. Little Desert NP, see p15
9. Mt Arapiles-Tooan SP, see p17
10. Wyperfeld NP, see p17
11. Murray-Sunset NP, see p18
12. Hattah-Kulkyne NP, see p19
13. Brisbane Ranges NP, see p21
14. Organ Pipes NP, see p21
15. Dandenong Ranges NP, see p23
16. Point Nepean NP, see p24
17. Kinglake NP, see p24
18. Cathedral Range SP, see p26
19. Fraser NP, see p28
20. Eildon SP, see p28
21. Mt Samaria SP, see p31
22. Mt Buffalo NP, see p31
23. Alpine NP, see p34
24. Burrowa-Pine Mountain NP, see p37
25. Wilsons Promontory NP, see p38
26. Tarra-Bulga NP, see p40
27. Morwell NP, see p42
28. Baw Baw NP, see p42
29. Mitchell River NP, see p42
30. The Lakes NP, see p45
31. Snowy River NP, see p45
32. Errinundra NP, see p49
33. Cape Conran, see p50
34. Croajingolong NP, see p51

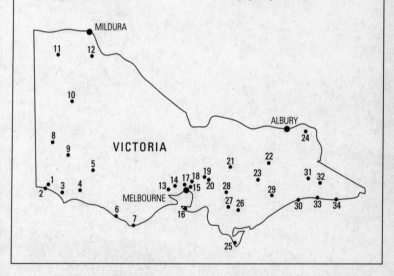

NOTE: Look through the chapter to the On the Way sections to see additional places to camp or visit.

NATIONAL PARKS SERVICE

Parks Victoria manage the 36 national parks, 3 wilderness parks, 31 State parks, regional parks and 3000 crown reserves in this state. This service was formerly known as the Department of Conservation and Natural Resources (CNR).

Parks Victoria 13 19 63
info@parkweb.vic.gov.au
www.parkweb.vic.gov.au

OFF-PEAK FEES

Many parks have two rates for camping. The 'normal rate' applies to the peak periods of Christmas holidays (usually the third Friday in December to the first Sunday in February), Easter, Labour Day weekend and Melbourne Cup weekend. Off-season rates are quite a bit cheaper and you probably won't need to book.

BOOKING

A ballot system operates in many of the popular parks over the Christmas holidays, Easter, long weekends and other school holidays.

To apply for a booking you must send in a deposit for the site — often for a minimum number of nights. Sites are then allocated through a random selection of applications.

ABORIGINAL HISTORY

In Victoria at the time of colonisation there were between 11,000 and 15,000 Aboriginal people. The population was made up of 38 tribes with 10 distinct languages. By 1886, the population had diminished to around 800.

Colonial settlement in Victoria was rapid and violent. In 1835 John Batman gave a few knives, tools and supplies to the Woi Wurrung and Boon Wurrung tribal chiefs and believed he had purchased the land where Melbourne is now situated. White settlers quickly followed and although resistance was strong, there was no remorse by colonialists who massacred Aborigines in order to force them from their lands.

Most Victorian Aborigines refer to themselves as Koori, meaning 'person' or 'people'.

PUB PATRON GUIDE

Pot	285ml
Glass	200ml

SOUTHWEST AND COAST

LOWER GLENELG NATIONAL PARK

If you're coming from South Australia you may be faced with the decision of whether to travel inland along the Glenelg River in Lower Glenelg NP or follow the coast in Discovery Bay Coastal Park. In my opinion the Lower Glenelg NP has a lot more to offer for the camper and walker, particularly if the weather is cool.

CAMPING AND TRAMPING

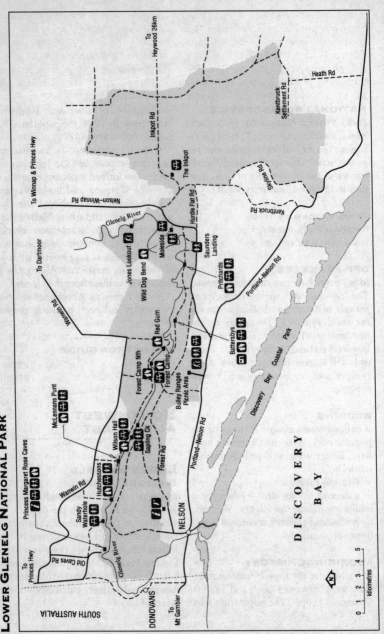

Location and access

Head north of Nelson township for 3km to the park information centre. North Nelson Track (unsealed) leads to River Rd, which follows the south bank. The attractions north of the river, including Princess Margaret Rose Caves, can be reached by turning off the Princes Hwy just inside the Victorian border, onto Old Caves Rd.

Wanwin Rd, which provides access to places on the northern side of the river, links up to Dartmoor. The Portland-Nelson Rd also provides several access points.

Camping and facilities

There are several campsites along the river, with basic facilities such as toilets and fireplaces. To camp in the park you need to contact the national parks office at Nelson (phone: (03) 8738 4171). Princess Margaret Rose Caves, on the northern bank, and Pritchards, on the southern bank, are suitable for caravans. The fee is $11 per site. The vehicle-based camping spots on the northern bank are Hutchessons, McLennans Punt, Wilson Hall and Red Gum. On the southern side are Forest Camp, Battersbys, Pritchards and Wild Dog Bend.

For canoe and walker access sites see the Glenelg River Canoeing Guide, available from the information centre.

Walks and attractions

The Princess Margaret Rose Caves are quite popular and there are several tours daily (cost is $6.20 for adults and $3.00 for children). The caves are sometimes closed on Fridays, so call the Nelson Information Centre to check. The visitor centre at the caves has displays and information on the area.

Hire a canoe in Nelson and paddle along the Glenelg River, downstream from the caves, to view the spectacular limestone gorge. Otherwise there are two pleasure cruises which leave from Nelson (phone: (03) 8738 4191).

The River View Nature Walk, a short self-guiding trail, begins at the caves and leads to views over the Glenelg River (pamphlet available).

Aboriginal history

The Dhauwurd Wurrung language group, of the Boandik tribe, occupied this area at the time of European colonisation. Plentiful resources existed for people in the area, with shellfish and crustaceans readily available, as well as lizards, snakes, wombats, emus and kangaroos. The pigface plant was considered a delicacy and was a rich source of salt.

DISCOVERY BAY COASTAL PARK

Although this is a coastal park, the campsites are located near pleasant freshwater lakes. In fine weather the coastal terrain can be dramatic and enjoyable. A variety of birdlife inhabits the park.

Location and access

The park stretches from the SA–Victorian border to Descartes Bay, only 30km from Portland. Lake Monibeong camping area is reached by turning off the Portland-Nelson Road, 17km east of Nelson, at a small street sign indicating Lake Monibeong. This 7km unsealed road initially passes through pine plantations and is quite rough in places (passable by 2WD).

Swan Lake is reached by a good road which leaves the Portland-Nelson Rd 34km west of Portland and 37km from Nelson. Again, a small sign indicates Swan Lake. It is a 6km gravel road, steep in some places, but generally good.

The Bridgewater Lakes day-use area may be reached easily from Tarragal, 27km from Portland.

CAMPING AND TRAMPING

DISCOVERY BAY COASTAL PARK

Camping and facilities

Lake Monibeong camping area has tables, water, fireplaces and toilets. Little wood is available so bring your own or use a fuel stove. It is a large grassy area which may be quite exposed in windy conditions.

Unlike Monibeong, Swan Lake camping area is not by the edge of the lake. This site is very large and grassy, dotted with fireplaces and tea-trees. There are also toilets and water.

A permit to camp must be purchased from Nelson or Portland Parks Victoria office (phone: (03) 8738 4051) beforehand. The fee is $12.30 per site or $9 during the off-season.

Walks and attractions

Nobles Rocks Inland Walk (8.3km rtn–mod–3.5 hrs), part of the Great South West Walk, may be completed as a circuit by returning along the beach. It begins at Lake Monibeong and water should be carried, especially in the warmer months. It provides a sample of the unspoilt coastal landscape typical of the park.

Bridgewater Lakes are often used for swimming, fishing and water skiing.

Aboriginal history

Hundreds of middens exist in this park, showing the importance of the area for hunting and gathering. Middens can be seen along the Great South West walk.

MT RICHMOND NATIONAL PARK

The extinct volcano of Mt Richmond is now a pocket of lush forest and heath which has picnic areas, toilets, lookouts and four easy walking trails. Camping is not permitted.

Turn off the Portland-Nelson Rd, 20km from Portland, and continue for 7.5km. The information board provides details of the walks. Koalas are often seen in the manna gums around the picnic area.

MT ECCLES NATIONAL PARK

From the dry stretches of western Victoria you suddenly find yourself in the crisp mountain forest surrounding Lake Surprise. The crater lake is formed from an extinct volcano.

Location and access

From the Henty Hwy, turn off 17km north of Heywood, toward the township of Macarthur. Turn right and follow the signs to the park. From Macarthur, a road leads directly to the park. Access is good all year as the road is sealed most of the way.

Camping and facilities

An excellent camping ground and picnic area is located a short walk from Lake Surprise. Hot showers, toilets, tables, fireplaces and firewood are all available. The park ranger will collect the fee of $13 per site (up to four people), or $9 in off-peak periods. Bookings can be made through the Macarthur office (phone: (03) 5576 1338). The campsite is very popular during Christmas and Easter.

A sheltered picnic area and playground equipment are located near the crater rim.

Walks and attractions

Information boards on the outside of the stone visitor centre provide details of the geological and Aboriginal history of the area.

The Crater Rim Nature Walk (2km rtn–easy–1 hr) follows the rim of the crater, including a steep section to the summit of Mt Eccles.

The easier Lake Walk follows the

Mt Eccles National Park

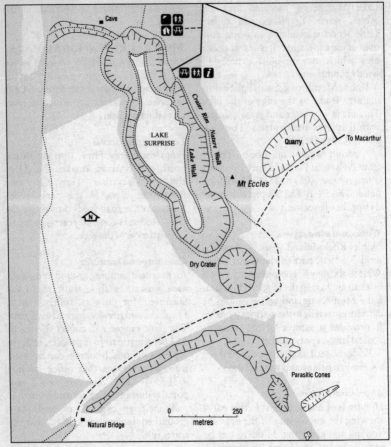

shoreline of the lake after descending the crater via steps.

In warm weather swimming is popular in the lake and I am told the fishing is not too bad either.

The Natural Bridge, a lava creation, can be reached on foot by diverting from the Crater Rim track, past Mt Eccles. By vehicle, you continue along the road from Macarthur, instead of turning right toward the camping area.

Aboriginal history
Mt Eccles is part of the traditional land of the Dhauwurd Wurrung tribe, more commonly known as Gunditjmara. Hut circles and fish traps are found in and around Mt Eccles.

🚙 ON THE WAY
ABORIGINAL HISTORY
The Gunditjmara people are the custodians of the Lake Condah area. Significant

GRAMPIANS NATIONAL PARK

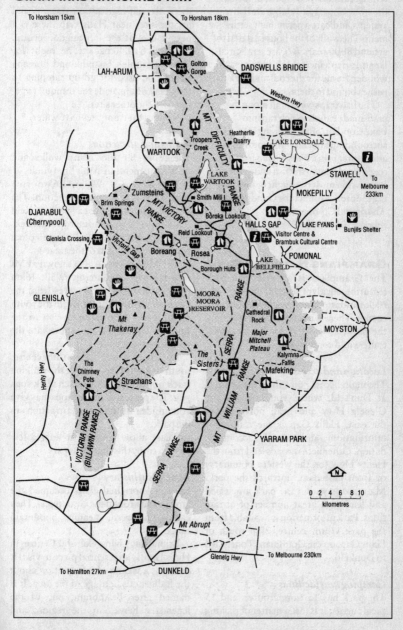

remnants of early occupation, such as the stone houses and elaborate fish trap systems, indicate a permanent settlement. The walls of the houses, dated to around 8000 years ago, are semi-circular and up to a metre high, with a wooden frame for the roof and bark or rushes bound to them.

The fish traps were built along the man-made canals which ran into Lake Condah, often draining the surrounding land after the autumn and winter rains. Nets woven from reeds would catch the fish and eels. Permission must be sought before visiting the area. Contact the Gunditjmara Aboriginal Co-operative (phone: (03) 5562 9729).

GRAMPIANS NATIONAL PARK

The Grampians is an extensive park featuring eucalypt forests, wildflowers, rock formations and waterfalls in every corner. There is a range of ways to enjoy the park, as it caters for bushwalkers, tourers and contemplators.

Location and access

The main access point from the south is at Dunkeld, where you turn off the Glenelg Hwy and head north. From the east, Halls Gap is the centre for information and motel accommodation. Other access roads lead from the Henty Hwy (on the western boundary) or from Horsham, north of the park. Main roads within the park are sealed and lead to a great number of attractions. Park information is available from the park visitor centre, 2km south of Halls Gap, on the Grampians Tourist Rd to Dunkeld.

Camping and facilities

The park has 15 campgrounds and 15 picnic areas. It is just a matter of picking the one you like best. In the outer area there are self-registration stations and for the sites near Halls Gap there is a permit box at the information centre. The fee is $10.40 per site, per night (for up to 6 people). Buandik and Boreang tend to be used for group camping so they may not provide the tranquil experience of the other sites.

None of the campsites have water.

Walks and attractions

There are far too many walks and features to mention in this brief guide.

The Balconies Walk (1.6km rtn–easy–1 hr) is a popular attraction. The walk begins from the car-park at Reid Lookout. The jagged outcrop and backdrop of Victoria Valley are often featured in postcards of the area.

The Mt Abrupt — also known as Mt Murdadjoog — Summit Walk (6km rtn–mod/hard–3.5 hrs) leaves from the car-park, off Mt Abrupt Rd, in the south of the park. Arrows direct you to the summit, where you can appreciate the grandeur of the park.

My advice is to go to the visitor centre, south of Halls Gap, and get the walking track notes and decide which walk suits you. The postcards in the shops may give you an idea of the scenic attractions in the park.

Please allow yourself at least a few days to enjoy this first-class park.

Aboriginal history

Several Aboriginal clans occupied the land in and around the Grampians. They call it *Gariwerd*, meaning 'mountain range'.

Brambruk Living Cultural Centre, in Halls Gap, is an essential place to visit. It contains a wealth of information about the Indigenous heritage of the area. It is named after Brambram, one of the legendary heroes in the region, and

PORT CAMPBELL NATIONAL PARK

Brambuk, the Djab Warrung word for white cockatoo, the totem for the area.

The physical form of the range is linked to creation stories from the dreamtime. There are many rock art sites in the park. One of the most impressive art sites is Bunjil's Cave, just outside of the park in Black Range. The site is 10km south of Stawell, off the Stawell–Pomonal Rd.

PORT CAMPBELL NATIONAL PARK

Probably one of the most recognisable attractions in Victoria is the Twelve Apostles. Port Campbell NP preserves the narrow stretch of coastline featuring the eroded limestone cliffs, which continue to change with each crashing wave.

Location and access
The park occupies the coast between Peterborough and Princetown. The viewpoints for London Bridge, Loch Ard Gorge and the Twelve Apostles are all sign-posted from the Great Ocean Rd.

Camping and facilities
There is a national park campground in Port Campbell which has powered sites, hot showers and laundry facilities. Fees are $15 for 2 people and $5 per person in addition. If you want more of a bush-style camping location you are better off staying in the Otway National Park.

Booking is essential for summer holidays, Easter and Labour Day weekend. Office opens at 2 pm.

OTWAY NATIONAL PARK

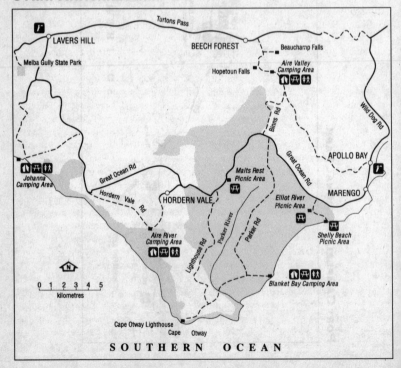

Walks and attractions
Sightseeing is the major activity in the park.

At Port Campbell there is the Port Campbell Discovery Walk (1.5 hrs– easy), which begins at Port Campbell Beach.

A coastal walking trail links Loch Ard Gorge to the Blowhole and Thunder Cave. It continues around the cliff edge to Broken Head, then joins the Sherbrook River Valley Walk.

During the summer holidays there are often activities organised by the national park rangers, such as viewing the mutton birds at dusk, a boat trip out to view the Twelve Apostles and various children's activities.

See the information centre at Port Campbell for more details.

Aboriginal history
The Girai Wurrung tribe, with its 21 associated clans, were the original inhabitants of the land between Princetown and Warrnambool. Shell middens and stone artefacts have been found in the area. Historical records show steps were cut into the limestone cliffs to provide access to the shoreline.

ON THE WAY
Melba Gully State Park, 3km southwest of Lavers Hill, has a good nature walk, passing by the Big Tree, waterfalls and lush green forests. There is a nice picnic spot at the start of the walk.

OTWAY NATIONAL PARK
This park features coastal attractions as well as deep forest for bushwalking. Changeable weather is not a problem in the Otways, as the forest is wonderful when it rains and the coast is glorious when the sun is shining.

Location and access
The Great Ocean Rd passes through the park. Roads lead from it to reach camping and attractions. The sealed road to Johanna Beach branches off 4km south of Lavers Hill and it is then 8km to Johanna campground. You can return to the Great Ocean Rd via another road which branches off 11km from Lavers Hill.

The Aire River campsite is midway along the Hordern Vale Rd, which leaves the Great Ocean Rd at Glenaire, and rejoins it just east of the Calder River Bridge.

Lighthouse Rd leads 17km south of Hordern Vale to the lighthouse. From there Blanket Bay Rd leads east to Blanket Bay campsite. The road is unsealed and can get boggy during winter. From there Parker Rd links back up with the Great Ocean Rd. Parker Rd is unsealed, narrow and slippery when wet. It is closed during winter.

The Aire Valley Reserve is 6km south of Beech Forest, north of the park.

Camping and facilities
The three camping areas — Johanna, Aire River and Blanket Bay — have toilets, tables and fireplaces. Blanket Bay is not suitable for caravans and water availability should not be depended upon. However, the site is in a sheltered location, making it a good spot during windy weather. The Aire Valley Reserve, to the north of the park, is a pleasant forest site with toilets, tables and fireplaces. No fee is charged to camp in the park or the Aire Valley Reserve.

Walks and attractions
From Johanna Beach you can walk south-east 4km to Rotten Point. Along the way you might get your feet wet crossing Johanna River and Brown Creek. Return by the same route.

LITTLE DESERT NATIONAL PARK

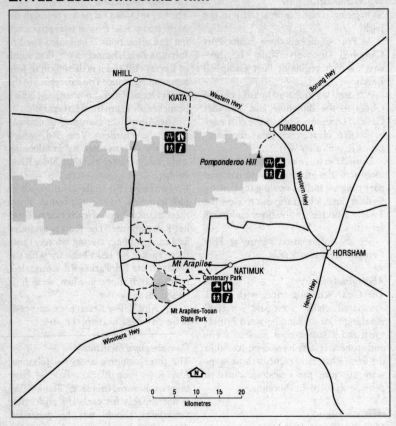

By turning right from Johanna Beach and heading north-west you can do the Sutherlands Beach Circuit (4km–mod–2 hrs), which leads to Slippery Point and into Sutherlands Beach (can only do this section at low tide). Return by the same route.

The Escarpment Walk (4km rtn–mod–2 hrs) begins from the Aire River campground and follows a 4WD track toward the beach then branches left up the hill for ocean views. Follow the escarpment for a kilometre in a westerly direction. Retrace your steps back to the campground.

The Cape Otway Lighthouse is a historic attraction worth visiting. The grounds are open from 10am to 4pm weekdays (closed on the weekends). No entry into the lighthouse is allowed.

For an excellent scenic drive head north from Apollo Bay on Wild Dog Rd for 16km then turn left into Turtons Track, which continues to Lavers Hill along Beech Forest Rd. From the Aire Valley Rd, which leads south from

> **MALLEE SCRUB**
>
> 'Mallee' is a term used to describe the growth form of some eucalypt species, as well as the formations largely comprised of these species. The term is also used to describe the dry country where these formations occur. In south-eastern Australia, mallee scrub tends to grow in inland areas, where annual rainfall varies from 200 to 600mm, and falls predominantly in the winter. Mallee scrub is very hardy, surviving in dry conditions in usually alkaline soils. The scrub, 3 to 5 metres high, is characterised by several stems growing into an umbrella-shaped crown.

Beech Forest, there are tracks branching off to Beauchamp Falls and further south to Hopetoun Falls. Both these spots are spectacular and have day-use picnic areas.

Elliot River picnic area, located off the Great Ocean Rd, is just within the eastern boundary of the park. From the picnic area you can undertake the Elliot River Walk (4km loop–mod–2 hrs). Follow the path across the river then 50 metres along turn right and continue north to Elliot River Rd. Turn right and walk along the Shelly Beach Track to the car-park.

Sign-posted off the Great Ocean Rd, 8km east of Hordern Vale, Maits Rest has a short rainforest boardwalk.

The Beauty Spot Scenic Reserve is just north of the road to Johanna. A 4km trail winds through the tall mountain ash trees and fern-covered forest floor. There is a nice picnic spot at the start of the walk.

Aboriginal history

At the time of European settlement the Katubanuut tribe occupied the coast and ranges of what is now Otway NP. Shell middens and artefact scatters show extensive use of the area for much of the year. Middens show that a significant camp was situated at Seal Point, overlooking the eastern end of Crayfish Bay. There are also 10 circular depressions thought to be the remains of huts.

THE MALLEE

LITTLE DESERT NATIONAL PARK

Contrary to its name, this park is not a featureless barren landscape, although it is dominated by heathland and mallee scrub, which may not appeal to everyone. It is an important conservation area, protecting the habitat for a number of plant and animal species in the area. During spring and early summer the area is ablaze with over 600 flowering species sprinkling the landscape with purples, yellows, pinks and blues.

To reach the main camping area, turn south from Kiata, on the Western Hwy, and travel for 10km to the picnic and camping area. An information board here details the walks and features of the park. The $10.40 camping fee can be paid at the self-registration station.

Another recreation area is 6km south of Dimboola along the Wimmera River at Horseshoe and Ackle Bends. Here you will find toilets, tables, fireplaces, water and information. Nearby Pomponderoo Hill has a good trail leading to its summit.

Due to flooding during winter,

WYPERFELD NATIONAL PARK

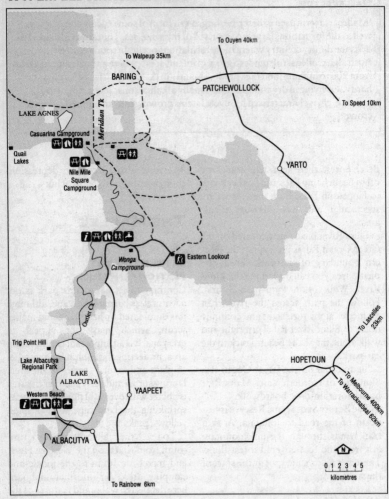

seasonal closures apply on selected roads from July to August inclusive.

Aboriginal history

The Wergaia tribe occupied the area to the east of the park from Wimmera River to Richardson River. Scarred trees can be found along the river banks and middens and mounds have also been recorded. Occupation tended to centre around the river and freshwater lakes.

Mt Arapiles—Tooan State Park

The sheer rock bluff of Mt Arapiles is a world-class challenge for rock climbers. It is a picturesque landmark just off the Wimmera Hwy. You don't have to be a rock climber to reach the summit of Mt Arapiles. A 2km loop trail leads from Centenary Park camping area to the summit. This track is quite steep in parts. If you want to enjoy great views for little effort you can drive along the Lookout Rd, from where a short walk leads to the summit. A new lookout suitable for to car-disabled visitors is also located on Lookout Rd.

Camping and picnic facilities are provided at Centenary Park, along Alfred Wright Lockwood Memorial Drive. The camp fee is $7.90 per site, per night (phone: (03) 5387 1260).

Aboriginal history

The Kanal gundidj clan, who occupied the area near Chetwynd River and Glenelg River, were the closest clan to the park. They were part of the Jardwadjali language group, whose lands covered the area west of the Grampians.

Wyperfeld National Park

This is a significant park in the Mallee region, famous for its chain of dry lake beds, linked by Outlet Creek. It is a tranquil and varied place, thriving with animal and birdlife.

Location and access

Travel to Yaapeet, either west from Hopetoun on the Henty Hwy, or north from Rainbow via the Western Hwy. Drive north of Yaapeet along the sealed road for 30km to reach the main (Wonga) camping area. A camping area in the northern section can be reached by driving to Baring (12km west of Patchewollock) then continuing another 9km before turning south into Meridian Track. The Casuarina camping area is 6km along this unsealed road. Nine Mile Square campground, a further 3km down Meridian Track, is accessible to walkers only. In the western extension of the park, Milmed Rock and Chinaman Well are popular 4WD destinations through the undulating heathland of the Big Desert.

Camping and facilities

The Wonga camping area is set in woodland and has toilets, tables, undercover shelter, fireplaces and water. The camping fee is $10.40 per night. The Casuarina and Nine Mile Square camping areas have a toilet, water, tables and fireplaces. Along Milmed Rock and Chinaman Well tracks, vehicle-based camping is permitted within 50m of the track. A remote campsite at Round Swamp has a fireplace and table.

Water should be used sparingly, and is often in short supply, so always ensure you have enough with you, particularly in summer. It is also useful to bring your own firewood.

An information centre is provided near the Wonga campground and there are remnants of the pastoral era dotted around the area.

Walks and attractions

A good view of the sand dunes can be had from Mt Mattingley, near the main campsite; on certain mornings you may see the mist hanging between the lunettes.

There are several walks starting from the main campsite. A good one is the Lake Brambruk Nature Walk (6km rtn–easy/mod–2.5 hrs). Obtain a walking brochure from the information centre for details on the other walks. The Eastern Lookout Nature Drive (18km) is a popular way to see the features of the park if you have limited time. It is an excellent route to undertake on a bicycle. This area, along with most of the mallee, is best visited in the cooler months, as summer can be relentlessly hot.

A longer walk along the freeway or Meridian Track follows the scenic Outlet Creek floodplain. Another walk follows Nine Mile Square Track, traversing heathland that displays wildflowers in spring.

Near by is Lake Albacutya Regional Park. The lake fills once every 20 years but is still a popular spot for camping. Western Beach camping area, 6km north of Rainbow, has toilets, water, fireplaces and tables.

Aboriginal history

People of the Wergaia language group lived a nomadic lifestyle in this region. They travelled along Outlet Creek in search of food. Middens and scarred trees are found near the lakes and water sources. Possums and kangaroos were skinned and made into cloaks or into bags to carry water.

The non-crystalline form of Gypsum, found in the Wyperfeld NP, was used to make the white plaster used as body paint in ceremonies.

The tribe had a north–south trade route through Big Desert NP. Camping points were approximately 16km apart, equivalent to one day of travel. Wirrengren Plain is where people from the south met and traded with those from the Murray River tribes. Artefacts from distant places have been found at this site.

MURRAY-SUNSET NATIONAL PARK

This is Victoria's second largest national park, a massive 633,000ha. The southern sector of this park features the delightful Pink Lakes. The salt lakes are pink due to the alga *Dunaliella salina*, which secretes a red pigment, resulting in this very picturesque and unusual sight. The lakes are dry in summer and covered with a white and pink salt crust.

The remainder of the park contains a very broad range of environments, including the riverine plains and wetlands of Lindsay Island and Lake Wallawalla, the grasslands and woodlands of Mopoke, the dry lake bed of Rocket Lake, and vast areas of heath and mallee scrub on undulating dunes.

Location and access

The only reliable 2WD access is via the Ouyen Highway to Pink Lakes, travel 16km north from Linga. Lindsay Island and Lake Wallawalla can be reached from the Sturt Highway in the north. A network of 4WD tracks throughout the park connects other points of interest. Popular routes are Underbool Track and Honeymoon Hut Track.

Camping and facilities

At Pink Lakes, there is a campsite at Lake Crosbie with toilets, tables, gas barbecue, fireplaces, and drinking water. However the supply of water and firewood is unreliable, so bring your own. There are remote camping sites with fireplaces and tables in the remainder of the park. Where there are no facilities, camping is permitted within 50m of a track. General fire regulations apply.

Walks and attractions

At Pink Lakes, there is a three-hour walk around Lake Crosbie, and nearby Lake Kenyon takes four hours to circuit. Lake Becking, 2km north of Lake Crosbie, takes one and a half hours to walk

MURRAY-SUNSET NATIONAL PARK

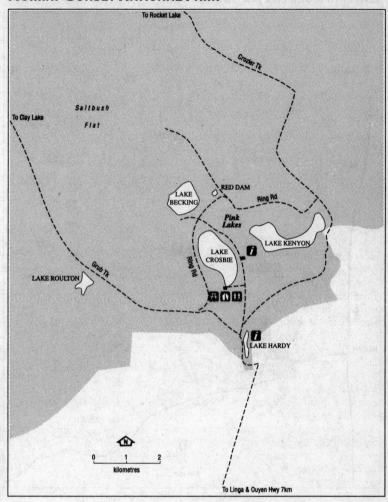

around. There is a display of old salt-mining equipment and photographs nearby.

For longer walks it is essential to be experienced and fully prepared. Walking can be particularly dangerous in summer.

HATTAH-KULKYNE NATIONAL PARK

Due to the Murray River — which fills nearby creeks and lakes during floods — there is flourishing vegetation and birdlife in this park. Stately river red gums edge the waterways, which are

HATTAH-KULKYNE NATIONAL PARK

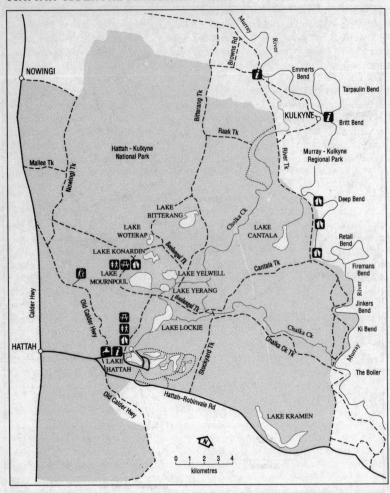

popular for swimming, fishing and other water-based activities.

Location and access

The Lake Hattah camping area is easily reached by travelling along the Calder Hwy and turning east for 4km from Hattah along the Hattah-Robinvale Main Rd. Unsealed roads lead through the park to the Murray River and Murray-Kulkyne Regional Park. The River Track, which runs alongside the Murray, heads south from Colignan all the way to the southern boundary of the park. It is unsealed and impassable after rain and during periods of high river.

Camping and facilities
In Hattah-Kulkyne National Park you can camp at either Lake Hattah or Lake Mournpoul. Both have toilets, tables and fireplaces. There is limited water and firewood available so bring your own. The fee is $6 per night. In the Murray-Kulkyne Regional Park you can camp between the River Track and the river. No facilities are provided and it is a popular place for locals to stay for Easter and Christmas. Please ensure you take out all your rubbish with you.

Walks and attractions
A short nature trail leaves just past the turn-off to Lake Hattah. There is a comprehensive network of tracks throughout the park which can be used for longer walks through a variety of landscapes. Some of these are open for car touring. The Hattah Nature Drive near Lake Hattah is an excellent introduction to the park. There are also opportunities for water activities in the lakes and in the Murray River. See the information centre near Lake Hattah for more activities.

Aboriginal history
The Latjilatji people occupied the land from Chalka Creek to Mildura for at least 5000 years. Occupational finds indicate a settled rather than nomadic lifestyle. Scarred trees show avid canoe-building and shield-making. A canoe tree can be seen along the 6km Lake Hattah Nature Drive departing from the visitor centre at Lake Hattah.

AROUND MELBOURNE

BRISBANE RANGES NATIONAL PARK
This small park, only 80km west of Melbourne, has several picnic areas and walking trails. The Boar Gully campsite, on the Bacchus Marsh-Mt Wallace Rd has tables, toilets and fireplaces. Bookings and fees are required for camping. Call the national park office for further information (phone: (03) 5284 1230). From there you can travel south along unsealed roads, passing Little River picnic area and Lower Stony Creek picnic area. South-west of the Brisbane Ranges is historic Steiglitz Courthouse (open Sundays and public holidays from 10am till 4pm) Major walking trails lead from Anakie Gorge picnic area (just off Staughton Vale Rd) and Lower Stony Creek picnic area.

Aboriginal history
The Wathaurong clan occupied the Brisbane Ranges prior to European settlement. They were part of the Kurung Nation who controlled 3400 sq km of land west of Port Phillip Bay. In 1859 the few remaining Wathaurong people were taken to Steiglitz Reserve, on the north bank of the Little River. The reserve was closed down in 1901. A commemorative plaque has been placed near Little River Picnic Area by the Wathaurong Aboriginal Co-operative.

ORGAN PIPES NATIONAL PARK
A group of basalt columns known as the 'Organ Pipes' forms a picturesque attraction just off the Calder Hwy, only 20km north of Melbourne. There are picnic facilities and a short walk leading along the creek to Rosette Rock and the Tessellated Pavement. Overall a good place to stop for lunch or to see on a day trip from Melbourne.

Aboriginal history
The Woi Wurrung tribe of the Kulin Nation occupied the land along the Yarra and Maribyrnong River systems.

22   **CAMPING AND TRAMPING**

BRISBANE RANGES NATIONAL PARK

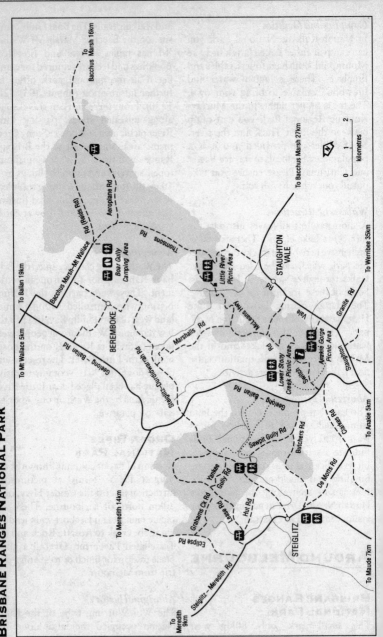

DANDENONG RANGES NATIONAL PARK

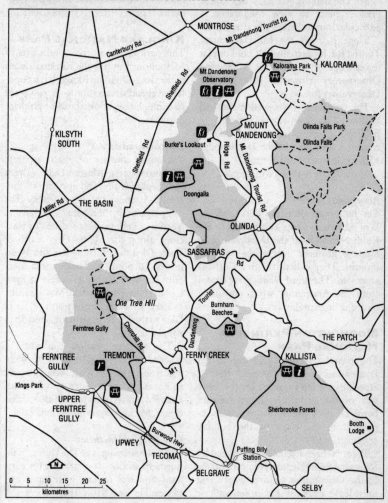

Jacksons Creek formed a boundary between the Marin-Bulluk and Wurundjeri-William clans.

DANDENONG RANGES NATIONAL PARK

Another good day trip from Melbourne is to the Dandenong Ranges, east of the city. The park consists of three sections — Sherbrooke, Doongalla and Ferntree Gully.

Burwood Hwy leads to the Ferntree Gully section of the park, where you will find the Lower Picnic Ground in which the ranger's office, and further information, is located.

Mt Dandenong Observatory is the premier place to view Melbourne, a particularly impressive sight after dark.

Ridge Rd, off the Mt Dandenong Tourist Rd, leads to Burke's Lookout (at the end of Eyre Rd) and Mt Dandenong Observatory (closes at 10pm), along Observatory Rd.

The terminus of the well-recognised Puffing Billy Railway is located in Belgrave township, so you may like to combine your visit to the Dandenongs with a ride on the historic train.

No camping is allowed in the park.

Aboriginal history

The Bunurong (Western Port) and the Woi Wurrung (Yarra Yarra) clans of the Kulin Nation used the Dandenongs as hunting grounds during the summer months. They called the area *Corhanwarrabul*. The word *Dandenong* comes from the Aboriginal word tanjenong meaning 'high mountains'.

MORNINGTON PENINSULA NATIONAL PARK

The coastal towns of Rye, Sorrento and Portsea are popular seaside resorts, especially during summer. On the other side of the peninsula, Point Nepean National Park provides a welcome retreat from the hype of the holiday season.

Point Nepean itself can be reached by following Point Nepean Rd past Portsea to the Orientation Centre, where you must leave your car and either walk or take the special transporter to the point. There is a fee and bookings are recommended (phone: (03) 5984 4276).

The Bushrangers Bay Nature Walk (2 hr rtn–easy/mod–3km) is a popular one leaving from the lighthouse at Cape Schanck.

There are several picnic areas in the park, but no camping is allowed. More information is available from the Dromana Tourist Office, (03) 5987 3078.

KINGLAKE NATIONAL PARK

This park on the northern outskirts of Melbourne features the forested slopes of the Great Dividing Range. It is a popular weekend destination so if you want to camp, either book ahead or go there during the week.

Location and access

The park consists of three separate sections: western (Masons Falls), eastern (Jehosephat Gully) and northern (Wombelano-Andrews Hill) sections. The camping area in the northern section and Yea River Park are best reached by travelling along the Melba Hwy north of Yarra Glen then turning left into Westbridge Rd. South of The Gums is Glenburn Rd which provides access to Jehosephat Gully, Kinglake and Masons Falls.

Steels Creek Rd leads north of Yarra Glen to the Mt Jerusalem area and up to Kinglake.

The western section can also be reached by travelling to Kinglake West, 13km north-east of Whittlesea, then east to Pheasant Creek. Turn into National Park Rd which leads to the information centre, Mt Sugarloaf and Masons Falls.

Camping and facilities

The only camping is at The Gums, in the northern section. It is suitable for caravans and has toilets, water and fireplaces. The fee is $10.20 per site.

Walks and attractions

From the camping area you can walk to the highest point in the park along the Andrews Hill Track (5.5km rtn–mod– 2 hrs). To make a circuit walk, return by the Andrews Hill West Track (2.8km– easy/mod–1 hr) or via Dusty Miller and Stringybark Tracks.

Kinglake National Park

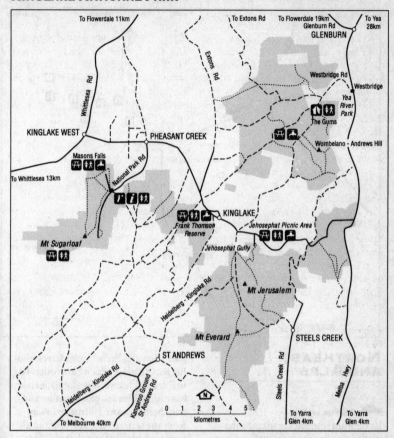

In the western section Masons Falls are a feature. From the information centre you can walk to the falls along Boundary Track (45 mins o/w) or along Wallaby Trail (2.5km o/w). This trail also leads to the start of the Running Creek Track (6.8km), a more challenging hike which eventually links onto the Sugarloaf Ridge Track (6km rtn from the park office). The final lookout offers limited views over the Yarra Valley and Port Phillip Bay.

More extensive views can be had from Frank Thomson Reserve, Main Rd, Kinglake.

From Jehosephat picnic area you can take the well-graded Shelley Harris Walk (3km rtn–easy–1 hr). The Everard Circuit Walk (22km–mod/hard–6 hrs) and Lavers Circuit Walk (easy–15 min rtn) also leave from here — consult brochure available.

See the information centre for more details and opportunities.

UPPER BIG RIVER VALLEY STATE FOREST

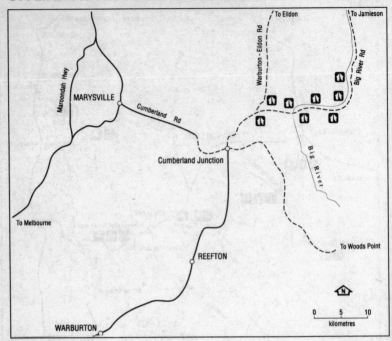

NORTHEAST AND ALPS

ON THE WAY

If you want somewhere to camp the night, in a pleasant forest environment, you might consider Upper Big River Valley State Forest.

Once you've driven through the magnificent Black Spur Range, between Healesville and Buxton, turn toward Marysville and continue along the Cumberland Rd then left into Warburton-Eildon Rd. A few kilometres further turn right into Big River Rd, where the campsites are located.

You can also reach the area by driving north-east of Warburton.

The main camping areas are at Stockmans Reward, Frenchmans Creek and Big River Camp, which have toilets and fireplaces. Cleared sites along the river have no facilities so please ensure you bury human waste 100 metres away from any watercourse and take out all your rubbish. No fee is charged to stay here.

CATHEDRAL RANGE STATE PARK

The jagged sandstone range, rising abruptly from the green farmland north of Buxton, is an impressive sight from the Maroondah Hwy.

Location and access

The road which climbs up and along the range can be reached from Mt Margaret Rd (which leaves the Buxton-Marysville

CATHEDRAL RANGE STATE PARK

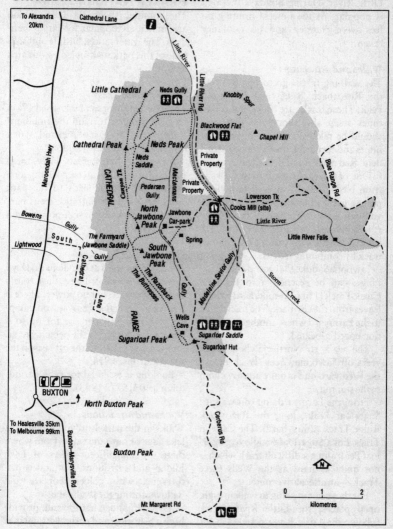

Rd) or from Cathedral Lane, just north of the landform, off the Maroondah Hwy.

The road is unsealed and may be impassable for conventional vehicles after rain.

Camping and facilities

The camping areas at Sugarloaf Saddle, Cooks Mill, Blackwood Flat and Neds Gully have toilets and fireplaces. Cooks Mill and Blackwood Flat are suitable for caravans. Water is available from

Little River. During holidays the area is popular. At the time of printing no fees were charged and no bookings taken.

Walks and attractions

The walking tracks go to points along the Razorback Ridge and Cathedral Peak. These tracks are rocky and sometimes steep and slippery. Great care should be taken; be aware of personal limits and turn back if you are not confident. Red markers guide the way.

One of the easiest and safest walks is from Neds Gully (1 hr o/w) to a viewpoint and information board. From here you can walk to Cathedral Peak (1 hr rtn–mod/hard) or Little Cathedral (1.5 hrs rtn–hard). You can make a circuit track by combining the two.

Jawbone Saddle, the central part of the range, can be reached from Jawbone Creek Track (1 hr o/w–mod/hard) which leaves from the car-park. The track leads to the Farmyard where another information board is located.

The walk to North Jawbone Peak veers off Jawbone Creek Track before the Farmyard and is quite an easy climb to the summit.

From the Farmyard you can walk to Sugarloaf Peak along the Razorback Ridge Track (2 hrs–hard). The Canyon Track links Sugarloaf Saddle to Sugarloaf Peak along a difficult track which is not quite as hard as the Wells Cave Track — an alternative route.

For those not wishing to walk in high, open places, the Little River Track follows the Little River between Neds Gully and Cooks Mill (40 mins o/w–easy).

Aboriginal history

The Tuangurong people occupied the area around Cathedral Range and the Acheron River Valley, west of the park.

FRASER NATIONAL PARK

The tranquil shores of Lake Eildon are immensely popular for family holidays. The watersports, birdlife and solitude of this park make it a pleasant area to visit.

Location and access

The park entrance can be reached 17km from Alexandra (turn off the Goulburn Valley Hwy 1km east of Alexandra) or a few kilometres north of Eildon.

From the Maroondah Hwy, near Bonnie Doon, you can turn south along Skyline Rd, which leads to the park entrance (a vehicle entrance fee is payable). The park is well sign-posted from any direction.

Camping and facilities

The camping areas at Candlebark, Devil Cove and Lakeside all have flush toilets and hot showers, but no power. There is room for caravans. Peak season camping rates are $16 per site for up to 4 people and $3 per extra person (maximum of 6 per site). In the off-season the site rate drops to $14.

Booking is essential for peak periods (phone: (03) 5772 1293).

Walks and attractions

Walks in the park lead you around the lake edge or onto the ridges from where there are magnificent views of Lake Eildon and surrounds. Autumn is picturesque, with golden poplars and willows dotting the landscape.

Two self-guided nature walk provide both a historical and natural insight into the area.

EILDON STATE PARK

Occupying the eastern and southern shores of Lake Eildon, this state park offers some similar attractions to Fraser National Park.

Eildon State Park and Fraser National Park

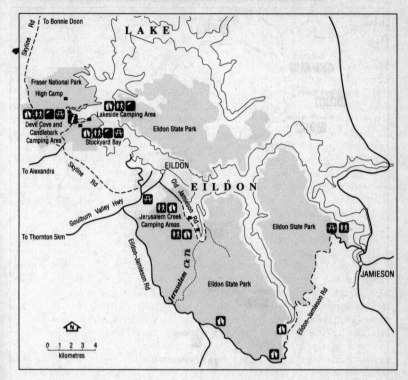

Location and access
The main camping area, at Jerusalem Creek, is reached by driving 10km east of Eildon along Old Jamieson Rd. The basic camping spots on the southern boundary of the park are reached by turning off the Goulburn Valley Hwy, 5km before Eildon, into the Eildon-Jamieson Rd.

Camping and facilities
The Jerusalem Creek camping ground is a large area with 70 sites. There are toilets and fireplaces. Cost is $8.50 per site and booking is essential during peak periods (phone: (03) 5772 1293).

The other sites have no facilities and no fee. Bury human waste 100m from waterways and carry out all rubbish.

Walks and attractions
From the Jerusalem Creek camping area you can take the Sheoak Creek Nature Walk which follows the creek for 2km. Other walks offering attractive views include the Pinnacles, Rocky Spur to Cable Track, and Wilsons Track.

On the way
The Upper Goulburn Historic Recreation Area has several camping reserves adjacent to the main road between

Upper Goulburn Historic Recreation Area

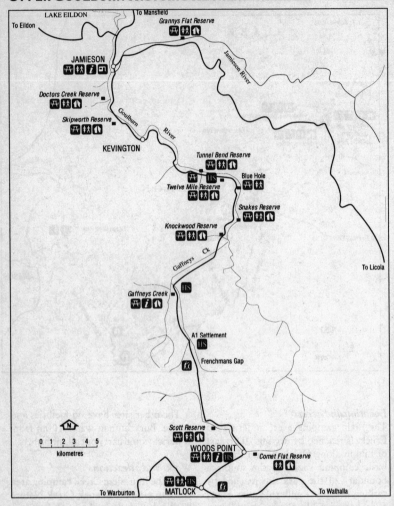

Jamieson and Matlock. They are Doctors Creek, Skipworth, Tunnel Bend, Twelve Mile, Blue Hole, Snakes, Knockwood, Gaffneys Creek, Scott and Comet Flat, in order south from Jamieson. Along the road are several historical points of interest.

Grannys Flat Reserve is east of Jamieson along the road to Licola. All the campsites have toilets, tables and fireplaces. There is a fee of $2 per site at the Doctors Creek and Skipworth Reserves. These two reserves are operated by a local committee of management in conjunction with the CNR. The other sites have no fee.

MT SAMARIA STATE PARK

This park north of Mansfield is a seldom-used retreat. It has some pleasant forest walks and low-key campsites.

Location and access

From Mansfield travel north on an unsealed road toward Wrightley, then after 17km veer left to follow Mt Samaria Rd. If you continue north a short distance you will reach a campsite in the Blue Range Creek State Forest.

Mt Samaria Rd is rough in places but passable by conventional vehicles when dry. Once onto the range there are walking trails leading from Mt Samaria Rd. At the northern end of the park you can turn right to reach the picnic area. The camping area is along a road which branches to the left once you're heading toward the picnic area.

The main access from the Midland Hwy is via Swanpool. A sign-posted all-weather road leads south to the park.

Camping and facilities

The Samaria Well camping area, near the northern boundary, is the only site accessible to vehicles. It is a lush, green area with a gurgling stream nearby and forest all around. There are fireplaces provided, but toilets are located at the picnic area 200m away.

On the range there are walk-in sites at Wild Dog Creek and Camphora, 800m and 500m from the road, respectively.

Walks and attractions

At the southern end of the park is a picnic area at Rocky Point Lookout where you can see Mt Buller, Mt Stirling and Mt Timbertop. The view is particularly good in winter when peaks of the alps are white from snow.

MT BUFFALO NATIONAL PARK

Although a snow-covered skifield in winter, after the snow melts Mt Buffalo is a wonderful area to camp and walk.

Location and access

A sealed road leads up to the mountain 30km from Porepunkah. An entrance fee of $9 ($12.50 if ski lifts are operating) is charged per vehicle.

Camping and facilities

The only camping area is at Lake Catani, open from November to May. It has hot showers, toilets and fireplaces. Peak season camping rates are $16.50 per site for up to 4 people and $3 per extra person (maximum of 6 per site). In the off-season the site rate drops to $10. You will need to book ahead over holiday periods (phone: (03) 5756 2328).

Walks and attractions

Walking and scenic lookouts are the highlights of the park. The View Point Nature Walk (4km rtn–easy/mod–1 hr) leaves from near the Lake Catani Dam wall and leads to Pulpit Rock. It features several lookouts along the way and the gorge itself is spectacular.

The Chalet Walk (11.5km loop– mod–5 hrs) leads from the chalet to the Monolith, where you can climb up the tor via a steep ladder to a lookout. Continue onto the Horn Rd and return via the track past Lake Catani to the chalet.

A popular stop-off on the way up the mountain is Eurobin Falls. A short walk leads from the car-park to the gushing stream of icy water at Ladies Bath Falls and then a little further to the larger Eurobin Falls.

A few kilometres further is the 2km walk to Rollasons Falls. There are dozens more sights and walks. See the national park office to get a *Walking Track Guide*.

Mt Samaria State Park

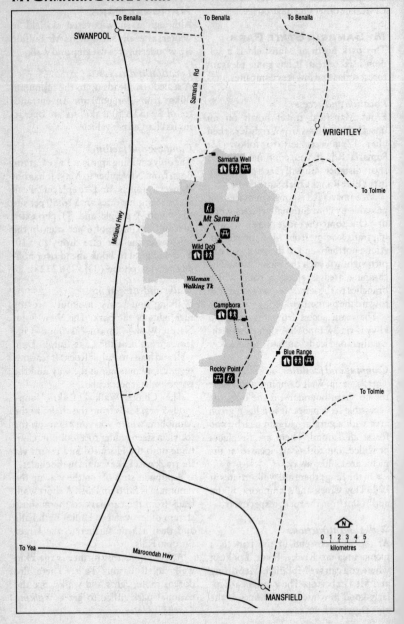

Mt Buffalo National Park

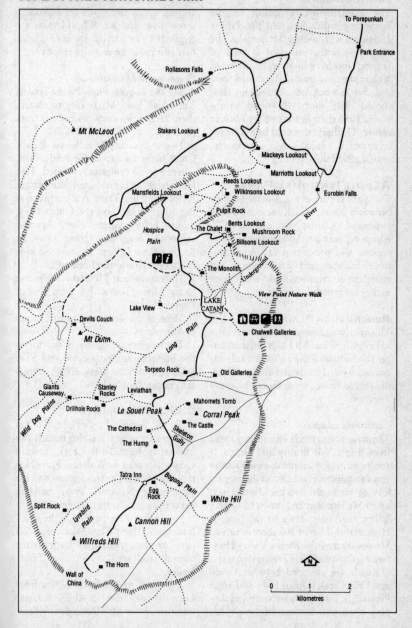

Aboriginal history
The Minjambuta, a group of the Pangerang tribe, occupied the valleys and plains surrounding Mt Buffalo. The summer months provided a feast of bogong moths which were collected high in the mountains. The moths were collected in a bag, put onto the fire then cooled. The nutty flavoured moths would have their heads removed before eating. The harvest would be a time for ceremonies such as corroboree, marriage and story-telling.

ALPINE NATIONAL PARK

This park is part of the Australian Alps National Parks, which includes alpine regions of Victoria, NSW and the ACT. Alpine NP is an amalgamation of several regions and presents a range of locations, facilities and attractions. I will group the descriptions under the regions as they are generally known.

BOGONG HIGH PLAINS

This area, containing the popular resorts of Falls Creek and Mt Hotham, is probably the feature of the alpine area. It has colourful heathlands and endless layers of jagged blue mountains in every direction.

Location and access
The main access roads into the area lead from Bright, Mt Beauty and Omeo. If you're visiting from north-east Victoria you can make a good circuit journey by leaving via Bright and the Ovens Hwy, up to Mt Hotham and down to Omeo; follow the Omeo Hwy to the Bogong High Plains Tourist Rd then return to Mt Beauty and the Kiewa Valley Hwy, passing through Falls Creek on the way.

Roads are unsealed between Omeo and Falls Creek (Omeo Hwy and High Plains Rd). Some parts are steep and slippery when wet. Sections of these roads are closed during the snow season. During winter the roads are subject to snow cover and ice. Wheel chains are required to be carried by law. Chains may be hired in the sub-alpine towns.

Camping and facilities
Along the Bogong High Plains Tourist Rd, which links Mt Beauty to Omeo, there are a few campsites not far from the road.

Twelve kilometres south-east of Falls Creek is the Langford West Aqueduct, where a small campsite is located. Two kilometres further is another campsite at Raspberry Hill. There is a campsite at Big River Bridge, on the Omeo Hwy, 3.5km before Glen Valley. Another campsite, near the Omeo Hwy, is Anglers Rest, next to the historic Blue Duck Hotel (no longer licensed).

The campsite at J.B. Plain is adjacent to the Alpine Tourist Rd, 2km west of Dinner Plain.

Most of the sites have toilets, tables and fireplaces.

The weather changes very quickly in the higher altitudes; ensure you have good equipment so that you stay warm if the weather turns cold.

Walks and attractions
From the Bogong High Plains Tourist Rd there are several walking tracks. Ten kilometres from Falls Creek, toward Omeo, is a trail to Wallaces Hut (2km rtn–easy–1 hr). The snow gums and the picturesque National Trust building make this a good walk to undertake.

Four kilometres further is the track leading to Mount Cope (4km–mod–2.5 hrs). An unmarked trail leads to the summit and good views over Pretty Valley.

The walk to Mt Loch begins from Loch car-park, just off Alpine Rd, one kilometre from Mt Hotham ski village.

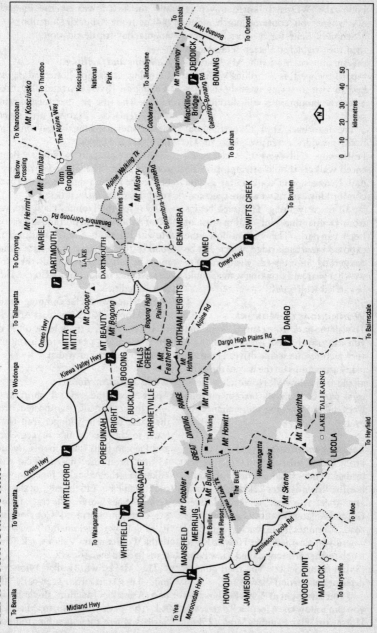

Follow the 4WD track 3km to snow pole 60, where you continue north along Machinery Spur for a short distance, then turn right for a steep scramble to the summit of Mt Loch. Mt Feathertop, to the west, is a thrilling sight; it's best to visit in spring or early summer when the mountain is still shrouded in snow.

The Razorback Trail (22km rtn–mod/hard) provides extensive views of Mt Feathertop. Only very fit and experienced walkers should attempt this in a day. I suggest you walk as far as you comfortably can, as views are spectacular all the way along. The track begins from Diamantina Hut, 1.5km west of Loch car-park. The walk follows the exposed razorback ridge, which can be dangerous in rugged weather. Wet weather gear and drinking water should be carried at all times.

WONNANGATTA-MOROKA

To visit the park from central Gippsland you can travel north of Licola along a very picturesque scenic drive. There are many attractions on the way to the semi-alpine area below Mt Howitt. It is a less-used part of the park (except on long weekends), providing more chance for escape.

Location and access

From Licola turn right just before the bridge. The sealed section of Tamboritha Rd ends after 22km and shortly after there is a walk to Dinner Creek Gorge and later Bennison Lookout. The road continues to Arbuckle Junction, where you turn left into Howitt Rd to reach further attractions and View Point (85km from Licola). The road quickly deteriorates beyond View Point.

If you turn right at Arbuckle Junction you can follow the Moroka Rd to reach Horseyard Flat camping area (25km) and the fire tower on the Pinnacles (34km from Arbuckle Junction) — a popular day-trip destination.

Camping and facilities

Camping areas are dotted along the Wellington River, starting 10km from Licola. The first site has toilets, tables and fireplaces. Beyond are several cleared sites along the river — some have fireplaces and tables.

The next campsite is 7km past Bennison Lookout. The Thomastown site is beside the river, a short distance off the road. There are no facilities.

To reach the Holmes Plain site, veer left at Arbuckle Junction and drive along Howitt Rd 4km. A track leads off the road to the left down to a gate (which must be left as it is found) then to a cleared area beside Shaws Creek. There are no facilities.

The Horseyard Flat camping area is along Moroka Rd, 25km past Arbuckle Junction. Again, a track leads off to the left and through a gate to reach a cleared area. A pit toilet is provided.

Walks and attractions

Apart from the several short trails and lookouts, all sign-posted from the road, there is a longer trail which leads to the spectacular Bryces Gorge and Pieman Falls (8km loop–easy/mod –3 hrs). From the Guys Hut car-park, 18km past the Arbuckle Junction, walk to Pieman Falls and the edge of the staggering Bryces Gorge. The track follows the cliff rim north to Conglomerate Falls. Follow Conglomerate Creek west to the Wonnangatta Valley track, which leads back to the car-park.

The Mt Howitt walk (14km rtn–mod–4 hrs) starts from a car-park 34km past Arbuckle Junction along Howitt Rd. The path leads up to Macalister Springs where there is a hut and good views. This is the midway point — for those not wanting to complete the whole journey this is a good point to reach before turning back. It is another hour's walk to reach the summit of Mt Howitt for excellent views of the surrounding landscape.

A more challenging walk is to Moroka Gorge (mod/hard–6 hrs rtn). The walk starts from the Horseyard Flat camping area.

COBBERAS-TINGARINGY

The most eastern section of the park borders with Kosciusko NP in NSW and the Snowy River NP in East Gippsland. It is a remote area, ideal for experienced bushwalkers and adventurers. Two spots you can reach in a conventional vehicle are the Native Dog Flat and Willis campsites.

Native Dog Flat is 31km north of Seldom Seen, along Black Mountain Rd (rough, unsealed). Willis campsite is 11km north of Suggan Buggan just near the state border. This unsealed road continues to Jindabyne. Contact the Bendoc national park office (phone: (02) 6458 1456), for more information.

Aboriginal history

Several Koori tribes used the high country during the warmer months to gather food, such as bogong moths, and for ceremonies. The Jaitmathang tribe was the largest and occupied the north-eastern alps around Tambo, Mitta Mitta, Kiewa and Gibbo Rivers. The Mt Buller–Mt Cobbler area forms the boundaries between the tribal territories. The Mitta Mitta River was a major route for trade and war between tribes. After European settlement the Koori population in the alps diminished rapidly due to disease and massacres. By 1860 few remained on the land.

BURROWA-PINE MOUNTAIN NATIONAL PARK

In an oft forgotten corner of Victoria, bypassed by commuters on the Hume Hwy, is a pleasant forest retreat.

Location and access

There are several gravel roads leading into various parts of the park. The easiest route to the camping areas is to head east from Tallangatta and onto the Cudgewa-Tintaldra Rd then veer off 10km north-east of Cudgewa. Falls Rd turns left and leads to Blue Gum and Bluff Creek camping spots. Or you can continue on an unsealed road to Hinces Creek campsite. This road continues north 14km to Walwa.

Camping and facilities

The camping sites have toilets, tables and fireplaces. At the time of printing no fees were charged.

Walks and attractions

There are many walking opportunities, from a comfortable 10-minute stroll to 3- to 4-day hikes. The walk to Bluff Falls (4km rtn–1.5 to 2 hrs), a gushing torrent of water during winter, begins at the Bluff Creek picnic area. Numbered points of interest correspond to the self-guide brochure, available from a pamphlet box at the picnic area and the falls. The Top Falls Walk (500m–30 mins) starts at the Bluff Falls car-park and is steep and rough. Its real attraction is the wet mountain gully. Another steep and rough walk to Campbells Lookout continues on from Top Falls (700m–1 hr rtn). There are fine views of the valley, Mt Mittamatite, Corryong and the distant Snowy Mountains. Most of the longer walks are also rocky and steep, and there is no water *en route*. For further information contact the ranger (Phone: (02) 6076 1655).

BURROWA-PINE MOUNTAIN NATIONAL PARK

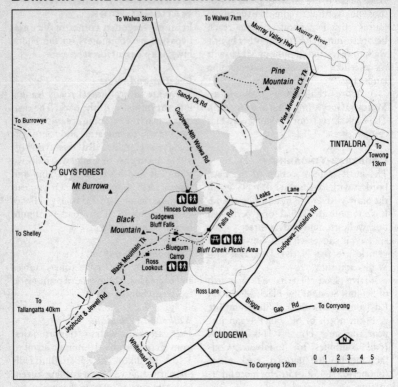

GIPPSLAND AND THE FAR EAST

 ON THE WAY

A very popular and well-known attraction is located at the tip of Phillip Island, south-east of Melbourne. The fairy penguin parade occurs each evening at about 6.15 pm at The Nobbies, on the far end of the island. It costs $14 per adult, $7 per child or $35 for a family pass for entrance to the viewing area and you may need to book ahead. For more information call the Phillip Island Information Centre (phone: (03) 5956 7447).

WILSONS PROMONTORY NATIONAL PARK

One of Victoria's best parks, 'The Prom' offers magnificent scenery, including huge granite boulders, idyllic beaches and rainforest. It is an easy park to explore and enjoy — wombats wander through the campsite, long walks end at isolated beaches. Few will leave this park without vowing to return.

Location and access

From Foster in South Gippsland, travel 25km south to the park entrance, where you will be charged $9 per vehicle. A sealed road leads 32km to the Tidal River camping area. Short roads veer off

VICTORIA

WILSONS PROMONTORY NATIONAL PARK

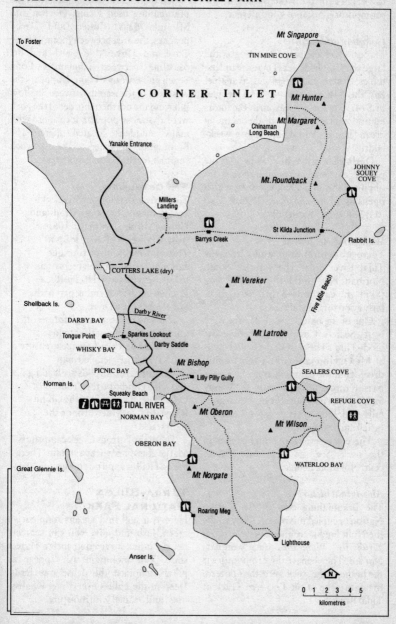

to beaches on the western side of the promontory. Access is good all year.

Camping and facilities

The only vehicle-based camping is the large site at Tidal River. There are toilets, tables, water and fireplaces available. Pay the $18 per site (up to 3 people) or $14.50 in the off-season, at the information centre just before the camping area. The normal rate applies on weekends.

During Christmas holiday periods the place is extremely popular and sites are obtained through a ballot system which opens on 1 June and closes 30 June. Call (03) 5680 9555 for details.

Walks and attractions

There are several short walks from the Tidal River area. The walk to South Norman Bay and Little Oberon Bay (8km rtn–easy/mod–3 hrs) is particularly good for coastal views.

One of the best day walks in the park is to Sealers Cove (9.5km o/w–easy/mod–3 hrs). The start of the walk begins at Mt Oberon car-park, a short uphill drive from the camping area. The walk passes through woodlands to Windy Saddle, then past rainforests with waterfalls and later emerges at a beautiful beach and tranquil cove.

There are several overnight hikes in the park. See the large information centre for more details.

Aboriginal history

The Brataualung clan of the Kurnai Nation occupied this region. They spoke the Nulit language, and called the prom *Yiruk* (or *Wamoom*) and wombats *Naroot*. They believe the promontory is the home of the spirit ancestor Looerrn, the namesake of the Loo-errn Track at Tidal River.

Occupational debris indicates that the Brataualung used Picnic, Oberon and Miranda Bays, Cotters and Darby Beaches, the area between Johnny Souey Cove and Three Mile Beach and the coastline between Chinaman Long Beach and Entrance Point. It appears the west side of the island, between Shallow Inlet and the northern border of the park were the most popular locations, with many middens located there. The Brataualung travelled to the alps each summer for the bogong moth feast.

ON THE WAY

To discover the glorious Strzelecki Forest, turn off the South Gippsland Hwy at Mirboo North Rd, 10km west of Foster. This road leads to Turtons Creek with picturesque camping spots and then veers right to link up with Grand Ridge Rd, a fascinating drive forming part of the Strzelecki Forest Drive.

The road passes through forests of tall trees, dripping with shredded bark. It can be a bit of a maze so ensure you have a fairly detailed map showing where the roads are leading and what condition they're in. Otherwise, if you follow the Grand Ridge Rd signs you will be on the right track.

The main Turtons Creek campsite is a large grassy area near a stream. There are no facilities and no charge.

TARRA-BULGA NATIONAL PARK

Here you will find an environment so green, lush and alive you can scarcely believe it has survived in such a perfect state. Tall mountain ash appear as pillars amongst the dense tree ferns. Deep in the gullies everything is moss-lined and beaded with moisture.

Tarra-Bulga National Park

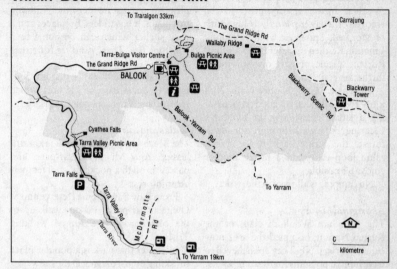

Location and Access
The park is 33km from Traralgon, along the Traralgon South Rd. This road joins The Grand Ridge Rd from where the picnic areas, car-parks and visitor centre are easily reached.

There are also several sign-posted access points from the South Gippsland Hwy, which lead north to the park.

Camping and facilities
No camping is allowed in the park, but there are two good caravan parks near the southern edge, along the Tarra Valley Rd.

Walks and attractions
Some short, easy trails lead from the visitor centre in Balook. The Lyrebird Ridge Track (2.4km rtn–easy) is suitable for wheelchairs. Ash Track veers off the Lyrebird Ridge Track, leading to the Bulga picnic area. From this spot, also accessible by vehicle, you can cross the suspension bridge and the walk through Fern Gully and forests of mountain ash.

Another great picnic spot is 5km from Balook on the Tarra Valley Rd, which turns off The Grand Ridge Rd. A short circuit (1.2km) trail leads through dark, moss-clad forest to Cyathea Falls.

If you're interested in longer day walks, such as the Diaper Track and Roberts Track, check with the ranger at the visitor centre for details and maps.

Aboriginal history
The Brataualung and the Brayakaulung co-existed in the South Gippsland area. They are part of the Kurnai Nation. A large number of sites have been recorded in the Monkey Creek, Traralgon and Gormandale–Hiamdale areas. The park is named after Charlie Tarra, an Aboriginal man who accompanied explorer Strzelecki, and *Bulga* is the word used for 'high mountain'.

MORWELL NATIONAL PARK

Another forest environment to be enjoyed on a day trip is only 16km south of Morwell. Travel via Churchill along Junction Rd then turn right into Jumbuk Rd; the picnic area is one kilometre further on your left.

The Fosters Gully Nature Walk (2km loop–easy–30 mins) is a good path, passing a small picnic area at Lyndon's Clearing. For a walk through more open forest, the Stringybark Ridge Track (3km loop–easy/mod–1 hr) is another enjoyable ramble.

No camping is allowed in the park.

Aboriginal history

The Woollum Woollum clan, of the Kurnai Nation, occupied the area now called Morwell NP. They are believed to have hunted possums for food and skins.

BAW BAW NATIONAL PARK

This sub-alpine park, enjoyed in winter by skiers, doubles as a good bushwalking location in the warmer months. Access is easy and the historic Walhalla area, just south of the park, is fascinating.

Location and access

Head north of Moe, 32km to Erica. From there you can drive east to Walhalla, from where an unsealed road twists 19km north to the Aberfeldy River camping area.

Otherwise, from Erica you can continue north to Mt Erica picnic area and further to Thomson Valley Rd and St Gwinear car-park. Both these points provide access to the Alpine Walking Track.

The Baw Baw Alpine Reserve is east of Tanjil Bren.

Camping and facilities

The Aberfeldy River campsite has toilets, tables and fireplaces. It is a remote site which you may have to yourself.

The North Gardens campground is a pleasant site just north of the Walhalla township. It has toilets, fireplaces and a cosy shelter which can be home to a welcome fire. There is no fee for either site.

Stop at the CNR office just north of Erica to get a map of the area which shows the 4WD-accessible campsites.

Walks and attractions

The Beech Gully Nature Walk (1km rtn) leaves from Mt Erica car-park and passes through a pocket of cool temperate rainforest.

From Baw Baw Alpine Reserve and St Gwinear car-park you can walk up to the plateau and the Alpine Walking Track.

In winter this park is a popular place for skiing or just playing in the snow.

Walhalla, steeped in gold-mining history, is a very interesting place to explore.

Aboriginal history

Aboriginal people lived around the river valleys at the base of *Baw Baw*, which is said to mean 'echo' or 'big'.

MITCHELL RIVER NATIONAL PARK

As you travel through the featureless country between Sale and Bairnsdale it may surprise you to find the spectacular Den of Nargun is only 30km north of the highway, surrounded by tangled warm temperate rainforest.

Location and access

Turn off the Princes Hwy 24km east of Stratford into Fernbank-Dargo Rd. Follow the signs to the park, passing through Fingerboards Junction and Glenaladale. The road is unsealed for the last part but fine for conventional vehicle access.

MORWELL NATIONAL PARK

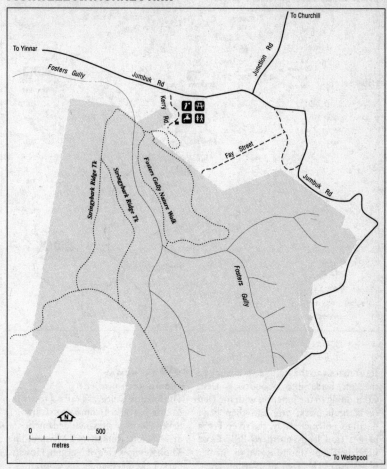

Camping and facilities
It is a popular day-use park with camping along the Mitchell River for walking or canoe access only. A good picnic area, located by the car-park, has toilets, tables, fireplaces and information.

Walks and attractions
The feature of the park is the mysterious Den of Nargun — a dark cave below a sandstone overhang. The Woolshed Creek topples over the rim, creating a curtain of water. Stalagmites and stalactites also guard the cave entrance.

The walk to the Den of Nargun can be completed as a loop track (3km–easy/mod–2 hrs), visiting other features of the park, or as a return trip of 1.5km.

The circuit track leads to Bluff Lookout then through the dense rainforest of Woolshed Creek Gorge. The red cliffs edging the Mitchell River are seen from a

Baw Baw National Park

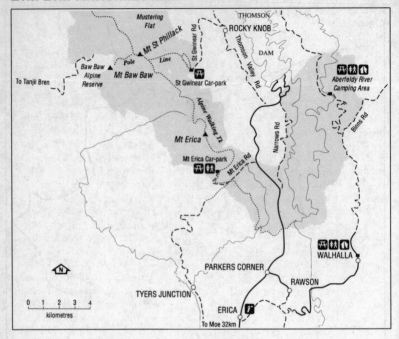

short detour to the right; a spur track to the left leads into Woodcock Den. Continuing to the junction with the Den of Nargun track, you can then head north to a picnic spot by the river. From here a trail leads north to Billy Goat Bend and the Amphitheatre (a further 6 hrs rtn); The Den of Nargun track leads to Woolshed Creek Gully, which you follow to reach the Den of Nargun.

Aboriginal history
The Brabuwooloong lived to the east of Mitchell River and the Brayakoloong to the west. These were clans of the Kurnai Nation. The Den of Nargun is believed to be a women's sacred site, where initiation and learning ceremonies took place.

ON THE WAY
ABORIGINAL HISTORY
The Bataluk Cultural Trail is a tour of Aboriginal places from Sale to Cann River. Heritage sites included on the drive include Ramahyuck Mission, The Knob Reserve, Den of Nargun, Howitt Park, Lake Tyers and Cape Conran. Also on the way is Krowathunkoolong Keeping Place, a cultural centre with displays and artefacts, open 9am–5pm Monday to Friday at 37–53 Dalmahoy St, Bairnsdale (phone: (03) 5152 1891). Further information and brochures about the trail are available from the Bairnsdale Tourist Information Centre, 240 Main Street, (phone: (03) 5152 3444).

The Lakes National Park and Gippsland Lakes Coastal Park

Most visitors passing through Gippsland appreciate the Gippsland Lakes from the excellent viewpoints near Lakes Entrance. For those who want to explore the area further, The Lakes NP may be a good way to do it.

Location and access
To reach the park you will need to drive south from Sale to Longford then continue to Loch Sport. The park is 63km from Sale, just east of Loch Sport. The Gippsland Lakes Coastal Park covers much of the coastal area between Seaspray and Lakes Entrance; many places are accessible by boat only.

Camping and facilities
In The Lakes NP camping is permitted only at Emu Bight. Here you will find toilets, tables, fireplaces and water. Pay the $10.40 camp fee at the park office near the park entrance. Bookings can be made through this office (phone: (03) 5146 0278). There are several picnic areas dotted around the coastline.

Gippsland Lakes Coastal Park has designated campsites between Paradise Beach and the Honeysuckles. Some sites have fireplaces and pit toilets nearby. Bring your own drinking water.

Campsites along the Bunga Arm are accessible by boat only. Enquire at the CNR office in Bairnsdale for details of this area.

Walks and attractions
From the park office you can walk to Pelican Point and Oil Bore Landing (5km loop–easy/mod). There are a few trails leaving from Emu Bight.

Sperm Whale Head can be explored by a number of short trails.

Both these parks, as with many coastal parks, require self-exploration and discovery.

Aboriginal history
The Tatungalung clan of the Kurnai Nation occupied the Gippsland Lakes area.

ON THE WAY
Another place to enjoy the lake system, while remaining on the northern edge, is at Nyerimilang Park.

Turn off the Princes Hwy 5km east of Swan Reach into Nungurner Rd and follow the signs to the park (only a few kilometres).

This is a day-use park (open 9am to 4pm each day) featuring the historic Nyerimilang Homestead and a picnic area.

There is a 4.5km walk which leads from the homestead to Cliffs Lookout then along the Cliff Top Walk to further lookouts and a bird-hide. From there you can follow the Saltmarsh Track back onto Homestead Track to return to the car-park.

Snowy River National Park

This park occupies a remote section of rugged country in East Gippsland. Driving in and exploring this region can be very rewarding. As with most touring in the East Gippsland area, visitors need to beware of log trucks which constantly use many of the roads. Seasonal road closures (during winter) and variable road conditions also need to be considered.

Location and access
To reach Buchan, turn off the Bruthen-Nowa Nowa Rd 7km west of Nowa Nowa and follow the sealed road to the township. Buchan can also be reached along the Orbost-Buchan Rd, a winding drive leaving from Bete Bolong

The Lakes National Park

Map showing Lake Victoria, Lake Reeve, and Ninety Mile Beach with features including Pelican Point, Oil Bore Landing, Park Office, lookout tower, Emu Bight, Cherry Tree, Trouser Point, Lake Victoria Tk, Lake Reeve Tk, Point Wilson, jetty, Sperm Whale Head, Murphy Hill, Trapper Point, Rotamah Island, Causeway, beach access, private property, To Loch Sport, To Ocean Grange.

Snowy River National Park

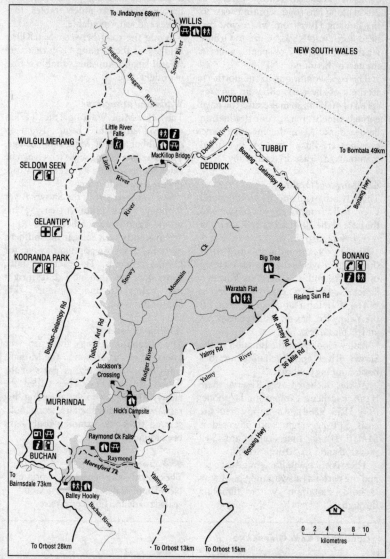

(sign-posted from Orbost). Five kilometres before Buchan along this road turn right into Basin Rd then right again to reach Balley Hooley campsite.

To get to MacKillop Bridge, travel north of Buchan along the Gelantipy Rd, unsealed after 20km, up past Seldom Seen to the Bonang-Gelantipy Rd. The campsite near MacKillop Bridge is 20km along this road. Continue east to the Bonang Hwy from where you can head north into NSW, return to Orbost via the Bonang Hwy, or spend a while in the nearby Errinundra NP.

The road conditions in the northern sections of the park allow an average speed of 40 km/h so make sure you have enough time to reach your destination before dark. Also, the mornings and evenings are busy times for nocturnal mammals so please drive carefully.

Camping and facilities

There is a basic campsite at Raymond Creek Falls, from where you can walk to the base of the 20-metre falls. A pit toilet is yet to be constructed.

The Hick's camping area is located on the Rodger River in the southern section of the park and is reached via Varney's Track. No facilities are provided yet.

The Waratah Flat camping area, off the Yalmy Rd, has pit toilets, barbecues and picnic tables.

Balley Hooley, at the junction of the Snowy River and Buchan River, has basic camping facilities.

At the Buchan Caves Reserve there is an excellent campground (phone: (03) 5155 9264). An unpowered site costs $11 per night and powered is $14.50. Peak time rates are $19 powered and $15.50 unpowered.

There is often wildlife around the sites and the park has a swimming pool with ice-cold mountain water tumbling through it.

There is a camping spot at MacKillop Bridge, which has toilets, tables, fireplaces and water available.

Along the road between MacKillop Bridge and the Bonang Hwy there are several small campsites suitable for an overnight stay.

Walks and attractions

The Silver Mine Walking Track (17km rtn–mod/hard–5 hrs) begins 100m on the Tubbut side of MacKillop Bridge. This is an interesting walk which can be extended to include an overnight stop. Ensure you carry water.

For a shorter stroll, the Snowy River Walking Track (2km rtn–easy–1 hr) provides good views of the area.

Raymond Creek Falls, in the southern tip of the park, is a popular day trip for Orbost residents. To reach the falls, drive along Jarrahmond Rd, turn right into Yalmy Rd and continue 37km along a dirt road.

Aboriginal history

The Krauatungalung lived in the lowlands of this area, and the Monaro clans occupied the higher parts of the Snowy River valley. They called the Snowy *Mowonbymoney*, meaning 'big rapid water'. Rock shelters, stone tools, scarred trees and grinding tools have been found in the park.

ON THE WAY

The coastal route between Victoria and New South Wales is well worn. Good sealed roads and fine scenery are

---

LOGGING IN EAST GIPPSLAND

The misty forests of Errinundra Plateau have been the cause of nearly two decades of dispute. Protests in the 1980s resulted in large areas of East Gippsland forests being registered as National Estate forests and the creation of Errinundra NP in July 1988.

probably the main reasons. I would like to offer an alternative for those wanting a challenge and a chance to explore the diverse areas of East Gippsland—take the less established route between Orbost and Bombala. The roads in this region are winding and often unsealed.

Travelling here is not really suitable for caravans, although it can be done.

Taking this way will leave you well placed to visit Kosciusko NP and still allow you to cross to the coast from Cooma.

ERRINUNDRA NATIONAL PARK

The beauty of Errinundra Plateau is hard to describe. As you follow the twisting road toward the plateau a motionless mist envelopes the landscape, creating an ethereal scene. The fringes of the plateau are more spectacular than the plateau itself. Tree ferns carpet the gullies and tall eucalypts appear as ghostly forms in the mist.

Location and access

The easiest access into the park is by travelling along the Bonang Hwy, from Orbost, to Errinundra Rd, 9km south of Bonang. Travel along this unsealed road 16km to Errinundra Saddle.

This spot is also reached by travelling north from the Princes Hwy, via Club Terrace, along Errinundra Rd—passing Ada River camping area, 25km north of Club Terrace.

Ten kilometres north of Club Terrace, where Errinundra Rd bears to the left, Combienbar Rd continues to the right,

ERRINUNDRA NATIONAL PARK

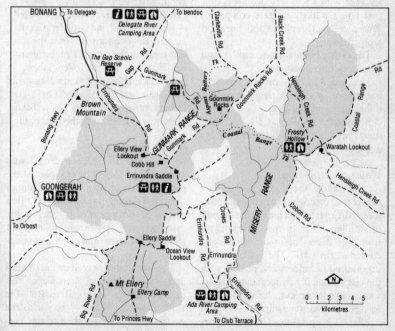

passing through Combienbar to Hensleigh Creek Rd and the Frosty Hollow Camp. This site is more easily reached by travelling south from Bendoc along Beasley Rd then Back Creek Rd into Hensleigh Creek Rd. At the intersection of this road with Coast Range Rd (difficult to identify) turn west and continue for 2.5km to a minor road on the right which leads to the campsite.

Most roads in this area are unsealed and can be boggy in places — unsuitable for caravans. Check conditions at the Orbost Rainforest Centre (phone: (03) 5161 1375). Many of the roads are also used by log trucks.

Camping and facilities

One of the easiest camping areas to reach is the Delegate River campsite. It is located along Gap Rd, midway between Errinundra Rd and Bendoc. It is a pleasant spot with a few secluded areas (not that you are likely to have company). Water, toilets, fireplaces and firewood are available.

The Frosty Hollow site has toilets and fireplaces, but no water.

The Ada River campsite is a remote forest spot by a small river. There is a toilet, table and fireplace.

Errinundra Saddle has a picnic area, toilets and an attractive information display.

Walks and attractions

At the Saddle there is a self-guiding nature trail through cool temperate rainforest. An interesting climb to the summit of Mt Ellery (4km rtn–mod– 3 hrs) leaves from Big River Rd in the south-west corner of the park. The walk involves negotiation of ladders and planks, with the last section involving scrambling up some rocks for spectacular views of the forests and distant coastline.

Ellery Camp, along Green Rd, has short walks to Sassafras Gully (20 mins) where you will uncover a deep rainforest environment, or to the Big Tree, a giant mountain grey gum.

From Gunmark Rd you can take the Spotmill Track (2km rtn–easy–1.5 hrs) which wanders through old shining gum forests and ends at regrowth forest, where you can return by the same route.

Goonmirk Rocks–Rooty Break Loop (2 hr rtn–easy/mod) begins from Goonmirk Rocks Rd, just east of Gunmark Rd intersection. The Aspens Battery Track also begins here.

ON THE WAY

Lind NP is located at the intersection of the Princes Hwy and Combienbar Rd. The main way to explore the park is along the Euchre Valley Nature Drive which follows the Old Princes Hwy, beginning (or ending) just west of the Bemm River bridge. The drive passes through Club Terrace and into Lind NP — where you will find Growlers Creek picnic area — and emerges onto the Princes Hwy 4km east of Combienbar Rd. The picnic area has toilets, tables, fireplaces and water. A 4km walking trail leads from here to the Princes Hwy. Either arrange a pick-up or just walk part of the way and return by the same path.

CAPE CONRAN

An easily accessible place to camp, swim and fish is at Cape Conran (part of the proposed Sydenham Inlet–Cape Conran Coastal Reserve). Banksia Bluff is 19km east of Marlo, unsealed just before the camping area. There are toilets, hot showers, fireplaces and cabin accommodation.

The swimming is excellent nearby and at Salmon Rocks, on West Cape. You can drive along Yeerung River Rd — or walk along the beach — to get to the warm, tea-coloured waters of the Yeerung River. It is an unusual and enjoyable place to visit.

A walking trail explores around the cape from Sailors Grove (5km rtn), offering excellent coastal views.

In summer the camping area is a thriving metropolis, so booking may be necessary (phone: (03) 5154 8438).

CROAJINGOLONG NATIONAL PARK

This is a remarkable park, protecting the coastal region between Sydenham Inlet and the state border.

There are excellent camping areas set amongst unspoilt coastal terrain. The pounding surf can be heard from the coastal camping areas, lulling you to sleep and waking you at sunrise. There is a great deal to enjoy in this park.

Location and access

To reach two of the camping areas, head south from Cann River along Tamboon Rd for 15km then veer left into Point Hicks Rd and continue for 25km to the Mueller River and Thurra River campsites. Point Hicks Road may be closed after rain.

If you continue on the Tamboon Rd you will reach Tamboon Inlet, which has campsites accessible by boat only (see the Cann River visitor centre for details, phone: (03) 5158 6351). The road is unsealed after a few kilometres south of Cann River, but is generally in good condition.

To reach the Wingan Inlet campsite turn off the Princes Hwy 19km east of Cann River and travel 34km south on West Wingan Rd. The road is unsealed and unsuitable for caravans; it may become impassable after rain.

Shipwreck Creek camping area is accessed via Mallacoota. Follow Betka Rd past the aerodrome then onto Centre Track and left into Betka Track, to the campsite, 16km from Mallacoota. The road is unsealed and not recommended for caravans.

Camping and facilities

The Thurra River, Wingan Inlet and Shipwreck Creek sites are well established and popular spots during holiday season. They have designated sites in private pockets of wilderness. Toilets, tables, fireplaces and firewood are provided. Mueller River campsite has pit toilets. All sites have fresh water nearby except Mueller River, where campers must go to the Thurra River for water. Bookings are required for holiday periods Phone the Point Hicks Lighthouse (phone: (03) 5158 4268 to book the Thurra River or Mueller River sites and the Cann River Information Centre (phone: (03) 5158 6351) for the other locations. Sites cost $11 off peak and $15 in peak season.

Walks and attractions

One remarkable feature of the park, often mentioned by travellers, is the vast area of sand dunes near the Thurra River campsite. The Dunes Walk (4km rtn–easy), sign-posted from the campsite, begins from Point Hicks Rd and leads to the edge of the dunes. You can explore them yourself—just don't forget the spot you left from, as you return by the same route.

A good track leads from the camping area to the historic Point Hicks Lighthouse (4km rtn–easy–1.5hrs), which, history has it, occupies the first point on the Australian mainland to be seen by Captain Cook.

For the walk to Mt Everard (8km rtn–mod), turn off Point Hicks Rd, 7km north of Thurra Camp, and travel a short distance to the start of the walk. The track involves some steep sections, leading to a granite outcrop where you can

52   **CAMPING AND TRAMPING**

enjoy a wide view, south to the sand dunes and north to Mt Ellery and the forest wilderness. A 17km 4WD track called the Cicada Trail (which links up West Wingan Rd) features a 1km walk to the Mueller River, which is worth a look.

Swimming is excellent on the beach near the Thurra River, particularly because you can walk a short distance to rinse off the salt water in the fresh water of the Thurra River. However, after heavy rain the river can cause a nasty rip along the beach.

Aboriginal history

The Krautungulung people once occupied the coastal area now covered by the national park. *Croajingolong* means 'looking eastward, high plains'. The Krautungulung people were competent warriors and fiercely resisted European settlement. They were part of the Kurnai people who were known enemies of the Kulin Nation.

Australian Capital Territory

NATIONAL PARKS SERVICE
The ACT Parks and Conservation Service controls the parks in this territory.

ABORIGINAL HISTORY
Canberra was a meeting place for the Ngunnawal, from the southern tablelands, the Wiiradjuri to the north, the Ngarigo from the Monaro tablelands and the Walgalu from the west. *Canberra* is an Aboriginal word meaning 'meeting place'.

Archaeological evidence shows occupation of this region for at least 21,000 years.

Axe-grinding stones have been found around Canberra and Tidbinbilla Valley. Basalt and other volcanic rocks were brought from the Monaro area and then made into the ground edge axes. Ochre is plentiful in the Canberra area and may have been used for trade. Bark huts were made for shelter from rain and frost.

CONTACT
ENVIRONMENT INFORMATION CENTRE
(02) 6207 9777
ENVIRONMENTACT@ACT.GOV.AU
WWW.ENVIRONMENT.ACT.GOV.AU

PUB PATRON GUIDE
MIDDY   285ML

NAMADGI NATIONAL PARK
The Australian Capital Territory consists of more than just Canberra. Namadgi National Park covers nearly 50 per cent of the south-western area of the ACT, sharing part of its border with Kosciuszko National Park in NSW.

Location and access
If you're coming from the south the best access is from Adaminaby, on the Snowy Mountains Hwy. Head west from Cooma toward Berridale. The Snowy Mountains Hwy veers right about 5km out of town. Just before Adaminaby turn right toward Bolaro and follow the signs to Canberra. This route is unsealed once you turn off the Snowy Mountains Hwy.

Otherwise you can continue north along the Monaro Hwy from Cooma until you reach Tuggeranong, a residential area south of Canberra. From Tuggeranong you can travel south along Tharwa Rd to reach Namadgi Visitor Centre and continue on Naas Rd to Orroral campground. The north-western section of the park is reached by heading west from Tuggeranong on Tidbinbilla Rd.

From Canberra, Cotter Rd leads west to Brindabella Rd and the Mt Franklin Rd, or south along Paddys River Rd to Tidbinbilla Nature Reserve.

Camping and facilities
A short way into the park from the southern entrance is the large, grassy Mt Clear campground. There are pit toilets and stone fireplaces. It is a little-used site containing several trees and alive with birds. The main camping area is the Orroral campground, further north from Mt Clear, and accessible from

NAMADGI NATIONAL PARK

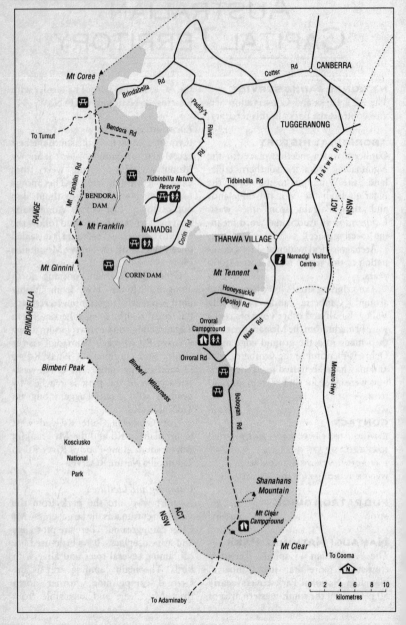

Canberra along a sealed road. It is a large area with designated sites, toilets, fireplaces and firewood, and a pleasant river nearby. This area is often used by groups (tents only) and there is a three-day limit for campers. No drinking water is available and no fee applies.

Walks and attractions

There are many walking trails in this park plus an excellent visitor centre, 2km south of Tharwa. I will list a few of the good walks but I recommend consulting the visitor centre for more information. An excellent map of the park, showing all the walking trails, is available for $2 from the visitor centre.

From the Mt Clear camping area you can walk from Naas Valley to Horse Gully Hut (16km rtn–mod–all day). It is a long but enjoyable stroll along the grassy riverside and woodland to the historic hut. Rainwater is available there. If you're not up to the entire distance you might like to turn back at post number 6, which will mean a 4km, 2-hour walk.

Further north is the Shanahans Mountain Circuit (3km–easy–1.5 hrs), a pleasurable walk to good views. The Yerrabi Track (4km rtn–mod–1.5 hrs) provides a 360° panorama across wilderness area.

Just north of the intersection of Old Boboyan Rd and the Boboyan Rd is Rendezvous Creek. There is no marked trail, but walking along the river bank can be very pleasant — particularly on a weekend, when some areas of the park are swamped by Canberrans escaping from the city. You can follow the creek north-west then climb over the ridge (north) to the Nursery Swamp. Alternatively the Nursery Swamp Walk (6km rtn–mod–3 hrs) is a pleasant stroll from the Orroral Valley.

A one-kilometre circuit track, through woodlands of snow gum and peppermint gum, leaves the Orroral campground.

The hike to the summit of Mt Franklin, on the western edge of the park, is very rewarding (3km rtn–mod–1.5 hrs). To reach the car-park follow Mt Franklin Rd along the western boundary of the park.

Aboriginal history

The Ngunnawal people occupied the area now used by the national park. *Namadgi* is the name they used for the mountains south-west of Canberra. Despite the conditions they lived here during the middle of the last ice age when snow covered the area for most of the year.

Ngunnawal people made stone arrangements, stone tools and rock art.

The seasonal Bogong moth migration was a rich source of food in spring.

A rock art site at Yankee Hat Rock is accessible to the public. To reach the site travel 29km south from the Namadgi visitor centre and turn west onto Old Boboyan Rd. The carpark is 3.7km along this road. Take the 2hr return walk to view the site (6km rtn easy).

ON THE WAY

Tidbinbilla Nature Reserve is a day-use park for visitors to enjoy pleasant picnic facilities and abundant wildlife. To reach the reserve, take Cotter Rd out of the city then head south along Paddys River Rd to the park. A visitor centre with information and displays is located near the entrance. Easy walking trails lead through forest environs.

New South Wales

1. Kosciuszko NP, see p63
2. Ben Boyd NP, see p64
3. Bourdna NP, see p65
4. Mimosa Rocks NP, see p65
5. Wadbilliga NP, see p67
6. Deua NP, see p67
7. Murramarang NP, see p69
8. Booderee NP, see p70
9. Seven Mile Beach NP, see p71
10. Morton NP, see p72
11. Budderoo NP, see p75
12. Macquarie Pass NP, see p77
13. Thirlmere Lakes NP, see p77
14. Royal NP, see p77
15. Botany Bay NP, see p78
16. Sydney Harbour NP, see p78
17. Blue Mountains NP, see p79
18. Kanangra-Boyd NP, see p80
19. Ku-Ring-Gai Chase NP, see p80
20. Brisbane Water NP, see p82
21. Bouddi NP, see p83
22. Wyrrabalong NP, see p84
23. Goulburn River NP, see p84
24. Cattai NP, see p86
25. Wollemi NP, see p86
26. Dharug NP, see p86
27. Yengo NP, see p89
28. Tomaree NP, see p90
29. Myall Lakes NP, see p90
30. Barrington Tops NP, see p92
31. Woko NP, see p94
32. Crowdy Bay NP, see p94
33. Hat Head NP, see p96
34. Werrikimbe NP, see p97
35. Oxley Wild Rivers NP, see p98
36. New England NP, see p99
37. Cathedral Rock NP, see p100
38. Guy Fawkes River NP, see p101
39. Gibraltar Range NP, see p102
40. Washpool NP, see p103
41. Boonoo Boonoo NP, see p104
42. Bald Rock NP, see p105
43. Dorrigo NP, see p106
44. Yuraygir NP, see p107
45. Bundjalung NP, see p108
46. Broadwater NP, see p111
47. Nightcap NP, see p111
48. Mt Warning NP, see p113
49. Border Ranges NP, see p113
50. Cocoparra NP, see p115
51. Weddin Mountains NP, see p116
52. Conimbla NP, see p119
53. Hill End HS, see p119
54. Warrumbungle NP, see p119
55. Warrabah NP, see p120
56. Mt Kaputar NP, see p120
57. Mungo NP, see p121
58. Willandra NP, see p123
59. Kinchega NP, see p123
60. Mootwingee NP, see p125
61. Sturt NP, see p126

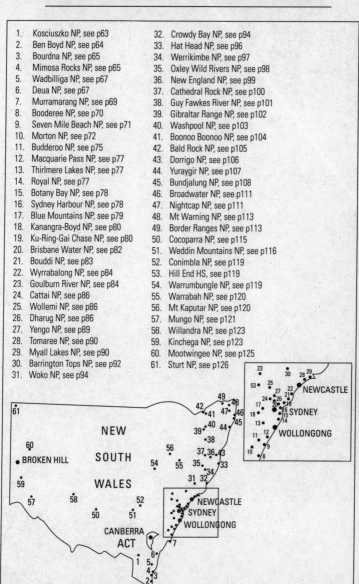

NOTE: Look through the chapter to the On the Way sections to see additional places to camp or visit.

NATIONAL PARKS SERVICE

The New South Wales National Parks and Wildlife Service (NSW NPWS) are your hosts for your trip through the parks in this State.

CONTACT

NATIONAL PARKS CENTRE
1300 361 967 (WITHIN NSW)
OR (02) 9253 4600
INFO@NPWS.NSW.GOV.AU
WWW.NPWS.NSW.GOV.AU/

102 GEORGE STREET
THE ROCKS, SYDNEY
OPEN 9AM - 5PM MON - FRI
9.30AM - 4.30PM SAT/SUN

PARK ENTRY FEES

Park entry fees are charged for most parks in NSW. The cost is $9 per car for parks in the Sydney Basin, and $5 per car for all other parks. An annual pass can be purchased for $60, or $80 including Mt Kosciuszko.

STATE FORESTS

Many of the state forests in NSW have excellent facilities for campers — and few have a camp or user fee. Inquire at Forestry Commission offices or tourist information centres to find out their location.

REST AREAS

Within the NSW national parks, 'rest area' means a place where you can camp. I have used this term throughout the chapter to maintain uniformity with sign-posts and maps you will see along the way.

PUB PATRON GUIDE

| MIDDY | 285M |
| SCHOONER | 425ML |

New South Wales is a vast State with a high density of parks near the coast and along the Great Dividing Range. In the greater area of the State, west of the dividing range, parks are long distances apart, requiring a determined commitment to reach them.

I have listed the parks in the west of the State under the categories of West and Far West. If you are taking the Newell Hwy between Albury and Queensland you can reach many of the parks in the West section. The Far West parks occupy the area nearer the South Australian border, between Mildura, Broken Hill and Tibooburra.

Before embarking inland to some of the more isolated parks, I suggest you obtain more specific and detailed information, to ensure your journey is worthwhile and safe.

ABORIGINAL HISTORY

In the 1770s, when the Europeans first arrived, it was noted how peaceful the Indigenous people were. Despite instructions to facilitate an amicable relationship, the first settlers where quick to introduce violence in order to control the Aboriginal tribes around Sydney Harbour. Smallpox ran rife amongst the tribes in the Botany Bay and Pittwater areas where the population was halved by 1870.

Over 18,000 Aboriginal sites have been recorded in New South Wales.

KOSCIUSZKO NATIONAL PARK

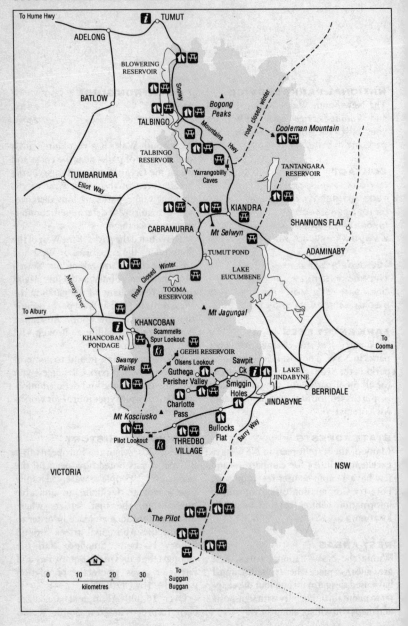

NSW now has the largest indigenous population of all the states and territories. Many indigenous people in NSW call themselves Koori, meaning 'person' or 'people'.

ALPINE

KOSCIUSZKO NATIONAL PARK

The Kosciuszko region is probably Australia's largest alpine playground. There is ample to see and do, with excellent visitor services to make it an easy trip. As with Victoria's alpine regions, you need to be prepared for rapid changes in weather. Tracks are often wet, so sturdy footwear is important.

Location and access

Thredbo Village is 37km west of Jindabyne along Alpine Way. To reach Sawpit Creek, Perisher Valley and Guthega travel north-west of Jindabyne. To reach Thredbo, turn left a few kilometres out of Jindabyne. From Albury you can travel east to Khancoban and follow Alpine Way up to Thredbo Village. The northern section of the park can be accessed from the Snowy Mountains Hwy, which starts from the Cooma–Jindabyne Rd 5km west of Cooma. The highway passes through Adaminaby, leading north to Yarrangobilly Caves, Talbingo and Tumut. An entry fee of $15 is charged per vehicle.

Camping and facilities

The Kosciuszko Mountain Retreat, near the visitor centre in Sawpit Creek, has camping and caravan sites, with amenities blocks and fireplaces. Booking is essential during school holidays (phone: (02) 6456 2224). The other campsites shown on the map mostly have tables, toilets and fireplaces. There is no camp fee.

Walks and attractions

One of the most popular walks during summer is to the summit of Mt Kosciuszko, the highest peak in Australia. Travel part the way up the mountain on the Crackenback Chairlift to Thredbo Village. From there to the summit is 12km return or to the lookout is only 4km return.

At Yarrangobilly Caves, in the northern part of the park, are cave tours, short walking trails and a thermal pool. You can walk through Glory Hole Cave (open 10 am to 4 pm daily) yourself. There are guided tours of the North Glory, Jillabean and Jersey Caves. Buy your ticket to enter the caves from the visitor centre. There is a thermal pool (constant 27°C) and a few short lookout walks.

To reach the caves, turn off the Snowy Mountain Hwy 109km from Cooma or 77km from Tumut. The caves car-park is 6.5km along an unsealed road.

Aboriginal history

Several tribes occupied the area of Kosciuszko NP including the Wiradjuri, Bidewal, Wolgal, Ngarigo and Ngunnawal people. They lived in the lowlands during the winter months with each tribe or clan living in a different valley. During the spring and summer they would travel to the high country to feast on bogong moths, which would migrate from southern Queensland and northern NSW. Huge numbers of the moths, considered a delicacy, were available at harvest time.

Many scarred trees can be found along the Lower Snowy River and the stony river beds provided materials for making tools. When sheep and cattle were introduced into the lower valleys in the 1830s Aboriginal tribes were driven out.

Ben Boyd National Park

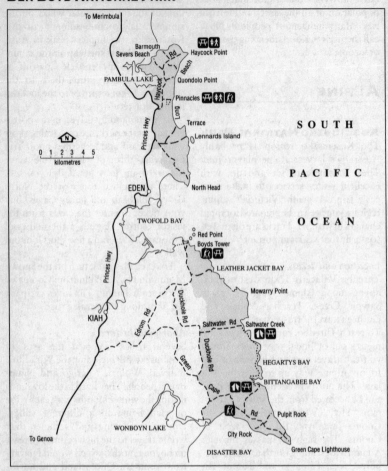

Southeast

On the way

The Cann Valley Hwy is a scenic route to take when travelling to NSW from Victoria. Turn off the Princes Hwy at Cann River. The road is sealed most of the way and passes through several quaint towns. Bombala, just inside the NSW border, is a good place to stay the night. The Bombala Shire Caravan Park, located just north of the bridge, charges $13.50 for an unpowered site or $15 for a powered site (phone: (02) 6458 3270).

Ben Boyd National Park

This park, in the southern corner of the State, preserves the coastal and historical features south and north of Twofold Bay.

Eden, the township in between, is an old whaling town with many relics from the past. The southern part of the park has more to offer the visitor, with two camping areas and a good walking trail.

Location and access
Roads leading into the park branch off the Princes Hwy. The southern access road turns off 18km south of Eden; from here it is 22km to Saltwater Creek or 27km to Bittangabee Bay.

Two roads, leaving the Princes Hwy 6km and 8km north of Eden, lead to North Head and the Pinnacles, respectively.

The access roads are unsealed and may become difficult to drive along after rain.

Camping and facilities
The two camping areas — Saltwater Creek and Bittangabee Bay — have toilets, tables and fireplaces. Camp fees exist and bookings are required. Calll the Merimbula NPWS (phone: (02) 6495 5000).

The day-use areas in the park, including Haycock Point and the Pinnacles, have picnic tables and toilets.

Walks and attractions
From the Bittangabee Bay camping area you can undertake a good coastal walk north to Saltwater Creek (10km o/w-easy/mod). It can also be undertaken in smaller sections. Bittangabee Ruins, near the camping area, is also worth a look.

Boyds Tower (erected in the 1840s) is at Red Point, where you can look over Twofold Bay and Eden township.

The rich red cliffs of the Pinnacles are the feature of the northern section. The multi-coloured display of erosion can be viewed from a loop track leaving the car-park.

Haycock Point, at the northern tip of the park, is another scenic feature.

Green Cape Lighthouse, at the southern tip of the park, is also worth a visit.

In fine weather swimming, surfing and fishing are popular.

Mt Imlay National Park is a good day trip to undertake from Ben Boyd. The summit trail (6km rtn–mod–3 hrs) starts from the car-park 30km from Eden, at the end of Burrawang Forest Rd. Turn west off the Princes Hwy, 19km south of Eden.

BOURNDA NATIONAL PARK
Midway between Merimbula and Tathra is the Bournda coastal park. Facilities and attractions can be reached by turning off Sapphire Coast Drive, 5km south of the Snowy Mountains Hwy.

White Rock and Chamberlain Lookouts are reached from roads which directly leave the Snowy Mountains Hwy.

Camping is at Hobart Beach (hot showers, laundry etc.) and is very popular during holiday periods. Booking is essential in those times. Call the Merimbula office (phone: (02) 6495 5000).

There are several picnic areas and walking trails.

MIMOSA ROCKS NATIONAL PARK
The unusual landscape in this park includes remnant rainforest almost to the water's edge. The rocks near the coastline are rusty-orange from lichen.

There are several camping areas, so during the off-season you may find a piece of secluded beach for yourself. See the map for location of sites. Cost is $5 per site (for two people). Bring your own drinking water.

The roads into the park are unsealed,

MIMOSA ROCKS NATIONAL PARK

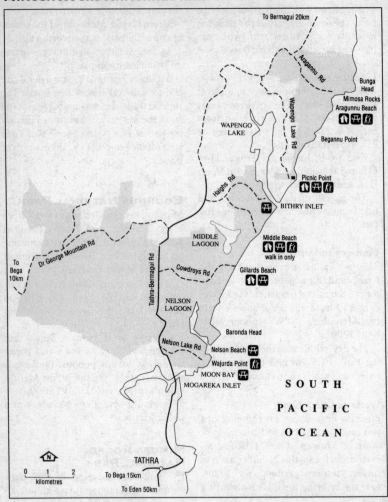

so you should check conditions after rain, or if you are towing a caravan (phone: (02) 4476 2888).

Aboriginal history
The territory of the Yuin people extended along the coast and hinterland. Descendants of the Yuin people live locally and in nearby Wallaga Lake, an Aboriginal community.

It is believed the Yuin had close contact with people from the Monaro Tablelands and there was a high level of trade between the groups.

WADBILLIGA NATIONAL PARK

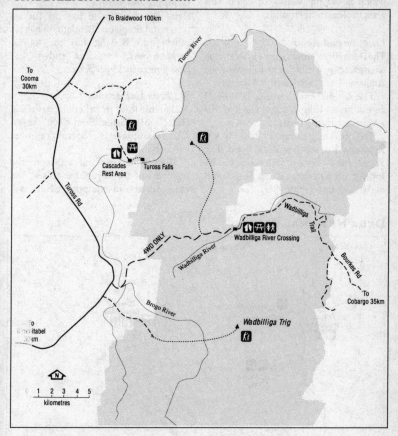

WADBILLIGA NATIONAL PARK

Like Deua NP to the north, Wadbilliga is largely undeveloped, remaining a pristine wilderness environment. There are two areas with facilities. The Cascades rest area, on the western side of the park, provides access to Tuross Falls. To get there take the Krawaree Rd south of Braidwood, then the Budjar Forest Rd, then Tuross Falls Rd. The Wadbilliga Crossing section is best reached from Cobargo, on the Princes Hwy. Take the Yowrie turnoff from the centre of the township. Follow the Wadbilliga Trail to the campsite. This site has pit toilets, tables and fireplaces. The Cascades rest area has tables and fireplaces only. No fees are collected in this park.

DEUA NATIONAL PARK

Although most of this park is confined to 4WD and walker access, there are a couple of places on the fringe of the park which allow the visitor to camp and walk in pleasant surrounds.

Location and access

The Deua River camping area is accessible to conventional vehicles by following the Araluen–Moruya Rd, west of Moruya.

The Bendethera campsite has 4WD access only. Take Little Sugarloaf Rd south-west from Moruya.

The Berlang camping area is off Krawaree Rd, south of Braidwood. The Wyanbene Caves day area is reached by turning off Krawaree Road 5km south of the Berlang turnoff.

Camping and facilities

Deua River campsite has pit toilets, tables and fireplaces. Bendethera has pit toilets and Berlang has pit toilets, garbage pits, fireplaces and tables. Camping costs $5 per person.

Walks and attractions

A 2km trail leads from Berlang to the Big Hole, a 50m wide, 96m deep chasm, which is quite a sight. The trail continues to Marble Arch.

There is unrestricted access to the first part of the Wyanbene Caves, but experienced and equipped cavers will

DEUA NATIONAL PARK

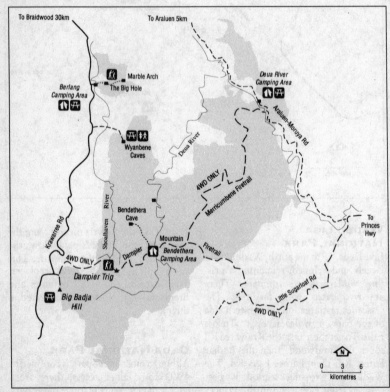

MURRAMARANG NATIONAL PARK

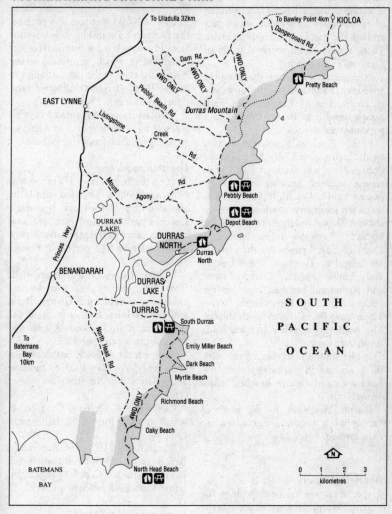

require a key and permit (available from the national park office in Narooma) to enter the restricted area.

MURRAMARANG NATIONAL PARK

This coastal park, north of Batemans Bay, has a number of small beaches and craggy headlands to explore and enjoy. A feature of the park is the large number of eastern grey kangaroos which laze around the picnic and camping areas. There always seems to be a group of them on Pebbly Beach.

Private operators run the camping grounds at South and North Durras and at Depot Beach. The national park campground is at Pebbly Beach and a park-use fee is payable.

Pebbly Beach is accessible via two roads. Livingstone Creek Rd leaves the Princes Hwy just south of East Lynne service station. Another road, signposted 'Pebbly Beach', leaves the highway a few kilometres north of the service station. Depot Beach is 14km off the highway. Turn off a few kilometres south of East Lynne. All these roads are unsealed. To reach South Durras and Emily Miller, Dark, Myrtle and Richmond beaches, turn off the Princes Hwy at Benandarah. Drive 12km along Durras Rd to South Durras. The road to the other beaches leads south from there.

In the southern section of the park there are rough paths exploring the headlands and various beaches below Wasp Head.

Durras Mountain, to the north of Pebbly Beach, has a walking trail leading to its summit.

Aboriginal history

A special reserve has been made to the north of Murramarang that protects the largest unmounded midden on the NSW south coast, at Murramarang Point. It also includes a lagoon waterhole, home to a dreamtime serpent associated with stories about the formation of the land. A self guiding walking track around the area provides Aboriginal heritage information.

BOODEREE NATIONAL PARK

The Australian Nature Conservation Agency (ANCA) manages this park on the Bherwene Peninsula, 30km southeast of Nowra. It is a substantial coastal environment which supported many Aboriginal clans in the past. Aborigines live at Wreck Bay and obtained land rights to this area in 1986.

There are many attractions for the visitor, such as swimming in clear waters or watching dolphins frolicking in the sea.

Location and access

Turn off the Princes Hwy 17km south of Nowra and follow the sealed road to the visitor centre at the park boundary. Collect a park brochure from here, as it contains a map of the peninsula. A park entrance fee of $10 per car per week applies.

Ellmoos Rd (unsealed) bears right from here, leading to car-parks and swimming spots along St Georges Basin and Sussex Inlet. It also leads to the Australian Railway Union Camp and Lumeah private campground.

To reach the national park camping areas and Jervis Bay Village, continue along Jervis Bay Rd from the visitor centre.

Cave Beach Rd leads to Cave Beach, which provides for walk-in lightweight camping.

Wreck Bay Rd leads to Summercloud Bay. Stoney Creek Rd turns off Wreck Bay Rd and leads to Cape St George Lighthouse, Moes Rock and Stoney Creek.

Camping and facilities

Green Patch is the main campsite, with hot showers, toilets, fireplaces and tables. Nearby Bristol Point has large sites with similar facilities and is suitable for large groups of over 20 people. Bookings essential.

The third national park campsite is at

Cave Beach. The site is 300 metres from the car-park and there are restrictions on tent size. Cold showers, toilets, tables and fireplaces are provided.

Bookings are needed during busy periods and can be made up to four months ahead. Call the visitor centre for information (phone: (02) 4443 0977).

Jervis Bay Village has food and petrol available.

Walks and attractions

Apart from swimming and snorkelling at the excellent beaches, there are walking trails and natural formations to explore. The several walking trails are detailed on a brochure provided at the visitor centre.

During spring the heathlands in the park are scattered with colourful flowers.

There are middens and cave shelters used by Aborigines who lived in the area.

The ruins of Cape St George Lighthouse can be photogenic at dawn and dusk.

Aboriginal history

The Jerrinja people lived around Jervis Bay. They called the area *Bouderee*, meaning 'large fishing ground, plentiful bay'. The park is jointly managed by the Wreck Bay Aboriginal Community and Environment Australia. Beecroft Peninsula features a rock shelter site which you can visit on Abrahams Bosom Reserve. Also on the peninsula is the Devils Hole, an 80 metre deep chasm leading down to the caves and the sea. The Jerrinja people believed that an ancestral being, Bundoola, drowned in this hole and now his spirit lives on there. A track leading to the Devils Hole can be found just north of Crocodile Head, and east of Lighthouse Road.

SEVEN MILE BEACH NATIONAL PARK

Seven Mile Beach stretches between Shoalhaven Heads and Gerroa. It is a pleasant coastal park with bush camping facilities at the northern end (a park-use fee applies). To reach the picnic area near the beach, turn off the Princes Hwy just north of Berry and follow Beach Rd to the end.

ON THE WAY

Just to the west of Morton NP is Bungonia State Recreation Area. Although access into the park is quite a detour from Fitzroy Falls, it is only a short deviation if you're driving along the Hume Hwy. There are excellent visitor facilities including a visitor centre, walking trails and a camping area with hot showers, toilets, fireplaces and communal kitchen facilities. The road into the park is sign-posted north-east of Bungonia. There are lookouts and an enjoyable walk which passes through Bungonia Canyon. For further information call (02) 4844 4277.

Aboriginal history

The Njunawal tribe, of the Yuin Nation, occupied the main area of Bungonia SRA. Neighbouring tribes were the Wandandian and Gundangarra people. The Bungonia ridgetops were likely to be travel routes used by Aborigines moving between the tablelands and the lowlands, gathering seasonally available food. *Bungonia* means 'creek that flows only in the rainy season'.

Various rock types from the region were used to make stone tools which have been found in the many open campsites found in the park. Caves in the area have shown evidence of burial rituals.

The totem for the Yuin Nation is the black swan.

BUNGONIA STATE RECREATION AREA

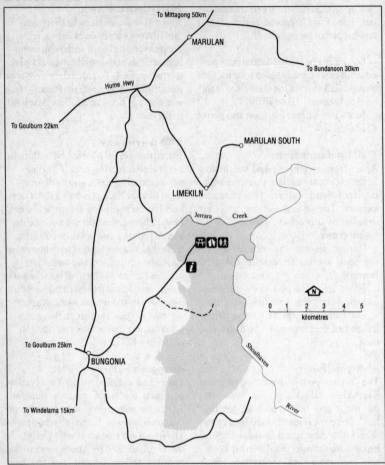

MORTON NATIONAL PARK

The twisting landscape of this park — bordered by sandstone escarpments — features waterfalls and rainforest and provides many opportunities for visitors to enjoy the surrounds. It is a remarkable park which reveals a different character each time I visit. The Bundanoon section of the park provides a variety of walking trails for easy wilderness enjoyment.

Location and access

There are several centres of activity in the park. The main area, where the visitor centre is located, can be reached by travelling to Fitzroy Falls from either the Illawarra Hwy or Kangaroo Valley. This road is sealed and the visitor centre is by the road.

To reach the Pigeon House Mountains Walk turn off the Princes Hwy 3km

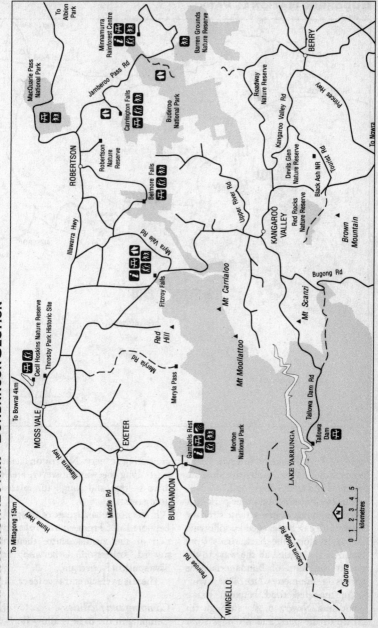

BUDDEROO NATIONAL PARK

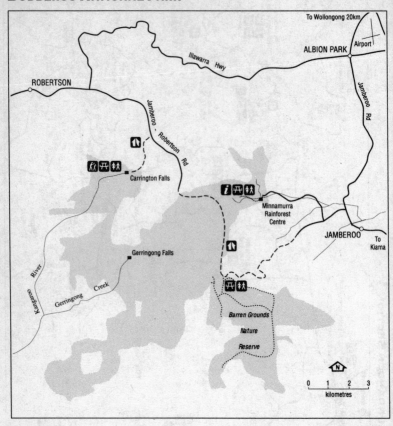

south of Burrill Lake on to Clyde Ridge Forest Rd. This is a 26km drive along an unsealed and fairly rough road.

The northern section of the park near Bundanoon has ample activities for the visitor and can be reached by following the signs along the back roads from Fitzroy Falls (sealed all the way) to the quaint township of Bundanoon. The park is one kilometre south of the town.

An unsealed road between Braidwood and Nowra passes through the centre of the park and provides some interesting scenery. No visitor facilities exist along the way, however, and the drive is long and rough for relatively little gain.

In the north-east fringe of the park is Belmore Falls. From Fitzroy Falls travel east of the visitor centre then turn toward Robertson. Otherwise, drive 8km south of Robertson.

There is a vehicle entrance fee of $3.

Camping and facilities

Camping in the park is allowed at two

locations. One, just south of the Fitzroy Falls Visitor Centre, is a small, basic site with fireplaces. A camp fee applies (pay at the visitor centre).

The other area is Gambells Rest, near Bundanoon, where there is a small number of pleasant sites with toilets and hot showers nearby. A fee applies — when we were there the fee was $10 per person. Booking is essential.

Walks and attractions

The walk to the summit of Pigeon House Mountains (2.4km rtn–mod/hard–4 hrs rtn) is in Flat Rock State Forest. There are a number of steep sections leading to the sheer-faced walls of the plateau. You must complete the walk, by climbing a series of vertical steel ladders, to be rewarded with excellent views of the surrounding escarpments.

At Fitzroy Falls there are short paths to lookout points to view the waterfalls and deep gorges. Belmore Falls has easy tracks leading to vistas of the falls and lookouts over Kangaroo Valley.

In the Bundanoon area there are 14 designated walking trails, all detailed on the information board in the Gambells picnic area. Vehicular tracks lead through the park to lookouts where you can view the sandstone escarpments fringing the valleys. On the valley floor, the dusty green of the eucalypts cloaks the undergrowth of ferns and vines. The walks leading down into the valley reveal the rich forest world below. The easy 40-minute walk to Erith Coal Mine is enjoyable and of historical interest.

Aboriginal history

The area covered by Morton NP was part of the territory of the Walbanja and Wandandian tribes, coastal people who used the mountainous area for trading and ceremonial purposes. Landforms of significance were Pigeon Mountain (called *Didthul*), Fitzroy Falls (called *Yaranga*) and Quilty's Mountain. Stone arrangements have been found in the park.

When settlers began arriving in the 1820s Aboriginal people were forced into the mountains and the population was decimated within a few decades.

BUDDEROO NATIONAL PARK

Carrington Falls is probably the main feature of this park for the fleeting visitor. A steep, winding road leads through the ferny terrain common to the area. If you want to travel between Robertson and either Kiama or Albion Park then this road is a scenic alternative to the highway.

Location and access

From Robertson turn into Jamberoo-Robertson Rd, 2.5km east of the township. Five kilometres along this road is a road to the right leading to the falls and a basic camping area. After visiting the falls return to the Jamberoo-Robertson Rd and follow the steep, unsealed road for 10km to Barren Grounds Nature Reserve. From there it is another 8km to Minnamurra Rainforest Centre.

Camping and facilities

A basic camping area is provided just off the road leading to Carrington Falls. No facilities are provided and no fee is charged for staying in this rather rough site. Further along, the picnic area near the falls has tables, fireplaces and toilets. Picnic facilities are also provided at Barren Grounds NR and the visitor centre.

Walks and attractions

There is a short walk leading to several good lookout points over the falls and the steep escarpment valley leading from it.

ROYAL NATIONAL PARK

Barren Grounds NR has interesting trails leading from the picnic area. The Timber Track (2.4km o/w) leads to an old flying fox, used for hauling timber out of the valley. The longer Griffiths Trail (8km rtn) is a circuit track leading to Illarawara Lookout, the Glen and Barren Grounds Trig. The Cook's Nose Track (6.4km rtn) leads to views over the Broger's Creek Valley. The Barren Grounds NR is best during spring and early summer, when the heaths of the 'hanging swamp' are in flower.

The Minnamurra Rainforest Centre has displays, information and a rainforest walk. A park-use fee of $10 per car is payable here.

Aboriginal history

The Wodiwodi tribal group lived a semi-nomadic lifestyle along the plateau and escarpment cliffline of what is now Budderoo NP and Macquarie NP. Corroborees are believed to have taken place on the river flats below Minnamurra Falls.

MACQUARIE PASS NATIONAL PARK

The region between Robertson and Albion Park, where this park is located, is a fertile environment. From the Illawarra Hwy the visitor may take advantage of this pocket of wilderness by enjoying the two walking trails located within the park.

The Cascades Rainforest Walk (2km rtn–easy–1 hr) leads to a 20 metre waterfall which gushes through dense rainforest. A picnic area is located at the start of the walk, 6km from Albion Park.

A couple of kilometres further west is the start of the Glenview Track, which follows an old road to the top of another cascade. This path is more difficult to negotiate and not as clearly marked.

No vehicle-based camping exists in the park.

CENTRAL

THIRLMERE LAKES NATIONAL PARK

This park, to the west of the Hume Hwy, is a popular place for family recreation. The five reedy freshwater lakes are used for water-based activities such as canoeing, power boating and swimming. To reach the park, turn off the old Hume Hwy onto the Thirlmere-Buxton Rd, either just north of Mittagong or 3km south of Picton. Two unsealed roads lead into the park from this road.

Camping is not allowed in the park.

Aboriginal history

The D'harawal and Gandangarra people lived around the Nattai system of reserves and Thirlmere Lakes. Aboriginal people collected nectar from the banksia flowers by washing them in water-filled coolamons. The area adjacent to the lakes, where the banksia grew in numbers, was called *Couridjah*, believed to mean 'nectar'. The area is rich in history of Aboriginal use, with many engravings, shelter caves, axe-grinding grooves and art sites within the park. Disease quickly spread amongst the indigenous population after European settlement. Massacres of the D'harawal people of Gwaigl, near Appin in 1816, forced tribes from the area.

ROYAL NATIONAL PARK

Its proximity to Sydney means Royal National Park is a popular place, especially on the weekends. Thankfully it is so well maintained there is little evidence of problems caused by overuse.

Impressive coastal scenery, as well as forest and rock pools, provide a diverse and interesting environment to explore. The Coast Walk, which stretches 26km between Bundeena and Otford is a spectacular track and can be accessed from several locations. Bush camping is allowed along the track at Curracurrong, Era and Werrong.

Location and access

From the south, travel to Stanwell Tops by diverting from the Princes Hwy, then follow the signs north to the park. From the north, turn off the Princes Hwy toward Audley. Most of the roads within the park are sealed. At both the northern and southern entry points there are gate keepers who collect the park-use fee of $10.

Camping and facilities

The only vehicle-based camping allowed in the park is at Bonnie Vale, where there is a campground with hot showers, toilets, laundry facilities and a few communal barbecues. Camping fee is $7.50 per adult and $4 per child. If you intend visiting during peak periods (Christmas, Easter and public holidays) you will need to book well in advance. Call (02) 9542 0648 for details.

The nearby township of Bundeena has fuel and supplies.

Walks and attractions

Several walking trails branch off the main road running through the park. One of the features in the south is at Burning Palms, which is reached by turning into Garie Rd, from Sir Bertram Stevens Drive, and walking south to the fascinating figure-eight shaped rock pools. The 3km walk follows the spectacular coastline south to the formations.

Curracurrong Creek is a vastly different scene, yet still near the coast. Wattamolla Rd, 6km north of Garie Rd, leads to the picnic area at Wattamolla from where you can easily walk to the forest-edged rock pools and carved gorges of the river.

An excellent visitor centre at Audley, near the northern access, can provide brochures and guidance on the many walks and sights in this park.

While you're there you may like to inquire about Heathcote National Park, located across the Princes Hwy from Royal NP. It is predominantly a bushwalking park and little is available for the vehicle-based traveller.

Aboriginal history

D'harawal is the language group of the Tharawal people who have occupied the area for 30,000 years. The visitor centre, 1km into the park from the northern entrance at Farnell Rd, has heritage information. Discovery tours of the park are with Aboriginal rangers and describe the culture and lifestyles of the D'harawal people. For bookings call the Discovery Coordinator (phone: (02) 9542 0649).

The Dharawal reserve, nearby Royal NP, has over 200 identified occupation sites, making it one of the most significant heritage places around Sydney.

BOTANY BAY NATIONAL PARK

If you travel north of Cronulla to Kurnell you can visit Botany Bay NP. It is a day-use park only with a visitor centre, walks and scenic lookouts. The park-use fee of $10 must be paid on entry.

ABORIGINAL HISTORY

People of the Gweagal and Goorawal nations occupied the area around Botany Bay at the time of European settlement. The Goorawal were in the northern section and the Gweagal were in the south. Explorers Cook and Banks noted an abundance of Aboriginal habitation, such as bark canoes, scarred trees, huts and fishing gear. Many occupation sites exist in the park including rock engravings, middens, axe-grinding grooves and shelters. For more information visit the interpretive centres at La Perouse Museum and the Discovery Centre at Kurnell and take a Discovery tour led by an Aboriginal ranger (booking and information call (02) 9542 0649).

SYDNEY HARBOUR NATIONAL PARK

Few cities in the world have such extensive areas of national park, nestled in and around them, like Sydney does. Sydney Harbour NP covers several of the headlands and all the islands you see from the ferry as you cross to Manly. Many of the park features can be reached by ferries or buses. Inquire at the national park office in the historic Cadmans Cottage (110 George Street, The Rocks) for details of the walks and sights, or call the park information centre (phone: (02) 9247 5033).

One of the most popular and easily accessible is the Gap, which is reached by travelling north of Bondi Beach to Watsons Bay. There is a short walk to Gap Bluff for great views of North Head and the harbour.

BLUE MOUNTAINS NATIONAL PARK

The rolling mountains of this park, fringed by strips of sandstone, are only one part of this magnificent park. Just west of Sydney, it is a significant place, preserving Aboriginal culture, rainforests and boundless escarpments. It is definitely a place not to be missed.

Location and access

Head west from Sydney along the Great Western Hwy. Glenbrook, where a visitor centre and one of the main camping areas is located, is the first stopover. To reach Ingar campsite, turn left at the top of Bodington Hill and follow Kings Tableland Rd until Queen Elizabeth Dve, where you turn left. Follow the signs to the campsite, which is 13km from the highway (11km is unsealed). Katoomba and Blackheath have lots of information and are close to attractions within the park. As the park is one of the most highly visited in Australia there are ample signs to guide you.

Camping and facilities

Euroka Clearing campsite is located near the visitor centre, 2km south of Glenbrook township. Follow the signs into Ross St then Bruce Rd. For information on how to book, which is essential, call (02) 4787 8877. A camping fee is charged.

The Ingar campsite has pit toilets and water. It is near a small dam and creek, which are suitable for swimming. No camping fee is charged.

The campsite at Perrys Lookdown near Blackheath is along Hat Hill Rd, north of Blackheath township. The site has pit toilets, tables and fireplaces. At the time of printing no fee was charged for this site.

Walks and attractions

One of the Blue Mountains' most famous attractions is the Three Sisters rock formation, which you can view from Echo Point, sign-posted from Katoomba.

Wentworth Falls is another impressive spectacle. The steep walk, some of it down steel steps, leads to views of the waterfalls and the dramatic horseshoe-shaped escarpment around it. The path divides, with one trail leading back to the highway and the other descending along a steep, rugged path to the valley floor. Otherwise you can simply turn around and begin the breathless climb back up.

If you stay at the private campsite near the scenic railway, just out of Katoomba, there are good walks leading from the base of the railway. You may like to integrate a ride on the railway with a walk.

There is a limitless variety of walks in this region. See one of the visitor centres for a walking trail map. The Heritage Centre, on Govetts Leap Rd, Blackheath, has displays and information about the history and natural features of the area (open 7 days).

Aboriginal history

The Dharug people lived in the central Blue Mountains area. The Wiradjuri were in the south-west, the Gundangarra people were in the lowlands, south of the park and the Darruk occupied the northern and central mountains. *Katoomba* is an Aboriginal word meaning 'waters tumble over hill'.

The park contains hundreds of

significant sites such as axe-grinding stones, rock art, shelters and stone arrangements. Publicly accessible sites include Walls Cave, Red Hands Cave and Campfire Creek. Walls Cave is a large sandstone shelter where archaeological work has shown Aboriginal people camped 12,000 years ago. Red Hands Cave contains stencil paintings aged between 500 and 1600 years old and on the same walk Campfire Creek has several axe-grinding grooves.

Aboriginal Discovery tours are available in the park.

KANANGRA-BOYD NATIONAL PARK

Although offering similar scenery to that of the Blue Mountains NP, Kanangra-Boyd is a bit more difficult to reach and is less serviced by quaint towns such as those dotted in the Blue Mountains. Fewer people visit the park, so there is more chance to enjoy the solitude and spectacular scenery on your own terms.

Location and access

The main road into the park turns off the Great Western Hwy, just west of Hartley, and leads 48km south to Jenolan Caves. From there, an unsealed road continues 13km to Boyd River camping area and a further 19km to Kanangra Walls Lookout. From Oberon, a partly unsealed road leads 31km to Jenolan Caves and continues into the park.

Camping and facilities

The only camping ground in the park is at Boyd River, 13km south of Jenolan Caves. It has toilets and fireplaces. Drinking water can be obtained from nearby Boyd River.

A picnic area and public phone are located at Jenolan Caves.

Toilets and information can be found at Kanangra Walls.

Walks and attractions

There are three walks beginning at the sheer-faced sandstone escarpment of Kanangra Walls.

The Echo Head and Gully View Lookouts (1km rtn–easy) are easily reached and provide excellent views.

The Waterfall Walk (1km rtn–mod) leaves from Echo Head lookout to follow a rough trail to the base of Kalang Falls.

The longer Plateau Walk (3km rtn–easy/mod) turns off the main track to the lookouts and leads to the plateau of Kanangra Tops, allowing fine views and often a grand piece of isolation. The area offers challenging overnight walks for the experienced bushwalker.

Aboriginal history

This area is believed to have been the territory of the Gundangarra, with some southern parts belonging to the Wiradjuri people. Jenolan Caves, Coxs River and Kowmung River are said to be spiritually significant to the Gundangarra people. Occupation sites and art shelters in the park reveal the area was used for at least 20,000 years.

KU-RING-GAI CHASE NATIONAL PARK

Ku-Ring-Gai Chase NP is a park nestled around the edges of the Hawkesbury River, on the outskirts of metropolitan Sydney.

Location and access

The Bobbin Head area can be reached by turning into Ku-Ring-Gai Chase Rd from Mt Colah or from North Turramurra, into Bobbin Head Rd. From the Mona Vale Rd, which passes along the south-east edge of the park (via Terrey

Ku-Ring-Gai Chase National Park

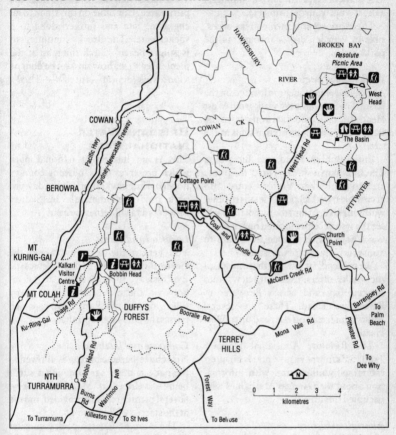

Hills), you can turn into McCarrs Creek Rd, which later veers left toward Cottage Point or right to West Head. McCarrs Creek Rd can also be followed from Church Point, heading west. Each vehicle entering the park is subject to the $10 park-use fee.

An interesting alternative for reaching Bobbin Head is to take the ferry from Palm Beach. Another enjoyable ferry ride goes across Pittwater to The Basin, Coasters Retreat and Mackerel Beach. These areas have no vehicular access, providing a motor-free haven to explore.

Camping and facilities

A great place to stay, if you can carry a few supplies and a tent across on the ferry, is at the Basin. It is a lovely grassy site, set amongst shady trees. Facilities include cold showers, toilets and tables. For information or bookings, phone Bobbin Head Information Centre (02) 9472 8949.

A shark net area, for safe swimming, is a short walk from the campsite.

There are several picnic areas accessible by vehicles, dotted throughout the park.

Walks and attractions

Aboriginal engravings are located on the Basin Track — an easy walk from West Head Rd, or a moderate walk from the Basin. There are interpretive signs at the site.

From Bobbin Head, the Birrawana Track (2.5km o/w–easy) links the picnic area to the Kalkari Visitor Centre (also accessible by vehicle). For details of other walks in this area and the rest of the park, see the visitor centre located on Ku-Ring-Gai Chase Rd. It is open from 9am to 5pm every day except Christmas.

West Head, at the northern peak of the park, offers excellent views into Broken Bay and across Pittwater to Barrenjoey Head. There are several walks which lead off the road up to West Head.

The Resolute Aboriginal Heritage Trail (3.5km rtn–easy–2 hrs) is an interesting self-guiding trail with information about the Garrigal Aborigines who occupied this area.

Aboriginal history

The Ku-Ring-Gai (or Guringai) people occupied the area from Sydney Harbour north to Broken Bay and then as far inland as Lane Cove River. The Garrigal clan lived around West Head and the Terramerragal clan lived near Turramurra. There are hundreds of rock art sites in the park. The sandstone in the area was well suited to engravings. It is thought that the artist first made a series of holes for the outline, then used a stone tool to carve a line between the holes.

The Red Hands Cave rock art site can be accessed from Resolute Picnic Area, West Head. The site is 100m from the picnic area. Continue on this track to an engraving site and further along to a shelter site. The track continues to Resolute Beach. Check the map at the picnic area to see how this can be done as a loop walk (3.5km — rtn easy — 3 hrs).

BRISBANE WATER NATIONAL PARK

This is an interesting national park which preserves the sandstone country north of the Hawkesbury. It is a day-use park used predominantly by Sydney residents as a wilderness retreat.

Location and access

You get to the park by taking the Gosford exit off the Sydney-Newcastle Expressway, then travelling to Girrakool via the old Pacific Hwy; or by following the old Pacific Hwy, which passes the Girrakool entrance.

Camping and facilities

No vehicle-based camping is allowed in the park at this stage although a site is being developed at Mooney Mooney. Several picnic areas are provided, mostly at the start of walking trails.

There are designated pack campsites for walkers using the Great North Walk.

Walks and attractions

From the Girrakool picnic area you can go on the Mooney Mooney Nature Walk (6km loop–easy/mod–3 hrs). Add another 3km if you follow the spur track down to Mooney Mooney Creek. North of Girrakool is Somersby Falls. Travel north on Wisemans Ferry Rd and veer left at the sign-post. From here you can walk to the base of the falls along a rainforest path. There are some Aboriginal axe-grinding grooves at the top of the falls. A

BRISBANE WATER NATIONAL PARK

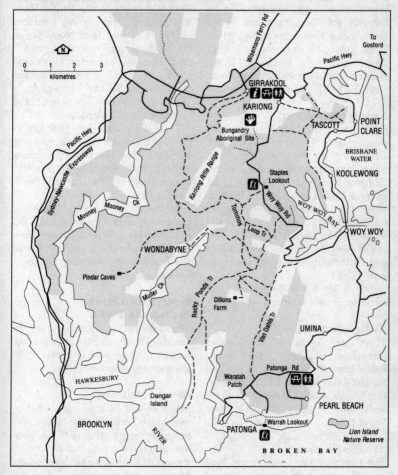

picnic area is at the start of the walk.

In the south of the park, reached by travelling through Woy Woy and along Patonga Rd, is Warrah Lookout. A short trail leads to fine views of Broken Bay and Ku-Ring-Gai Chase NP.

The Great North Walk runs north-south through the park. The main access points can be reached by taking the ferry to Patonga or the train to Wondabyne Station.

BOUDDI NATIONAL PARK

This charming coastal park, a short drive from Gosford, has low-key camping areas and good coastal walks. It occupies a beautiful area, making walks here particularly enjoyable.

Location and access

From Gosford, head south-east along the Entrance Rd. Turn right into Avoca Drive, then at Kincumber turn right into Scenic Drive. To reach the park from Woy Woy, get onto Empire Bay Drive, via Rip Bridge, then turn right into Wards Hill Rd, which joins onto Scenic Drive.

Camping and facilities

At the north end of Putty Beach is a small camping area. Travel to Killcare then along Putty Beach Drive. There are toilets, fireplaces and drinking water. Camping fee is $7.50 per person or $5 off-peak. You are required to book in advance if you want to stay in the park. Call the Gosford office (phone: (02) 4324 4911) for more details.

The two other sites — Tallow Beach and Little Beach — require campers to walk in.

Tallow Beach costs $3 per adult and Little Beach costs $7.50 or $5 off-peak.

Walks and attractions

There are dozens of short walks throughout the park. Several walks begin from the Scenic Drive itself. I suggest a visit to Mailand Bay Information Centre, which has details on all the walks and is easily accessible from Scenic Drive.

Aboriginal history

The Guringai Aboriginal people lived along the coast to the north and south of Broken Bay. Rock art in the area depicts fish, wallabies and shields. Other evidence of occupation includes axe-grinding grooves and rock shelters.

WYRRABALONG NATIONAL PARK

This coastal park north-east of Gosford is only newly established and has no camping facilities. There are some good walks and lookouts to appreciate on an alternative route to the Pacific Hwy. Wyrrabalong Trig, in the southern section, is reached from North Scenic Rd, which veers off Forresters Beach Rd. From here you can enjoy fine views. Crackneck Point Lookout, further north, is reached by turning down Shakespeare Ave then Burrawong St and into Hilltop St to the lookout.

There is a coastal walk from Crackneck Point through the park and on to Toowoon Bay. There is an extensive walking track system in the northern section between The Entrance North and Toukley.

In the northern section (over the Entrance Bridge) there are short walks sign-posted from Wilfred Barrett Drive, the main road through the park. Bateau Bay is a popular swimming and snorkelling spot.

GOULBURN RIVER NATIONAL PARK

The sandstone escarpment cut by the Goulburn River is a dramatic sight, and visitors can take extended, easy walks along the beautiful river valley.

Location and access

Much of the park is surrounded by private land requiring the landowners' permission to pass through to the park. For most travellers the best access is via Ringwood Rd, which links Merriwa and Mudgee, passing through Wollar. It is unsealed part of the way. This route provides access to Lee's Pinch and White Box Camp. Four-wheel drive vehicles can make it along Mogo Road (north of Wollar) to Spring Gully camping area.

Camping and facilities

No facilities are provided but cleared camping areas are located at White Box camping area, off Ringwood Rd, and

GOULBURN RIVER NATIONAL PARK

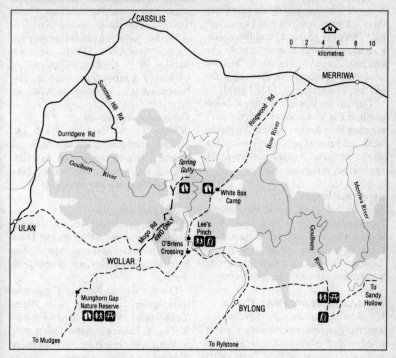

Spring Gully (4WD only). Bring your own everything, and take your rubbish out with you.

Walks and attractions
Walking along the sandstone gorge edging the river can be very enjoyable. Rocky Creek Gorge and O'Briens Crossing can be reached from Ringwood Rd. Lee's Pinch, just north of O'Briens Crossing, has a loop track to the top of an escarpment for views of the park (1km rtn–mod). Remember, this park is not set up for vehicles or tourists; it is a park where you need to find your own way around. Contact the Mudgee NPWS for further information: (02) 6372 7199.

Aboriginal history
The area is known as *burbong* to the Wiradjuri people of this region. Hundreds of occupation sites have been found in this park. The Drip hand stencil rock paintings can be found to the west of Goulburn River NP. The site, also called Hands on Rock, is located 40km north-west of Gulgong.

ON THE WAY
Marramarra NP, 18km south of Wisemans Ferry, provides opportunities for canoeing, bushwalking and overnight camping for walkers. It has no visitor facilities and access is often through private property. Inquire at a national park office for information if you intend to go there.

CATTAI NATIONAL PARK

Between Windsor and Wisemans Ferry there is a quiet park you may enjoy visiting. There are historical buildings, easy walking trails and a visitor centre. The camping ground has full facilities (including hot showers). To book a site call the parks service (02) 4572 3100.

Turn off the Wisemans Ferry Rd 6km north of Pitt Town. Gates into the park are open from 8am to 4.30pm during the week and 8am to 6pm on the weekend or public holidays. A park-use fee of $6 applies; pay at the visitor centre.

Aboriginal history

Two Dharuk clans, the Cattai and the Berooerongal, lived in this region. There are many art sites and rock engravings in the park, including one of a sailing ship. Adjacent to the Cattai farm main road access there are many axe-grinding sites.

WOLLEMI NATIONAL PARK

Considering its proximity to Sydney it is a marvel that this park remains a largely undeveloped wilderness area. Facilities and recreation areas have been established at Colo River, Newnes and Dunns Swamp. Roads which lead into the park are rough and difficult to follow.

Location and access

The access points provided here may vary in quality, so check on road conditions beforehand. In the south-east corner of the park the Wheeny Creek camping area is along Comleroy Rd, between Kurmond and Upper Colo. North of this spot, along Putty Rd, is Colo Heights (fuel available). Just north of here is the start of a good day walk.

On the western edge of the park you can travel north from Lithgow along Mudgee Rd. Pass through Wallerawang and continue to Lidsdale, where you turn right and follow the signs for 35km to the campsite at Newnes. From this road you can walk to the Glow Worm Tunnel and the shale mine ruins.

Further north you can access the park from Rylstone, via Olinda, to reach Kandos Weir. Continue 7km east of Olinda to a turn-off on the left. The camping area is 2km down this road.

Camping and facilities

Wheeny Creek, Dunn's Swamp and Newnes camping grounds have pit toilets, fireplaces (bring your own firewood), and no drinking water. Take your rubbish out when you leave.

Walks and attractions

One of the easier routes to the dramatic Colo River is by Bob Turners Track (8km rtn–mod–3 hrs) which starts 700m north of Colo Heights, sign-posted from the road.

On the way to Newnes a sign-post indicates the track to the Glow Worm Tunnel. It is a long walk, so allow at least half a day. Take a torch and some water.

Many people explore the ruins of Newnes, a once-prosperous mining town. Pamphlets on this area and the Glow Worm Tunnel are available from the Blackheath national park office.

For more information call the Blackheath office (phone: (02) 4787 8877).

DHARUG NATIONAL PARK

Adjoining Yengo NP, Dharug is far more accessible and provides some interesting features for the visitor. The whole area around Wisemans Ferry and along the Hawkesbury River is superb and should not be missed on your journey through NSW.

Location and access

Continue through the township of Wisemans Ferry to cross the Hawkesbury River. Once across, you can drive 500m

NEW SOUTH WALES

WOLLEMI NATIONAL PARK

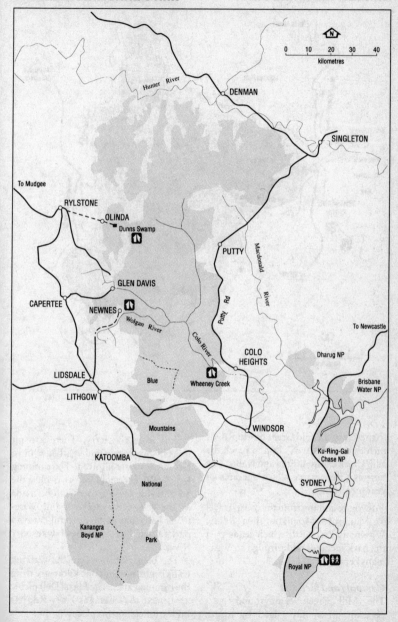

DHARUG NATIONAL PARK

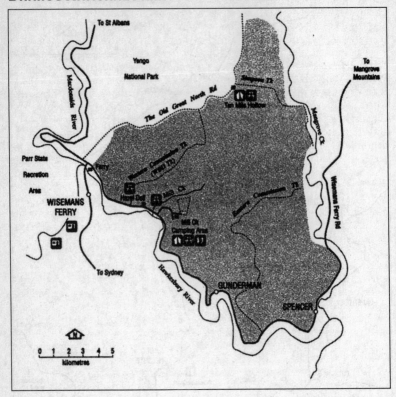

to the left to the Old Great North Rd, or turn right and drive 7.5km to reach the Mill Creek camping area and walks. The ferry is a free service which operates all year for all hours.

If you're coming from the coast, travel to Mangrove Mountain then follow Wisemans Ferry Rd, which leads past the park facilities and through to Wisemans Ferry.

Camping and facilities
The Mill Creek campground is a pleasant grassy site edged by forest, 7.5km from the ferry. There are pit toilets, fireplaces and garbage bins. No caravans are allowed. The camping fee is $10 per night for two plus the $6 park-use fee. Payment can be made at the self-registration station. Wisemans Ferry has some peaceful caravan parks along the edge of the Hawkesbury River.

The picnic area, where the walking trails begin, is about one kilometre from the camping area. The Hazel Dell picnic area, next to Wisemans Ferry Rd, has tables, toilets and fireplaces.

A walk-in camping area is at Ten Mile Hollow. The walking trail follows the Old Great North Rd for about 15km to the campsite.

Walks and attractions

From the Mill Creek camping area either walk or drive to the picnic area, from where two walks begin. The Grass Tree Circuit (1.4km–easy–30 mins) is a pleasant stroll and allows you to appreciate the bushland and wildlife this park preserves. You might catch a glimpse of a startled lyrebird, scuttling for cover. The Mill Creek Circuit (11km–mod–5 hrs) is along an undulating track, making it strenuous at times.

The Old Great North Rd is the most promoted feature of the park. The road begins just north of the ferry. A locked gate prevents vehicle entrance. You'll soon see why as you begin the gentle rise up the escarpment. The convict-built road has fallen away in many parts. The magnitude of the project is evident as you pass sections of the road where huge sandstone blocks, over 13m deep, have been dug out. You can explore as far as you like, as the road continues for many kilometres.

Aboriginal history

The Daruk Aboriginal people lived south of the Hawkesbury River and the park itself is believed to be on the land of the Darkinung group. The preservation of Aboriginal sites was one of the main reasons for the establishment of this park. Several hundred rock engraving sites have been recorded in the park. The Hawkesbury sandstone is well suited to engraving and some of the artwork is believed to be 5000–8000 years old. One of the most significant sites, known as the Group 6, contains about 150 engravings of figures such as emus, kangaroos and people.

YENGO NATIONAL PARK

Yengo NP is located between Dharug and Wollemi NPs. The roads through the park are generally rough but some features are accessible by conventional vehicles. Apart from two basic camping areas, there are few facilities. It is a rugged area mainly suitable for overnight walkers. 4WD vehicles can follow several of the trails throughout the park.

Location and access

Access is via Simpsons, Yango and Settlers Tracks. Call the Gosford office (phone: (02) 4324 4911) or the Bulga office (phone: (02) 6574 5275) for more details. Although scenic, the road up to St Albans and beyond is rough, making a lengthy drive on gravel roads.

Camping and facilities

Mogo Creek camping area, 10km southwest of Bucketty, is a basic site with pit toilets, tables and fireplaces. It is a remote spot so you may have the place to yourself.

The other vehicle based camp site is at Finchley, with pit toilets, dam water and fireplaces. Travel 12km west of Laguna along the unsealed Finchley Track. Many campsites are available to overnight walkers.

Walks and attractions

There are few marked walking trails in the park. At Finchley Trig you can take a short walk to enjoy good views of the park. Some Aboriginal rock carvings are nearby.

Aboriginal history

The northern part of Yengo NP was part of the territory of the Wonnarua people. The Macdonald River area was used by the Darkingjung people.

Hundreds of sites have been recorded in the park. Mt Yengo itself has spiritual significance to the Aboriginal community. Burragurra (Devils Rock) and Finchley are two significant engraving sites which are accessible. Burragurra appears to contain information about Aboriginal family kinship and relates to Mt Yengo. The Darkingjung Local Aboriginal Land Council request that sites are visited with a local guide. Call the land council for more information or to arrange a tour (phone: (02) 4351 2930).

TOMAREE NATIONAL PARK

This fringe of coastal land on the Tomaree Peninsula is worth exploring if you're staying in Nelson Bay. The main attractions are the fine beaches as well as the dramatic Tomaree Head. A steep climb to the top reveals incredible views. Be warned, it is a challenging climb.

MYALL LAKES NATIONAL PARK

The lakes system is a pleasant coastal environment which is a popular summer retreat. The predominantly freshwater lakes (occasionally saline through tidal movements) offer an alternative to the surf swimming spots along the beach. Marked walking trails add variety to the activities in the park.

Location and access

There are three main roads to the park. In the south, turn off the Pacific Hwy toward Hawks Nest and Tea Gardens.

MYALL LAKES NATIONAL PARK

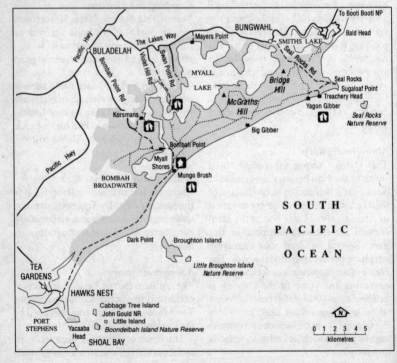

From Hawks Nest drive north to reach Mungo Brush and Bombah Point. These spots can also be reached by travelling 15km along Bombah Point Rd from Bulahdelah to Myall Shores, then crossing on a vehicular ferry to Bombah Point (the ferry operates from 8am to 6pm daily). The third access road into the park is The Lakes Way. Turn off the Pacific Hwy, north of Bulahdelah, and head toward Forster. Eight kilometres along, a gravel road to the right leads to Violet Hill (10km). Further along The Lakes Way is Mayers Point. At Bungwahl turn right to reach Seal Rocks and Yagon Gibber.

Camping and facilities

Unless you want to share with 6000 others, you may like to avoid the park during the summer holidays. At other times of the year there is ample room to find a pleasant place to camp at either Mungo Brush, Broadwater Foreshores, Myall Shores, Violet Hill, Korsmans and Yagon Gibber. Mungo Brush and Myall Shores cater for caravans. They have drinking water, as does Yagon Gibber and Violet Hill. Bring your own firewood, except to Mungo Brush, where fires are not allowed; gas barbecues are supplied both here and at White Tree Bay, however. Fuel and limited food supplies are available from Myall Shores (previously Legges Camp).

Walks and attractions

There are two main walking tracks in the park. The Moors Track begins 1.5km from Bombah Point and heads northeast, midway between the coast and the lake. Several tracks branch off the main track to Johnsons Beach, Tickerabit, Shelly Beach and Kataway Bay, all on the edge of the lake. The shortest walk from Bombah Point is to Johnsons Beach (8km rtn–mod).

The other main walk requires an overnight stop to complete as a whole. It begins at the southern end of the park and stretches 21km to Mungo Brush.

A short, easy walk leads from Mungo Brush into a patch of coastal rainforest. The Rainforest Track is a self-guiding tour which takes about 30 minutes.

A scenic feature of the area is Seal Rocks to the north of the park. It is a rugged coastal headland with a pleasant beach nearby.

At the southerly extreme of the park, not far from Hawks Nest, you can climb Yacaaba Head for views of the lake system and Tomaree National Park just to the south. The track is very rough and steep in parts.

As this is a popular park, attracting many people, there are a range of things for hire, such as canoes and wind-surfers, from either Myall Shores or Tea Gardens.

Aboriginal history

The Worimi people occupied the territory north of the Hunter River as far as Forster–Tuncurry and inland to Gloucester. Middens, scarred trees, stone arrangements and fish traps indicate an active fisher/hunter/gatherer lifestyle.

ON THE WAY

North of Myall Lakes along the Lakes Way you will pass through Booti Booti NP. Pristine beaches, coastal rainforest and dramatic headlands typify the area. Camping and facilities are located at the Ruins; turn off The Lakes Way just past Booti Point. There are hot showers, toilets and drinking water provided. Two kilometres further on is a picnic area, Santa Barbara, which has electric barbecues, toilets, drinking water and tables. No wood fires are allowed in the park.

For more information visit the park office in the camping area (phone: (02) 6591 0300).

BARRINGTON TOPS NATIONAL PARK

This park forms a blanket of dense forest set in the misty altitudes of Barrington Plateau. A great deal of the park is limited to 4WD and overnight walker access. Conventional vehicles can access the park at three separate points, considerable distances apart.

Location and access

The southern access is via Dungog. It is 43km along a sealed road from Dungog to the Barrington Guest House. Continue on the forestry road then veer left to reach the Allyn River forestry camping areas.

The popular Gloucester Tops area is reached by turning off the Gloucester-Stroud Rd, 9km south of Gloucester, and travelling 33km to the Gloucester River rest area. This road is unsealed for the last 23km and has a number of creek crossings which may rise to impassable depths after heavy rain. The climb up to the plateau to various lookouts and the Gloucester Falls walk involves a further 19km on a steep, winding road.

You can drive along Barrington Tops Forest Rd between Gloucester and

BARRINGTON TOPS NATIONAL PARK

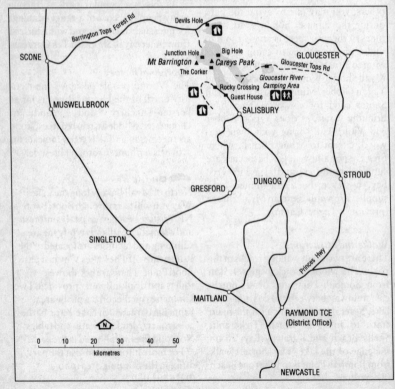

Scone which provides access to forestry camping areas and attractions. The northern access from Barrington Tops Forest Rd into the park is 4WD only.

Trails within the park are not to be used by 4WD vehicles between 1 June and 30 September each year, or after heavy rain. This is to prevent damage and erosion.

Camping and facilities

The main camping area in the park is at Gloucester River; a pleasant grassy area in a clearing surrounded by dense rainforest. There are tables, toilets and fireplaces. Camping fee is $5 per person. As the park is surrounded by state forest there are several opportunities to stay in camping areas provided by the Forestry Commission. The Allyn River area has several sites with standard facilities at some of them. To reach another camping area in the southern section, head north from Dungog along the Chichester Dam Rd, and continue to the Telegherry Forest Park, instead of veering left to the Barrington Guest House. The camping areas are sign-posted and have tables, toilets and fireplaces. No fees are charged for camping in the state forest.

To the north of the park there are campsites not far from the Barrington Tops Forest Rd, including Polblue Swamp and near the Devil's Hole Lookout.

Walks and attractions

In the southern section of the park the main walk is the Rocky Crossing Walk (6km o/w) including several small spur tracks to sights along the Williams River. See if you can organise a vehicle pick-up, otherwise return by the same track, making it a 4 hr return journey by omitting the spur trails. The path links Rocky Crossing and Barrington Guest House and takes about 4 hours return.

The Fern Tree Creek Walk (1 hr rtn) leaves from the guesthouse and passes over two picturesque swing bridges.

Inquire at the guesthouse about other short walks which lead to ridges and lookouts nearby.

Just before the Gloucester River camping area, the Sharpes Creek Walk (1 hr) follows the creek and emerges back onto the road, from where you can return to the camping area by the road.

The Gloucester Tops area has some good walks. Along the steep drive up to the plateau take time to stop at the lookouts — they are like windows which open up the dense rainforest canopy to endless views.

The Gloucester Falls Walk (2km–easy–1 hr) is an enjoyable path which should be walked in a clockwise direction. Features along the way include Laurie Lookout and views over the tiered cascades of Gloucester Falls, surrounded by lush vegetation. Nearing the end of the walk the track divides; the path to the left, sign-posted 'River Walk', leads you onto the Gloucester Tops Circuit — detailed on the information boards at the start of the walks. If you are not up to the whole distance just follow the River Walk to the picnic area and return to your car along the road.

Antarctic Beech Forest Walk is also part of the Gloucester Tops Circuit but can be undertaken on its own. It begins near the picnic area adjacent to the road leading to the Gloucester Falls Walk. As the name suggests, the path leads through Antarctic beech forest.

Sign-posted walks leave from several of the state forest areas. There are many opportunities for overnight hikes within the park. For information on the Forestry Commission areas contact the office in Newcastle (phone: (02) 4927 0977) or in Gloucester (phone: (02) 6538 5300).

> **HASTINGS RIVER MOUSE (*PSEUDOMYS ORALIS*)**
>
> The Hastings River mouse is a relatively new find in Australia. In 1969 only the third of the species had been trapped. Several more were found in the Hastings River area, which is now part of the Werrikimbe NP. The brownish-grey mouse has a distinctive rounded snout, large eyes and a white belly and feet.
>
> Skeletal remains have been found along the Great Dividing Range in NSW, Queensland and Victoria, indicating the species was far more widespread than current representation shows.

Aboriginal history

The territories of the Worimi, Dainggati, Geawegal and Birpai people overlapped at Barrington Tops. Although the plateau of Barrington Tops was not well suited to permanent habitation, due to climate and topography, it was used for ceremonial and hunting purposes.

WOKO NATIONAL PARK

If you aren't sick of dirt roads then this park, north-east of Barrington Tops NP, is a pleasant hideaway for camping, swimming and walking.

Location and access

From Gloucester take the Walcha Rd 16km north-west to the Curricabark turn-off, just past Rookhurst. Follow this road 13km to the causeway and the park entrance. Beware of rapid flooding of the causeway after rain.

Camping and facilities

The camping area is close to the edge of the Manning River, just within the park boundary. Pit toilets, tables and fireplaces are provided. The fee is $5 per person.

Walks and attractions

From the camping area you can go on the Scrub Turkey Walk (1km loop–easy–30 mins) through low-altitude rainforest. For a more energetic hike go on the Cliff Face Walk (2 hrs–mod), which begins with a steep path into an interesting forest environment.

CROWDY BAY NATIONAL PARK

This low-key coastal park features an excellent walk and is good for general relaxation by the sea.

Location and access

Turn off the Pacific Hwy at Kew then drive through Laurieton, over the bridge, and along an all-weather gravel road for 9km to the Diamond Head camping area. There are other routes into the park but they are rough and difficult to follow.

Camping and facilities

There are three camping areas all within a few kilometres of each other. Diamond Head is a large grassy area with a few shady trees. Kangaroos often graze here in the morning and evening. Indian Head and Kylie's rest areas are small sites sprinkled with banksias. All have toilets, tables and fireplaces. No water is available in the park. Camping fees are $5 per person.

WOKO NATIONAL PARK

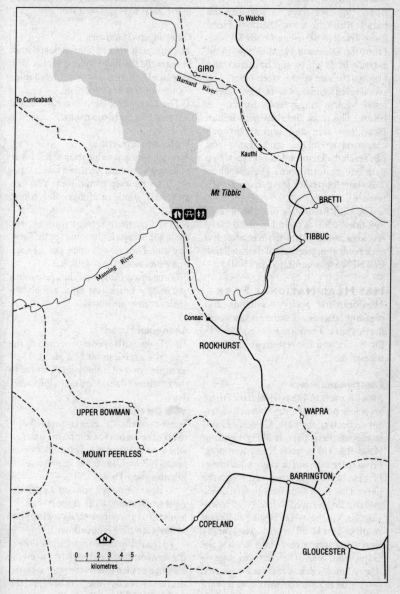

Walks and attractions

Apart from water-based activities the park features the scenic Diamond Head Loop Track (4.8km–easy/mod–2.5 hrs). From the Diamond Head campground a track leads up to the headland and follows the rim of the steep cliffs. The swirling turquoise waters beat relentlessly against craggy rock formations below. The track links up with Indian Head rest area and returns through casuarina woodlands and heath. You can reach the Diamond Loop Track by a path leading north from Kylie's Beach.

A short loop track leaves from Kylie's rest area.

The Cliff Base Walk must be done at low tide. It leaves from Diamond Head rest area and explores the reef edge and rock pools along the base of the headland. Call NPWS (phone: (02) 6586 8300).

HAT HEAD NATIONAL PARK

The dramatic rocky headlands and pleasant beaches are the main drawcard for this park. There are some good walking tracks and the rest areas are easily accessible.

Location and access

As with most of the coastal parks there are a few points of entry to reach different sections of the park. Crescent Head, in the southern part, is along Crescent Head Rd, 18km from South Kempsey. From there turn north along Gladstone-Hat Head Rd, which passes through the park. This road continues to Gladstone and can be followed to Hat Head township via Kinchela-Hat Head Rd. Travel south of Hat Head township to Hungry Beach rest area or east of the town to the Gap picnic area. The northern part — where Smoky Beach rest area is located — can be reached by travelling toward South West Rocks, turning right into Arakoon Rd (just north of Jerseyville) then right into Lighthouse Rd.

Camping and facilities

The camping area at Smoky Beach and Hungry Beach have toilets, tables and fireplaces. There is no water available. Camping costs $5 per person.

The Gap picnic area is on the coast just past Hat Head township.

Walks and attractions

A rough but enjoyable loop track leads to Korogoro Point, Arch and Cave, leaving from the Gap picnic area. You can also walk south to Hungry Beach rest area.

In the northern section you can visit the Smoky Cape Lighthouse (open Tuesday and Thursday), where you can see fine views along the coastline.

Some interesting sandhills, just south of Hungry Beach rest area, are photogenic at dawn and dusk.

Aboriginal history

The Dainggatti people occupied the coastal area, including Hat Head. Their territory covered from Point Plommer to the north and inland to Kemps Pinnacle.

ON THE WAY

For some scenic delights you may like to take the detour to Comboyne from where you can travel 6.5km to Boorganna NR or 32km to the impressive Ellenborough Falls.

At Boorganna NR you can see Allans Falls and Rawson Falls. A short walk leads through rainforest to viewing platforms. Camping is not allowed.

To reach Ellenborough Falls follow the sign south of Comboyne for a few kilometres then follow the signs west to the falls. It is a day-use park only and the 157m waterfall is well worth seeing.

NEW ENGLAND REGION

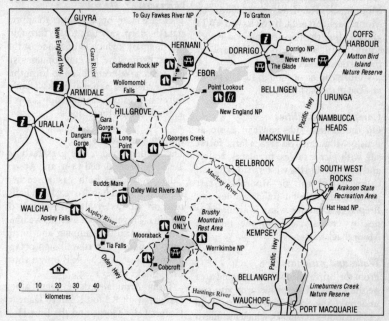

NEW ENGLAND AND ESCARPMENT FORESTS

WERRIKIMBE NATIONAL PARK

Long gravel roads lead to this park which may mean that if you make the effort to get into the park then chances are you will have it to yourself. If you're in no rush and take the time to explore the area, or just stay a few days in the remote camping area, I don't think you will be disappointed.

Location and access

There are roads into either side of the park but the park itself may only be crossed by 4WD or intrepid walkers. If you are coming from the coast and want to visit the eastern side of the park, turn right toward Beechwood just after you pass through the township of Wauchope (pronounced War-hope). Follow the signs to Werrikimbe NP. It is 65km from Wauchope to Brushy Mountain rest area (45km unsealed). The most direct route to the eastern side is from the Oxley Hwy, north to Yarras and Birdwood, along the Forbes River Rd, then along Cockerawombeeba Rd. This is a rougher but shorter (40km) route. If coming from the coast, the western side of the park can be reached by turning off the Oxley Hwy into Fenwicks Rd, 67km east of Walcha. Follow Cobcrofts Rd nearly 30km to Cobcroft rest area. Continue 16km north to Mooraback rest area. To reach the park along a different route travel along Kangaroo Flat Rd, which turns off the Oxley Hwy 56km east of

Walcha. This road leads 32km to where Mooraback Rd leads left, 6km to Mooraback rest area. If you have a 4WD you can link the two sections via Racecourse Trail, which circles the park on the northern boundary.

Ensure you have enough fuel to get in and out of the park.

Camping and facilities

On the eastern side you can camp at Brushy Mountain rest area, a large forest site with picnic tables, fireplaces, toilets and a shelter. On the western side you can camp at Cobcroft or Mooraback rest areas. Both have pit toilets, tables and fireplaces. Drinking water is available at nearby creeks, or from the tank at Mooraback hut.

Walks and attractions

From the Brushy Mountain camping area or the Grassy Tree picnic area you can undertake the Scrub Bird Walking Trail (4.9km loop–easy/mod), which includes a short hike up to Spokes Lookout. You can omit this spur track and simply do the 3km circuit, which passes through a forest of unusual grass trees, Antarctic beech forest and cool temperate rainforest. The variety of vegetation along the way makes this a very pleasant walk.

From the Plateau Beech picnic area, 3km from Cockerawombeeba Rd, a 2km loop trail leads through some beautiful Antarctic beech forests and past the King Fern Falls and Filmy Fern Falls.

An easy 1.5km loop track leaves from Cobcroft rest area, passing through open forest and warm temperate and sub-tropical rainforest. From Mooraback rest area the Mooraback Trail (9km rtn–mod) runs beside the creek then up a steep section (called Dingo Knob) to views all around the park.

OXLEY WILD RIVERS NATIONAL PARK

There are many opportunities to appreciate the deep, yawning gorges throughout this park, which is now one of the largest in the State. Several popular visitor areas have been linked to form this vast wilderness national park. Thankfully it has easily accessible spots, as well as ample chance for escape.

Location and access

The southern end of the park features Tia Falls (pronounced Ty-a) and Apsley Falls, which are both easily reached from the Oxley Hwy. To reach Tia Falls, turn off the Oxley Hwy 38km east of Walcha. Travel along a 5km all-weather gravel road to the camping and picnic spots. Apsley Falls is well sign-posted 19km east of Walcha. It is only a short drive off the Oxley Hwy.

From Armidale, drive south along Dangarsleigh Rd for 22km to Dangars Gorge. Gara Gorge and the Blue Hole are at the end of Castledoyle Rd; turn off the Coast Rd just east of Armidale and follow a mostly sealed road for 16km.

To reach Long Point, turn off the Coast Rd, 23km east of Armidale, and travel 26km to the park (unsealed past Hillgrove). Wollomombi Falls and Chandler Gorge are only 2km off the highway; turn off 35km from Armidale.

East Kunderang Homestead is in a remote area in the north-east of the park, 112km east of Armidale. Access is by 4WD only, along Raspberry Rd, which leads off the 'Big Hill' road, south-east of Wollomombi.

Camping and facilities

The camping areas at Tia Gorge and Apsley Gorge are set in open woodlands with fireplaces, pit toilets and river water available.

Dangars Gorge, Long Point and Wollomombi Gorge have pleasant camping spots with similar facilities. Tank water is not available at Dangars so bring your own. After dry periods the river water, which supplies the other sites, cannot always be depended on.

Walks and attractions

After driving past the lush roadside vegetation of Werrikimbe NP and the Oxley Hwy, Tia Gorge is a stark contrast. However, the dramatic wedge-shaped cliffs of the gorge are an impressive sight. An easy gravel path follows the edge of the escarpment, offering good viewpoints of the gorge.

At Apsley Gorge there are easy strolling tracks and lookout platforms from which to admire this astounding gorge and its two waterfalls. Similarly, Dangars Gorge, Long Point and Wollomombi have paths following the gorge rims. You will be treated to extensive views of the deep chasms, with the river beds barely visible from the heights where you are standing (in some places over 500m from the bottom of the gorge).

Dangars Gorge has a good walk to Mihi Falls (4.5km o/w). From this track you can take the 1.5km walk to McDirtys Lookout along a narrow spur, allowing steep views either side of the track — a particularly thrilling spot.

The Blue Hole and cascades in upper Gara Gorge are popular spots to swim and explore. The Threlfell Walk at Gara Gorge features the remains of the first hydro-electric scheme to power an Australian town. At Long Point you can embark on a 5km return walk along the gorge rim, and also a short walk through dry rainforest.

East Kunderang Homestead is available for guest accommodation. Bookings are essential and can be made through the Armidale district office (phone: (02) 6776 4260). The homestead offers easy access to the Macleay River for fishing, swimming and canoeing as well as walks around the former cattle station — now surrounded by the Apsley Macleay Gorge Wilderness Area.

Aboriginal history

The Anaiwan people occupied the area around Oxley Wild Rivers. There is a red ochre rock painting site that can be accessed at Mt Yarrowyck. To reach the walking track travel west from Armidale on Bundarra Rd for 28km to the Uralla–Bundarra Rd turn-off. Take this road north for 1km to the Mt Yarrowyck Nature Reserve. The 3km loop walking track to the site is signposted.

NEW ENGLAND NATIONAL PARK

This park is a superb place to camp and undertake scenic and forest walks. It is a huge wilderness area. From the lookout you can view hazy, blue valleys and mountains filling the landscape to the horizon.

Location and access

The park is sign-posted off the Armidale-Grafton Rd, 67km east of Armidale and 13km from Ebor. An 11km gravel road leads to the park boundary. On the steep section to the lookouts, the road is sealed.

Camping and facilities

There are two camping areas for people to use. One is the Styx River rest area, which lies just outside the park boundary. The other is Thungutti, a very pleasant spot in the forest with cold showers provided. The Styx River area is suitable for caravans. Both areas have pit toilets, tables and fireplaces. No fee is charged as yet.

The Thungutti camping area is a short detour from Point Lookout Rd, which passes through the park, just inside the park boundary.

Picnic areas are at Berarngutta and Banksia Point. An enclosed shelter is located at Point Lookout, which is ideal for lunch on a cold day.

Walks and attractions

The park is somewhat deceptive when you first enter it, as the vegetation near the highway is dry bushland. Soon after entering the park you are enveloped in cool, damp rainforest.

From the Thungutti rest area you can go on the Tea Tree Falls Walk (1.5km o/w–easy), which wanders through open forest and Antarctic beech forest, past cascades of the Styx River, and finishes on Point Lookout Rd, near Tom's Cabin.

Other longer walks include Lyrebird Nature Trail (7km rtn–mod–3.5 hrs), Cascades Walk (7km rtn–mod–3.5 hrs) and the steep Eagles Nest Walk (2.5km rtn–mod/hard–1.5 hrs). All walking trails are designed to be walked in a clockwise direction. The national park brochure detailing the walks is available from carparks and the main office. There are also excellent track signs (with maps) at every track head and intersection.

The Point Lookout area has several short tracks for you to gain strategic viewpoints over the sweeping Bellinger River Valley and out toward the coast.

Aboriginal history

The park straddles the border between the Dainggatti and the Gumbainggir tribes.

Point Lookout has special significance in relation to creation stories in the area. For heritage information visit the Aboriginal Cultural Centre and Keeping Place in Kentucky Street, Armidale, next to the Art Centre (phone: (02) 6771 1249).

CATHEDRAL ROCK NATIONAL PARK

Although this park is relatively small and less dramatic than its vast neighbours of New England NP and Guy Fawkes River NP, it has pleasant places to camp and a good walking trail.

Location and access

The Barokee rest area is along Round Mountain Rd. Turn off the Armidale-Grafton Rd 2km south of the Guyra Rd intersection or 5.5km north of the signpost for New England NP. Follow this all-weather gravel road 8km to the camping area.

The Native Dog Creek rest area is reached from Guyra Rd, 7.5km west of the Armidale-Grafton Rd.

Camping and facilities

Camping is allowed at Barokee and Native Dog Creek rest areas. Pit toilets, tables, creek water (can dry up in spring) and fireplaces are provided. Barokee is particularly pleasant, set in the forest with well-spaced sites. No fee is charged as yet.

Walks and attractions

From Barokee camping area the Cathedral Rock Track (5.8km loop–mod– 3 hrs) leads to the giant rocks (tors) assembled in an interesting array. A 400m trail leads off the main track to the top of Cathedral Rock.

From Native Dog Creek there is an equally impressive journey to Woolpack Rocks (7.4km rtn–mod–3.5 hrs). Some consider this stack of boulders to be more impressive than Cathedral Rocks. For the agile it is worth climbing to the top. No marked tracks exist so you will need to find your own way up.

A 10.4km trail links Barokee with Native Dog Creek, which is a good walk if you can arrange vehicle pick-up from the other side.

GUY FAWKES RIVER NATIONAL PARK

This park is largely a wilderness area, providing great opportunities for overnight hikers who want to immerse themselves in remote escarpment country. For vehicle-based travellers there are pleasant spots in the park where you can camp, walk and explore one of the less used parks in NSW.

Location and access

From the Ebor-Grafton Rd turn into Marengo Rd at Hernani, 16km north-east of Ebor. Travel along this unsealed road then veer right into Hardens Rd. Continue to a T-intersection at Chaelundi Rd, where you turn left, and follow this road 7km before veering left again,

GUY FAWKES RIVER NATIONAL PARK

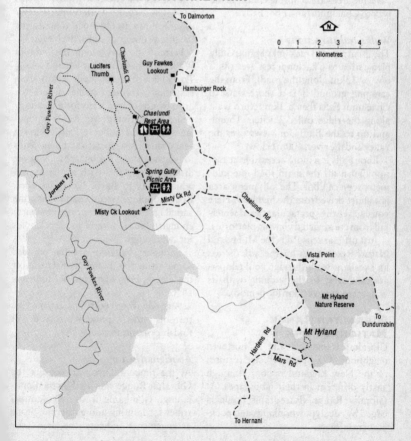

into Misty Creek Rd. Follow this to Chaelundi rest area, 35km from the Ebor-Grafton Rd. If coming from the north, turn off the Ebor-Grafton Rd at Dundurrabin and follow the Sheep Station Creek Rd to Misty Creek Rd. Beware of log trucks which frequently use these roads.

Camping and facilities
The Chaelundi rest area has pit toilets, tables and fireplaces. There is no charge for camping at present and fresh water is readily available from the creek nearby.

Picnic areas are at Spring Gully (on the way to Chaelundi) and Ebor Falls.

Walks and attractions
The Escarpment Track links Spring Gully picnic area to Chaelundi rest area (8km o/w or 13km along the road). From the camping ground it is a short walk to Chaelundi Falls then a 3km return walk along the ridge called Lucifers Thumb and up to the Bluff, for views over the valley and the river, 600m below.

Ebor Falls is a more accessible attraction. Turn off the main road one kilometre west of Ebor. The falls picnic area is a short drive from the highway. Here you can see the spectacular tiered waterfall from constructed viewing platforms.

Just off Hardens Rd is the Mt Hyland Nature Reserve. Within the park there is an excellent walk through cool temperate rainforest to the summit, with its widespread views (3km loop–mod).

GIBRALTAR RANGE NATIONAL PARK

Gibraltar Range NP and its northern neighbour, Washpool NP, are features of the New England region, although vastly different in their landscapes. At Gibraltar Range NP are granite boulders edged by eucalypt woodlands and pockets of rainforest.

Location and access
The road into the park leaves the Gwydir Hwy 4km west of the road into Washpool. Travel along the unsealed Mulligans Drive 10km to the rest area and the start of the walking trails.

Camping and facilities
The large camping area near Mulligans Hut has toilets, cold showers, fireplaces and tables. No bookings are taken and no fees are charged.

Walks and attractions
The walks are the real feature of this park. The Needles Trail (6km rtn easy/mod) follows an old stock route to the six granite outcrops called the Needles.

Part of the way along the Needles Walk you can veer to the left and follow Tree Fern Forest Walk (8km rtn– easy/mod), through gullies where the huge fronds of tree ferns form a canopy which blocks out the sky. Another popular walk is to Dandahra Falls (5km rtn –easy/mod). A steep path at the end leads to views of the 240m falls. A short distance along this path is a spur trail which leads to Barra Nula Cascades. Rock hopping is required to reach the actual cascades. If the weather is warm enough there are several good rock holes for swimming.

Boundary Falls are another popular scenic attraction. Boundary Rd turns off the Gwydir Hwy 8km west of Mulligans Drive.

A good visitor centre is located at the turn-off into the park, where you will find information and displays.

Aboriginal history
At the time of European contact the Gibraltar Range was used by the Bundjalung, Gumbainggir and Yokumbal tribes for hunting and gathering. Stone arrangements indicate the area may

> **RAINFOREST**
>
> Rainforest (or closed forest) occurs from the north-west of the Northern Territory down the east coast to southern Tasmania. It is mostly on the eastern side of the Great Dividing Range and is scarce in Victoria and southern NSW. Even before clearing, rainforest only covered 1 per cent of Australia.
>
> Rainforests are characterised by a closed canopy, with 70–100 per cent of the sky blocked out by leaves. They are biologically diverse and usually have no single, dominant tree species.
>
> There are a number of different types, ranging from tropical to littoral (coastal). They tend to grow in richer soils, although this does not imply that where rainforest occurs the soil is rich. Most rainforest nutrient is locked in the ecosystem and when the forest is cleared (e.g. by logging) the soil is usually fertile for only a few years.
>
> Rainforests don't necessarily occur in regions of high rainfall. However, year-round access to water is needed. Shelter is also important. This is why rainforests often line valleys and gullies with eucalypt forests on the ridges.

have been used for ceremonies. The rugged terrain provided a refuge to the Bundjalung people who were forced to leave the lowlands when the area around the Clarence River was colonised by white settlers.

WASHPOOL NATIONAL PARK

This is a particularly enjoyable park which combines easy access with superb camping and walking trails. Having lyrebirds stalk nonchalantly through your campsite makes this an unforgettable place to visit.

Location and access

From the Gwydir Hwy, between Grafton and Glen Innes, turn into Coombadjha Rd, 73km east of Glen Innes. The road to Granite picnic area veers to the left not far from the highway. An all-weather road leads to Bellbird camping area, 3km from the highway. Beyond this point the road is steep and not recommended for caravans. It is little over a kilometre to the end of the road and Coombadjha rest area. A bus parking bay is located adjacent to the Bellbird rest area.

Camping and facilities

The Bellbird rest area is a large grassy site which caters for large groups and caravans. It has toilets, undercover shelter, tables and fireplaces. The Coombadjha rest area is set in dense rainforest and has toilets, tables and fireplaces. Water is available at both sites. No fees are charged. There are several pleasant picnic areas in the park.

Walks and attractions

The best way to explore the area is by the Washpool Walk (10km loop–mod–4 hrs). Leaving from Coombadjha rest area, it meanders through warm temperate rainforest, past lookouts and subtropical rainforest. One kilometre past Cedar Creek is a short spur track leading to Summit Creek Falls. On the return journey another side track leads to Twin Red Cedars.

The Cedar Valley Track (5km o/w–mod) links Hakea picnic area — just off

WASHPOOL NATIONAL PARK

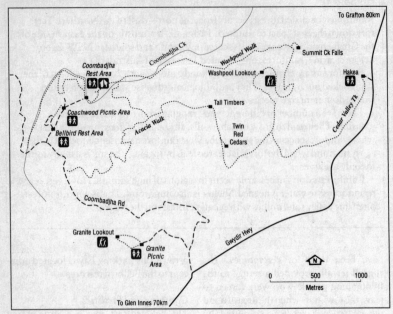

the Gwydir Hwy — with Coombadjha Rd. The central part of this walk follows the Washpool Walk. The start of the walk between Hakea and the Washpool Walk can become very boggy, so suitable footwear is required. The last section, called Acacia Walk, veers off the Washpool Walk one kilometre before the camping area and winds its way to Coombadjha Rd.

The Granite picnic area has a short loop walk to Granite Lookout, which can be quite steep in sections.

BOONOO BOONOO NATIONAL PARK

Pronounced 'bunna bun-noo', this park, east of Bald Rock, is well worth a look. It is particularly nice in warm weather, as it has some good swimming spots.

Location and access
To reach Boonoo Boonoo Falls, turn off Woodenbong Rd (previously Mt Lindesay Hwy) 22km north of Tenterfield. From here it is 14km to the falls along an all-weather gravel road. Cypress rest area is 10km before the falls.

Camping and facilities
Camping is allowed near the falls and at Cypress rest area. Basic facilities, including toilets, tables and fireplaces, are provided. Those towing caravans are advised to stay at Cypress rest area. Leave the van there before continuing to the falls, as the road is not suitable for caravans. No fee is charged for camping.

Boonoo Boonoo Falls camping area is more popular due to its proximity to the walking trail and good swimming holes. There are some small spots near

Cypress which are refreshing for a dip on a hot day.

Walks and attractions
The 210-metre falls can be viewed from a constructed platform near the top of the falls. Agile people can walk down the gorge to the base of the falls. It is not an easy descent and you must scramble and rock hop to make your way down.

The major attraction here is the serene environment. You can enjoy forests and clear flowing creeks in a pleasant, warm-weather retreat.

BALD ROCK NATIONAL PARK

The feature of this park, a giant dome of Stanthorpe adamellite, provides visitors with a challenging climb and a worthy scenic attraction.

Location and access
Bald Rock is 35km from Tenterfield. Take the sign-posted turn-off just north of the township and travel along Woodenbong Rd 29km to the turn-off to the rock. It is 6km along a gravel road to the picnic and camping area. Access is fine all year.

An alternate route from the north is via Stanthorpe.

Camping and facilities
Near the rock there is a pleasant rest area which can be used by short-term campers only. There are toilets, picnic tables and fireplaces. Drinking water is obtainable all year from Bald Rock Creek. No fees apply at time of printing.

Walks and attractions
There are two ways to reach the top of the great monolith. Once you have crossed the wooden bridge across the creek the track divides. The path to the left is the 2.5km Bungoona Walk, which is a gradual ascent through pleasant woodlands and approaches the rock from the eastern side. Your other option is to confront the rock head-on. The path to the right leads to the base of the rock and a 1.2km direct scramble up the rock awaits you. Shoes with good grip are important for safety on the steep sections. I would recommend the Bungoona Walk for the way up then a slow return along the rock face. White paint guides your way on the rock, although there are ample opportunities to deviate to explore the many rock caves and gullies on the summit.

Another walking trail begins 2km before the picnic area. The walk is easy and leads to Fairy Valley (approx. 2km o/w–easy), providing good views and better photo opportunities of the rock. An access trail begins one kilometre from Woodenbong Rd, leading to Carroll's Creek. The 1.5km path passes through dry sclerophyll forests and once you reach the creek you can follow it upstream for about one kilometre.

Aboriginal history
The area north of Tenterfield was part of the territory of the Jukambal people. Bald Rock itself was a meeting site for the Githabal, Wahlebal and Dinggha- bal. The rock formed the border between the nations, allowing people to gather without crossing the land of the other tribes. European settlement from the 1840s forced Aboriginal people to leave the area.

NORTH COAST AND HINTERLAND

ON THE WAY
An interesting place to stay the night, before or after visiting Dorrigo National Park, is next to Bellingen Island Flora and Faunal Reserve, in the Bellingen Caravan Park. From December to

March this is a thriving centre for a maternity colony of grey-headed flying foxes. Thousands of shrieking bats darken the sky at dusk as they go out to feed. The island is a dense, green sanctuary teeming with wildlife. To reach the park, turn off the main road through town at the Post Office and follow the signs. Camping is $15.50 per night for two people (phone: (02) 6655 1338).

DORRIGO NATIONAL PARK

The enchanting rainforest within Dorrigo NP is easily accessible and can be explored by a number of trails. Travellers often remark on this park when recounting memorable travel experiences.

Location and access

The Dorrigo Rainforest Centre and the Glade picnic area are reached by turning off the Dorrigo-Bellingen Rd into Dome Rd 2km east of Dorrigo township. A sealed road leads to the visitor centre. Veer right to reach the Glade picnic area or continue along Dome Rd for 11km to the Never Never picnic area. Park maps that show all the walking trails can be collected from the visitor centre.

Camping and facilities

No camping is allowed in the park. Private caravan parks are in Dorrigo or 30 minutes away in Bellingen (described above in On the way). Tables, fireplaces, firewood and undercover shelters are provided at the Glade and Never Never picnic areas.

Walks and attractions

From the Glade you can undertake the Wonga Walk (5.5km loop–easy/mod–2 hrs) which begins from the Satinbird Stroll (600 metres). The path passes behind the Crystal Shower Falls, so that you are encased by an overhang and the fine waterfall streaming from its edge. It is an enjoyable walk featuring sub-tropical rainforest, strangler figs and coastal views.

From the Never Never picnic area there are four walking trails of reasonable length. Some overlap and can be completed simultaneously.

For example, the Blackbutt Track (6.4km o/w–mod–2.5 hrs) leads past the impressive Casuarina Falls and back on to the Dome Rd, 4.5km from the picnic area. If you can't organise a lift back you might like to just undertake the first section of the walk to Casuarina Falls (4.8km rtn–mod–1.5 hrs).

The other main track is the 5.5km Rosewood Creek Track, which is an easy loop walk through rainforest and features the Coachwood Falls. To add a bit more challenge you can take the steep journey down to the base of Cedar Falls. I recommend that you undertake this walk (6.4km rtn–mod) by following the Rosewood circuit in an anti-clockwise direction then, a little over midway, veer off at the sign-posted path. The track is quite steep, particularly near the bottom. The sound of the waterfall echoing around the gorge and the sight of the giant red cedar crutched at the base of the falls make this a magical place to be.

The Dorrigo Rainforest Centre is an important stopover for detailed information on the park and interesting displays. It has the popular Skywalk, which takes visitors high into the rainforest canopy. Short informative walks leave from the centre.

Leeches are quite friendly in this park, so while you're walking, regularly check there are none in your boots and clothing or on your skin.

Aboriginal history

The coastal dwelling Gumbainggir people, who occupied the area from Coffs Harbour to Nambucca Heads, were believed to use the Dorrigo Plateau in summer to harvest seasonal food resources. *Dorrigo* means 'stringy bark tree'.

YURAYGIR NATIONAL PARK

This is another coastal park which is popular with holiday campers. It protects about 60km of coastline and offers many recreation opportunities. The rocky headland and sweeping beaches, typical of the northern NSW coast, make this a good place to visit.

Location and access

There are four separate access points to the park.

To reach Station Creek rest area in the south, turn into Barcoongere Forest Way (well sign-posted) off the Pacific Hwy, 15km north of Woolgoolga. The road is unsealed and leads 15km to the rest area.

The next access is via Wooli Rd, 15km south of Grafton, leading to the central section where Minnie Water, Diggers Camp and Wooli are located. The road is sealed for the 25km to Minnie Water.

To reach the northern section where Sandon River rest area is located, turn off the Pacific Hwy at Maclean and travel along the Brooms Head Rd 25km to Brooms Head. Ten kilometres south is Sandon River and the rest area. Seven kilometres north of Brooms Head are the Lake Arragan and Red Cliff rest areas.

To reach Mara Creek and Angourie Bay picnic areas, at the northern tip of the park, travel to Yamba and south toward Angourie. Just north of Angourie turn right along Lakes Boulevard, which leads to the park.

Camping and facilities

Camping is allowed at Station Creek, Illaroo (one kilometre north of Minnie Water), Sandon River, Red Cliff and Lake Arragan rest areas, as well as Shelley Head (walk in only).

Sandon River and Illaroo are popular because they have drinking water. Illaroo has reticulated town water to the park boundary and Sandon River has tanks. Provisions may be found at the small townships of Minnie Water, Brooms Head and Wooli.

Most sites have pit toilets, tables, fireplaces and firewood. Fees are $5 for two. No bookings are taken and the maximum stay is six weeks (in any six-month period). Bring your own drinking water for Station Creek, Lake Arragan and Red Cliff rest areas.

Walks and attractions

From the Station Creek camping spot you can embark on an easy one kilometre walk to a tea-tree stained freshwater creek. This track is called the Corkwood Walk. A longer walk leads from the beach near Station Creek past Pebbly Beach and on to Freshwater Beach.

Two short walks leave from Illaroo rest area: the Angophora Grove Walk (1km rtn–easy) and the Rocky Point Walk (2km rtn). The latter is a more scenic coastal walk and the former explores the vegetation in the area.

From the Boorkoom picnic area, below Diggers Camp, you can embark on the Wilsons Headland Walk (2km o/w–easy), which is a scenic walk following the coastline past Stony Beach, Bare Point and Hungary Cove. You can return either via this route or by the road back to Boorkoom.

Another feature of the northern section is the sandstone caves which have formed deep below the Shelley headland. To reach them you can walk 5km north from Lake Arragan rest area, along a pleasant path passing Lake Arra-

YURAYGIR NATIONAL PARK

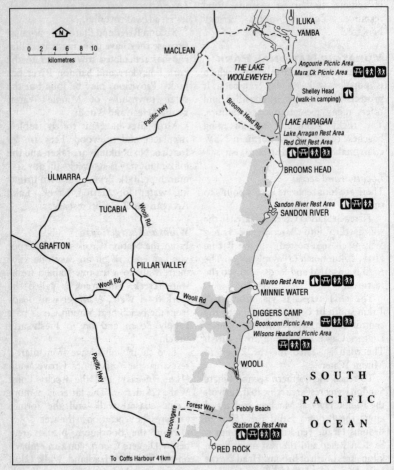

gan. Otherwise take the Angourie Walk, a 5km path south of the Mara Creek picnic area. This path leads to Shelley Beach and the headland, from where you need to drop down to the beach, if it is low tide, to explore the caves.

You can get more information from the Grafton District Office (phone: (02) 6642 0613).

BUNDJALUNG NATIONAL PARK

Unlike Broadwater National Park, this coastal park is far more established for visitor use. It features unusual coastal rainforest and magnificent coastal scenery.

BUNDJALUNG NATIONAL PARK

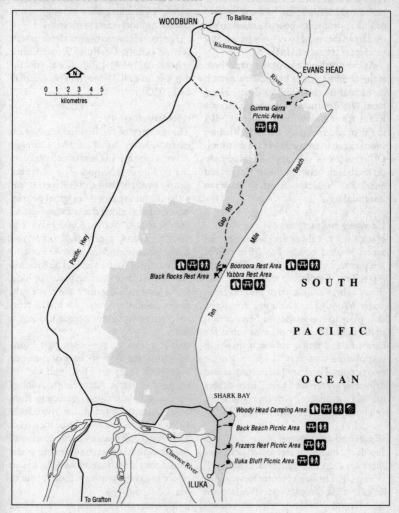

Location and access
There are three main areas for recreation in the park. The less-visited retreat is in the central part, where you will find Black Rocks, Yabbra and Booroora rest areas. This part is reached by turning into Gap Rd, sign-posted off the Pacific Hwy, 5km south of Woodburn. Gap Rd is an all-weather gravel road leading approximately 20km to the rest areas.

In the southern end there are several beaches, Woody Head camping area and access to Iluka Nature Reserve. To reach these spots, turn off the Pacific

Hwy just north of the Clarence River. A sealed road leads 15km to the township of Iluka; short sign-posted gravel roads lead from this road to various beach and rainforest attractions in the park.

At the northern end of the park there is the Gumma Garra picnic area, which is reached by travelling to Evans Head from Woodburn; after the bridge across Evans River follow the Bundjalung Rd to the picnic area (sign-posted). Visitors should keep to formed roads at all times. Off-road use of vehicles is allowed only on the beach between Black Rocks and Shark Bay. Vehicles are not to leave the intertidal zone.

Camping and facilities
Black Rocks, Yabbra and Booroora rest areas, located beside Ten Mile Beach, are pleasant places to camp. There are pit toilets, fireplaces, tables and firewood. There is no charge and no fresh water. Woody Head camping area is the only place to stay in the southern section of the park. The camping area caters for caravans and tents, although there are no powered sites. It is $10 per night for two people. There are full amenities and drinkable water available. Three cabins are also available. Advance bookings can be made (phone: (02) 6646 6134).

Walks and attractions
Beside the endless water-based activities there are a few enjoyable walks in Bundjalung NP. The Iluka Nature Reserve has an easy walk through coastal rainforest (the largest remaining area of coastal rainforest in NSW). Turn left opposite the golf course and follow the road a short distance to the Iluka Bluff carpark, where the walking track begins.

There is an easy walking trail from the Booroora rest area to the mouth of Jerusalem Creek.

The Gumma Garra Nature Trail (4km rtn–easy) leaves from the Gumma Garra picnic area and passes through some coastal rainforest and mangroves.

For more information on the southern section call the Grafton District Office (phone: (02) 6641 1500). For the northern section call Alstonville (phone: (02) 6627 0200).

Aboriginal history
The territory of the Bundjalung Nation extends from north of the Clarence River. There are 13 clans which make up the Bundjalung Nation. The Gidgabul people lived south of Evans River. It was a significant area for Aboriginal people, with middens along the coast indicating use of the area for over 6,000 years. The Gumma Garra nature trail takes you past extensive midden systems consisting mainly of oyster shells. The location was also a major meeting place for local tribes who would gather and trade salt, seafood and stone tools, for inland treasures such as quandong seeds and bunya nuts.

If you walk up the beach past Evans River, toward the Salty Lagoon, you can look back at Evans Head and see the shape of a goanna. According to Aboriginal legend, the goanna spirit came from Swan Bay, travelled down river from Corika and chased a snake to the coast. They fought all the way to the headland. Before the snake was chased out to sea he took a couple of the goannas eggs, and so now the goanna is always looking out to sea.

Massacres to the south of Evans Head in 1842/43 wiped out 150 people of this clan.

BROADWATER NATIONAL PARK

If you like empty beaches and large areas of undisturbed coastal terrain, then this is the park for you. The park is mainly a conservation zone for this undeveloped area. A sealed road passes through the park between Evans Head and Broadwater townships.

There is a car-park at the southern end of the park where you can embark on the 3km (rtn) walk to Salty Lagoon. In the north of the park there are picnic facilities at the main lookout as well as by the coast near Broadwater Headland. There is no drinking water available. Camping is allowed away from roadsides and picnic areas. You can get more information from the Alstonville office (phone: (02) 6627 0200).

Aboriginal history

Aborigines of the Bundjalung tribe lived along the coastline. The contents of the middens, found in several locations, shows a diet of fish, shellfish and turtles. The park would have also been a rich source of snakes, wallabies, birds and honey. Some of the descendants of the Bundjalung people live on Cabbage Tree Island, north of the park. Traditional ceremonies and lifestyles were still carried out up until around 1922.

ON THE WAY

Whian Whian State Forest, which shares a border with Nightcap NP, has a great camping area at Rummery Park, with the spectacular Minyon Falls nearby. If you're coming from Lismore or Terania Creek, drive to Dunoon and continue north-east and follow the signs to Minyon Falls (small section unsealed), for approximately 20km.

From the coast you can head to Goonengerry then drive south for a few kilometres to the turn-off into the park. Walks leave from the camping ground to Minyon Falls along Boggy Creek Track (2km–easy–45 mins) or to Peates Mountain (3km o/w–easy/mod–1 hr). Slightly more challenging is the Eastern Boundary Track (2.5km–easy/mod–45 mins), with some steep sections along the way, ending at a good views over Byron Bay and Coopers Creek Valley.

From Minyon Falls you can walk 2km to Quandong Falls. The walk to the base of Minyon Falls leaves from this path just before Quandong Falls. It is a steep 4km descent, but generally well formed. Alternatively the base can be reached from a walking track which leaves Minyon Grass Picnic Area — 2km from Minyon Falls along Minyon Drive. The walk itself is 2km one way, of moderate difficulty.

NIGHTCAP NATIONAL PARK

This park forms part of the southern caldera rim. The park was the site of strong protest against logging in the area. In 1979 protesters were successful in halting logging in the Mt Nardi area. Soon after, most of the surviving rainforests in the area were protected. For the visitor there are good walks and scenery plus a pleasant camping ground at Terania Creek (overnight only).

Location and access

Two main recreation areas in the park are at Mt Nardi and Terania Creek. To reach Mt Nardi take the sign-posted road east of Nimbin for 13km along a sealed road. Terania Creek access is from Lismore via the Channon, from where Terania Creek Rd winds 14km to the camping area (the Channon is 25km north of Lismore). You will have to cross two causeways on this route so take care after heavy rains (or if you are in the park, watch out, as the causeways flood quickly).

Camping and facilities

A pleasant camping area is at Terania Creek. Toilets and tables are provided. There are no fireplaces due to the

Nightcap National Park & Whian Whian State Forest

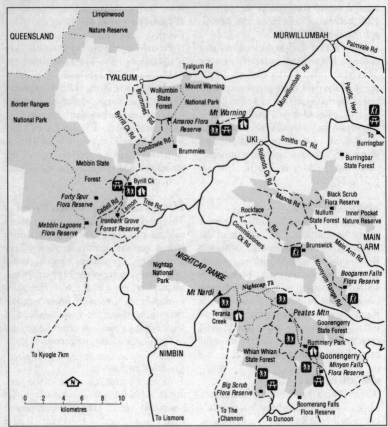

dampness of wood in the area. Campers should have their own portable stove. There is no camping fee and campers should only stay one night. A picnic area is provided at Mt Nardi.

Walks and attractions
From Terania Creek you can walk 500m to Protestors Falls as well as a 4km (rtn) walk alongside the creek to the Terania Creek Basin, a valley of dense subtropical rainforest.

From the Mt Nardi picnic area you can walk 2 hours to Mt Matheson then return via a loop track through subtropical rainforest along the base of the mountain. It is a good walk of moderate difficulty which provides splendid views and interesting forest environments. Some other walking tracks branch off this one, such as Pholis Walk, which branches off the Mt Matheson Track 600m from the car-park. Pholis Gap Lookout is 1.5km along this track.

Mt Warning National Park

The distinctive landmark of Mt Warning, used as a navigational aid by Captain Cook, mesmerises me every time I visit the northern NSW area. The formation is the core of an ancient volcano which is thought to have been active for around 3 million years. The dense rainforest at the base of the peak is wonderful. Walking to the summit, to be the first on the mainland to see the sunrise, is an unforgettable experience.

Location and access

To reach the park, follow the signs from Murwillumbah, 18km away. The road is sealed all the way to the Breakfast Creek car-park. You can head south-west on the Kyogle-Murwillumbah Rd, 12km to the turn-off. From the south, make your way to Uki then continue 3km toward Murwillumbah to the turn-off.

Camping and facilities

No camping is allowed in the park itself. The closest camping spot is at the Mt Warning Caravan Park, on Mt Warning Rd (phone: (02) 6679 5120) Camping costs $14 for two (unpowered) or $16 for a powered site.

Otherwise bush camping is available at the Mebbin State Forest. To reach this spot take the road past Uki toward Nimbin, turn off at either Byrrill Creek Rd or Lemon Tree Rd (9km and 19km from Uki respectively), which will lead you to Byrrill Creek camping area. There are toilets, tables, fireplaces and cold showers.

Picnic facilities are available at Breakfast Creek, at the base of Mt Warning.

Walks and attractions

The walk to the summit of Mt Warning is 8.8km return and can take around 5 hours. The track is often damp and slippery, so wear good footwear and watch out for leeches. The walk is steep in parts but if taken slowly it is manageable by most people. At the top you can enjoy views up and down the coast as well as a clearer picture of the significant caldera (an eroded volcanic crater) of which Mt Warning is the central core.

An enjoyable alternative, if you don't have the time or energy, is the Lyrebird Walk. This easy path leads to a wooden platform set in a dense forest of tall palms. The tranquillity of the setting is likely to be broken by scuttling bush turkeys, fossicking about in a demented fashion.

Aboriginal history

The Murwillumbah and Moorung-Moobar clans, of the Bundjalung Nation, lived close to Mt Warning. Mt Warning is called *Wollumbin*, meaning 'cloud maker' or 'weather maker'.

The forests around Mt Warning supplied abundant resources, such as edible fruits and berries. Brush turkeys, possums, pademelons and bats provided ample meat. Palm fronds, vines and fibres from giant stinging trees provided materials for making bags and water carriers. The semi-tropical rainforest is also rich in medicines.

Most Aborigines do not climb the mountain out of respect for its sacred nature.

Nearby, the Minjungabal Aboriginal Cultural Centre, cnr Kirkwood Rd and Duffy Streets, South Tweed Heads, is a good place to find out about local Aboriginal culture. It is open 9am–5pm weekdays and 10am–2pm Saturday (phone: (07) 5524 2109).

Border Ranges National Park

The hinterland of northern NSW is one of my favourite places in Australia. It is a rich landscape of valleys and ridges. The Border Ranges NP provides many opportunities to appreciate the area.

Location and access

If you're coming from the south, the easiest access is by the Murwillumbah Rd, which passes through Uki and heads toward Kyogle. This road is only partly unsealed before the park. The sign-posted turn-off (25km from Kyogle) leads you onto a narrow, gravel farming track which winds through green farming country to the park. Conventional vehicle access is fine except after heavy rainfall. From the turn-off it is 31km to the Pinnacle carpark and a further 7km to the Forest Tops camping spot. The roads within the park can be slippery and are not recommended for caravans. You can leave them at Sheep Station Creek and explore the park from there.

Camping and facilities

Forest Tops camping area is a pleasant grassy area, in a pocket of deep rainforest. It has a communal shelter with a fireplace, firewood and tables. Tank water is available.

The Sheep Station Creek camping

BORDER RANGES NATIONAL PARK

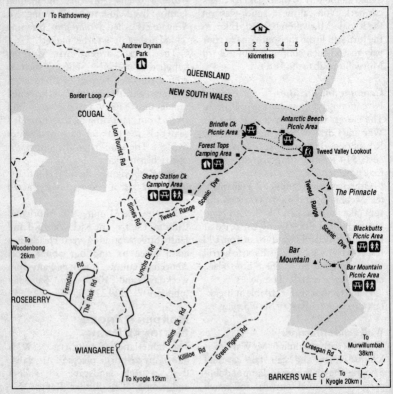

area is much larger, with defined sites set in woodland. Most have tables and fireplaces and there are toilets and a shelter area. Currently no fee is charged to camp in the Border Ranges. En-sure you have enough fuel, as none is available within close proximity to the park.

Walks and attractions

By far the most popular feature of the park is The Pinnacle landform. A thrilling walk takes you out along a ridge and onto the outcrop itself, providing uninterrupted views of the valley and Mt Warning. Try to go there on a clear day so you can appreciate the unique shape of Mt Warning and the glorious Tweed area.

A word of caution: the walk is quite difficult and strenuous. It is not so much fitness the walker requires, but the agility to climb up and down rock steps and cope with slippery spots. Many people walk only the first muddy section to the plateau before the track descends toward The Pinnacle. However, The Pinnacle is not visible from here and the view is not as good as from the Blackbutts picnic area. So if you're not going to go all the way, it's probably not worth going at all. For those who do make the journey it is a wonderful experience. Allow 2 hours to complete the 2km (rtn) journey.

Another good walk is the Bar Mountain Loop (3.5km rtn–mod), starting at Bar Mountain picnic area, which leads to views of the western escarpment and overlooks Mt Warning on the return journey.

Brindle Creek Walk (5km o/w–mod–2.5 hrs) is more of a rainforest walk and goes from Brindle Creek picnic area to Antarctic Beech picnic area. If you don't want a 10km walk you will need to arrange a vehicle pick-up.

From Sheep Station Creek you can embark on the Palm Forest Walk (2km rtn–easy).

The Rosewood Loop (8km rtn–mod –4 hrs) is another walk which starts at Sheep Station Creek. It explores rainforest areas and follows part of the longer Booyong Walk (11km o/w–mod–6 hrs).

Aboriginal history

Prior to European settlement the Galibal language group of the Bundjalung Nation lived in the Border Ranges. The main clan of the Galibal people were the Walungmira, who knew the secret of turning the poisonous starch of the cunjevoi root into edible bread. The Walungmira also used the fibres from the stinging tree to weave nets that were used to catch pademelons.

The lush rainforest offered many resources to Aboriginal clans in the area, such as palm fronds for weaving baskets and carrying water, fibres from the stinging trees to make nets for fishing, and food resources such as possums, birds, bandicoots and echidnas.

WEST

ON THE WAY

The Rock Nature Reserve is a large rock outcrop which you can climb to the summit (3km–hard) for fine views of Mt Kosciuszko and the Victorian alps. It is visible — and sign-posted — from Olympic Way, which links Albury and Wagga Wagga. The picnic area and start of the walk are 6km from The Rock township, 31km south-west of Wagga Wagga.

COCOPARRA NATIONAL PARK

The bushland and rugged terrain of this park allow self-exploration and solitude. There are camping and picnic facilities and an interesting gorge walk. If you're in the Griffith area this park is worth a visit.

Location and access
From Yenda, 16km east of Griffith, head north along the Whitton Stock Route. About 8km along, Barry Scenic Drive veers to the right and leads to a picnic area near Falcon Falls. Otherwise continue 5km to Store Creek picnic spot and another kilometre to Ladysmith Glen picnic spot. A few kilometres further is the road into Woolshed Flat camping area. All roads are unsealed in the park and after rain they can become impassable.

Camping and facilities
Camping is allowed at Woolshed Flat. There are pit toilets, tables and fireplaces. No water is available.

Walks and attractions
At Steamboat Creek, along the Whitton Stock Route, you will notice the remnants of an old bridge used by Cobb & Co. coaches, which used the old stock route late last century on their run between Queensland and Melbourne.

A walking trail leads from Ladysmith Glen picnic area, near Jack's Creek, to an interesting gorge. It is a short and easy loop trail.

Contact Griffith District Office for more information about the park (phone: (02) 6966 8100).

Aboriginal history
The original occupants of the Cocoparra and Koonadan region were the Wiradjuri people (the largest tribe in NSW). Occupation sites in the park indicate intense land use during winter and spring when water was available. Cocoparra is derived from the Aboriginal word *cocupara* which refers to the kookaburra.

In the late 19th century Aboriginal people in the area were forced to move to a mission.

Ruins of this place can be seen at Koonadan Historical Site, located north-west of Lecton. From Lecton travel west toward Griffith for 15km. Turn right onto Cantrill Rd, which runs parallel with the railway track, and continue for 9km to the site.

WEDDIN MOUNTAINS NATIONAL PARK
This park is surrounded by farming country. It is a low-key area where you shouldn't be bothered by too many other people. Ben Hall, a famous bushranger, had his hideout in a cave on the western side of the range.

Weddin Mountains, Conimbla and Hill End are part of the Central Region. Inquiries should be directed to the Forbes NPWS (02) 6851 4429.

Location and access
To reach the cave and nearby camping area, turn off the Mid Western Hwy 5km north-west of Grenfell, into Back Piney Range Rd, and continue 22km to the turn-off to the cave. Follow this road 4km to Seatons Farm campsite.

Holy Camp picnic area, on the eastern side of the range, is reached by turning into Holy Camp Rd, one kilometre south of Grenfell, and following the road directly there.

Camping and facilities
The Holy Camp picnic area is suitable for camping and has toilets and fireplaces. Seatons Farm camping area is a grassy, cleared site where you can find shade, some toilets, a fireplace and little else. Both sites are tranquil and in-frequently visited. Enjoy the solitude and bring your own drinking water.

Cocoparra National Park

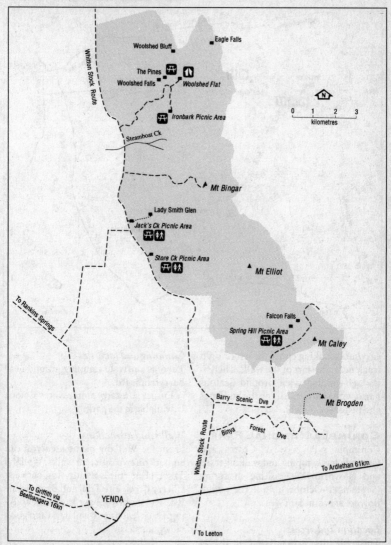

Walks and attractions
From Holy Camp you can walk to Peregrine and Eualdrie Lookouts. There is a steep section up the escarpment to Peregrine Lookout then the path continues quite a distance to Eualdrie Lookout. Allow 3 hours to complete the entire walk.

The walk to Ben Hall's Cave can be completed as a loop track (1.5km rtn–

WEDDIN MOUNTAINS NATIONAL PARK

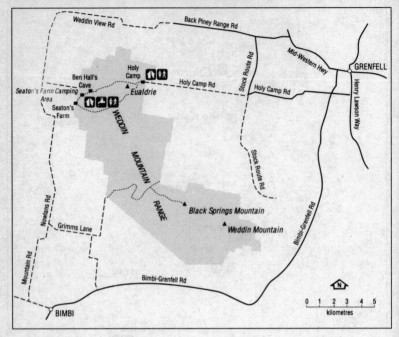

easy/mod), taking either the left or right track near the start of the walk. There is the self-guiding walk around Seatons Farm with signs describing the buildings and history of the site.

CONIMBLA NATIONAL PARK

Conimbla NP, between Cowra and Grenfell, has camping and walking trails and is worthwhile visiting in spring (September–October), as the wildflowers are abundant

Location and access
Turn off the Cowra-Grenfell Rd at the sign-post 9km west of Cowra. Barryrennie Rd runs through the main section of the park. It is 16km along a gravel road to the Wallaby picnic area.

Camping and facilities
There is a private camping ground near Barryrennie Rd.

Ensure you carry ample water as none is available in the park.

Walks and attractions
From the Wallaby picnic area you can embark on two different walks. Wallaby Track (1 hr rtn) is a loop trail between Cherry Creek Fire Trail and Barryrennie Rd. The slightly longer Ironbark Walking Track leads up to a plateau and good viewpoints.

HILL END HISTORICAL SITE

An interesting alternative to bush walks and natural scenery can be found at this partly deserted, old gold-mining town. Hill End was a booming gold-rush town in the late 1800s. There are rustic old homes, idle stamper batteries (used for crushing rocks) and derelict carts scattered around.

Location and access
From Bathurst travel to Sofala and the site is 35km along a gravel road, signposted from Sofala. Otherwise travel from Bathurst via Turondale.

Camping and facilities
There are three places to camp in Hill End. The Village and Glendora sites have hot showers and the Village has some powered sites. The Trough camping area has toilets, tables and fireplaces.

Walks and attractions
An extensive visitor centre, with information, displays, a museum and a short film about the history of the area, is located in the town.

The self-guiding walk to Bald Hill (2km) takes you through the mining area (be careful while exploring the old settlement).

WARRUMBUNGLE NATIONAL PARK
Great reviews of this park are being spread by word-of-mouth, so that the Warrumbungles are fast becoming an essential stopover for many people. It's not hard to see why as you watch the jagged outcrops (the feature of the park) turn purple and gold, silhouetted against a hazy morning sky.

It is an excellent park with extensive walking trails, stunning views and pleasant camping and picnicking environs.

Location and access
From Coonabarabran it is 35km (signposted) to the park along a sealed road. You can return that way or follow the road west through the park then south to Gilgandra. If you're coming from the west the park is 77km from Coonamble. Entry is also via Gilgandra and Tooraweenah, with about 15km of unsealed road. From either direction you can simply follow directions to the visitor centre where you can collect a park brochure that shows all the walks and facilities in the park.

Camping and facilities
Camp Blackman is the main camping area, which has powered and unpowered sites. There are hot showers, laundry facilities, flush toilets and fireplaces. Firewood is extremely scarce so you will need to bring your own or face a $75 fine for collecting it within the park. Just outside the park boundary, if you've come from Coonabarabran, there is firewood for sale. Another spot for vehicle-based travellers is Camp Wambelong (also used for group camping). There are fireplaces provided. Other camping areas in the park with facilities are Camp Pincham (a short walk from the carpark), Camp Burbie (4WD only), Woolshed and Camp Elongery (both group sites only). There are also several sites that can be reached by overnight walkers.

The fee for camping in the park is $10 for two people and $2 for each extra person for anywhere except the overnight walking campsites, which are $2 per person. The fees are to be paid at the visitor centre, or self-registration station nearby. A pleasant picnic area can be found at Canyon picnic area.

Walks and attractions
There are so many walks and attractions that you need to consult the visitor centre for advice on their suitability for you.

The most popular walk is the Grand

High Tops Circuit (14.5km–mod/hard–5 or 6 hrs) which is steep and difficult in places but provides extensive views of the Belougery Spire, the Breadknife and Bluff Mountain.

If you're short on time, but high on energy, you might like to walk to Fan's Horizon (3.6km rtn–mod–2 hrs). A steep path of 1100 steps leads to Fan's Horizon. The view of the Belougery Spire and the Breadknife is slightly obscured by the foreground. A little further along, the view of Bluff Mountain is unmarred and quite impressive. This walk does not fully illustrate the splendour of the Warrumbungle Range, but it is a good sample.

Both these walks start from the Camp Pincham car-park, a short drive south of the main road through the park. The distance shown on the national park sign at the start of the walking trails is one-way only.

Less fit visitors or family groups with children may enjoy the easy access tracks at White Gum Lookout and the Gurianawa Track at the visitor centre. For more information contact the district office in Coonabarabran (phone: (02) 6842 1311) or the visitor centre (phone (02) 6825 4364).

Aboriginal history

People of the Weilan, Kamilaroi and Kawambarai language groups occupied this area. *Warrumbungle* is a Kamilaroi word for 'crooked mountains'. The park contains many Aboriginal sites including shelters, axe-grinding grooves, stone tools and organic deposits.

WARRABAH NATIONAL PARK

This is a largely undeveloped park with a rough gravel road leading to it. Namoi River Rd, just north of Manilla, leads 35km to the park. A basic campground with toilets, tables and fireplaces has been provided near the Namoi River, at the park entrance. It is a popular fishing spot.

MT KAPUTAR NATIONAL PARK

The rugged landscape protected in this park can be explored by many walks, mostly starting from the main recreation area in the southern part of the park. The spectacular Sawn Rocks are on the Bingara Rd, east of Narrabri, with a small picnic area adjacent.

Location and access

The main area is 53km east of Narrabri and the road is mostly unsealed and not

---

YELLOW-FOOTED ROCK WALLABY

The yellow-footed rock wallaby was once hunted for its pelt. Its main threat now is from introduced predators such as the fox, as well as competition with feral goats for food and shelter.

In the early 1980s Mootwingee NP was established primarily to preserve the habitat of the endangered yellow-footed rock wallaby, as the numbers in the area were thought to be as low as 250. The rock shelters of the Bynguano Range provide a valuable habitat for the species. A small colony of yellow-footed rock wallabies is now found at the Cooturandee Nature Reserve. Access to the reserve is extremely limited, and the area is not open to the public.

suitable for caravans. The Sawn Rocks is along the Bingara-Narrabri Rd and can be used as a short cut if you're passing between Narrabri and Inverell. This route requires driving 100km on a gravel road which is generally in good condition.

Camping and facilities

Bark Hut and Dawsons Spring are the main camping areas in the park and are located 7km apart. Both have hot showers, flush toilets, fireplaces and tables (Dawsons Spring has electric barbecues and laundry facilities). The camping fee is $10 per person.

Walks and attractions

From Dawsons Spring you can walk to the summit of Mt Kaputar (2km rtn–easy–1 hr) or to Lindsay Rock Tops (2km rtn–easy–1 hr). Both provide good views and pass through snow gum forests.

The Bundabulla Circuit (3km–easy/mod–2.5 hrs) is another walk which leaves from Dawsons Spring and is popular for all ages and fitness levels. It features Bundabulla Lookout and Eckford's Lookout.

A challenging walk for fit, keen walkers is to Scutts Hut and Kurrawonga Falls (19km–hard–all day). The walk begins at the Bark Hut campsite.

For a challenging hike, the Yulludunida Crater Walk (4km rtn–mod/hard–3 hrs) leads to one of the most impressive sights in the park. The walk begins from the Green Camp car-park, 14.5km west of Dawsons Spring.

There is more information and individual park brochures available within the park.

If you make the journey to Sawn Rocks you should find them spectacular. It is an 800 metre walk to the base of the organ-pipe shaped landform. There is a picnic area, tank water and toilets at the start of the walk.

Contact the Narrabri District Office (phone: (02) 6792 4724) for more information.

FAR WEST

ON THE WAY

If you are travelling west along the Barrier Hwy from Dubbo you may like to visit the Mt Grenfell Historic Site, 40km west of Cobar. For information call Cobar National Park Office (phone: (02) 6836 2692).

Aboriginal history

The Mt Grenfell site is part of the territory of the Wangayuwan people. This reserve contains over 1300 rock art pictures. The Ngiyampaa Walk (5km rtn — mod — 3 hrs) takes you to significant sites in the park. There is a shorter trail of 2.5km rtn taking you to the caves. It is recommended you wear sturdy shoes and long pants to protect you from the burrs.

MUNGO NATIONAL PARK

The exquisite formation of the Walls of China is only one feature of the park, part of the Willandra Lakes World Heritage Region. The area has revealed historic remains indicating life here 40,000 years ago.

Location and access

From Mildura it is 110km north-east to the park, via Arumpo Rd, with little in

Mt Kaputar National Park

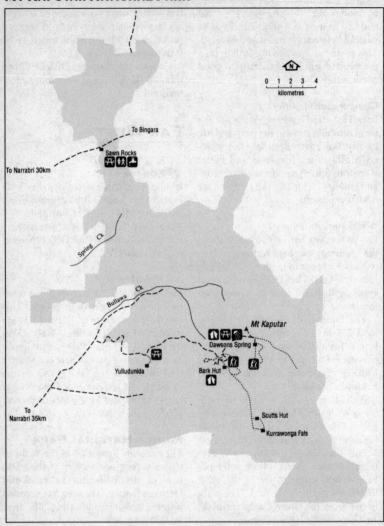

between. The park is 150km from Balranald. Once you reach the park, signs will direct you to the visitor centre, where you can collect a map of the park. Ensure you have enough fuel, food and water for a round trip of 300km. There is a vehicle entry fee of $6 per day.

Camping and facilities
Just within the park boundary, as you enter along Arumpo Rd, there is a basic campsite with toilets, tables and fireplaces. Another site is Belah Camp, located midway along the 60km circuit drive around the park, which has similar

facilities. Limited water is available, so bring your own. Bunk accommodation is available at the shearers' quarters next to the visitor centre.

Walks and attractions

The visitor centre has displays and information about the park and the remains which have been uncovered here. The 60km anti-clockwise tour has a number of stops including the Walls of China — particularly impressive at daybreak or dusk.

For information call the NPWS, Buronga District Office (near Mildura) (phone: (02) 5021 8900).

Aboriginal history

The Barkindji, Ngiyaampa and Muthi Muthi people lived in the area now called Mungo NP. Carbon dating in the park has revealed occupation sites between 40,000 and 60,000 years old. In that time the climate was cooler and Lake Mungo was full of fresh water, providing plentiful supplies of fish, yabbies and shellfish. The changing climate gradually turned the area into a dry, arid claypan, perfectly preserving evidence of prior land use. Lake Mungo is now world heritage listed because of archaeological finds there. Occupation sites indicate that autumn and winter were when Aboriginal people camped beside Lake Mungo. They used ground ovens to cook the game that was caught, including wallabies and lizards. The emu is said to be one of the totems for the region.

WILLANDRA NATIONAL PARK

The 64km of gravel road from Hillston leads to the old homestead on what used to be Willandra Station. There are basic camping facilities available and some walking trails. Willandra Creek attracts many animals and birdlife to its edges. Access is often limited during wet periods.

Aboriginal history

It is likely that Willandra Creek formed the boundary between the Wiradjuri people to the south and Wongaibon people to the north. The Wongaibon people lived in a semi-traditional way right up until 1933. The Wongaibon are often referred to as the Ngiyampaa. *Willandra* is an Aboriginal word meaning 'little waters, creek'.

KINCHEGA NATIONAL PARK

As you approach Kinchega NP from Broken Hill, what looks like a mirage before you broadens to such an extent you know it won't evaporate in an instant. With the scarcity of water in the outback it is no wonder the Darling River attracts such a wealth of wildlife.

Location and access

The 109km from Broken Hill to Menindee is sealed; from there it is 10km to the first of several camping sites set along the Darling River. Roads within the park are gravel and may become impassable after rain.

Camping and facilities

There are 35 campsites dotted along the Darling River, as well as several on the shores of Lake Cawndilla. Toilets, fireplaces and garbage bins are provided. Hot showers are available at the shearers' quarters of the Woolshed, near Emu Lake. The $3 camp fee per person ($2 for children) is payable through the self-registration station. A day-use fee of $6 applies if you don't have an annual entry permit.

Food and fuel are available from Menindee.

Bunk and group accommodation is available at the Kinchega Shearers' Quarters, at $16.50 per person per night.

Walks and attractions

The visitor centre can provide a detailed description of the area and its history.

KINCHEGA NATIONAL PARK

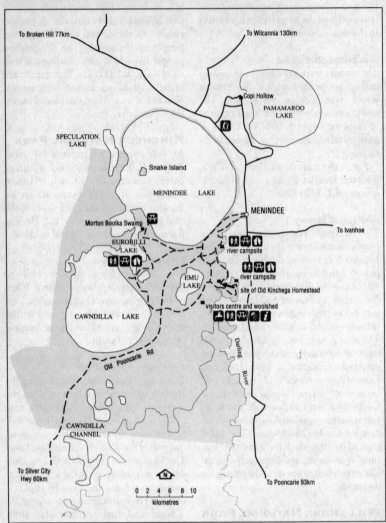

The unusual landscape and abundant wildlife make it an ideal place to relax and observe the surrounds.

The Kinchega Woolshed is an interesting place to explore. A self-guided walk will help you discover the woolshed's secrets.

Middens and old campsites reveal the long occupation of the area by Aborigines.

Contact the Broken Hill District Office (phone: (02) 8088 5933) for more information.

Aboriginal history

The Paakantji people lived in this region. Scarred trees along the Darling River, near Menindee, and middens show active use of the water. Stone axes and wooden wedges were used to cut large sheets of the bark off the trees that now bear the ancient scar.

Over 220 Aboriginal sites have been recorded here.

MOOTWINGEE NATIONAL PARK

The most remote parks seem to harbour the best treasures. There are gorges, creeks lined with river red gums and Aboriginal rock paintings and engravings to see in this park.

Location and access

The park is 130km north-east of Broken Hill on an unsealed road. Turn off the Silver City Hwy, 54km north of the township onto White Cliffs Rd. Follow this road in a north-easterly direction for 76km to the visitor centre, where you can collect a park map. After rain access may be restricted; contact the NPWS district office or the RTA office in Broken Hill.

Camping and facilities

The only camping area is at Homestead Creek set among river red gums. There are cold showers, toilets, tables, fireplaces and bore water. Bring your own drinking water. Camping is $10 a night for two, plus $2 for each extra person. A day-use fee of $6 applies if you don't have an annual permit; pay at the campground.

Walks and attractions

At the beginning of the Homestead Gorge parking area, the easy 400m Thaakaltjika Mingkana Walk leads to a natural rock overhang, which has Aboriginal rock paintings and engravings. The Homestead Gorge Trail (7km rtn–easy/mod) follows the dry creek bed through the gorge. Along the way you will pass several rock pools and some art sites. Nearing the end of the walk you can divert onto the short Rockholes Loop, which passes some Aboriginal carvings and leads to spectactular views of the area and the Bynguano Range. Instead of returning via the Homestead Gorge Trail you might like to continue on the Bynguano Trail, which is a scenic route back to the car-park; allow an additional 2 hours on this section, which is a bit more challenging. Wear comfortable footwear and take drinking water.

A short drive leads to Old Mootwingee Gorge where there is a picturesque rock pool bordered by deep, red cliffs. A 2km return walk enables you to experience the magical tranquillity of the area.

At sunset you might like to do the Western Ridge Trail, which overlooks the Bynguano Range and the endless plains beyond (it is advisable to take a torch for the return walk).

Aboriginal history

The Wandjiwalgu people occupied the place now called Mootwingee NP. The area is steeped in Aboriginal history, with many rock paintings, carvings and occupation sites found there.

Visiting the Mutawintji Historic Site, rich in rock art and ceremonial sites, is by organised tours departing from the amenities block at 11am Eastern Standard Time on Wednesday and Saturday. The tour is $20 and goes for 2–3 hours. Contact the Mutawintji Heritage Tours for information (phone: (08) 8088 7000). The Homestead Gorge trail passes painting and engraving sites.

The park was handed back to the traditional owners in 1998 and is jointly managed by the Mutawingji Local Aboriginal Land Council and the NPWS.

STURT NATIONAL PARK

This park in the north-west corner of NSW shares its border with Queensland and South Australia. Although it is in a highly remote area, bordering the Strzelecki Desert, it is accessible by 2WD vehicles, except after rain.

The landscape in this region is vast and rust-red, setting a perfect scene for a memorable experience.

Location and access

The park is not far from Tibooburra, 330km north of Broken Hill along the Silver City Hwy. From Bourke it is 430km. The roads are gravel and suitable for conventional vehicles, but become impassable after rain. Visitors should be self-sufficient and be prepared to stay as long as necessary if they become stranded after rain. Fuel and supplies are available from Tibooburra. Collect a park brochure, which shows a map of the park, from the visitor centre in Tibooburra.

Camping and facilities

A camping ground is provided at Dead Horse Gully (just north of Tibooburra township), Mt Wood, Olive Downs and Fort Grey, where there are toilets, fireplaces and water. Campers should bring their own wood, as supplies in the park are dwindling.

Walks and attractions

There are several walks in Sturt NP. At Dead Horse Gully there is a walk (4km–2 hrs rtn) through the granite outcrops. At Olive Downs a walk (3.5km–2 hrs rtn) takes you to the edge of the Jump Ups for panoramic views. Fort Grey is the start of a walk (7km–3 hrs rtn) across the dry lake bed of Lake Pineroo to see Sturt's Tree, marked by the famous explorer in 1845.

For the less energetic there are two self-guided drives. The Gorge Loop Drive, 100km and 2 hours driving time, winds over the rolling downs of Mt Wood and through Mt Wood Gorge before returning to Tibooburra. The Jump Up Loop Drive, 110km and 3 hours driving time, passes through the vast Mitchell grass plains and small ephemeral creeks which find their source at the Jump Ups. The additional elevation provides excellent views of the park. A very popular drive is to Cameron Corner, 140km from Tibooburra, where you can stand at the intersection of the three state borders.

This area of the State is rich in flora and fauna, including red kangaroos, wedge-tailed eagles, bearded dragon lizards and, in good seasons, carpets of wildflowers, including Sturt's Desert Pea.

See the visitor centre for details of other activities in the park. Or call the Tibooburra District Office (phone: (08) 8091 3308).

The park is best visited during winter.

Aboriginal history

The Brothers Rocks at Tibooburra have spiritual significance as they relate to a dreamtime story about two brothers who brought the Wongkumara tribe from Cooper Creek to the Tibooburra area. *Tibooburra* is the Aboriginal word meaning 'a heap of granite rocks'.

Queensland

1. Girraween NP, see p130
2. Queen Mary Falls NP, see p131
3. Main Range NP, see p131
4. Mt Barney NP, see p133
5. Bunya Mountains NP, see p134
6. Auburn River NP, see p137
7. Cania Gorge NP, see p137
8. Carnarvon NP, see p138
9. Blackdown Tableland NP, see p140
10. Springbrook NP, see p140
11. Lamington NP, see p143
12. Tamborine Mt NP, see p145
13. Brisbane FP, see p145
14. Glasshouse Mountains NP, see p146
15. Kondalilla NP, see p148
16. Mapleton Falls NP, see p148
17. Booloumba Creek SF, see p149
18. Charlie Moreland SF, see p149
19. Noosa NP, see p149
20. Cooloola NP, see p149
21. Fraser Island RA, see p152
22. Burrum Coast NP, see p154
23. Mon Repos EP, see p155
24. Eungella NP, see p155
25. Cape Hillsborough NP, see p156
26. Conway NP, see p157
27. Bowling Green Bay NP, see p158
28. Magnetic Island NP, see p158
29. Mt Spec NP, see p159
30. Jourama Falls NP, see p161
31. Lumholz NP, see p161
32. Edmund Kennedy NP, see p162
33. Wooroonooran NP, see p162
34. Goldsborough Valley SF, see p164
35. Daintree NP, see p165
36. Cape Tribulation NP, see p165
37. Davies Creek NP, see p168
38. Danbulla Forest Drive, see p168
39. Crater Lakes NP – Lake Barrine, see p169
40. Crater Lakes NP – Lake Eacham, see p169
41. Mt Hypipamee NP, see p169
42. Chillagoe/Mungana Caves NP, see p169
43. Millstream Falls NP, see p171
44. Undara Volcanic NP, see p171
45. Porcupine Gorge NP, see p171
46. Lawn Hill NP, see p173
47. Camooweal Caves NP, see p174

NOTE: Look through the chapter to the On the Way sections to see additional places to camp or visit.

NATIONAL PARKS SERVICE

The Queensland National Parks and Wildlife Service (QNPWS) is part of the Department of Environment (DOE). Maps, signs and uniforms display the QNPWS logo.

CONTACT

NATURALLY QUEENSLAND
INFORMATION CENTRE
(07) 3227 8197
NQIC@ENV.QLD.GOV.AU
WWW.ENV.QLD.GOV.AU/ENVIRON-
MENT/PARK

160 ANN STREET,
BRISBANE
OPEN 8.30AM TO 5.00PM

PARKS

Queensland has a great deal of land bound up in national parks (3.4% of the State or 5.9 million hectares). Many of them are yet to establish visitor facilities and access is often difficult (4WD or walking). I have included details of the most accessible parks which feature walks, camping and other attractions. The *Discover National Parks* booklets produced by DOE and provide details of other places to visit in particular regions.

At the time of European contact Queensland was home to the largest concentration of Aboriginal people. Torres Strait Island people lived on the islands to the north of Cape York Peninsula. The invasion was fast and fierce. The brutality of persecution against Aboriginal people in Queensland was noted throughout the nation. In 1992 the historic Mabo judgement, made by the High Court, recognised native title, over-ruling the previous doctrine of *Terra Nullius*. Large areas of land in Cape York are declared Aboriginal lands. Many Aboriginal people in south and central Queensland refer to themselves as Murris.

STATE FORESTS

The Queensland Department of Natural Resources manages many excellent state forests which feature camping and picnic spots throughout the State. I have covered a few of the sites. If you want to go to more there are small booklets, produced by the service ($2 each), which cover six separate regions, mainly for the coast and hinterland.

TROPICAL ISLANDS

There are countless idyllic islands to visit around Australia, particularly along the Queensland coast. Although many of these are partly, or wholly, national parks, I have included only Magnetic Island, as only it has vehicle access. Ample information is available from tourist bureaus or national park information centres on access, accommodation and what to see and do.

PUB PATRON GUIDE

POT	285ML
SCHOONER	425ML

GIRRAWEEN AND SUNDOWN NATIONAL PARKS

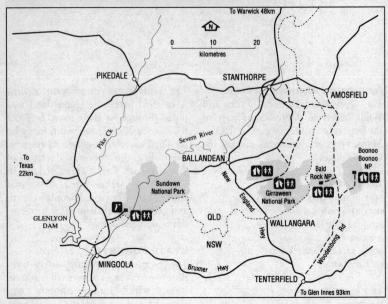

SOUTHWEST

GIRRAWEEN NATIONAL PARK
Featuring similar granite landscape to Bald Rock NP across the border, Girraween is easier to reach and has greater scope for camping and walking. Precariously balanced granite tors provide scenic enjoyment along several walks.

Location and access
The park is sign-posted from the New England Hwy, 7km south of Ballandean. From there it is 9km to the campground, sealed all the way.

Camping and facilities
There are two separate camp areas offering quite different environments. The Bald Rock Creek camping area, on your left as you enter the park, is a forested shady area with fireplaces, toilets and showers. The Castle Rock camping area, on the right once you pass the visitor centre, is a larger, open campground with grassy sites and occasional trees. It has showers, toilets and fireplaces. Drinking water is available and the camping fee is $3.50 per person per night.

A public phone is located at the visitor centre. There are ample picnic facilities for day visitors. Camp bookings are essential for long weekends and holiday periods (phone: (07) 4684 5157).

Walks and attractions
The most popular walk is the Pyramid Track (3km rtn–easy/mod–2 hrs). This walk leads to the base of the huge granite dome called the Pyramid. You can walk the steep path to the top for fine views

around the park and beyond. On the way, or way back, you can detour to see the Granite Arch.

Another popular walk is to Mt Norman and Eye of the Needle (10.4km rtn–mod–6 hrs). This leaves from the Castle Rock camping area with the first turn-off to the right leading to Sphinx and Turtle Rock (7.4 km rtn from the campground). The turn-off to the left leads to the summit of Castle Rock (5.2km rtn–mod–2.5 hrs). I doubt you will be disappointed if you do make the journey to Mt Norman when the towering granite slopes rise before you. Reaching the summit can be tricky — seek advice from the ranger beforehand.

Brochures detailing all the walks are available from the visitor centre.

ON THE WAY

Sundown NP, to the west of Girraween, is mainly a wilderness park for self-exploration and adventure. There is one area in the south-west corner which is accessible for conventional vehicles. Broadwater camping area is reached by a sealed road to the park boundary north of the Bruxner Hwy. Turn off the New England Hwy and follow the Bruxner Hwy 54km west to the Mingoola turn-off, then towards Pikedale. Otherwise travel west of Stanthorpe 35km to Pikedale then travel south to the road into the park. It is near a permanent waterhole of the Severn River and has designated sites with tables, fireplaces, firewood, toilets and showers nearby.

To reach the eastern boundary travel west from Ballandean along a gravel road. From there you need a 4WD to reach the river.

QUEEN MARY FALLS NATIONAL PARK

Ten kilometres east of Killarney, not far north of the border, is Queen Mary Falls. The pleasant touring environment around this area may explain why the falls are so popular. Between Killarney and the falls you may like to stop to see Browns Falls and Daggs Falls, both close to the road and sign-posted.

There is no camping allowed in the park. Opposite the road into the park there is the Queen Mary Falls Kiosk-Caravan Park, which has full caravan facilities.

In dry weather, those with 4WDs can drive along Condamine Gorge, as an alternative route back to Killarney.

MAIN RANGE NATIONAL PARK

If you decide to travel between Warwick and either Brisbane or the Gold Coast then the Cunningham Hwy is an enjoyable route. The park covers a section of the Great Dividing Range so get ready for wildly overgrown vegetation and steep valleys. There are good camping spots and walks not far from the highway, which passes through the centre of the park. Main Range NP and Mt Barney NP are part of the south-eastern region. For more information on Main Range NP, call the ranger (phone: (07) 4666 1133).

Location and access

Cunninghams Gap camping area is the closest to the highway, opposite the Fisher Park Service Station.

The Spicers Gap camping ground is reached by turning into Moogerah Dam Rd, 5km west of Aratula or 18km east of Cunninghams Gap. It is 15km to the camping area along a gravel road which is unsuitable for caravans.

For a place a little more out-of-the-way you can stay in Goomburra State Forest. If coming from Toowoomba, heading toward Warwick, go through Allora, turn east onto the Inverramsey

MAIN RANGE NATIONAL PARK

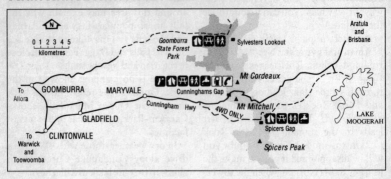

Rd and follow the Goomburra Valley to the camping area. From Brisbane you pass through Cunninghams Gap and turn north at Clintonvale toward Goomburra, then turn east when you reach Inverramsey Rd (gravel for the last 20km). For information call the Warwick Forestry Office (phone: (07) 4661 6600).

Mt Mistake, to the north, is accessible to bushwalkers only.

Camping and facilities

The Cunninghams Gap and Spicers Gap camping areas cost $5 per night. The Goomburra camping site costs $2 per person per night. They all have toilets, tables and fireplaces. Water supplies are limited at all sites, so take your own drinking water.

Walks and attractions

The walks in the Cunninghams Gap area start from the car-park at the Crest, a few kilometres east of the camping area. If you want to reach the Crest without using your car, the Box Forest Track (4.2km o/w) links the two, passing through rainforest and open forest along the way. Of course the path is downhill from the Crest back to the campground and is much easier.

If you only have time for short walks, the Fassifern Valley Lookout (880m rtn) or the Rainforest Circuit (1.4km rtn) provides a good sample of the area.

For a longer walk, the Palm Grove Circuit (4.4km rtn–2 hrs) is interesting. The Mt Cordeaux Track (6.8km rtn–mod–2.5 hrs) is a good hike through rainforest to reach a lookout point from the top of a high cliff (take care near the edge).

The Gap Creek Falls Track (9.4km–hard–6 hrs), Morgans Lookout/Bare Rock Track (12.4km rtn–mod/hard–4 hrs) and the Mt Mitchell Track (10.2km rtn–mod/hard–3 hrs) are long trails requiring a good degree of fitness, particularly the Gap Creek Falls Track. Mt Mitchell is the only path to explore south of the Cunningham Hwy.

The only marked trail from Spicers Gap is to Mt Matheson (3.6km rtn–mod–1 hr). You can continue along a rough path to make a circuit track of 8.1km back to the camping area.

Overnight bushwalking to remote areas of the park is possible. Walkers should be experienced and well prepared. Bush campsites must be booked in advance by contacting the ranger, as sites are limited and group size restrictions apply.

Mt Barney National Park

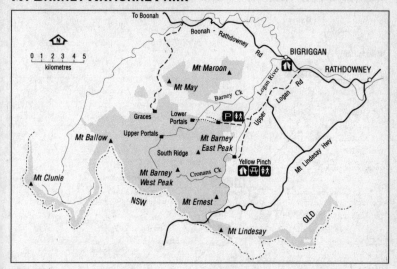

Mt Barney National Park

This park, one of several parks edging the NSW border, is best suited for experienced hikers. Yellow Pinch is about the only place accessible by conventional vehicles. Turn off the Woodenbong Road 11km south of Rathdowney. Follow this road 9km to the Upper Logan Rd where you turn left and continue 9km to the camping area. Beaudesert Shire Council maintains the Yellow Pinch site just outside the park boundary. There are toilets, tables and fireplaces. They also provide another site at Bigriggan, along the Boonah-Rathdowney Rd. This site has showers and a kiosk, and is better suited to family groups.

From a car-park 6km before the camping area, a 3.7km walking trail to the Lower Portals begins. The track leads to a spectacular rock pool in Barney Creek, with sheer cliffs either side.

On the way

Ravensbourne NP is a day-use park with a picnic area and about 3 hours worth of walking trails. The park is sign-posted from Hampton, 17km away. Otherwise it is 33km south-west of Esk.

Crows Nest Falls NP is probably a more scenic place to embark on some easy walks and to stop for lunch or stay the night. Turn off at the police station in the township of Crows Nest and the park is 6km away along a sealed road. There are some pleasant places to camp with toilets, tables and fireplaces provided ($3.50 per person per night). The walking trails leave from the picnic area and follow the Crows Nest Creek to some lookout points. The track down to 'the pool' involves rock hopping and may be a bit difficult for children and the less than sure-footed. You can swim here but don't dive as it is very dangerous. The cascades nearer the picnic area are also suitable for swimming.

BUNYA MOUNTAINS NATIONAL PARK

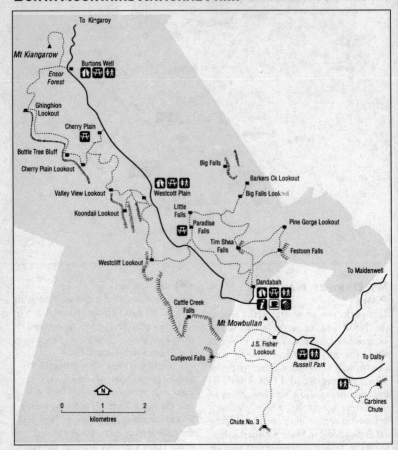

BUNYA MOUNTAINS NATIONAL PARK

The dry scrubby terrain you pass on the way to Bunya Mountains is soon replaced by snaking vines and dense rainforest once you ascend the steep roads to the plateau area. The park protects the largest remaining forests of Bunya Pines (characterised by their unusual dome-shaped crown). I think it is one of the best parks in south-eastern Queensland, but don't take my word for it — see for yourself.

Location and access

There are three main routes to the Bunya Mountains, but whichever direction you approach from, you should find there are ample signs to direct you. From Dalby, the park is 60km via Kaimkillenbun. This route is unsealed for about 6km. From Kingaroy it is 60km via Kumbia and the road is fully sealed. If travelling from Toowoomba it is not necessary to travel to Dalby. Turn off at Jondaryan then travel north to Maclagan. From Jondaryan to the Bunya Mountains is 60km with some unsealed sections. From Nanango or Yarraman the park is 60km via Maidenwell, about 10km of this being unsealed. Towing caravans or trailers on any of these routes is not recommended due to the steep and narrow road climbing the mountain.

Camping and facilities

There are three main camping areas high on the summit area. The main one, with hot showers and flush toilets, is at Dandabah, near the visitor centre. It is a popular family site with a large grassy space suitable for caravans and tents (no powered sites). The camping fee is $3.85 per person per night.

The other sites are Westcott and Burton's Well, both near the road to Kingaroy. These have toilets, tables, fireplaces and firewood. Burton's Well has bush showers (boil your own water in the boiler provided and pour into a canvas shower bag). If you have a solar shower you will have no trouble. The fee for these areas is $3.95 per person per night.

Drinking water is available at Dandabah. Be prepared for the cold nights, even in summer, but don't be disheartened, as the cold and mist usually clear up by about 10am. There are ample picnic facilities for day visitors. Camp bookings are essential for long weekends and holiday periods (phone: (07) 4668 3127).

Walks and attractions

There are several excellent walks for you to appreciate the habitat and fine views. The walks to the south of the road are generally for views out to Darling Downs and the coast and those to the north lead through rainforest to some lookouts. One of the best walks is to the summit of Mt Kiangarow (2.4km rtn–easy/mod–1 hr) which can be started from the Burton's Well campsite.

Otherwise the scenic circuit, which starts from Dandabah, is an enthralling walk which passes huge trees — the trail even goes through an old fig tree (look out for the owl inside). The walk also features waterfalls and Pine Gorge Lookout.

Brochures detailing all the walks are available from the park office information boards throughout the park.

Aboriginal history

The Dalla, Jarowai and Kaiabara people lived around the base of the Bunya Mountains, as conditions on the mountain were not suited for permanent habitation. The Bunya pines were an important food source and every three years the abundant harvest was a time of celebration where several hundred people from clans in southern Queensland and northern NSW would travel to the Bonye Bonye feast, staying for up to three months.

Each clan lay claim to a collection of the pine trees and ownership was passed from father to son. Only the owner was permitted to climb the tree which was done using footholds cut into the trunk with stone axes and using rope made from vines.

The kernels from the cones are sweet and floury and can be eaten raw, roasted, or made into a flour for cake.

Corroborees and other tribal ceremonies, such as marriage, would take place at this time. Sawmilling from the 1870s cut down many of the sacred trees. The last Bonye Bonye feast happened in 1875.

CANIA GORGE NATIONAL PARK

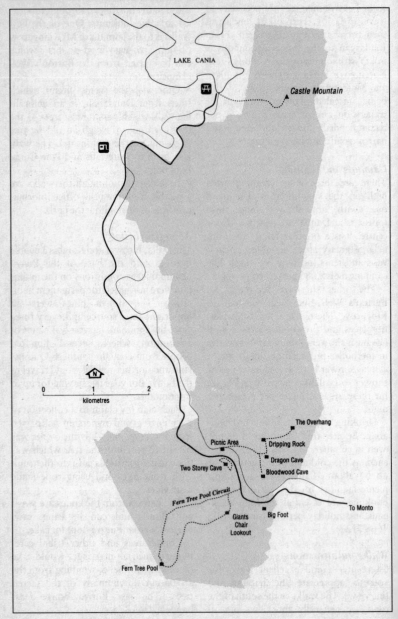

Auburn River National Park

Auburn River and Cania Gorge NPs are part of the Central Coast region. Inquiries can be made to the Bundaberg office (phone: (07) 4131 1600) or Monto office (phone: (07) 4167 8162).

Although largely undeveloped for visitors, Auburn River does have a basic campground, set amongst dry, open woodland. Travel 28km south-west of Mundubberra along the Hawkwood Rd then turn left at the sign-post and follow this road 7km to the campsite. There are toilets, tables and fireplaces but no water. It is $2 to camp and permits can be obtained from the self-registration stand at the park.

Beside the river you will see some interesting granite formations, with some worn so smooth they look like giant eggs.

Cania Gorge National Park

Although Cania Gorge is a day-use park only, its ease of access and wonderful walks make it an enjoyable place to visit. There is something deeply satisfying about driving for many kilometres through featureless country, to be suddenly plunged into an unusual and interesting environment, as is the case with this park.

Location and access

From Monto travel north 12km on the Burnett Hwy then turn off and continue 13km to the picnic area and car-park where most of the walks begin.

If you're coming from the coast and heading inland to visit Carnarvon Gorge, a good alternate route is to turn off one kilometre north of Gin Gin and travel to Mt Perry then north to Monto. This way involves long unsealed sections, but is very scenic.

Camping and facilities

There is no camping in the park itself. Seven kilometres north of the picnic area is a private caravan park. If you want to camp for free there is a council rest area 15km north of the turn-off into the park, along the Burnett Hwy. There are toilets, a table and fireplace provided.

Walks and attractions

From the picnic area, one of the best walks is to the Dripping Rock (1.1km rtn) and further along to the Overhang (1.6km rtn). The easy trail takes you into the tangled coolness of the sub-tropical rainforest. There are intensely coloured sandstone formations opposite palm trees and ferns.

Two Storey Cave (1.3km rtn), on the other side of the road, is probably better than Dragon and Bloodwood Caves (although they are just a short detour from the Overhang walk).

The Fern Tree Pool Circuit (5km–mod) is probably the hardest of the walks as it involves a steep climb to Giants Chair Lookout. The walk begins 900 metres south of the picnic area. From the same spot you can walk 500m to Big Foot (a foot-shaped imprint on a sandstone wall).

ON THE WAY

If you happen to be travelling along the Leichhardt Hwy you might like to stop at Isla Gorge NP for views and a picnic lunch near the lookout. This area is a short distance off the highway, 35km south of Theodore. An undercover picnic area, toilets and water are available. No camping is permitted.

A 400m walk follows along a ridge to better views of the rugged escarpments.

For more information contact the Ranger at Taroom (07) 6273 3358.

CARNARVON NATIONAL PARK

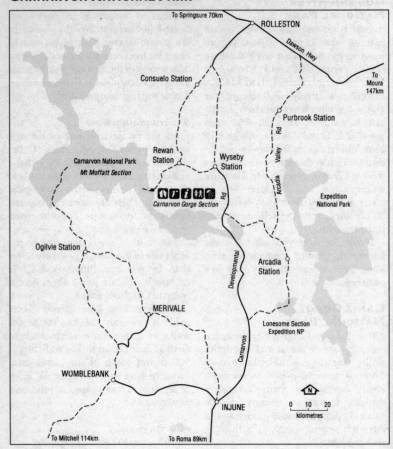

CARNARVON NATIONAL PARK

This is the type of park that you have to go way out of your way to reach, but you won't regret one inch of it. It is a grand place preserving Aboriginal rock art and huge sandstone escarpments which hide pockets of dripping rainforest. The park itself is divided into a number of sections, the most popular for visitors being the Carnarvon Gorge. It warrants a week of exploration (and after the long drive to get there you will want to stay a while).

Location and access

From the north the park is accessible via Rolleston or from the south via Injune. From Rolleston you face about 75km of unsealed roads; from the south only the last 45km from Wyseby is unsealed.

From Injune travel north 94km to Wyseby where you turn left. From Rolleston veer off the Carnarvon Developmental Rd toward Consuelo and follow the road south to the park. Both turn-offs are sign-posted. The gravel roads may become impassable after rain.

The Mt Moffat section of the park is 160km north-west of Injune along a rough, unsealed road. Conventional vehicles can make this journey but, once in the park, 4WD is needed to visit many of the attractions.

The more remote Salvator Rosa section of the park may be reached by turning west from Springsure for 119km then turning left toward Cungelella Station and continuing 53km to Nogoa River camping area. This region is very remote and intending travellers should seek advice on visiting the area and be totally self-sufficient if they do.

Camping and facilities

The main camping ground in the Carnarvon Gorge section has toilets, cold showers, tables, drinking water and a public phone. The camping fee is $3.95 per person per night. There is no firewood available so ensure your fuel stove is working or bring you own firewood (a few fireplaces are provided). The Oasis Lodge, 3km away, has fuel, gas, and limited food available.

You will need to book well in advance if you intend visiting during school holidays. There is a maximum stay of five nights during Queensland and New South Wales school holidays. Whenever possible arrange to take out rubbish such as plastics, tins, glass and cartons. The creek water in the park is unsuitable for drinking. Use a drinking container on walks. Enquire about availability of sites before heading out to the park (phone: (07) 4984 4505 or fax: (07) 4984 4519).

There are four basic sites available in the Mt Moffat section (phone: (07) 4626 3581).

Camping is allowed at Nogoa River (4WD only, no facilities) in the Salvator Rosa section. Visitors are advised to bring extra food and suitable camping gear in case of wet weather.

Walks and attractions

Moss Gardens is one of the closest features to the campsite (3.6km o/w). It is a damp enclave, lined with delicate moss and ferns, with a rock pool at the centre, fed by a small waterfall.

One of the most enchanting places to visit is the Amphitheatre (4.1km– mod), which involves climbing a steel ladder to the narrow entrance. Once through the crevice you enter a large chasm which resounds with exquisite acoustics.

The Wards Canyon and Aljon Falls Track (4.8km o/w–easy/mod) leads through the dark passage of Wards Canyon where the sunlight glances in for only 20 minutes each day. The track continues along to a group of giant king ferns spanning metres across, ending at a rock pool at the base of the Upper Aljon Falls.

The Art Gallery (5.6km from the campsite) and Cathedral Cave (9.3km) both display a number of Aboriginal rock paintings. At these sites there are boardwalks so you can easily view the art without fear of damage.

These features and several others are found by branching off from the main track. A number of sites can be visited on a day walk.

The park brochure and the visitor centre will give you more ideas on where to go.

Aboriginal history

The Nguri people occupied the lowlands and the Bidjara people occupied the high northern areas of this park. A dreamtime story about Moondungera, the Rainbow Serpent, tells about how he caused a large spring to flow from the range, creating the Maranoa River.

The Tombs was a significant burial site, where bodies were wrapped and bound ornately in bark. Kenniff Caves is a significant location with archaeological research showing human habitation dating back 11,500 years. The cave also contains several examples of stencil art, the most dominant art form in Carnarvon. Over 5,500 paintings have been recorded in the park. Two-thirds of them are in the Art Gallery and Cathedral Cave.

The 500m Aboriginal Cultural Trail, beginning 2km before you reach the camping area, leads to Baloon Cave. Sign-posts provide information about plant use and traditional lifestyles in the park. *Baloon* means 'axe' and the cave was likely to have been a supply of rock for axe-making.

BLACKDOWN TABLELAND NATIONAL PARK

To get to this park, turn off the Capricorn Hwy 11km west of Dingo and follow the gravel road 30km to the South Mimosa Creek camping area. At the camping area toilets, fireplaces and tables are provided. Carry your own firewood into the park and take your rubbish out. No drinking water is available.

A short walk (2km rtn) leads from the campground to an art site. Drive south of the camping area to reach the Rainbow Falls car-park. A 2.2km trail leads to views of the falls.

A rough vehicle track veers right from the road to Rainbow Falls, leading to a car-park from where you can walk to Stony Creek Falls (10km rtn–mod).

Blackdown Tableland NP is part of the Central Coast region. For general inquiries call Rockhampton (phone: (07) 4936 0511).

Aboriginal history
The Gangulu Aboriginal people lived in the Blackdown Tablelands. Rock art sites near upper Mimosa Creek show hands, weapons and tools. It is unlikely the tablelands were permanently occupied due to scarce food resources.

The sign-posted Mimosa Cultural Circuit walk leads to an art site in a sheltered rock overhang (2.8km rtn — easy).

SOUTHEAST

SPRINGBROOK NATIONAL PARKS

A very pleasant way to enter sunny Queensland from northern NSW is by travelling north-west of Murwillumbah, to Numinbah, then across the border; making Natural Bridge one of your first stops.

Another feature of the area is the two outstanding lookouts (Best of All and Bilbrough's) which peer south, from the scenic rim, over the beautiful Tweed region.

Location and access
The Nerang-Murwillumbah Rd leads past the Natural Bridge and up to a turn-off, 6km north of Numinbah Valley, where you turn right and drive in a southerly direction for 18km to Springbrook. If you are coming from the Gold Coast, Springbrook is 29km along a sealed road from Mudgeeraba.

Camping and facilities
The only camping ground is next to the Gwongorella picnic area, off Springbrook Rd. It has toilets, tables and fireplaces and the fee is $3.95 per person per night. Children under the age of five are free.

Walks and attractions
From the campground you can take the short walk to Purling Brook Falls, a spectacular cascade falling 109m. Waringa Pool, downstream of the falls, is a pleasant spot in the warmer months. As you drive further south along Spring-

BLACKDOWN TABLELAND NATIONAL PARK

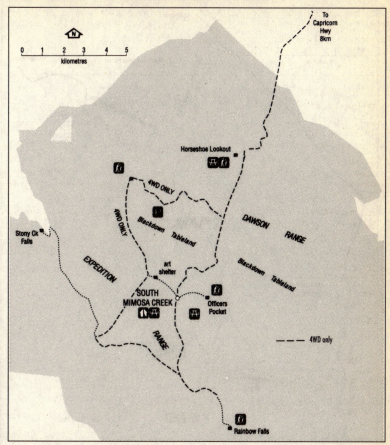

brook Rd and Lyrebird Ridge Rd you will see sign-posts for the Best of All and Bilbrough's lookouts. The Best of All lookout lives up to its name. A 300m walk leads through moss- and lichen-clad forest to a panoramic vista over the coast and the craggy form of Mt Warning.

The Twin Falls Circuit (4km–easy/mod) can be accessed at Tallanbana picnic area and follows the rim before dropping to the base of the falls.

The Natural Bridge is a great place to visit. A short walk leads down to the eroded archway. You can walk into the large cave surrounding the pool and waterfall. Once inside, the thundering of the water is deafening. Take your swimmers in case you are tempted to plunge in, but be warned, although supremely invigorating, it is icy cold. If you visit after dark you can see the sprinkling of glow-worms on the walls of the cave.

Mt Cougal is another section of the park, for day use only. Closer to the

SPRINGBROOK NATIONAL PARKS

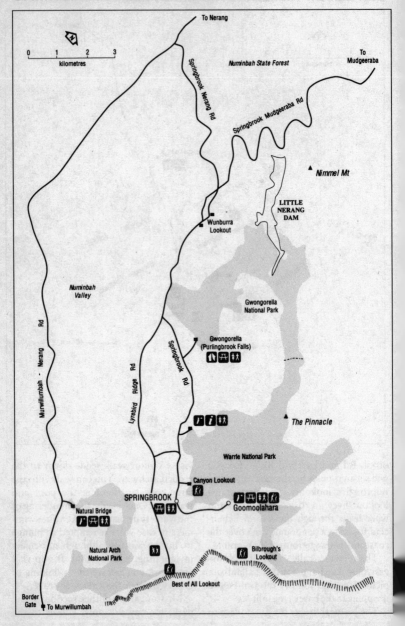

Gold Coast than Springbrook, it is a good place to walk in rainforest or swim in clear mountain pools. Turn off the Gold Coast Hwy along Currumbin Creek Rd for 21km to the picnic area. A constructed walking trail follows Currumbin Creek past Cougals Cascades to Mountain Pool. The path continues to an old sawmill which has been restored and is worth a look.

LAMINGTON NATIONAL PARK

Visiting the limitless beauty of the subtropical rainforests of Lamington NP does not have to be an uncomfortable experience. Sealed roads lead all the way to high-quality camping areas, with rainforest resorts nearby, if you want to treat yourself. Yet once you set off into the dense, misty rainforest, civilisation quickly fades away.

Location and access

The two main areas, Green Mountains and Binna Burra, are long distances apart so you may need to decide which one you will go to beforehand. O'Reilly's Guest House, within the Green Mountains section, is 36km south of Canungra. Binna Burra Mountain Lodge is 26km from Canungra or 35km south-west of Nerang. The last section, south of Beechmont, is winding and steep. Once you arrive at either O'Reillys or Binna Burra you can collect a walking trail map from the national park office.

If you are entering Queensland after visiting the Border Ranges you can do so via the Lions Tourist Rd, which begins just west of Sheep Station Creek camping area. The Lions Tourist Rd is a scenic drive and passes a good picnic and camping area at Andrew Drynan Park, just north of the border. The road leads to the quaint town of Rathdowney, from where you can head west to Mt Barney NP or turn right to Beaudesert and Canungra.

Camping and facilities

The national park camping area is located near O'Reilly's Guest House. There are hot showers, toilets, tables and fireplaces. Camping fee is $3.95 per site and booking is recommended for any time of the year but is essential for weekends and holiday periods. Phone (07) 5544 0634 between 2pm and 4pm for details. Binna Burra has a private campground. Public phones and limited supplies are available from the guesthouses. No fuel is obtainable in the park.

Walks and attractions
GREEN MOUNTAINS

One of the features of O'Reilly's is the Tree Top Walk. A suspended boardwalk leads high into the canopy of the rainforest so you have a better chance of seeing the birds who make all the exquisite racket.

The walk to Moran's Falls (6km rtn-mod) begins from the main road about one kilometre before the camping area. Python Rock can be seen along the Western Lookouts Walk (5km rtn-easy), which begins near the start of Moran's Falls Walk. This walk also leads to Pats Bluff, perched on a steep cliff with expansive views beyond.

The Blue Pool (9.8km rtn-mod) is a popular walk and can be crowded on weekends. Another 1.7km past the Blue Pool are the Stairway Falls. Otherwise you can make a 14km circuit track by visiting Elabana Falls on the return journey.

BINNA BURRA

The Binna Burra region has much to reveal to those who explore its many trails. One of the unusual features of this area is the Senses Trail, designed for the visually impaired. It can be an enlightening experience for everyone. The Bellbird Lookout Walk (2km loop) and the Caves Circuit (5km rtn-2 hrs) are good

TAMBORINE MOUNTAIN NATIONAL PARKS

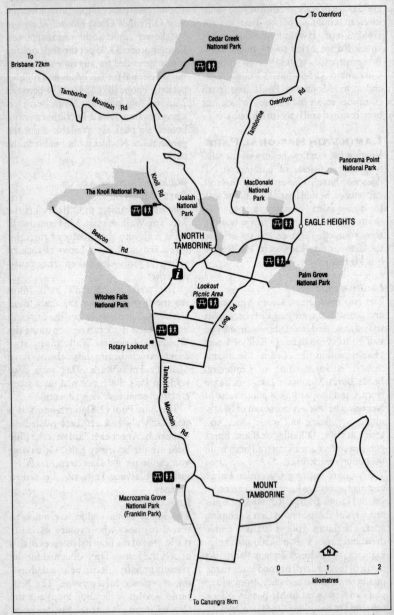

easy trails which may offer glimpses of elusive koalas. The Bellbird Lookout provides views over Egg Rock, Turtle Rock and Ships Stern.

If you can handle a bit more of a challenge, the Gwongoorool Pool (6km rtn–half day) is a popular walk.

A feature of the area are the spectacular Coomera Falls (11km rtn–mod), which drop 64m through lush, green ferns and rainforest.

The information centre has all the walk details and maps to carry with you.

Aboriginal history

The Wangeriburra clan, associated with the Kombumberri tribe, occupied this area. *Burra* relates to a clan group and *Binna* means 'cliff' or 'escarpment'. The Cooking Cave, near Binna Burra, contains remains of cooking fires and other occupational debris. Bushrangers Cave, a large shelter situated below Mt Hobwee, was most likely used as a short term camp for groups travelling across the ranges. A walking track to the site departs 1.5km north-west of the QLD–NSW border gate.

TAMBORINE MOUNTAIN NATIONAL PARKS

Several small national parks dot the plateau of Tamborine Mountain. They offer fantastic views, good short walks and pleasant places to picnic. Access is easy and I don't think you will regret a visit to this unusual area. They are all day-use parks which excel in picnic facilities, lookouts and short strolls.

Location and access

From Canungra, Mt Tamborine is 10km north along a sealed road. From Brisbane it is 77km to North Tamborine along Tamborine Mountain Rd. You can reach the parks by turning west off the Pacific Hwy at Oxenford to reach Eagle Heights and North Tamborine.

Camping and facilities

There is no camping allowed in the national park. Private caravan parks operate on the mountain. There are several picnic areas dotted within the parks.

Walks and attractions

If you want to do some walking, Palm Grove has the greatest number of tracks in the area. A feature is the spectacular palm forests. It's here that you realise you are in sub-tropical Queensland. The Joalah section is also dramatically beautiful with a maze of narrow trunks capped by a canopy of green palm leaves.

Lepidozamia Grove preserves the unusual cycad, a primitive and beautiful plant.

Cedar Creek is a popular picnic and swimming area and you can take the 3.5km Cedar Creek Circuit, which wanders through open eucalypt forest.

For more information visit the Tamborine Mountain Natural History Information Centre in Doughty Park, North Tamborine.

BRISBANE FOREST PARK

This region comprises national parks, state forests and council lands north-west of Brisbane. The recreation opportunities provided allow the visitor to explore the beauty of the D'Aguilar Ranges. Naturally it is a popular area on the weekends and holidays, so try to time your visit during the week if you can.

Location and access

From Ashgrove in Brisbane travel along Waterworks Rd, past the Enoggera Reservoir to the information centre at The Gap. From there follow the Mt

Brisbane Forest Park

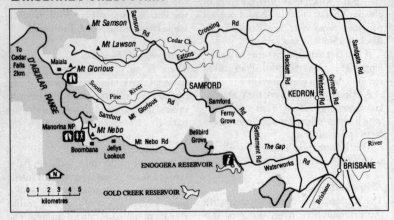

Nebo–Mt Glorious Rd to reach Manorina NP where the camping area is located, 40km from Brisbane.

Camping and facilities
The only vehicle-based camping area in the park is at Manorina NP, where there are septic toilets, drinking water and fireplaces. Stop at the visitor centre (open 7 days, 10am–4.30pm) to pay the $3.95 camping fee and get some more information on what to see and do. A private campground is located at Mt Glorious.

Walks and attractions
A good walk (6km rtn) leads from the campground through rainforest and eucalypts to Mt Nebo lookout.

The walk to Greene's Falls, in Maiala NP, is popular (5km rtn–easy/mod) passing through rainforest before the falls. Cedar Creek Cascades are good for swimming. They are located outside the park in the Samford Valley, along Upper Cedar Creek Rd off the Samford-Dayboro Rd, 6km north of Samford.

Glass House Mountains National Park
As you travel north of Brisbane it is impossible to ignore the presence of these mountains, which rise prominently from the flat surrounding terrain.

Location and access
From the Bruce Hwy take the Beerburrum/Maleny exit. Mt Tibrogarggan is reached by turning off the Glass House Mountains Rd and crossing the railway line, 2km south of the township of Glass House Mountains. Follow this sealed road 3km to the picnic area.

Mt Beerwah is reached by driving west from Glass House Mountains along Coonowrin Rd. Turn left after 4km into Old Gympie Rd. After 400m turn right and follow Mt Beerwah Rd to the picnic area.

Camping and facilities
There are no camping facilities provided. Private caravan parks are situated in nearby townships. Good picnic areas are located at the base of the mountains.

Glass House Mountains National Park

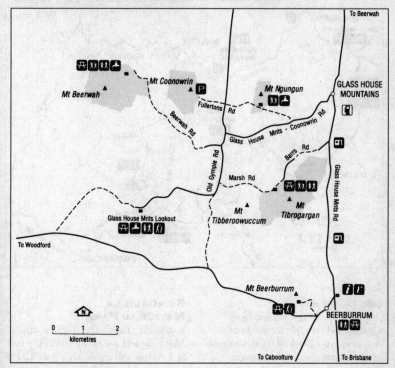

Walks and attractions

Mt Beerwah can be climbed but it is a difficult climb and should only be attempted by the fit and agile (3 to 4 hours return).

Mt Coonowrin can be climbed but only by skilled rock climbers.

Aboriginal history

The Gubbi Gubbi, or Merri River, people occupied the territory around the Glass House Mountains. The boundary between the lands of the Undambi and Nelbo clans is the Old Gympie Hwy, which used to be a common route extending as far north as Cooktown.

The dramatic landforms relate to a dreamtime story about a son Coonowrin, who cowardly ran away when his mother, Beerwah, needed him when the family was threatened during a flood. His father, Tibrogarggan, was so angry that he struck Coonowrin on the neck, dislocating it and forming the crooked shape. Tibrogarggan now looks toward the sea, with his back turned to his son.

The Beerburrum bora ring can be found 2.7km south-east of Glass House Mountains township. The bora ring is sign-posted from the Bruce Hwy. Turn west along Johnston Rd for 2km and then north 600m to near a pine plantation. A circular area, 22m in diameter, can be seen.

BLACKALL RANGE AND SURROUNDS

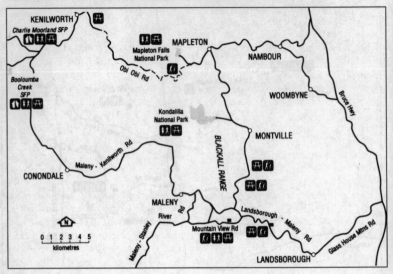

ON THE WAY

As part of any journey in southern Queensland I would recommend the detour into the Blackall Ranges, considered the hinterland of the Sunshine Coast.

In this region you will find the charming townships of Maleny, Montville and Mapleton. For great views of the Glass House Mountains make sure you stop at Mary Cairncross Scenic Reserve, located along Mountain View Rd. This road is sign-posted off the Maleny-Landsborough Rd one kilometre south-east of the road to Montville.

Once you've had a stroll through Maleny township you can either head north to Montville, visiting Kondalilla Falls and Mapleton Falls on the way, or continue west to explore more of the region and camp in some lovely state forests as well.

KONDALILLA NATIONAL PARK

Kondalilla Falls are 3km north of Montville and are easy to find. The falls and a large waterhole are about 1.5km from the car-park. If it's warm enough a paddle here is wonderful, in a lovely forest environment. The Kondalilla Falls Circuit (4.4km–mod), leads past the falls and through the surrounding rainforests.

MAPLETON FALLS NATIONAL PARK

To reach this park, which has similar attractions to Kondalilla, travel along Obi Obi Rd 4km from Mapleton then turn right and go a further one kilometre to the car-park. It has a good picnic area and it is a short walk to a lookout over the falls.

BOOLOUMBA CREEK STATE FOREST

From Maleny travel west for 32km to the turn-off to the park or, if coming from Kenilworth, the turn-off is 5km south of Little Yabba Creek. From the turn-off it is 6km to the Area 1 campsite, a very pleasant place with designated sites set in pockets of forest with a stream nearby.

You can continue to Area 2 (day-use only) or further to Area 3, a lovely place to camp with sites dotted along the river edge. Area 4 is the last, and least appealing, of the camping areas. It is on the other side of the road, occupying a large grassy area. All sites have toilets, tables, fireplaces and cold showers. The camping fee is $2 per person per night.

The Gold Mine Creek Circuit (3.3km) is a short trail leading to the historical site.

CHARLIE MORELAND STATE FOREST

The turn-off for this park is just north of the impressive bridge over Little Yabba Creek. A private caravan park operates on the south bank of the creek. From the turn-off it is 5km to a pleasant camping ground near a swimming area. Stopping for a picnic and swim is definitely recommended if you're travelling in the area.

There are toilets, tables and fireplaces in the big campground and it is $2 per person per night. The forestry office is located along the road to Charlie Moreland so stop and collect a brochure on the Kenilworth Forest Drive and walks in the area if you're interested.

ON THE WAY

If you cut back to Mapleton from Kenilworth along Obi Obi Rd you can enjoy the scenic drive. However, it is gravel in places and steep and bendy. It is not suitable for caravans. From Kenilworth you can continue north to the Bruce Hwy via the Kenilworth-Eumundi Rd.

NOOSA NATIONAL PARK

Although only a day-use park, several hours can be spent enjoying the coastal splendour of this park. On the edge of the up-market holiday retreat of Noosa Heads, the park is a mixture of superb beaches, easy walks and enchanting views.

Head north of the township to Noosa Beach then right, to get to the car-park and picnic area where the information centre is located. Pick up a walking map here and ensure your water bottle is full, as you will probably want a drink along the way. There are several walks which traverse the park but my favourite is the coastal track leading to Hells Gate (2.7km o/w– easy/mod). As you walk you can enjoy the view of the clear water, rolling toward the shore in long gentle waves, often littered with surfers. From Hells Gate you can walk down to Alexandria Beach (a discreetly nudist beach).

Aboriginal history

The Undumbi people occupied this area prior to the arrival of Europeans. Abundant food resources were available such as fish, shellfish, turtles, dugong, goannas, kangaroos, wallabies and possums. Midden sites have been found on the shores of Lake Weyba.

GREAT SANDY NATIONAL PARK

The park features extensive waterways in the southern section along the Noosa River, as well as the dramatic coastal scenery in the north near Rainbow Beach. Most areas in the park require 4WD. A popular alternative in the southern area

GREAT SANDY NATIONAL PARK—SOUTHERN END

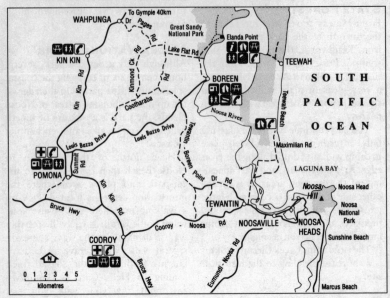

is to hire a canoe and paddle your way into remote and beautiful spots.

Location and access

One of the larger camping areas in the park is the privately run place at Elanda Point. Turn off the Bruce Hwy at the Cooroy turnoff and follow signs to Pomona. Alternatively take the Pioneer Rd turnoff, located north of Cooroy on the Bruce Hwy, and follow it to Pomona. Veer right before the township toward Boreen Point, turn left before Boreen Point and follow the gravel road 5km north to Elanda Point.

To reach Harry's Hut camping area, 35km from Elanda Point, you need to negotiate several forestry roads. It would be wise to obtain a visitor information sheet, with the route highlighted, from the national park office at Elanda Point.

If you have a 4WD you can reach the northern section of Great Sandy National Park by travelling to Tewantin and crossing the Noosa River by a vehicular ferry then, with care, driving along Teewah Beach north to Freshwater campground or Rainbow Beach. It is advisable to check tides and conditions first. Access via Double Island Point is dependent on tide times, heights and prevailing weather conditions.

Alternatively, to reach the Freshwater campground from Rainbow Beach take the turn-off 4km before the township and travel 16km along Freshwater Rd to Freshwater — 4WD needed after Bymein picnic area.

Rainbow Beach is 55km from Gympie, sealed all the way. Information on beach conditions and access can be

GREAT SANDY NATIONAL PARK – COOLOOLA SECTION

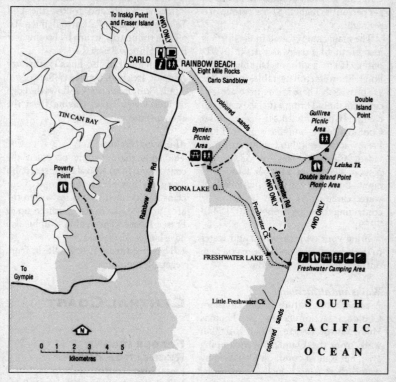

obtained by phoning the national park office at Rainbow Beach (phone: (07) 5486 3160).

Camping and facilities

Camping within Great Sandy National Park costs $3.95 per person per night with a maximum of $14 per family per night.

Camping at Elanda Point (run by a commercial leasee) costs $7 per person per night. It has hot showers (located near the kiosk), toilets, tables and fireplaces. You can hire canoes and the kiosk has a few food supplies. This place becomes a tent city during the holidays so if you visit then, don't expect a wilderness experience. Contact Elanda Point private camping ground (phone: (07) 5485 3165).

Several camping areas are located along the Noosa River and are accessible by water only. If you think you can pack a few essentials into a canoe, then contact the park office at Elanda Point on (07) 5485 3245. During peak periods these campsites can quickly become booked out so do check first. All campsites along the Noosa River must be booked prior to your visit.

Camping fees vary at these sites from $2 per person per night to $5 for a group of 6 per night.

The main campground in the north is just north of Freshwater Lake (4WD only), 10km south of Double Island Point. Showers, toilets, tables and water are provided. There are no fireplaces, so campers should bring a fuel stove. Beach camping is permitted north of the Noosa/Cooloola Shire boundary up to Little Freshwater Creek. No facilities are provided. Camping fees of $3.95 per person, maximum $14 per family per night. Bookings for camping at Freshwater camping area can be made by contacting the ranger (phone: (07) 5449 7959).

Bring your own firewood and water to these beach sites and ensure you take out all your rubbish with you.

Walks and attractions

A remarkable feature in the southern Cooloola section is the Sir Thomas Hiley Visitor Centre, which is a 2km walk from the Elanda Point camping area, but is most commonly reached by water (there is no vehicle access to the centre).

The area at Elanda Point offers many water-based activities. If you're into overnight hikes, check at the national park office about the Cooloola Wilderness Trail (46.2km o/w).

In the northern section an interesting place to visit is the Carlo Sandblow, just east of Rainbow Beach township, from where you can view the coloured sands. Travel to the water tower and from here a 600m trail leads to the edge of the natural sandblow.

From the Freshwater Rd you can take the Poona Lake Track (2.2km o/w – easy/mod), which begins at Bymien picnic area and leads to the tea-coloured lake edged with white sand.

For a full-day hike you can leave from Rainbow Beach and follow the Old Telegraph Line for 7.2km to Bymien. To make a round trip, return by Freshwater Rd to Rainbow Beach Rd.

A walking trail also links Freshwater camping area with Bymien (7.3km o/w).

A 2.7km circuit track follows the edge of Freshwater Lake, leaving from the campground.

Aboriginal history

The Dulingbara people occupied the coastal land from Noosa to Fraser Island living in clans of 30–160 people. Four clans had defined territories within the area from Noosa to the southern tip of Fraser Island. The Gubbi Gubbi also have links with the area.

They lived from fish, shellfish, fruit, vegetables and game.

CENTRAL COAST

FRASER ISLAND RECREATION AREA

Fraser Island consists of the Great Sandy National Park, occupying the northern section, and vacant crown land in the lower half. It is the largest sand island and a world heritage area. The clear freshwater lakes, magnificent rainforest and coastal features make the island one of the most popular destinations on the Queensland coast.

Location and access

Driving on the island requires 4WD. These can be hired from Maryborough, Hervey Bay, Rainbow Beach and from the three resorts on Fraser Island. Day trips operate from Rainbow Beach, Hervey Bay and Noosa.

The vehicle barge at the southern tip operates from Inskip Point (drive north

Sand-mining on Fraser Island

Sand-mining occurred on Fraser Island from 1966 to 1976 and logging was only halted when the area gained world heritage status in 1992.

The Fraser Island Defence Organisation (FIDO) has fought relentlessly to protect the area. John Sinclair made great personal sacrifices when he took the issue to court, representing the public interest. The Federal Government Inquiry stopped the sand-mining. Now that the threats from mining and logging have been alleviated, QPWS now manages the island to protect it from destruction caused by the influx of tourists.

---

along Rainbow Beach). The ferry departs on demand from 6.00am to 5.30pm, seven days a week. The return fare for vehicle and driver is $20 or $10 one way (phone: (07) 5486 3154).

The ferry from Urangan Boat Harbour leaves at 8.30am and departs from Moon Point (to return to the mainland) at 9.30am. In the afternoon the ferry leaves at 3.30pm from Urangan and 4.30pm from Moon Point. Call the Fraser Venture Tours office for information and bookings (phone: (07) 4125 4444).

The other ferry leaves from River Heads at 9.00am, 10.15am and 3.30pm and lands at the end of Wanggoolba Rd (phone: (07) 4125 4444). Both cost $82 return for vehicle and driver plus $5.50 per passenger.

To take a vehicle onto the island you require a permit, which you should purchase in advance from one of the Queensland DEH offices in the region or through the Rainbow Beach QPWS office (phone: (07) 5486 3160). The cost is $30 per vehicle (or $40 if purchased on the island), valid for one month, or $150 for a yearly pass.

The beaches at low tide provide the most efficient passage on the island.

Camping and facilities

In the south there is a pleasant, grassy area in Central Station (no caravans allowed). Also Lake Boomanjin, Lake Allom and Lake McKenzie have designated camping areas nearby.

In the Great Sandy NP there are camping facilities at Waddy Point, Wathumba Creek and Dundubara.

Some sites have showers, toilets, tables and fireplaces. The camping fee is $3.50 per head (maximum fee of $14 per family) and should be paid beforehand, whereby you will be issued with a permit to camp. If you request particular camping areas on certain nights you are likely to be assured of a site on your arrival.

A private campground operates at Cathedral Beach.

Walks and attractions

The attractions of the island are many and varied and I can list only the highlights.

The clear waters of Lake Wabby, Lake Birrabean and Lake McKenzie are an incredible sight. White sand appears through blue waters similar in clarity to the water at Cape Le Grand in Western Australia. As I swam in Lake McKenzie I half-expected to gulp a sour mouthful of salt water — instead, the pure, fresh water left me in wonder.

The 'perched' lakes, which have formed above the sea level on a bed of organic matter, are tea-coloured from tannins. The water is still fresh and drinkable. Lake Boomanjin and Lake Benaroon are perched lakes with picnic areas nearby.

Central Station contains tall, green rainforest with the clearest of creeks running through it. Information shelters provide history and facts about the island. Further north, along Seventy-Five Mile Beach, there are the scenic attractions of the *Maheno* wreck, the Pinnacles and the Cathedrals. The coloured Teewah sands have formed into natural sculptures, creating a spectacular sight at the Cathedrals.

Further north there is a good climb to the crest of Indian Head, from where you can peer down the steep cliffs to the brutal waters below. On your travels upon the island you are sure to see wild brumbies grazing and roaming around. The purest strain of dingo now exists on the island, through the lack of inbreeding with dogs. They appear shy, but are cunning enough to grab your food given half the chance. Please don't feed them, as they are native animals.

Aboriginal history

The Badtjala people lived on Fraser Island. They called the island *K'gari*, meaning 'paradise'. K'gari was a spirit who helped the Great Spirit, Beeral, to create the earth. K'gari wanted to live on earth so Beeral turned K'gari into an island paradise. The lakes on the island represent K'gari's eyes looking up to heaven.

The island supported an estimated 2,000 people prior to European invasion. Occupational deposits indicate the island was used for more than 30,000 years. Numbers dropped dramatically by the 1860s and the final survivors were taken from the island in 1904.

Scarred trees can be seen at Boomanjin and middens exist along the east coast.

BURRUM COAST NATIONAL PARK—WOODGATE SECTION

This is a 6,000 hectare coastal park set around the township of Woodgate and requires 4WD to access the campground at Burrum Point. Bookings (well in advance) are required for school and public holidays for the Burrum Point camping area, which has toilets, cold showers (pulley system for solar and bush showers) and town water. Fires are not permitted. Camping costs $3 per person per night for anyone over the age of five, or if more than four persons over the age of five in one family, a family rate of $12 applies.

There are four walking tracks which are accessible by two wheel drive. The Banksia Circuit (5.2km) and Boardwalk (400 metres) start at the rear of the town between Fifth and Sixth Avenues. The Boardwalk is wheelchair accessible.

The Melaleuca Circuit (1.7km) and the Birdhide (3.4km return) are both accessible from Walkers Point Road. All walking tracks are signposted.

KINKUNA SECTION

Kinkuna is a 13,300 hectare coastal plain with a sandy landscape which requires 4WD for access. Kinkuna can be accessed from Woodgate Road or Coonarr Road off the Goodwood — Bundaberg Road. Access roads are signposted. Camping is primitive and all campers have to be totally self-sufficient. Camping is permitted only in the areas behind the frontal foredunes. Campers must bring their own firewood, water and toilet facilities and must remove all rubbish from the park when leaving. Do not bury rubbish. Camping costs $3 per person per night for anyone over the age of five, or if more than four persons over the age of five in one family, a family rate of $12 per night applies. There are no official walking tracks in Kinkuna. Those visitors wishing to go walking in the park need to contact the ranger at Woodgate.

Mon Repos Conservation Park

The feature of this park is the marine turtle rookery. Nesting occurs between late November to late January. Hatchings emerge between mid-January and late March. You can view the hatchlings as they make their way to the ocean. There is also a turtle rookery at the Mon Repos beach, 14km east of Bundaberg. A fee is charged for the beach tour and the visitor centre, which features scientific-based displays, also charges a fee. Private caravan parks are located next to the park, in the nearby coastal villages, or in Bundaberg.

On the way

Deepwater NP, 15km south of Agnes Water, and Eurimbula NP, 14km west of Agnes Water, are unspoilt areas requiring 4WD to travel within them. Deepwater has exposed ocean frontage and so attracts people who enjoy surf environments. Bustard Beach at Eurimbula is protected and offers a quiet sheltered beach adjoining Eurimbula Creek Estuary. There are basic camping facilities at Wreck Rock (Deepwater) and at Bustard Beach (Eurimbula).

For more information contact the Central Coast Regional Office, corner of Yeppoon and Norman Rds, Rockhampton (phone: (07) 4936 0511).

To reach Seventeen Seventy and Agnes Water you can turn off just north of Bundaberg and follow Rosedale Rd to Berajondo. Signs from here guide you along gravel roads to Agnes Water. A better alternative is to continue through Gin Gin along the Bruce Hwy then turn off at Miriam Vale. Fifty-five kilometres of mixed sealed and unsealed road lead to Agnes Water.

North

Eungella National Park

It may be difficult for me to sound unbiased while I describe one of my favourite parks in the country. Eungella (pronounced young-ge-la) is an enchanting area of rainforest which you are unlikely to forget. As the park forms part of the Clarke Range, rising to over 1200m, the popular southern part of the park is misty and damp for most of the year.

Location and access

Travel 60km east of Mackay to Finch Hatton along the Pioneer Valley Rd, via Marian. Just before Finch Hatton township is a turn-off north to Finch Hatton Gorge. The 12km road is unsealed part of the way and crosses causeways which flood after high rainfall. To reach the Broken River area, where the campsite is located, continue along the valley, east of Finch Hatton, and follow the steep road leading up the Clarke Range to Eungella township (also known as Dalrymple Heights). Turn left and follow the Eungella-Broken River Rd for 5km to the camping areas and visitor centre (where you can collect a map showing walking trails).

Camping and facilities

There are two campsites at the Broken River area. The first one you see, before the bridge, is the Broken River camping area, which has cold showers, toilets, tables, fireplaces and firewood. The better area is at Fern Flats — past the visitor centre — which has separate sites and a modern amenities block with hot showers and toilets. The sites have tables, fireplaces and firewood.

Camping fee is $7.50 per site. For booking or enquiries call (07) 4958 4552.

There are picnic facilities at Finch Hatton Gorge.

Walks and attractions

For an unusual and extremely pleasurable walk I recommend the Wheel of Fire Falls Track (4.2km rtn–easy/mod– 2 hrs). The path leaves from the picnic area and winds its way through lowland tropical rainforest to Callistemon Cascades and along Finch Hatton Creek. The last part of the walk is like a snippet from an Indiana Jones film — you walk up weathered stone steps, reminiscent of ancient ruins, ducking below vines and thick foliage, to finally emerge at a rock pool edged by rainforest and sheer stone walls. A cool swim finishes off an exceptional walk.

Hopefully the track will be open when you visit (the track has been closed for a long time due to upgrading).

There is another swimming spot near Araluen Falls, along a path which branches off the main track 1.1km from the picnic area.

On top of the range there are walking trails through the rainforest running parallel with the road between Broken River and Eungella, then along Broken River to Credition Creek. Several lookouts are sign-posted from the road. See the visitor centre for a walking track guide. At dawn and dusk sneak down to the river to view platypuses busily feeding.

Aboriginal history

Eungella means 'land of clouds'.

CAPE HILLSBOROUGH NATIONAL PARK

This park, occupying a rugged headland north of Mackay, is a good place to stay near lovely beaches; it has the added attraction of containing some interesting and challenging walks.

Location and access

The park is only a short detour from the Bruce Hwy: turn into Seaforth Rd (sealed) and travel 20km north to the park turn-off. Another road to Seaforth leaves the Bruce Hwy just north of Mt Ossa. From the turn-off it is 10km to the park.

Before entering the park, a sign-post to the left indicates Smalleys Beach, 1.5km away. If you continue on the same road for 4km you will reach the council camping area, the resort and the national park office, where you can collect a park map.

Camping and facilities

There are 10 secluded and peaceful sites in the Smalleys Beach camping area. There are *Clivus Multrum* toilets, tables, fireplaces and limited water available. The fee is $5 per night. The national park camping ground has a limited number of sites so call the ranger to check availability (phone: (079) 59 0410). If that is full, there may be sites in the large council camping area near the end of the road. It has showers, toilets and water. A private tourist resort, catering for caravans, is also located in this area. It has a kiosk and a small restaurant.

Walks and attractions

The Aboriginal Awareness Walk (1.4km –easy–1 hr), beginning at the very end of the road, has a self-guiding brochure and information signs along the way. It leads through a pocket of rainforest protected by sheer rock walls and filled with gnarled vines and a bustling ecosystem.

A good walk for coastal scenery is the Andrews Point Track (2.5km o/w–easy/ mod), beginning at the far end of the tourist resort. The first section is steep,

> **BUSH STONE CURLEW**
>
> This unusual bird has a significant presence on the island, especially at night when you will hear its eerie wailing. The curlew does live in other regions in Australia, but few places require the same level of shared habitat with civilisation. Curlews are highly territorial and live in the lowland grassy areas on the island which are privately owned and are being developed. Unfortunately this means that the survival of the curlew is threatened because of cars, dogs and cats (particularly the high population of feral cats) killing them and their young chicks.
>
> The adult birds mate for life and breed once a year. As they are totally ground-dwelling birds they are particularly vulnerable to attack.
>
> For these beautiful, haunting birds to remain on Magnetic Island there needs to be greater awareness among residents and visitors to ensure control of pets and care on the roads at night.

leading to views of Wedge Island and Cape Hillsborough. The track continues over the ridge to Turtle Lookout where you should catch a glimpse of a turtle in the clear water below. The walk then descends to the causeway where, at low tide, you can cross to Wedge Island, or return along the beach to the camping area. If it is high tide you will need to retrace your steps back to the resort.

The Beachcombers Cove Track (1.6km o/w) leads from the picnic area to the beach. At low tide you can return to the visitor centre along the beach. The water at Smalleys Beach is generally still and pleasant for swimming.

Aboriginal history

The Juipera people lived on Cape Hillsborough. A self-guiding trail at Hidden Valley points out various plants and how they were used by Aboriginal people. The trail is 1.2km long and departs from the picnic area.

CONWAY NATIONAL PARK

The incredible scenery between Airlie Beach and Shute Harbour is part of the northern tip of Conway National Park. The area is a major tourist centre due to its proximity to the several tropical islands not far from the coast.

Location and access

The main recreation area is easily accessible from the Proserpine-Shute Harbour Rd, 9km east of Airlie Beach.

Camping and facilities

The large national park camping area is on the right of the road. There are hot showers, toilets, tables, electric barbecues and water. Camp fee is $7.50 per site. There is a four-day limit for camping during busy periods.

Walks and attractions

From the campsite a 1.5km circuit track leads through lowland rainforest and mangroves. From this track a 1.5km spur trail leads to Hayward Gully. Here you will see a stinging tree; beware of the large, heart-shaped leaves which can inflict a painful sting.

The Mt Rooper and Swamp Bay Trails begin 800m along the road towards Shute Harbour from the campsite.

The walk to Mt Rooper lookout can be completed as a 6.4km circuit. The path leads through woodlands and grass trees to views of the Whitsunday Islands and the aqua-coloured waters surrounding them. Follow the path downhill to a rocky outcrop from where you can view Swamp Bay. Then return via the Swamp Bay Track.

The path to Swamp Bay (6km rtn– easy/mod) leads to the beach, from where you can view nearby islands and fossick amongst the broken coral scattered on the beach.

A 1km trail leads north from Shute Harbour township to Coral Beach, which is good for snorkelling. Be mindful of marine stingers during summer.

Outside the park boundary are the wonderful Cedar Falls. Turn into Conway Rd from the Proserpine-Airlie Beach Rd, 5km east of Proserpine. After 9km turn left at the sign-post indicating Cedar Falls. The road leads 3km to a large swimming hole at the base of the falls.

BOWLING GREEN BAY (MT ELLIOT) NATIONAL PARK

The main attraction of this park is the pleasant campground with friendly kangaroos, wallabies, bush turkeys and possums which cheekily invade your campsite. A very enjoyable park.

Location and access
Turn into Alligator Creek Rd, 28km south of Townsville or 59km north of Ayr. The park is 6km off the Bruce Hwy. Sealed roads to the park mean access is good all year round. When approaching the turn-off, keep a close lookout for the national park sign-post, as it is not easily seen from the highway.

Camping and facilities
There are 20 sites with picnic tables, campfires, as well as toilets and hot showers. It costs $7.50 per site.

Walks and attractions
Alligator Falls Walk (8.5km o/w–easy–5 hrs rtn) is quite long and boring, as the track is mostly flat, grassy and follows power lines. However, the last section is through thick, vine-covered foliage alongside a bubbling creek and the waterfall at the end is indeed spectacular. There are a few creek crossings which require shoes off. It is a long walk but rewarding in the end.

There is a good swimming spot near the campsite.

Aboriginal history
The Bindal people occupied the area around the Mt Elliot foothills. Rock art, shelters and middens have been found in the area.

MAGNETIC ISLAND NATIONAL PARK

Situated 25km offshore from Townsville, Magnetic Island is almost half national park. The name originated when Captain James Cook believed the disturbances to the magnetic compasses on his ship, *Endeavour*, were caused by the granite boulders covering the island.

It is one of the few islands on the Queensland coast where you can take your car, by way of a vehicle barge. Although there is no national park camping, there is a variety of accommodation and lots to do on this scenic island.

Location and access
The cost of the barge is $87 return, so you would need to be staying quite a few days to make this option worthwhile. They go four times a day during the week and twice a day on weekends. Contact Capricorn Barge (phone: (07) 4772 5422). Alternatively, passenger ferries

cross regularly and cost $15 per person return.

To get around on the island there are several buses and courtesy buses, as well as scooters, bicycles and mokes ($40 per day plus 30c per kilometre) for hire.

Camping and facilities
There are no national park camping sites, but there is a variety of budget accommodation. Sharkworld in Nelly Bay has camping for $5 and there is a campground in Horseshoe Bay.

Walks and attractions
Swimming and exploring the beautiful beaches is best during the winter when marine stingers aren't a problem. The various walks provide great views of the island and beyond.

The most popular walk starts from the turn-off to Magnum's, from Horseshoe Bay Rd, to the Forts (1.4km o/w-easy-1.5 hrs rtn). The walk is on a wide, slightly graded track, from which koalas are frequently sighted.

The view from the Forts — a number of constructions used in World War II for observation and attack of enemy ships — is especially spectacular on a clear, sunny day.

Of course, one of the greatest attractions of the island is its coral reefs.

All four of these are easily accessed from the island. A pamphlet with maps and advice on snorkelling is available from the QNPWS office in the GBR Wonderland, where you catch the passenger ferry.

MT SPEC NATIONAL PARK
There are some short rainforest walks leaving from Paluma, high up in the mountain range. The Big Crystal Creek camping ground is just off the Bruce Hwy and has excellent amenities and a swimming hole nearby.

Location and access
Turn off the Bruce Hwy onto a service road, 65km north of Townsville, where a sign indicates Paluma 22km. Travel for 2km along this road to a Y-intersection where the road veers left for Paluma and right toward Crystal Creek. Veer right. Continue for 2km and turn left at Speigehauer Rd. The signs say Mt Spec National Park — Big Crystal Creek. Follow this road 4km to the Big Crystal Creek campsite.

Camping and facilities
There are 15 sites with tables and good fireplaces. The exceptionally clean amenities block makes the campsite very pleasant. The camp fee is $7.50.

CASSOWARY

I hope you are luckier than I was and that you catch a glimpse of this unusual rainforest dweller. The cassowary is the third largest bird in the world and sports a hard growth on its head which it uses to push through dense vegetation. This flightless bird has black plumage with red and blue colouring around its head.

Interestingly the male bird incubates the eggs and cares for the chicks. The main threat to the cassowary is the destruction of its rainforest habitat. It is a territorial bird and the diminishing area means that the chicks are finding it hard to establish their own territory.

Cars, domestic animals and feral animals are also killing the adults and chicks.

> **MANGROVES — COASTAL**
>
> The term 'mangrove' applies to both an individual species and a particular type of community. Traditionally the two meanings are interchangeable. Mangrove communities can survive in rather unstable and difficult environments. They tend to grow in the sheltered tropical and sub-tropical coastlines where air temperature is above 20°C at the coldest and seasonal range is less than 10°C. Along the Queensland coast there are the most highly developed communities due to the large amount of shelter from the barrier reef, warm water and many estuaries entering the sea. The best communities are found in the areas where annual rainfall is greater than 1200mm, which is generally next to elevations of over 700m, in close proximity to the coast.
>
> Mangroves act as important nursing and feeding grounds for most of the coastal fish taken by commercial and amateur fishermen. Many species of migratory waterbirds roost and feed in these areas. With much of the Australian population on the eastern seaboard, more and more pressure will be placed on mangrove areas and may threaten their existence. We need to keep this in mind and ensure we treat these important and diverse areas with respect.

Walks and attractions

Paradise Waterhole is only a short walk from the campsite and is a nice spot for a swim.

Midway up the winding drive to Paluma be sure to stop at Little Crystal Creek for a look at the historic and picturesque stone bridge. To reach the start of the walks, turn right just before the township of Paluma.

McClellands Lookout is a short walk through damp rainforest and gives

MT SPEC NATIONAL PARK

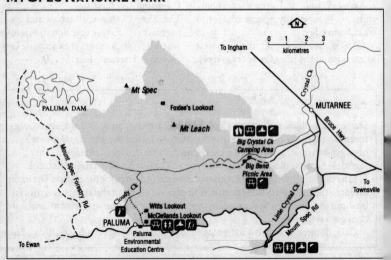

a good view of the nearby coastal islands. Further along you can veer to Witts Lookout (350m), for another view of the range and out to sea. The path to the left leads one kilometre to Cloudy Creek. The track is easy to moderate and takes you to a pleasant spot by small, cascading waterfalls and rock pools.

JOURAMA FALLS NATIONAL PARK

The lush green campsite and the gentle creek flowing through it make Jourama Falls a relaxing place to stop. It is a comfortable drive from Mt Elliot and Townsville and has good walks and swimming holes.

Location and access
The turn-off to Jourama Falls is clearly sign-posted 91km north of Townsville and 24km south of Ingham. The road to the park is 6km, part of which is unsealed but suitable for conventional cars and caravans. The two causeway crossings may become to impassable during the wet season.

Camping and facilities
There are around 20 sites with tables, campfires and toilets provided. There are no showers and you are asked to bring your own firewood. The campsite is clean, grassy and well maintained. Camping costs $5 per site.

Walks and attractions
This pleasant walk to Jourama Falls Lookout (1.2km o/w–easy/mod–1 hr rtn), steep at times, takes you to a spectacular view of the watercourse, which falls over 300m along varied terrain of sheer rockfaces, colourful boulders and rock pools. There is a second lookout a further 480m uphill, which provides a closer view of the waterfall and the lush green gorge below.

The base of the falls is only a 600m walk from the campsite and is a good spot for swimming and relaxing.

LUMHOLZ NATIONAL PARK
Seeing Wallaman Falls, Australia's largest permanent clear drop waterfall (305m), is not the only attraction in this park set in Queensland's coastal ranges; there is a good chance you will see the rare and unusual cassowary and you can also observe platypuses in the creek near the campsite.

Location and access
The park is a bit of a drive out of your way but I don't believe you will regret the detour. From Ingham head west to Trebonne. Good signs make the park easy to find. Most of the 48km drive is unsealed. Be careful of the sharp corners and straying cattle on the way. Once you near the end of your journey you will see a road to the right, which leads to the falls. The campsite is less than 1km away, continuing on the road from Ingham.

Camping and facilities
A couple of things make this camping ground unusual. Firstly, there are undercover gas barbecues you can use (handy when all the wood is wet) and secondly, you can't park your car near your campsite, but if you're lucky you will be able to park only a few metres away.

A shower has been built recently — there was cold water only when I was there but perhaps they have installed a hot water system by now.

There are around 20 sites for camping and a designated area for campervans. The camp fee is $5 per night.

Walks and attractions
The walk to Waterfall Base (2km o/w– mod–1.5 hrs rtn) is very popular. The ritual for viewing the waterfalls involves descending the steep path to the base of

the waterfall before 10am. This means you can witness the rainbows emerge as the sun creeps over the gorge rim and catches the mist from the water. The walk does require a fair degree of fitness for the climb back up the gorge, but most people can do it if they take their time. There are excellent viewpoints only 300m along the track for those who don't wish to complete the whole distance.

ON THE WAY

If you're following the Bruce Hwy then the national park office in Cardwell is a good stop for further information about the area and to view any current displays.

There is also a worthwhile detour along the Cardwell Forest Drive (turn at the BP service station in the main street and continue along this road). As you leave the township you will see a leaflet box on the left where you can pick up a guide to the drive. There are a number of swimming spots along the way — my favourite is the spa pool, about midway around.

EDMUND KENNEDY NATIONAL PARK

This park preserves an important area of coastal terrain. There is a camping area a short drive off the Bruce Hwy, but because of the proximity to large areas of mangroves, the mosquitoes can become unbearable. The site has toilets, tables and fireplace and costs $5 per site.

FAR NORTH

WOOROONOORAN NATIONAL PARK — PALMERSTON SECTION

Palmerston is one of the best places to camp and walk in the beautiful rainforests of North Queensland. There are two scenic, long-distance walks leaving from the camping spot in the thick rainforest.

Location and access

The Henrietta Creek camping area is located just off the Palmerston Hwy, 38km from Innisfail and 25km from Millaa Millaa.

Camping and facilities

There is an undercover area with picnic tables which is in the open, grassy part of the campsite, but there are some great spots tucked into the rainforest further from the highway. There are a few tables and fireplaces but wood is not to be collected from the forest. A coin-operated gas barbecue is provided. The site has fairly minimal facilities, with only two single toilet blocks. Nonetheless it is a very popular spot due to the enchanting surrounds and proximity to walks. There is no camp fee.

Walks and attractions

There are several options to chose from when deciding which walks to undertake in this park.

If you have two days to spare and are feeling energetic try both the Crawford's Lookout Walk (9km o/w–easy–3 hrs) and the Nandroya Falls Circuit (7km rtn–easy–2.5 hrs).

The walk from the campsite to Crawford's Lookout is divided into a few sections, which is good for those who are in a hurry or don't feel up to the total distance.

It is probably best to embark on this walk from the campsite, although you will need to arrange to be collected or have to hitch or walk back.

Watch out for the creek crossing a short way along the track from the camp-

WOOROONOORAN NATIONAL PARK – PALMERSTON SECTION

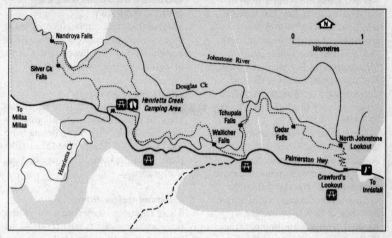

site. Take a short detour from the track to view Wallicher Falls before returning to the track where you must cross a creek to continue towards the highway.

Further along, the Tchupala Falls are spectacular, with large pools for a cold dip if you're game. Nearing the end, the view over North Johnstone River is better than Crawford's Lookout, which you reach after a steep, uphill climb.

Nandroya Falls Circuit is less spectacular but still interesting. You can take the shorter track to the falls and return by it or via the longer circuit track.

Be sure not to miss the platypuses at dawn and dusk; the viewing spot is a short walk from the campsite.

Aboriginal history

The Mamu people lived around the Bellenden Ker area, with the five main clans being the Mandubara, Bagingabara, Waribara, Dyiribara and Dulgubara. *Wari* means 'gorge' in the Mamu dialect and *dulgu* means 'thick scrub'. The Wari clan lived around the steep escarpment areas and the Dulgu occupied the catchment area of South Johnstone River.

ON THE WAY

When travelling north to Cairns you have the option of continuing on the easterly route or going up through the Tablelands. My recommendation would be to travel on the Bruce Hwy going north then south through the Atherton Tablelands so you have the option of cutting down to Porcupine Gorge NP and the Flinders Hwy (via the Kennedy Developmental Rd) heading west to the Northern Territory.

If you decide to continue north along the Bruce Hwy there are two attractions worth visiting on your way.

The turn-off to the Josephine Falls is about 24km north of Innisfail. Continue for 8km to the picnic area. An 800m walk leads to the falls — a magnificent series of falls and large rock pools. The falls are on the edge of the Bellenden

Ker Section of the Wooroonooran NP. For fit hikers there is a walking trail up to Broken Nose (10km rtn–mod–8 hrs) or to the south peak of Mt Bartle Frere, Queensland's highest peak, (15km rtn–hard–12 hrs). For information on the walks and the overnight camping spots call the ranger at Josephine Falls (phone: (07) 4067 6304).

Seven kilometres west from Babinda is the scenic Boulders picnic area. A short walk takes you to the fascinating carved formations caused by floodwater over the years. This section is very dangerous and people have been killed, so swimming is banned. A large waterhole near the picnic area provides a refreshing swimming spot.

GOLDSBOROUGH VALLEY STATE FOREST

This is a tranquil camping spot tucked at the base of the magnificent Bellenden Ker Range. A good stepping stone to Cairns or west to the Atherton Tablelands.

Location and access

The turn-off to the park is on the Gillies Hwy, 6km south-west of Gordonvale or 3km past Little Mulgrave (coming from the Tablelands). Most of the 15km to the park, from the turn-off, is unsealed but well graded.

Camping and facilities

There are about 10 sites, each with a fireplace and a few with tables. It costs $2 per person to stay the night. A day-use area has picnic tables and fireplaces with

GOLDSBOROUGH VALLEY STATE FOREST

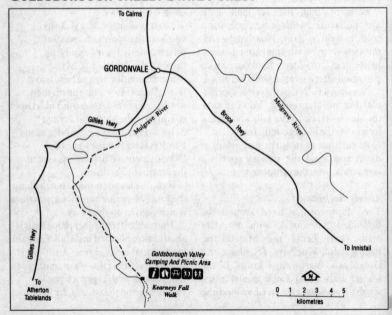

> **PRESERVING THE DAINTREE**
>
> Although this area is one of the most significant rainforest locations in the world, its future is uncertain. There are over 1,500 privately owned subdivisions between the Daintree River and Cape Tribulation. Should these become fully developed, the impact of waste, effluent, domestic animals and clearing of land will be devastating.
>
> In the past the dust caused by the high volume of traffic seriously depreciated the beauty of the roadside rainforest. The sealed road will alleviate the problem of erosion and excessive dust caused by the heavy number of vehicles using the road. However, there is likely to be a dramatic rise in development on the private blocks, due to easier access.
>
> There is also concern for the welfare of the area's wildlife, including the endangered Cassowary. The sealed road means that motorists can drive too fast for wildlife to escape.
>
> It is ironic that the area is so heavily promoted overseas and is expected to bring millions of tourists to Queensland, when in reality the Daintree rainforest may be on the brink of environmental devastation.
>
> The only way the area will survive is through restrictions on visitor numbers, greater public knowledge, and intervention by government authorities and conservation groups.

wood supplied. The two toilet blocks are located at either end of this large area.

Walks and attractions
The Kearneys Fall Walk (870m o/w– easy–40 mins rtn) takes you to the base of a nice but unexciting waterfall. The walk is good for a stroll in the morning before heading to Cairns or the Tablelands.

The Mulgrave River, which runs next to the campsite, is deep and good for swimming or watching wildlife.

For information contact the Department of Primary Industry Forest Service in Atherton (phone: (07) 4091 1844) as they manage the park.

DAINTREE NATIONAL PARK
Mossman Gorge, sign-posted from Mossman, is part of the Daintree NP. It has a day-use area with some delightful walks, picnic areas and swimming spots. It is a very easy way to experience the rainforest. A loop trail (2.7km-easy) across the suspension bridge provides an easily accessible rainforest experience

CAPE TRIBULATION SECTION
Cape Tribulation, at the gateway to the Cape York Peninsula, is about as far north as you can go on the coast road in a conventional vehicle. Visiting this area is certainly worth it for the sense of rugged tropical wilderness which it exudes. The beauty of the beaches and steep rainforest-covered ranges contributes to its special quality.

Location and access
Turn off the Mossman-Daintree Rd, approximately 100km past Cairns, at the

DAINTREE NATIONAL PARK

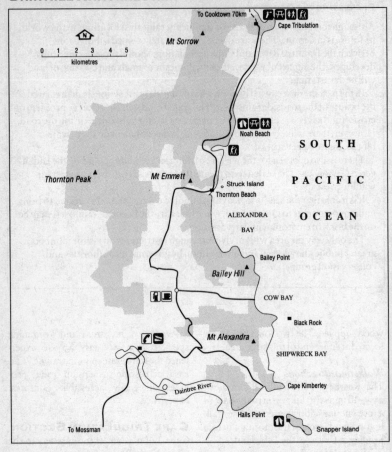

sign indicating the Cape Tribulation ferry. It is 6km to the ferry, which operates from 6am to midnight every day except Christmas and Good Friday. Cost is $10 per vehicle for the return journey.

Continue a further 28km to the Noah Beach camping area along the mostly sealed road.

Camping and facilities
The camping sites at Noah Beach are not as well equipped as many other national park campgrounds. This is easily compensated for by the 10m walk to the beach. There is a toilet block and cold-water shower and the camping fee is $5 per night per site. There are only 16 sites and it is a popular place, so you may need to call ahead and check the availability.

Atherton Tableland

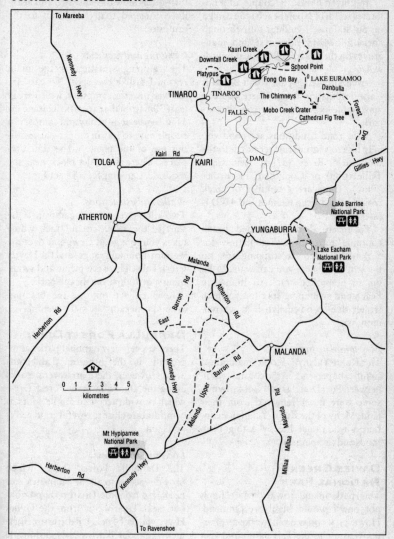

Walks and attractions
Unfortunately there is a lack of the long-distance rainforest walks which you would expect in such a significant location such as this. However, we have been promised that they are being 'planned'. Perhaps they will have eventuated by the time you visit.

At Oliver Creek, a couple of kilometres south of Noah Beach, you can go on an 800m self-guiding tour through ancient lowland rainforest and mangroves on the Marrdja Botanical Boardwalk.

Seven kilometres past Noah Beach is Cape Tribulation itself, where you can walk to the lookout, 350m from the car-park.

If the road conditions are good you may like to venture further north to the Bloomfield River (32km past Cape Tribulation) or Cooktown (a further 70km). There are a number of creek crossings and steep inclines and 4WD is essential.

To reach a nice, secluded beach continue past Cape Tribulation for 5.5km to a roadside stopping area on the left. From here you can walk 250m on an unmarked track to Emmagen Beach and swimming spot (only safe in winter due to box jellyfish in warmer months).

Aboriginal history
The Kuku-Yalanyji people maintain a significant presence in the coastal region between Port Douglas and Cooktown as some were never removed from their land. Many of the Kuku-Yalanyji maintain a traditional life by eating bush foods and camping out.

DAVIES CREEK NATIONAL PARK
This park inland toward Mareeba is not one I would highly recommend. However, if you wanted to take an alternative route to the Tablelands and visit Mareeba then it can be a convenient place to stop.

Location and access
From Cairns take the scenic drive through Kuranda and continue on the Kennedy Hwy for about 25km to the turn-off. Follow this unsealed and heavily corrugated road for 10km to the campsite.

Camping and facilities
The camping situation is the main reason I dislike this spot. No cars are allowed near the campsites, which are at least 30m from the car-park. This means a fair degree of difficulty and campervan people have to stay in the car-park without use of the picnic tables and fireplaces. There is a toilet block near the roadside. Camping fee is $5 per site.

Walks and attractions
Two kilometres past the campsite is the start of the 850m circuit track which takes you to a good viewpoint over the western mountain ranges and the Davies Creek Falls. There is a picnic and swimming spot 300m from the car-park.

Keep an eye out for the bettongs around your campsite in the evening.

DANBULLA FOREST DRIVE
There are very few national park campgrounds in the Atherton Tablelands area. However, there are several parks along the Danbulla State Forest Drive which provide access to ample spots to camp and are close to several good walks and sights.

Location and access
The Danbulla Forest Drive, which provides access to all the campsites, can be started from the Tinaroo Dam Lookout, near Tinaroo, or from the Gillies Hwy, via Ball Pocket Rd (turn off the highway about 5km toward Gordonvale from Lake Barrine).

Camping and facilities
There are five camping areas along this 31km drive. My favourite is the Fong On Bay site, which is the largest and offers a bit more room to set up an isolated camp-

site. It is less prone to the heavy sightseeing traffic than other campsites closer to the forest drive. The turn-off to Fong On Bay is the first you will encounter if coming from the Gillies Hwy and the camp is 6km once you turn off the forest drive. There are large, clean toilet blocks as well as fireplaces and tables.

Walks and attractions
Only a few kilometres from the Gillies Hwy, along the forest drive, there is the magnificent Cathedral Fig, only a short walk from the car-park. This is a spectacular example of a huge strangler fig.

A short drive further is the Mobo Creek Crater. A 600m circuit walk through rainforest leads to the crater — an extremely deep waterhole almost too cold to swim in.

Along the forest drive you can also stop at the Chimneys, for some local history, or Lake Euramoo, where carbon dating of sediment samples outlines the diverse biological changes in the landscape over time. A short walk at Lake Euramoo focuses on rainforest fruits and food sources. Detailed brochures on both the Goldsborough Valley State Forest and the Danbulla Forest Drive are available through contacting the Department of Primary Industry, Atherton, on (07) 4091 1844 or writing to PO Box 210, Atherton, Qld 4883.

CRATER LAKES NATIONAL PARK – LAKE BARRINE SECTION

An interesting 6km walk follows the lake perimeter, passing through tropical foliage with lots of birdlife. This waterfilled crater was formed by volcanic explosions around 95,000 years ago. The walking track begins near the water, 100m from the car-park. A spectacular feature of the walk is the two huge Kauri pines which can be found a short way along the track.

This is a day-use park only, with tea rooms and cruise operators on the lake edge.

CRATER LAKES – LAKE EACHAM SECTION

There is a nice picnic and recreation area by the lake, but no camping is allowed. The walk around the lake is shorter (4km) than the one at Lake Barrine, but with similar scenery and wildlife. Musky rat-kangaroos may be seen if you are quiet.

MT HYPIPAMEE NATIONAL PARK

Another example of the incredible amount of volcanic activity in the Tableland area is the Crater, which is part of the Mt Hypipamee NP.

The Crater is a huge volcanic pipe, 70m in diameter. Sheer granite walls accentuate the 58m drop from the rim to the water surface. The stagnant green lake below continues to a depth of 82m.

The Crater was formed by a build-up of gases produced by the molten rock deep below the earth's surface. The pressure resulted in an explosion and the natural formation to marvel at today.

From Atherton travel south on the Kennedy Highway 24km to the park. Or from Malanda go past the Malanda Falls and take the Upper Barron Rd for 16km (mostly unsealed) to the Kennedy Hwy and continue south. If you're travelling north it is 29km from Ravenshoe (pronounced Ravens-hoe).

CHILLAGOE/MUNGANA CAVES NATIONAL PARK

If you wish to venture inland and you enjoy caves then Chillagoe/Mungana Caves present a good opportunity. The features of the park don't lie exclusively underground. Giant spears of limestone dominate the landscape and protect small pockets of semi-deciduous vine thicket in otherwise dry surrounds.

CHILLAGOE/MUNGANA CAVES NATIONAL PARK

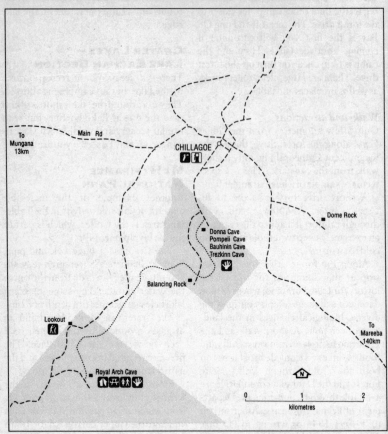

Location and access
From Mareeba travel 144km west to the township of Chillagoe. Royal Arch Cave is sign-posted 5km out of town and Mungana caves are 15km west along Main Rd.

The road is unsealed for 45km before Chillagoe; well-graded gravel roads mean access is fine except after heavy rain.

Camping and facilities
The national park campsite is located near Royal Arch Cave. There are toilets, tables, fireplaces and limited water. Visitors should bring ample water themselves. The camping fee is $5 and booking may be required during busy times. Call (07) 4094 7163 for details.

Nearby, the township of Chillagoe has fuel, food and ice for sale.

Walks and attractions
Cave tours are the main feature of the area. Guided tours are held at 9am and 1.30pm daily. The availability and booking times are posted outside the

national park office in Chillagoe. Tours of Royal Arch and Donna Caves cost $4 per adult and $2 per child. Trezkinn Caves cost $2 per adult and $1 per child. Make sure your torch battery is charged as you will need it for the Royal Arch tour.

An above-ground trail links Royal Arch Cave with Donna Cave (4km o/w– easy), passing the unusual Balancing Rock along the way.

Consult the national park office for details about the caves.

Millstream Falls National Park

For views of reputedly the widest waterfall in Australia (in full flow), this is a worthwhile stopping point, although unfortunately no camping is allowed.

Views of the falls are a short distance from the car-park.

On the way

About 15km from Ravenshoe, heading toward Mt Garnet on the Kennedy Hwy, is a popular roadside campground run by the Herberton Shire Council. No fee is charged and there is a toilet block and a large area of cleared land near the Millstream River.

Further west are the Innot Hot Springs. A private caravan park is next to the small creek with shallow holes where you can lie in the warm water.

Continuing on the Kennedy Hwy will take you past the 40 Mile Scrub NP, which is undeveloped for visitors at this stage.

Inland

Undara Volcanic National Park

The fascinating network of tube-like formations, caused by lava flows hundreds of years ago, make for an interesting place to visit. Visitation is by the privately run tour only. It is $70 for a full-day tour, $52 for a half-day and there are budget tours for $18. Many interesting facts about the specially adapted species in the caves and the visual aura of the place make the trip worthwhile.

From Mt Garnet travel 65km southwest on the Kennedy Hwy, then west along the Gulf Development Rd. Turn left at the Undara Experience sign-post and follow this road 16km to the lodge.

Tours operate from here. There is a campground as well as unusual accommodation in old train carriages or in Swag's Tent Village. Call the lodge (phone: (07) 4097 1411) for more details.

Porcupine Gorge National Park

If you are heading west, this place may be one of your first samples of the red earth and dramatic gorges characteristic of the outback regions. It can be conveniently located if you are travelling the inland route north or south. If not, it is a 150km detour from Hughenden.

Location and access
The Porcupine Gorge campsite is 75km north of Hughenden along the Kennedy Developmental Rd. This road can take you straight down from the Lynd Junction, where it leaves the Kennedy Hwy. If you can handle a long, and in places uneven, corrugated road this route will save you a lot of time and kilometres if you intend heading west.

Drive 196km south of Lynd Junction and turn left to get to the Pyramid and the camping area or continue to the gorge lookout and Hughenden.

The road is dirt most of the way with several sections being heavily corrugated. When dry it is suitable for

PORCUPINE GORGE NATIONAL PARK

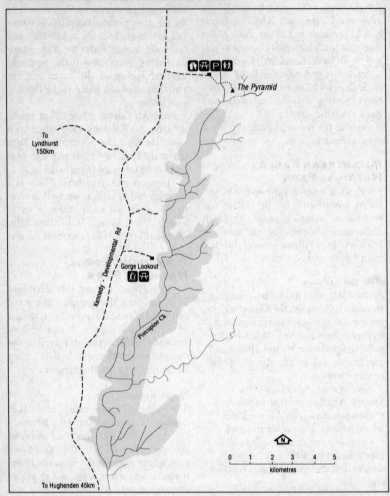

conventional vehicles, but after rain access is severely restricted.

Camping and facilities
There are no fireplaces or tables and you are advised to collect your own firewood on the way in as there are scarce supplies around the site. There is a limited supply of drinking water so it may be safest to have ample with you. The camp fee is $5.

Walks and attractions
There are many unmarked tracks leading from the campsite to the rim of the gorge and the rocky outcrops which are fun to explore yourself.

The main walk in the park is to the bottom of the gorge, along a rocky path. The base of the Pyramid is 500m along the base of the gorge, past dramatic swirling formations in the sandstone, caused by the rushing waters of the wet season.

Lawn Hill National Park

The deep red rocks of the gorge here contrast vividly with the emerald waters of Lawn Hill Creek. The plethora of wildlife, coupled with scenery you can witness from the several walks or by

Lawn Hill National Park

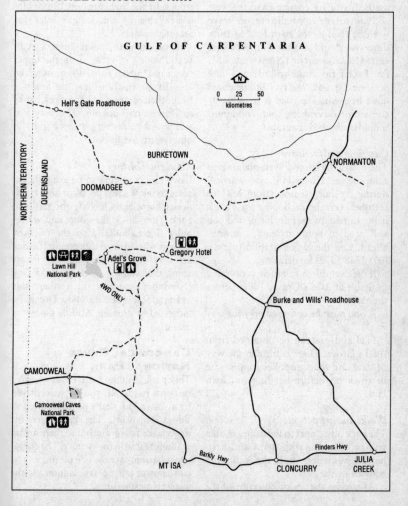

paddling down the gorge in a canoe, make this park exceptional.

Location and access

The park may be reached by a variety of routes. The most popular is by leaving the Flinders Hwy at Julia Creek or Cloncurry and driving to Gregory Downs, via the Burke and Wills Roadhouse. From there you will only have to travel 100km on dirt roads. If you are coming from the west and wish to take a more direct route, there is a dirt road to the park leading from Camooweal and another turn-off 68km east of Camooweal or 120km west of Mt Isa. Taking this route will mean a long drive on dirt roads and tyre problems are quite frequent. The road is passable by conventional vehicles, but conditions should be checked after rain.

Camping and facilities

There is a large and well-maintained campsite at Lawn Hill. Be warned, during the busy season (from May to October) you should book a site or risk being turned away. For this period you will need to book at least 3 months ahead. Call the ranger station (phone: (07) 4748 5572) for details.

If the campsite is full there is camping available at Adel's Grove, 10km before the park.

Wood must be collected on your way in.

Fuel and gas can be obtained from Adel's Grove. There is little in the way of food and other supplies so it is wise to stock up before heading to Lawn Hill.

Walks and attractions

The park office next to the camping area will provide you with maps and firsthand information about the walks and activities in the park.

At sunrise the rocky outcrops of the island stack glow deep red. The walk is 1.7km return, but this is increased somewhat once you have walked along each lookout path. So if you do it in the early morning you may like to take some breakfast to keep you going.

Another essential activity is to hire a canoe and paddle the length of the gorge. Again, early morning is the best time, as the wildlife is still quite active and the colours on the rocks are best. Canoe hire is available by the water's edge for reasonable rates.

If you intend to undertake the Circuit Walk, taking in views from the upper gorge and Indarri Falls, it is most advisable to go firstly along the Spinifex Ridge then return along the creek banks to Duwadarri Lookout. This way you will avoid some very steep climbs in often warm conditions.

Aboriginal history

Lawn Hill continues to be a significant place to the Waanyi people whose traditional homelands include the national park. They called the gorge and waterholes *Boodjamulla*, after the rainbow serpent who formed this country. Rock art sites can be accessed by visitors along the walking track to Wild Dog Dreaming, located on the northern side of Island Stack, and Rainbow Dreaming (accessed by crossing Middle Gorge by canoe).

CAMOOWEAL CAVES NATIONAL PARK

This park is quite a drive out of town on dirt roads. If you've just driven from Lawn Hill that's probably the last thing you want. The caves are for experienced cavers only and there are no walking tracks in the vicinity. The campsite is barren, save for one pit toilet. You can camp near a pleasant lagoon and the sunset is mesmerising.

The sign from town indicates 8km to the park. This is correct, but the campsite is 22km from Camooweal. Turn south at the hotel and travel 8km (count 5 cattle grids), turn left and follow the signs. The campsite is a good option if you dislike staying in caravan parks and aren't bothered by dirt roads.

NORTHERN TERRITORY

1. West MacDonnells NP, see p180
2. Finke Gorge NP, see p182
3. Alice Springs Telegraph Station HR, see p182
4. Emily and Jessie Gaps Nature Parks, see p182
5. Trephina Gorge Nature Park, see p183
6. N'Dhala Gorge Nautre Park, see p184
7. Arltunga HR, see p184
8. Chambers Pillar HR, see p185
9. Rainbow Valley CR, see p185
10. Henbury Meteorites CR, see p185
11. Watarrka NP, see p186
12. Uluru-Kata Tjuta NP, see p187
13. Elsey NP, see p189
14. Nitmiluk NP, see p190
15. Umbrawarra Gorge NP, see p191
16. Douglas Hot Springs Nature Park, see p191
17. Butterfly Gorge NP, see p192
18. Gregory NP, see p192
19. Keep River NP, see p193
20. Kakadu NP, see p195
21. Wildman Reserve, see p199
22. Gurig NP, see p199
23. Litchfield NP, see p200

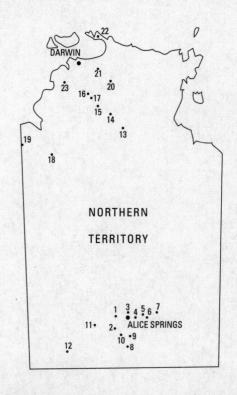

NOTE: Look through the chapter to the On the Way sections to see additional places to camp or visit.

NATIONAL PARKS SERVICE
The Parks and Wildlife Commission of the Northern Territory (formerly the Conservation Commission) administers most of the parks in NT. Uluru and Kakadu are managed by Parks Australia, Environment Australia (formerly Australian Nature Conservation Agency).

CONTACT
PARKS AND WILDLIFE COMMISSION
(08) 8951 8211
WWW.NT.GOV.AU/PAW

ABORIGINAL HISTORY
Over half of the Northern Territory has been handed back to the traditional custodians. The number of Indigenous people stands at a quarter of the total population. Settlement of the Northern Territory happened 50 years later than the southern parts of the country. Traditional life has been able to be sustained so that many communities keep their language and laws intact.

MONEY
You will find most supermarkets and service stations have facilities for EFTPOS transactions to allow payment and cash withdrawals.

SPEED
In some places there is no speed limit on those long stretches of highway from Alice Springs to Darwin. Of course, the temperature often restricts you from travelling too fast and risking overheating your engine.

CAMPING
Many camping areas near popular features of the Territory are leased to 'concessionaires', so that maintaining campgrounds doesn't need to be a priority for the Parks and Wildlife Commission. The concessionaires are still accountable to the Parks and Wildlife Commission so if you are not happy with the service you have received (at the price you have paid), let the nearest national park office know and they will record your complaint and act upon it.

PUB PATRON GUIDE
If you want to do as the Romans do you will order a can of beer in most pubs you visit.
POT   285ML

THE CENTRE

ON THE WAY
The Devils Marbles Reserve, 393km north of Alice Springs and 139km south of Three Ways Roadhouse, presents another icon of the centre.

A basic campsite with toilets and tables is located near the collection of huge granite boulders which lie waiting for creative photographers.

There are self-guided walking tracks for you to explore.

Aboriginal history
The Devils Marbles is significant to the Kaytej, Anmatyerre, Alyawarre and

West MacDonnells & Finke Gorge National Parks

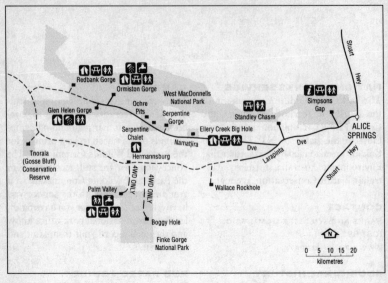

Warumungu people. They call it *Karlwe Karlwe*, meaning 'round'. Creation stories tell of ancestral beings living in the caves below the rocks.

West MacDonnells National Park

This large region spans most of the West MacDonnell Ranges and includes many gorges, walks and places to camp. It typifies the centre and allows you to explore the region without the tourist hype surrounding other places further south. It is also home to the well-known Larapinta Trail — over 220km of walking tracks along the splendid ridge. It can be undertaken in overnight sections. A sealed bicycle path has recently been constructed which links Alice Springs with Simpsons Gap.

Location and access
From Alice Springs travel west along Larapinta Drive for 47km then veer right into Namatjira Drive to reach the many sights in the area. This road is sealed for most of its length. The last section to Redbank Gorge is unsealed (25km), but accessible by conventional vehicles except after heavy rain.

Camping and facilities
Camping fees apply to all CCNT-managed campsites except Serpentine Chalet.

ELLERY CREEK BIG HOLE
Ellery Creek Big Hole, 93km west of Alice Springs, is the first spot in the park where you can camp. The waterhole nearby is often very cold in winter but refreshingly cool in the warmer months. There are tables and toilets provided. The high cliffs which shade the waterhole provide a fascinating display of rock folding, dating back 350 million years.

SERPENTINE CHALET

The name of this basic camping area is misleading. 'Chalet' refers to the ruins of an attempted tourist resort built in the 1960s. Half of the campsites, just off Namatjira Drive, can be reached by conventional vehicles. A 4WD track leads to the rest of the sites. Only fireplaces are provided. Walking tracks leading from the camping area are detailed on the information board.

ORMISTON GORGE

Ormiston Gorge has a well-established camping area which is a popular base for exploration. The proximity to a good swimming hole and Ormiston Pound are the real advantages of this spot. Fees are $4 per adult or $10 per family a night. Toilets, tables and water (always available although drinking water is limited) and heated showers are provided.

REDBANK GORGE

The last camping area in the park is Redbank Gorge, where a basic camping area, with tables and toilets, is located. Fees are $1 per adult or $3 for a family. A chilly waterhole, which is shaded most of the day, is good to paddle along on a lilo or inner tube.

Walks and attractions

SIMPSONS GAP

Simpsons Gap, only 18km from Alice Springs, is a day-use area. It has an information centre with details of the walks and features.

STANDLEY CHASM

At Standley Chasm, crowds gather to see the spectacle of the midday sun shining into the narrow chasm, briefly revealing its coloured walls. So if you want to avoid crowds, morning and afternoon are better times to visit. Standley Chasm is managed by the Angkerle Aboriginal Corporation on behalf of the Iwupataka Land Trust.

SERPENTINE GORGE

A short but rough drive from Namatjira Drive leads to the car-park, from where an easy 25-minute walk to the gorge begins. It is a narrow, cool gorge, with deep and chilly waterholes at the entrance. A short climb leads to good views. If you can endure the icy swim you will be offered solace in this protected gorge.

THE OCHRE PITS

As the name suggests, this site has large quantities of yellow and red ochre. A short walk leads to the creek bank where the traditional painting medium used by the Western Arrernte Aboriginal people is located. The ochre is used in many ceremonies and medical remedies.

ORMISTON GORGE AND POUND

The visitor centre at this well-known site provides detailed information on the walks and features here. Ormiston Pound is a 3 hour, 7km loop walk so if you're visiting in the warmer months it may be worth camping overnight and embarking early on this trip. There is a short walk to the waterhole which is a good swimming spot. Another short trail leads to the Ghostgum Lookout, overlooking the waterhole. Overnight walks are offered here — register and obtain maps and information from the visitor centre. Sealed roads leading into this site make access good all year unless flooding occurs.

GLEN HELEN GORGE

This gorge, not far off Namatjira Drive, has some impressive sandstone cliffs, a sandy waterhole edged by green vegetation. The Glen Helen Lodge and tourist facilities are closed until further notice.

A short track leads through the gorge alongside the Finke River.

REDBANK GORGE

Another narrow gorge and chilly waterhole can be found in this spot. From the camping area and car-park you walk part the way along the large, dry creek bed which involves rock hopping in some sections. Once you get to the sheer, red cliffs of the gorge you may not be able to proceed further unless you have a lilo or inner tube, as the water is often freezing.

Aboriginal history

The West MacDonnell Range is part of the traditional lands of the Central and Western Arrernte people. Standley Chasm (called Angkerle) is close to the boundary between their territories. The waterholes throughout the park are significant hunting places and have mythological significance. Many of the deeper waterholes are occupied by a large water snake who will kill anyone who stays too long at the edge of the pool or dares to swim there.

Simpsons Gaps is known as Tyunpe. Glen Helen Gorge (called Yalpulpa) has information signs about Itye, the Moon Man, who came there looking for a bride. The main waterhole in Ormiston Gorge (called Kwartetweme) is a sacred site relating to an emu ancestor.

Information displays about Aboriginal heritage can be found at Redbank Gorge and the Ochre Pits.

FINKE GORGE NATIONAL PARK

The Palm Valley oasis is the best-known feature of this park. Access is restricted to 4WD vehicles only. Rust-coloured cliffs and weathered formations, cool waterholes and ancient Red Cabbage Palms can be seen.

The road into the park follows a sandy creek bed part of the way, restricting access to 4WD vehicles only. Private tour companies provide day trips into the park from Alice Springs. For those with 4WDs the park is reached by travelling to Hermannsburg along Larapinta Drive and continuing south 13km to the park. There is a good camping area with tap water — although be prepared in case resources are depleted. The park is inaccessible if flooded.

Aboriginal history

The Western Arrernte people have lived in the Finke Gorge area for over 20,000 years. They called the Finke River *Larapinta*, meaning 'running water'. The underground river was an important water source and lured game during long droughts. The river was an important trading route between the centre and South Australia.

Palm Valley is called Mgulungkinya. The 5km Mpaara walking track has sign-posts containing Western Arrernte stories relating to the area.

ALICE SPRINGS TELEGRAPH STATION HISTORICAL RESERVE

Only 5km north of the current township is the original settlement of Alice Springs. Historic stone buildings remain and visitors can explore the remnants of the previous town. It is open daily and has picnic facilities and toilets. Regular guided tours are offered throughout the year.

EMILY AND JESSIE GAPS NATURE PARKS

Only 15km from Alice Springs, these narrow gorges feature Aboriginal rock art. They are popular picnic areas for Alice Springs residents. No camping is allowed. Follow the signs east of Alice Springs.

Aboriginal history

The Eastern Arrernte people occupied this area. Several sites in the park relate

TREPHINA GORGE NATURE PARK

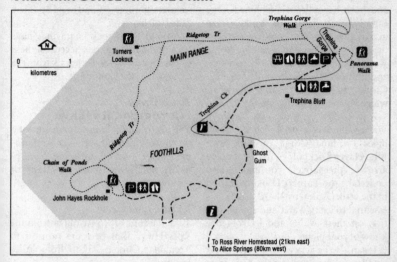

to Yeperenye (caterpillar) dreaming, where Intailuka stopped to cook and eat caterpillars on his dreamtime journey. Emily Gap features some significant totemic art paintings where interpretive signs and protective fencing have been erected. At the Udnirr Ingita site you can see caterpillar dreaming figures painted with red and yellow stripes, which reflect the decorative designs painted on men during ceremonies.

TREPHINA GORGE NATURE PARK

Easy access, good camping opportunities and stunning scenery make this one of the best places to visit in the centre.

Location and access
The park is accessible by conventional vehicles for most of the year. Turn off the Ross Hwy 68km east of Alice Springs. From there it is 9km to the Trephina Gorge car-park and camping area. A further 13km along the Ross Hwy past the turn-off is the Ross River Homestead, with fuel supplies and camping and cabin accommodation.

Camping and facilities
There are three small camping areas in the park: there is one near John Hayes Rockhole, another at Trephina Bluff and the third at Trephina Gorge. They are very popular from June until September — you may have to continue to the Ross River Homestead (phone: (08) 8956 9711) if they are full. There are toilets, tables and fireplaces provided. Tap water and gas barbecues are provided at the Trephina Gorge and Bluff campgrounds.

Walks and attractions
The variety and pleasurable quality of these walks contribute to the good memories I have of this place. There are four main walks, each identified by different-coloured markers to guide your way.

The Trephina Gorge Walk (2km rtn–easy–1 hr) is marked by orange markers, the Panorama Walk (1.5km rtn–easy/mod–1.5 hr) has red markers and both begin from Trephina Gorge camping area. Panorama Walk is steep in parts but provides excellent views of the gorge and the bluff. Trephina Gorge Walk meanders onto the escarpment and returns by the bed of Trephina Creek (can be done the opposite way), which is often dry during winter.

A more difficult walk is the Ridgetop Walk (10km o/w–hard–7 hrs), which links Trephina Gorge car-park with John Hayes Rockhole — follow the blue arrows. Alternatively you may like to undertake the Turners Lookout section of the walk (7.5km rtn–hard–6 hrs). It is essential to carry water and sun protection on these walks and let someone know of your plans.

It can also be very enjoyable to simply wander along the creek bed from Trephina camping area or the bluff to enjoy the serene environment with river red gums lining the waterway.

The local Eastern Arrernte Aboriginal name for the John Hayes Rockhole gorge is Atnaperke (ut-ne-per-ke) and a Dreamtime story tells of two spirits who fought here. One spirit, a Euro, ripped the intestines from a dingo, its opponent, and thus the winding gorge and rock pools were created.

N'DHALA GORGE NATURE PARK

The feature of this park is a number of Aboriginal rock engravings. The park is accessible by 4WD only. Follow the road south of Ross River Homestead 8km to the picnic and camping area. There are picnic tables, toilets and fireplaces. A short, easy walk leads to the engravings.

Aboriginal history

Eastern Arrernte people depended on the water supply at N'Dhala Gorge which was available even when the surrounding country had dried up. They called it *Irlwentye*.

Around 6000 rock engravings have been found in the gorge. Several of these can be seen along the 1km walk from the carpark into the main gorge.

ARLTUNGA HISTORICAL RESERVE

The historical buildings, fragments of a previous settlement, provide a refreshing change from all the gorges, escarpments and other grand creations of nature.

Location and access

Take the turn-off to Arltunga from the Ross Hwy, 5km past the turn-off to Trephina Gorge; 73km from Alice Springs.

A gravel road, suitable for conventional vehicles for most of the year, leads 40km to the visitor centre. Collect a map of the reserve from there.

Camping and facilities

No camping is allowed in the reserve itself. Many people stay at Trephina Gorge and do a day trip to the reserve. There are shaded picnic areas for day use.

Walks and attractions

Most people recommend that at least four hours be spent driving and walking within the reserve. In this time you can undertake self-guiding tours, including one around an old mine site (the settlement evolved around gold fossicking in the late 1800s).

The visitor centre, just within the park boundary, will provide you with information, self-guiding pamphlets and interesting displays — open 8am to 5pm daily.

Aboriginal history
Arltunga was occupied by the Karolinga people of the Eastern Arrernte tribe prior to European invasion. Paintings and rock engravings have been found in the park. Ceremonies were conducted here as recently as 1950.

ON THE WAY

Ewaninga Rock Carvings Conservation Reserve is 39km south of Alice Springs via Old South Rd (past the airport). Conventional vehicles may use this route, but check conditions beforehand. It is worth stopping at the site if you are going to Chambers Pillar (4WD only) or wanting an off-beat route which passes by the James Ranges and links back onto the Stuart Hwy, further south. It is a day-use area only and has a short self-guiding walk to observe the rock engravings.

Aboriginal history
The Eastern Arrernte people are the traditional custodians of this site. *Ewaninga* means 'place of rocks with small cave hollows'. The sandstone outcrops circling the claypan were used as camping places by Aboriginal people. The shelters have now crumbled in but the rock engravings can still be viewed.

CHAMBERS PILLAR HISTORICAL RESERVE

This park, 165km south of Alice Springs, is recommended for 4WD only. The distinctive pillar is not unlike the shape of a giant chef's hat. It has been a valuable landmark and reference point for travellers for many years. Private tour operators can take you to the park from Alice Springs. The track to the base of the pillar is very rough and involves sand dune crossings. Intending 4WD drivers should enquire about conditions and be prepared.

Aboriginal history
The Southern Arrernte people lived in this region and called the pillar *Itirkawara*, after a dreamtime gecko ancestor. He turned into the pillar after being banished for taking a girl of the wrong skin group as his bride. She now stands 500m away in the form of Castle Rock.

RAINBOW VALLEY CONSERVATION RESERVE

An equally impressive landscape can be found at this reserve not far from the Stuart Hwy. Rainbow Valley is a cathedral-shaped formation of coloured sandstone which can be mesmerising at sunset.

Turn off the Stuart Hwy 85km south of Alice Springs and travel 15km on an unsealed road. There is a basic camping area with toilets, tables and fireplaces.

Aboriginal history
The Southern Arrernte are the traditional custodians of the Rainbow Valley area. They call the rock massif *Ewerre*. There are sacred sites in the reserve.

HENBURY METEORITES CONSERVATION RESERVE

You will find a string of 12 meteorite craters, 15km from the Stuart Hwy (13km unsealed). Turn off 132km south of Alice Springs and follow the signs along the unsealed Giles Rd. Information provided along a short walk tells how the craters were formed many thousands of years ago.

Aboriginal history
The Arrernte people call the crater *Tatyeye Kepmwere* (*Tatjakapara*) and its formation is told through creation stories.

On the way

If you want to make a loop track through the West MacDonnell NP and return to the Stuart Hwy via Hermannsburg, continue for 17km past the Redbank Ernest Gorge turn-off. Turn left onto a rough track which leads down to Hermannsburg (check conditions and accessibility). By taking this route you can go to the giant crater of Gosse Bluff, an Aboriginal sacred site. A 4WD road leads into the crater. Check with the Parks and Wildlife Commission about how to gain access into the bluff.

WATARRKA NATIONAL PARK

This park is fast becoming as popular as Uluru, and in many ways it offers more for the visitor. The dramatic scenery of Kings Canyon, the main feature of the park, can be appreciated from the many walks and lookouts in the park. The new resort can provide a welcome dose of comfort in an otherwise barren and remote place.

Location and access

Turn off the Stuart Hwy 110km south of Alice Springs. It is 208km to the canyon and a further 7km to the resort. This road is sealed for all but 100km.

Camping and facilities

The only camping within the park is at the Frontier Kings Canyon Resort, which has room for 400 campsites. Thankfully the resort adopts conservation measures such as growing plantations for firewood. There is a bar and swimming pool, so you can enjoy taking time-out from roughing it (for bookings phone: (08) 8956 7442). Camping costs $16 per night for two (unpowered). Camping is also available at Kings Creek Station, just outside the park. The fee is $5 per adult per night (phone: (08) 8956 7474).

Walks and attractions

The walks into and along the canyon begin from the car-park, 7km before the resort.

The Kings Canyon Walk (6km loop–mod–4 hrs) is an excellent way to appreciate the formations and grandeur of the place. Arrowed markers guide the way in a clockwise direction. Midway along the walk is the idyllic Garden of Eden. Green cycads and ferns fringe cool rock pools in the exquisite amphitheatre. You need to be reasonably fit and take water and sun protection. Sturdy footwear is also recommended.

If you're not feeling up to the Kings Canyon Walk, the Kings Creek Walk (1.5km rtn–easy/mod–1 hr) is a good alternative. The path follows the creek through the heart of the canyon to a good lookout point. Again, it can be rough underfoot as well as hot and dry, so be prepared.

TRADITIONAL OWNERSHIP

The Pitjantjatjara and Yankuntjatjara people finally regained the title to Uluru in October 1985. They are now recognised as the traditional owners. The park is leased to the ANCA under a joint management agreement. Aboriginal culture and traditional land use are the focus of education and information in the park.

These developments have led to Uluru-Kata Tjuta National Park being recognised internationally as culturally and biologically significant. The park has been accepted as a Unesco Biosphere Reserve since 1977 and has been on the World Heritage List since 1987.

The Kathleen Springs Walk (2.6 km–easy–1 hr) is a pleasant walk among lush ferns to a cool waterhole.

From the resort you may like to inquire about informative tours around the area. One recommended to me is by the local Aboriginal company, Kurkara, who hold evening tours in the area. It may be a good way to get some insights into the history and Aboriginal traditions of the area.

Aboriginal history

The Luritja people are the traditional owners of the area surrounding Kings Canyon.

Many sacred sites listed in the park relate to creation stories and the Kuningka ancestors who travelled through this land. The path they followed is called *Watarrka*. The waterhole along the Kathleen Springs walk is the home of the giant water serpent, the guardian of all waterholes in the park.

Guided tours within the park are available. Enquire at the Kings Canyon Resort.

ULURU – KATA TJUTA NATIONAL PARK

What can I say about the icon of outback Australia, famous around the world, that hasn't already been said? Perhaps that few Australia-wide tours are considered complete without visiting 'the rock'.

Location and access

The Lasseter Hwy joins the Stuart Hwy at Erldunda, 75km north of the NT–SA border and 188km south of Alice Springs. From there a sealed road leads 244km to Yulara. It is a further 20km to Uluru (Ayers Rock) or 31km along a sealed road to Kata Tjuta (the Olgas). Access from Kings Canyon is via Luritja Rd, which leads south from Wallarah Roadhouse and connects with the Lasseter Hwy 140km east of Uluru.

Camping and facilities

The only camping available near the park is at Ayers Rock Resort, in Yulara village (phone: (08) 8956 2055). The fee is $9 per adult and $4.50 per child for a

ULURU – KATA TJUTA NATIONAL PARK

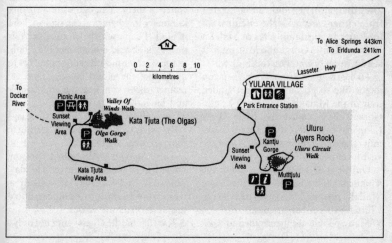

> **RIVER PANDANUS (*PANDANUS AQUATICUS*)**
>
> In accordance with its name, this species tends to occur along the banks of freshwater creeks and streams. The distinctive sword-like leaves create a crown, often with many dead leaves dropping from the base. The straight, light-brown trunk generally grows between three and five metres, its numerous tube-like roots showing above the water and ground. Unlike the *Pandanus spiralis* (or screw palm), the fruit of which is used by Aborigines for many medicinal and food purposes, the fruit of the river pandanus is inedible. However, the tough leaves can be used for weaving baskets, rope and mats. The fruit is a valuable food source for cockatoos and turtles.

tent site. Powered sites cost $6 extra. Again, the resort and its associated luxuries mean you can take a rest from bush camping.

There are picnic facilities, toilets and drinking water available at Uluru car-park. It is $10 per adult (over 16 years) for a 5-day pass into the park.

Walks and attractions

A good walk to appreciate the magnitude of the rock is the Uluru Circuit Walk (9km–mod–4 hrs), which follows the perimeter and can be started from either car-park. The circuit walk leads to the aboriginal sites of Malaku Wilytja, Kantju Gorge and Mutitjula. It is wise to carry water on this long walk.

To learn more from your visit you might like to go on the ranger-guided tour of the Malaku Wilytja and Kantju Gorges. It is called the Mala Walk (2km–easy–1.5 hrs) and leaves at 10am in winter and 9am in summer, from the visitor centre.

On the tour visitors learn about the Tjukurpa (Dreamtime) of the Hare Wallaby people (Mala) who travelled to Uluru for special ceremonies.

Many people are determined to walk to the summit of Uluru (Ayers Rock). Few realise that doing so is offensive to the traditional owners of the park. The Aboriginal term 'Nganana tatinja wiya' — we never climb — illustrates their sentiment.

The climb to the summit (1.6km rtn–hard–2 hrs) is steep and difficult. A chain runs alongside the path to assist walkers. The journey up is likely to take about 45 minutes. Once you reach the summit the pock-marked plateau lies before you. After rain the small craters often have water in them. You can walk a further kilometre to where you can sign an 'I did it' book. People with respiratory or heart problems should not attempt the climb. In the warmer months you should try to undertake the climb before 10am, as temperatures can become unbearable and dangerous.

The Liru Walk (2km o/w–easy–30 mins) leads from the ranger station to the start of the climb.

The Anangu (Aboriginal person) guided Liru Walk is held on Tuesday, Thursday and Saturday at 9.30am in winter or 8.30am during summer. Booking is essential for this tour.

Kata Tjuta (the Olgas) offer not only a

welcome respite from the busloads of people at Ayers Rock, they are a fascinating place to visit in their own right. There are marked walking trails which meander around the huge domes, some taller than Uluru. Visiting in the morning is wise, as temperatures are cooler, and you will also avoid the several tour groups which tend to visit Uluru in the morning and Kata Tjuta in the afternoon.

The Olga Gorge Walk (2km rtn–easy –1 hr) is a good path into the corridor between some huge domes. If you have more time and energy, the Valley of the Winds Walk (6km rtn–easy/mod– 3 hrs) leads deeper into the heart of the Olgas.

Extensive information is available from the information centre (phone: (08) 8956 2299).

Aboriginal history

The Pitjantjatjara and Yankuntjatjara people are the traditional custodians of Uluru and Kata Tjuta. They refer to themselves collectively as *Anangu*. The land was handed back to the Anangu people in 1985 and is now jointly managed with the CCNT. Kata Tjuta means 'many heads'.

The landforms in the area relate to Tjukurpa creation stories. Many rock art sites can be seen along the Mutitjulu and Mala walks along the base of the rock. The track leading to the top of Uluru relates to the traditional paths of ancestral Mala men and has strong spiritual values. Anangu people prefer if visitors do not climb the rock.

Visit the national park cultural centre, situated along the road from Yulara, 1km before Uluru (phone: (08) 8956 2299). The Yulara visitor centre also features displays and information on walks.

KATHERINE REGION

ELSEY NATIONAL PARK

This is a good place to sample the thermal springs of Mataranka, as well as undertake other activities such as canoeing and bushwalking.

Location and access

Turn off the Stuart Hwy into Homestead Rd, 5km north of the Roper Hwy and 1km south of Mataranka township. Continue on this road for 4km and then turn right into John Hauser Drive to get to the 12 Mile Yards camping area or continue to the thermal springs and Mataranka Homestead.

Camping and facilities

The national park campground is privately run by Clearwater Canoe and Camping. The cost is $5 per adult and $10 per family. It is a pleasant, green campsite near the Roper River.

Alternatively camping is available at Mataranka Homestead. Cost is $7 for adults and $3.50 for children, with a few facilities such as tables and fireplaces. There is a pub and shop located at the homestead.

Walks and attractions

The swimming hole at the thermal springs is popular. To avoid the crowds, an early morning swim is best. You can continue past the pool to the river for a bit more room.

From the 12 Mile Yards campsite you can walk to Mataranka Falls (8km rtn–easy–2.5 hrs). The walk follows the Roper River to a small waterfall and bubbling spring with waters rising up from under the ground. Swimming is pleasant, but be careful of the sharp sandstone formations on the river bed.

NITMILUK NATIONAL PARK

KATHERINE GORGE

The gorge itself is beautiful and there are several walks to explore in the area that take you to viewpoints overlooking the gorges. It is a good place to begin a several-day trek or undertake a long canoe trip. If you like to avoid tour buses and commercialism this is not the place to do it.

Location and access
Turn into Giles St in the centre of Katherine, where a sign indicates 29km to Katherine Gorge. Access to the park is fine all year.

Camping and facilities
There is a private campsite at the main access point to the gorge. The charge is $6.50 per adult. A few fireplaces and tables are available. If you are unhappy with the price or service, lodge a complaint with the national park office, as this is the only way things will be changed. Cheaper camping is available in the caravan parks in Katherine or at Springvale Homestead (inquire at the tourist information office).

Walks and attractions
The national park office is open from 7am every day and can provide you with maps and information on walks or canoeing in the area. You must register here before embarking on any of the walks.

The best way to see the first few gorges is to hire a canoe for the day and paddle up as far as the third gorge. Alternatively, if you have a lilo you can do one of the walks which take you to various points upstream, then float back to the camping area.

The Butterfly Gorge Walk is an interesting one (11km rtn–easy/mod–2 hrs) along a secondary gorge which has a large population of butterflies — a shady walk through the sparse rainforest. The walk ends at a fork in the river, providing a spectacular view of the second gorge.

Aboriginal history
The Jawoyn people lived nomadic lifestyes in the region around the Katherine River catchment, Mary River and upper South Alligator. The gorge itself has dreaming stories associated with it. Several rock paintings can be viewed along walking trails.

Nitmiluk is jointly managed by CCNT and the traditional custodians, the Jawoyn people. The land was returned to them in 1989. Traditional land use and ceremonies are conducted in the park.

EDITH FALLS

Edith Falls is a relaxed campsite with a nearby waterhole to swim in. There are several walks, but they will not provide gorge views comparable to those at Katherine Gorge.

Location and access
Continue north on the Stuart Hwy, 42km past Katherine, to the turn-off on the right. It is 20km into the park along a sealed road. Firewood should be collected on the way.

Camping and facilities
Edith Falls is a privately run campground charging $4 per person or $10 per family. Showers are available.

Walks and attractions
Walking information is available from the signs at the start of the walks or from the manager of the park.

At night you can see the snapping turtles in the waterhole.

UMBRAWARRA GORGE NATIONAL PARK

In sharp contrast to Katherine Gorge, this small but fascinating gorge is ideal to explore and enjoy the solitude.

Location and access

Three kilometres south of Pine Creek watch out for a large sign for Copperfield Recreation Dam, below which is a smaller sign indicating Umbrawarra Gorge. Turn here and continue on the well-graded dirt track for 22km, heading in a south-westerly direction. The campsite is on your left and the walk to the gorge begins 100m further on.

Camping and facilities

There is a small camping area with a pit toilet, a few fireplaces and tables ($1 per person or $3 per family).

Walks and attractions

The walk into Umbrawarra Gorge is about 600m long. From here you can rock hop down the gorge several kilometres further. There is some Aboriginal rock art on the ledges near the first swimming hole, then more further down. You can be rewarded with great views by climbing to the top of the gorge. There are several points where the climb is relatively easy.

DOUGLAS HOT SPRINGS NATURE PARK

The fascinating spectacle of water boiling up from the earth combined with a pleasant campground and blissful bathing places make Douglas Hot Springs a good stopping point.

DOUGLAS HOT SPRINGS NATURE PARK

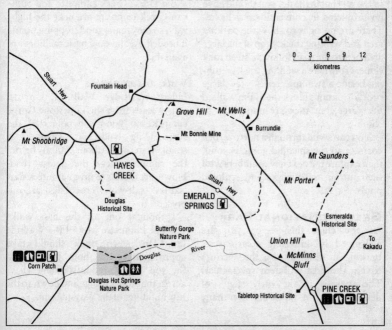

Location and access
The park is 26km off the Stuart Hwy; take the turn-off just north of Hayes Creek. Part of the road is well-formed gravel so access in the wet season may be limited.

Camping and facilities
There is a large camping area with pit toilets and a few fireplaces and tables.

Walks and attractions
Swimming in the springs is probably the most popular activity. Where the water bubbles up from the creek bed it is about 60°C. Further downstream are the cooler areas suitable for bathing.

BUTTERFLY GORGE NATIONAL PARK

The gorge is only 17km past the hot springs. It is a good day-trip activity as there is no camping available. The road says 4WD but in the dry you should have no problems in conventional vehicles. There are no signs to show the parking area and walking track. Stop in the large area before the road follows a steep rock slope. From here a walking track continues beside a swampy creek. A few large rock formations block the 500m walk to the gorge, but they are quite easy to climb.

You can swim through a narrow rock corridor to the splendid gorge beyond, then explore the next few chambers with their jutting rock ledges and sculpted pools.

GREGORY NATIONAL PARK

As you enter this region you are welcomed by imposing escarpments, twisting in tandem with the Victoria River. The area is indeed spectacular. The park is in the early stages of development, so there are not many established walking tracks or scenic access points.

Location and access
Most of the park and attractions lie south of the Victoria Hwy. To reach Limestone Gorge and Bullita campsites, turn off the highway 11km east of Timber Creek or 82km west of the Victoria River Wayside Inn. From here it is 59km to Limestone Gorge and 52km to Bullita. This road is gravel, so access is limited in the wet.

Fuel is available from the Victoria River Wayside Inn and Timber Creek.

Camping and facilities
Both the campsites mentioned are fairly basic with no suitable swimming holes nearby, so if you are visiting late in the dry season the flies and heat are a bit overwhelming. There are pit toilets, tables and fireplaces.

Big Horse Creek campsite and Sullivan Creek campsite are near the highway, so they make good stopping points if needed. Again, only basic facilities are available.

Walks and attractions
Limestone Ridge Walk (1.5km rtn –easy) leads from the Limestone Gorge campsite to good viewpoints of the surrounding landscape. There is a small waterhole about 600m before the campsite near the access road. However, there are no guarantees that 'salties' (salt-water crocodiles) are not present.

I thought one of the best walks was one kilometre west of the Wayside Inn. This steep track should take approximately one hour (rtn). From the top there are outstanding views across the Stokes Range and down to the tiny buildings of the Wayside Inn.

Gregory National Park

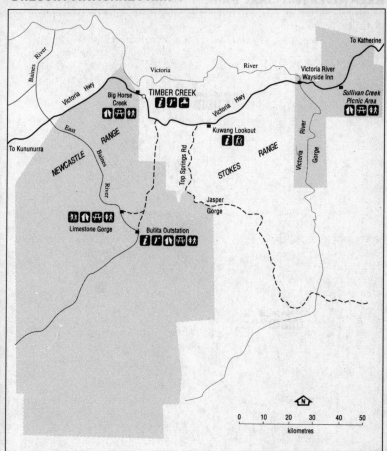

Another feature near the park is Jasper Gorge, 60km south of the Victoria Hwy. If you are travelling via Top Springs on Hwy 182 you will pass through it. A basic camping area is provided.

Keep River National Park

This well-managed park has incredible scenery coupled with fine examples of Aboriginal art work. There are good medium-distance walks and the deep-red sandstone ridges, dominant in the park, glow at sunrise and sunset.

Location and access

The road into the park is only 3km inside the NT–WA border. From here it is 18km to the first campsite. A short distance into the park there is an information booth worth visiting.

KEEP RIVER NATIONAL PARK

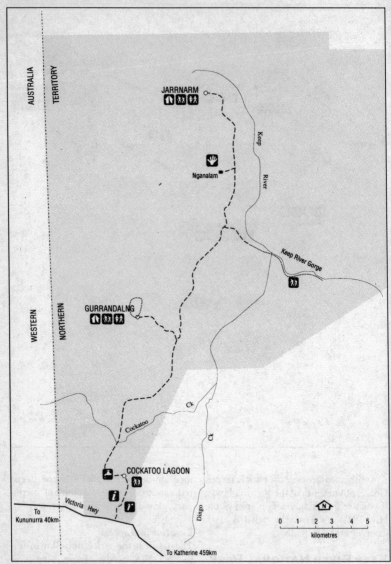

Camping and facilities
The Gurrandalng camp ($1 per person or $3 family) is 3km off the main road through the park. There is a monolithic escarpment overlooking the sites like a giant, faceless sphinx. There are pit

toilets, campfires and a few tables.

The Jarrnarm campsite is a further 16km, with similar facilities.

Drinking water can be obtained from a tap on the left-hand side of the road, 5km from the highway.

Walks and attractions
GURRANDALNG WALK
This walk (2.5km loop–easy) begins at the camping area and is best undertaken in the early morning or sunset, as the colours are magnificent at these times. The track winds up part of the way toward the giant, jutting rock faces to provide a view over the softly carved sandstone ridges in the distance. A walk guide is available at the start.

KEEP RIVER GORGE
Five kilometres after the Gurrandalng turn-off is a road to the right toward the gorge. The walking trail (4km o/w –easy–2 hrs rtn) meanders along the base of the gorge past several Aboriginal art sites and impressive rock formations.

NGANALAM
Five kilometres further is the road to the left for the Nganalam art site. A short walk from the car-park takes you to some interesting paintings on the underside of a large rock ledge.

JARRNARM WALK
A further 5.5km takes you to the Jarrnarm campsite. From here you can take a 24km (rtn) walk to a gorge and swimming hole or a 2.5km (rtn) walk to some Aboriginal art sites.

COCKATOO LAGOON
This circular walk takes about one hour and features the wetlands around the lagoon. Best during or soon after the wet season.

KAKADU NATIONAL PARK
Although this park is well known and very popular there are opportunities to get away and discover your own special places in Kakadu. It is an area of high cultural and environmental importance, so your visit is sure to be enlightening. The most important consideration is to allow yourself enough time to truly explore and appreciate this huge park.

Enquiries should be directed to Parks Australia, Darwin Office (phone: (08) 8946 4300) or the Park Headquarters in Kakadu (phone: (08) 8983 1100).

Location and access
You can enter the park from two points. If coming from the south, the turn-off is 1km north of Pine Creek. Then there is a 59km drive to Mary River where you can get fuel. A further 9km takes you to the southern entry station where you can stop to collect information and maps and pay the park fee of $10 per adult (over 16 years). From Darwin it is 150km to the northern entry station on the fully paved Arnhem Hwy.

Camping and facilities
Visiting Kakadu can be inexpensive if you take advantage of the many free bush camping areas. They don't have showers, but usually have pit toilets, tables and fireplaces and are less populated than the places with facilities.

The major camping grounds, with hot showers but no powered sites, have a nightly fee of $7 per site.

Walks and attractions
There are many walking tracks to explore and places to visit in Kakadu. Information obtained from the national parks office, at each entry point, or the park visitor centre near Jabiru, is thorough and easy to follow. I have written about the walks and features I enjoyed most that might help you plan your visit.

GUNLOM–WATERFALL CREEK FALLS
This attraction is located at the southern

KAKADU NATIONAL PARK

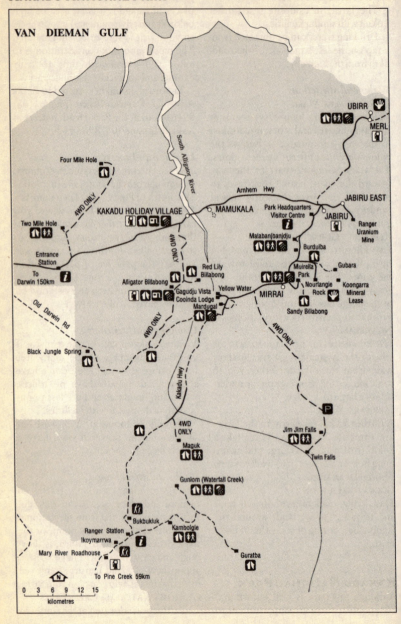

MINING

The prospect of mining near Coronation Hill, in the South Alligator Valley, should strike fear into all our hearts. The Dreamtime spirit Bulla lives here and if disturbed could inflict its angry wrath on the world. The Jawoyn people fear the ramifications if a mine should go ahead.

Another local resident who is likely to be worried is the totally aquatic pig-nosed turtle which lives in the South Alligator River catchment. The Resource Assessment Commission (RAC) found that there is a risk of pollution of the water system if a mine were to be built in the area.

Although Kakadu is listed as a World Heritage site, there is still a chance that the uranium-rich ground will be mined.

---

end of the park and can be reached by a dirt road 39km past the Kakadu Hwy. Turn off the Kakadu Hwy and follow the sign-posts to the campsites. Although rough and steep, the walk to the top of the waterfall is well worth it for a swim in the rock pools at the top, with the distant backdrop of the Kakadu landscape.

At Gunlom there is camping for $7, or down the road at Kambolgie the basic campsite is free.

MAGUK

The road to Maguk is marked for 4WD only. The bush camping sites are well spaced in pleasant bush surrounds. One kilometre past the camping area is the start of the one kilometre walk to the plunge pool, which is edged by sheer rockfaces.

COOINDA

Gagadju Lodge, Cooinda, offers camping at $3.50 per person (unpowered) or $6.50 per person (powered) with excel-

---

FIRES

While in Kakadu you may notice areas of blackened woodland or a trail of smoke rising in the distance. Controlled burning of the bush is a crucial part of the management of Kakadu, as it is in many regions throughout Australia.

The issues which exist in Kakadu concern the maintenance of traditional burning regimes as well as the restriction of the late season 'big' wildfires.

The burning takes place after the wet season so that there is enough moisture to limit the intensity and spread of the fire. The main purpose is to clear up the dry fuel on the ground to prevent wildfires during the late dry season, which can cause extensive damage.

The burning is also beneficial to many of the birds and other animal species; for example the agile wallaby feeds on the new shoots after the fire.

The concern about the fires mirrors many of the problems faced by park management. They must achieve a balance between maintaining conditions for park visitors (who contribute substantially to funding) and ensuring minimum damage to the environment, as well as heeding the advice of the Aboriginal people who have preserved the land for so long.

lent facilities, a swimming pool and bar. This is a good retreat from the wilderness if you feel like you need it (phone: (08) 8979 0145). An incredible experience may be had on the Yellow Water cruise through the wetlands of Kakadu. Cost is $22.50 for the two-hour cruise. Sunset and morning are probably the best times as the wildlife is active and the colours of the sun on the lush green surrounds are brilliant.

JIM JIM FALLS

Jim Jim Falls and Twin Falls are difficult to reach if you're in a conventional vehicle, but thoroughly rewarding once you make it. If you can stand rough, corrugated roads you will be able to drive 50km to the parking place, where you can leave the car and hike or catch a lift for the last 9km.

When you get to Jim Jim Falls the plunge pool and the steep gorge walls make an awesome sight. Twin Falls is a further 12km and you will need to swim or paddle on a lilo quite a way to get to them.

The Barrk Malam Walk (8km rtn) is hard for the first part to the top of the gorge. There are good vantage points as you are nearing the plateau. A long walk leads through scrubby terrain to the top of the falls, overlooking the gorge. The views are well worth the effort.

SANDY BILLABONG

Six kilometres past the Muirella camping area, along a sandy corrugated road, is a picturesque place to camp. There are no facilities and no fee. The clearings for camping are close to a large wetland, which is a haven for a variety of birds. Apart from the determined flies, which are followed by vicious mosquitoes at sunset, this spot is wonderful, but don't be tempted to swim.

The excellent 5km Buba Wetland Walk begins near the Muirella campsite.

NOURLANGIE ROCK

This area was an important site where Aboriginal clans used to live. There are many art sites you can view on walks in the area. Ranger-guided tours of Nourlangie Rock and Ubirr, conducted from May to October, will add to your understanding of the history and culture of the Aborigines in the area.

UBIRR

In the north-east section of the Kakadu is one of the most spectacular and informative places in the park. There are many Aboriginal rock paintings to see and learn about. The lookout is magical at sunset. The Merl camping ground is good, with hot showers. Nearby the Manngarre Monsoon Rainforest Walk is being revegetated after a fire in 1993, but is still a good walk in the cool of the morning.

MAMUKALA WETLANDS

During late August and September great flocks of magpie geese migrate to this expanse of water, creating a spectacular scene.

Aboriginal history

This region was originally inhabited by as many as 30 different clans. The Bunitj clan and others on the west bank of Alligator River, spoke Gagudju. The Jawoyn and Gundejehmi language groups also occupied the Kakadu NP region prior to colonisation. The Bunitj people are the traditional owners of the park.

The wetlands provided abundant food resources, including crocodiles, fish and turtles. During Gunumeleng (the wet season), building from mid-October to December, Aboriginal people moved to the higher ground of the escarpment.

Rock paintings in the park are considered the most signficant in the country, with some of them dating to 20,000 years. Over 7,000 paintings have been

> **CYCAD (*CYCAS ARMSTRONGII*)**
> It was wonderful to find so many of these plants scattered throughout northern Australia, particularly in Litchfield NP. The straight, black stump, growing up to 4m, contrasts with a thick clump of green, spiny leaves. The plants grow in colonies and regenerate quickly after fire, creating a vibrant rush of new leaves. Between March and September a hard nut-like fruit is produced by the plant. The Aborigines used the nuts, after careful preparation to remove toxins, to make flour or eat directly.
>
> A similar cycad found in Litchfield NP is the *Cycas calcicola*. It features more bluish-grey fronds and tends to grow between one and three metres.

recorded. Occupational debris in Deaf Adder Gorge, in the south of the park, has been dated to between 50,000 and 60,000 years old. Aborigines call this site *Nauwalabila*.

The Bowali Visitor Centre, located on Kakadu Hwy 2.5km south of Arnhem Hwy, is an essential stopping point to collect information prior to your visit to the park (phone: (08) 8938 1121). It is situated on Mirrar clan land and is open 8am–5pm daily. The Warradjan Aboriginal Culture Centre, near Cooinda (phone: (08) 8979 0051), is another place to learn about Aboriginal heritage. The centre is named after the pig-nosed turtle, whose shape is reflected in the design of the building.

THE TOP END

WILDMAN RESERVE

At Couzens Lookout bush camping is permitted. The small loop track provides a panoramic view of the Mary River and its wildlife. A boat ramp is close by a North Rockhole.

Turn off the Arnhem Highway on to the Point Stuart Road for 17km then on to the Rockhole Road for 19km.

The dirt road may become impassable for short times in the wet season.

SHADY CAMP RESERVE

Shady Camp is 55km north of the Arnhem Highway; turn off just west of Kakadu. The graded dirt road is occasionally impassable in the wet season. The campground is open and ideal for bush camping. There are two toilet blocks and two boat ramps. No drinking water is available. Camping fees apply. There are many birds and crocodiles around, so you can conduct your own wildlife safari on the various tracks in the Reserve (from the safety of your vehicle). This is predominantly a fishing place and boats can be hired from Shady Camp Boat Hire.

GURIG NATIONAL PARK

Spanning almost the entire Cobourg Peninsula, this park is a precious wilderness sanctuary. Access requires 4WD, self-sufficiency and a permit, as you will need to pass through Aboriginal land. There are strict controls on the number of vehicles allowed to enter the area at the one time; permits can be obtained from the Cobourg Peninsula Sanctuary and Marine Park Board, PO Box 496,

Palmerston, NT, 0831 (phone: (08) 8922 3394).

There are opportunities for walking, fishing, photography and bird watching in this remote, untouched sanctuary.

ON THE WAY

To reach Howard Springs Nature Park, a day-use park, turn off the Stuart Hwy 35km south of Darwin. It has an excellent swimming area and some short rainforest walks. It is open from 8am to 8pm every day. One of the most interesting spectacles the park has to offer is the giant barramundi which swim in the spring-fed pool and can be seen clearly from above.

Berry Springs Nature Park is located on the Cox Peninsula Road, 65km from Darwin, so it makes a good stopping point if you're heading to Litchfield National Park. The picturesque swimming hole is the main attraction. Again, it is for day use only, with toilets, tables, barbecues and a large, grassy picnic area.

LITCHFIELD NATIONAL PARK

Litchfield is an easily accessible park close to Darwin with a variety of attractions. Campsites near large waterholes make it pleasant even when the temperatures are high.

Location and access

The park is about 100km south-west of Darwin. From the Stuart Hwy you can take the northern access road into the park along the unsealed Cox Peninsula Rd (46km south of Darwin) or by sealed road through Batchelor (turn off another 47km south). From the start of the Cox Peninsula Rd it is 90km to the Wangi Falls camping area. Conditions on the gravel road should be checked after rain (phone: (08) 8922 3394. Access may be possible via the bitumen road from Batchelor. However, heavy rains can close the park at the Reynolds and Finniss Rivers.

Camping and facilities

Wangi Falls campsite is a short walk from a lush, tropical swimming hole. There are showers and toilets provided and the cost is $4 per person or $10 per family.

Sandy Creek campsite, a short walk from Tjaynera Falls, is a remote area of the park, but worth the detour. Head south along the main road from Wangi Falls for 10km, and at the junction take the right 4WD track. Follow this for 14km until you see the Tjaynera Falls turn-off. Check road conditions with the ranger. There is a small camping area with toilets and water available. The sites cost $5 per person or $12 per family.

Florence Falls has a shady campsite that is 2WD accessible. Showers are available and it is the closest place to Florence Falls (600m). It costs $5 per person or $12 per family. A second campsite is accessible by 4WD only, 800m from the falls.

Buley Rockhole also has a campsite, with toilets provided. The camp fee is $5 per person or $12 per family. It is close to a series of rockpools which are good for a swim.

Walks and attractions

At Wangi Falls there is a 2km circuit track around the large waterhole, taking you to the top of the waterfall. A boardwalk leads up and around the falls, making it fairly easy considering the steep grade in parts.

Tjaynera Falls is 1.7km from the campsite. It is an even walking track which leads to a magical pocket of water, red rock and rainforest. The walk

LITCHFIELD NATIONAL PARK

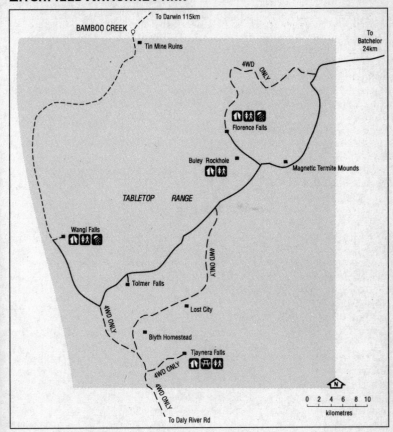

takes you through sections thick with the unusual cycad plant.

At Tolmer Falls a pathway leads 400m to a lookout of the falls and surrounding landscape. To explore the area further, take the path to the left from the car-park. You can follow a 1.6km loop track which brings you around to the lookout through interesting sandstone country. Walkers are not permitted to descend to the base of the gorge due to the colonies of orange horseshoe bats and ghost bats which live in the caves throughout the gorge and are vulnerable to disturbance.

Florence Falls has a good swimming spot with permanent falls creating a pleasant atmosphere. It is 600m from the car-park along a steep trail. You can also walk to the falls from Buley Rock, approximately one kilometre.

The Magnetic Termite Mounds, near the sealed road toward Batchelor, are a good spot to take a close look at the tombstone-shaped monuments which dot the landscape.

WESTERN AUSTRALIA

1. Mirima NP, see p206
2. Purnululu NP, see p206
3. Wolfe Creek Crater NP, see p207
4. Geikie Gorge NP, see p209
5. Tunnel Creek NP, see p209
6. Windjana Gorge, see p210
7. Karijini NP, see p210
8. Millstream-Chichester NP, see p214
9. Cape Range NP, see p215
10. Mt Augustus NP, see p219
11. Francois Peron NP, see p219
12. Monkey Mia Reserve, see p220
13. Kalbarri NP, see p220
14. Nambung NP, see p222
15. Avon Valley NP, see p223
16. Walyunga NP, see p223
17. Lane Poole Reserve, see p225
18. Yalgorup NP, see p225
19. Wellington Forest, see p227
20. Leeuwin-Naturaliste NP, see p227
21. Blackwood River Forest, see p229
22. Beedelup NP, see p230
23. Warren NP, see p230
24. D'Entrecasteaux NP, see p230
25. Shannon NP, see p231
26. Mt Frankland, see p231
27. Walpole-Nornalup NP, see p232
28. William Bay NP, see p234
29. West Cape Howe NP, see p234
30. Torndirrup NP, see p234
31. Porongurup NP, see p236
32. Stirling Range NP, see p236
33. Fitzgerald River NP, see p240
34. Stokes NP, see p240
35. Cape Le Grand NP, see p242
36. Cape Arid NP, see p243

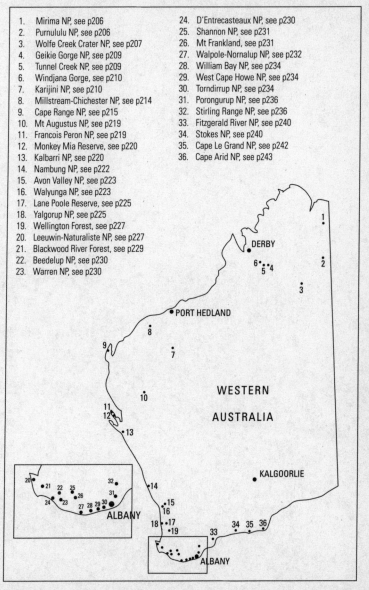

NOTE: Look through the chapter to the On the Way sections to see additional places to camp or visit.

NATIONAL PARKS SERVICE
The controlling body is called the Department of Conservation and Land Management — commonly referred to as CALM.

CONTACT
CALM
STATE OPERATIONS, COMO
(08) 9334 0333
WWW.CALM.WA.GOV.AU

TOURIST BUREAUX
The national parks service has a close relationship with the tourist bureaux in Western Australia. Most of the time it is easier to enquire at a tourist bureau for information and maps rather than a national park office. If you are having difficulty locating the information, or you need specific details, then call the CALM regional office and they will be able to give you the right contact address for your needs.

PARK ENTRANCE FEE
Some parks charge an entrance fee. These are mainly day-use parks near Perth. You can buy an annual pass for $51 which then exempts you from the fee. The pass is available from CALM State Operational Headquarters and selected park offices.

The four week All Parks Pass ($22.50) is a good option for those visiting several parks in the state during a holiday period.

ABORIGINAL HISTORY
There are six nations in Western Australia, the Jinyila, Bibbulmun, Karratjibbin, Nor'West, Kimberley and Central Areas. Within these nations are clans and tribes, and they are referred to in various ways, for example, the Aborigines of the south-eastern area collectively call themselves Nyoongars, the people of the Pilbara call themselves Mulba, the Wongi live around the Kalgoorlie region and people in the Murchison River area call themselves Yamitji.

Rottnest Island was made a prison for Aborigines in 1839. Diseases and forced removal of children devastated the Western Australian Aboriginal population within 50 years of white settlement.

FUEL
Unless you go way off the beaten track you will find fuel is obtainable fairly regularly. Even so, it does pay to have a jerry can in case of an emergency.

MONEY
Most service stations and supermarkets have EFTPOS facilities, enabling you to purchase goods as well as withdraw cash.

PUB PATRON GUIDE
MIDDY	285 ML
BAZZA	425 ML

> **BAOBAB (*ADANSONIA GREGORII*)**
> This distinctive tree, commonly referred to as the 'boab', is from the family Bombacaceae. The baobab can grow to 14m and develops a huge, swollen, bottle-like trunk. The white pith of the fruit is edible and the trees are found naturally in the northern regions of Western Australia.

THE KIMBERLEY

MIRIMA NATIONAL PARK

The park previously known as Hidden Valley, is 2km east of Kununurra, via Barringtonia Avenue and Hidden Valley Rd. The rock formations and colouring are said to be similar to the Bungle Bungle formation. This may be a good alternative for those not able to reach the Bungle Bungles on their trip to the Kimberley.

The Didbagirring Walk Trail (1km rtn–mod) involves a steep climb to a delightful viewpoint.

The Wuttuwutubin Walk Trail (500m rtn–mod) provides excellent views of the rock formations and Kununurra township.

CALM staff conduct guided walks and slide nights in the park during the dry season.

Aboriginal history

The Miriwoong people lived in this area. They call it *Mirima*. The Lily Pool Trail is an easy 100 metre return walk that passes axe-grinding grooves where the Miriwoong would grind the blades of stone axes.

ON THE WAY

The Grotto, 30km south of Wyndham, is interesting. An impressive stone pathway curls down to a narrow rock pool, boxed in by sheer walls.

PURNULULU (BUNGLE BUNGLE) NATIONAL PARK

The Bungle Bungle range, with its famous beehive-shape formations, is the feature of this park. It is a scenic wonder comparable to the best attractions in the world. As access is limited to 4WD, most people choose to fly over the gaping sandstone gorges and chasms.

Location and access

The Spring Creek Track, leading to the Bungle Bungle range, is located 50km south of Warmun Aboriginal Community (formerly Turkey Creek) or 109km north of Halls Creek. The ranger station and Three Ways Junction is 53km along this rough, unsealed track. Collect a map of the park from the station, which shows all tracks, walks and facilities. The park is closed from 1 January to 31 March due to the wet season. The park entrance fee of $11 per adult, $1 per child under 16, is payable at the self-registration bay opposite the ranger station.

Camping and facilities

There are two campsites that can be used by travellers in the park. Kurrajong is 7km north of the ranger station. Walardi camping area is 13km south of the ranger station. There are pit toilets, water and barbecue facilities available at both sites. There is no rubbish collection so you must take your rubbish away with you.

> **ECOTOURISM**
>
> In 1992, Purnululu National Park was awarded an international environmental tourism award. It won because of the ability of CALM and the Purnululu Aboriginal Corporation, who jointly manage the park, to integrate the needs of the local people and the preservation of the environment with the demands of tourism.
>
> The environment of Purnululu National Park is fragile. The outer crust of the sandstone formations of the massif are easily damaged by pedestrian traffic. Once this crust is broken, the exposed soft sandstone rock underneath erodes rapidly. It is important that visitors cooperate in protecting these structures by ensuring that no climbing on the rock surfaces occurs.

Walks and attractions

A popular option for viewing the Bungle Bungle massif is by helicopter. Heliwork WA (phone: (08) 9168 1811) runs a Tour B flight from the Turkey Creek Roadhouse costing $200 per adult, $110 per child, and the Tour A flight leaves from the airstrip inside the Bungle Bungles, costing $180 per adult and $100 per child.

There are various options of combined 4WD tours, helicopter and plane flights available from tour operators in Kununurra or Halls Creek.

From inside the park you can explore Echidna Chasm, 20km left of Three Ways Junction. A 750m path passes through the narrow gorge.

An overnight walk can be done in Piccaninny Gorge (30km rtn–mod). From Three Ways it is 25km to the Piccaninny car-park. The shorter Cathedral Gorge Walk (2km rtn–easy/mod) can also be undertaken from here.

Aboriginal history

The Bungle Bungle massif is part of the territory of several language groups including the Kija, Malngin, Jaru and Miriwoong. In the Kija language, *Purnululu* means sandstone. Aboriginal people call the Bungle Bungle Range *Kawara*, and every feature of the massif has an Aboriginal name. The fringe of the massif was used by Aboriginal groups after heavy rain when the run-off would form large waterholes.

The nearby Ord River was a hub of Aboriginal life. It was significant for trading, ceremonies and hunting, with a rich network of names and stories connecting all parts of the landscape.

The park is rich in Aboriginal art and it contains many burial sites.

WOLFE CREEK METEORITE CRATER NATIONAL PARK

Two to two-and-a-half hours south of Halls Creek, via the Tanami Rd, is an 850-metre wide crater caused by a meteorite about 300,000 years ago. Camping is available at Carranya Station. There is no water and no fires are allowed. You need to take your rubbish out with you. There are pit toilets and an information bay is located at the campsite. A short, steep walk leads to the crater rim. For more information call Kununurra CALM (phone: (08) 9168 4200).

Aboriginal history

The Djaru clan lived in this area and refer to the craters as *Kandimala*. Creation stories explain how it was formed by a rainbow snake emerging

GEIKIE GORGE, TUNNEL CREEK AND WINDJANA GORGE NATIONAL PARKS

from the ground before travelling with another rainbow snake across the land to form Sturt and Wolfe Creeks.

GEIKIE GORGE NATIONAL PARK

Geikie Gorge, Windjana Gorge and Tunnel Creek form part of an ancient ocean reef formed in the Devonian period, 350 million years ago. As well as being unique and significant geologically, they are an integral part of the Kimberley region and should not be missed.

Location and access

Geikie Gorge, the most accessible section, is 16km north-east of Fitzroy Crossing via a sealed road. From Fitzroy Crossing, turn off the Great Northern Hwy and follow signs to the park.

Camping and facilities

There is no camping at Geikie Gorge but very pleasant camping conditions can be found at the Fitzroy River Lodge, just east of Fitzroy Crossing (phone: (08) 9191 5141). Unpowered sites are $19 for two people; powered are $23. Toilets, gas barbecues and picnic facilities are provided at the gorge.

Walks and attractions

The Reef Walk Nature Trail (2.5km rtn–easy/mod) leads to the edge of the west wall. Take the path to the left where the sign indicates 'short walk'. This path winds along the base of high rock walls then straightens out to follow the gorge wall. At this point the Short Walk trail (1km rtn) veers to the right and returns to the picnic area.

The longer walk continues to the west wall, from where you cannot proceed any further. If you want a strenuous walk back, you can pick your way along the edge of the river for great views of the interesting gorge wall on the other side. Wet-season floodwaters have bleached the lower part of the 30-metre wall, so it contrasts vividly with the deep-red colouring above.

CALM operates a river cruise twice a day during the dry season, at 8am, 11am and 3pm ($17.50 adults, $2 children). The Darngku Heritage Cruise, led by an Aboriginal ranger, departs Monday to Friday at 8.15am during the dry season ($80 per person includes morning tea and lunch).

Aboriginal history

The Bunaba occupied this area, calling it Darngku. A range of boat tours are run by the Darlngungunaya Aboriginal Corporation and CALM. These are led by Bunaba guides and range from 1.5 hours to half day tours. Tours run from April until October and the short cruises leave at 8am, 11am and 3pm. Call the Fitzroy Crossing Tourist Bureau for more information (phone: (08) 9191 5355).

TUNNEL CREEK NATIONAL PARK

This park provides a remarkable contrast to other activities of the 'top end' — instead of gorges, vistas and sunshine there are caves, tunnels and darkness. It is located 70km from the Great Northern Hwy. Turn off 42km west of Fitzroy Crossing. From Derby travel 120km along the Gibb River Rd then turn right. Follow this road 25km to Windjana Gorge and another 42km to Tunnel Creek.

Pit toilets and an information sign are provided and no camping is allowed.

The main feature is the cave-like tunnel which channels through the Napier Range. The 800m tunnel leads to the other side of the range.

Take a torch and wear shoes and clothing which you don't mind getting wet, as the walk involves wading across some chilly waterholes. When you reach the first large amphitheatre (approximately 50m into the tunnel), keep to the left side to avoid a rather deep section.

You may see the red eyes of the harmless 'johnsoni' crocodile. Watch out for the colonies of bats and the fascinating cave formations on the ceiling.

Aboriginal history
The cave of Tunnel Creek is famous as the popular hideout for Aboriginal rebel leader Jandamarra (also known as Pigeon). Jandamarra tried to defend his land and people for over three years before he was tracked down and killed at Tunnel Creek in 1897.

WINDJANA GORGE NATIONAL PARK
This impressive gorge, with sheer 100-metre high walls for most of its length, is considered by geologists to be a world-class example of a fossilised coral reef.

Location and access
Windjana Gorge is 145km from Derby and 150km from Fitzroy Crossing. From Tunnel Creek continue north-west along the gravel road. Conventional vehicles can make the journey from Fitzroy Crossing to Tunnel Creek, Windjana Gorge and along the Gibb River Rd to Derby. On the section between the Gibb River Rd and the Great Northern Hwy beware of the 'razor rocks', which can slice the side of your tyres. Access is limited in the wet season.

Camping and facilities
Hot showers, pit toilets, tables, firewood and fireplaces are provided. The park is open all year, but facilities (such as showers) are available only in the dry season up until mid-November. The fee of $5 per person, plus $2 per child, is collected by the ranger who resides in the park.

Walks and attractions
The walk along Windjana Gorge (7km rtn–easy) requires at least 2 hours to properly explore the several deviating paths which traverse the creek beds and wide banks. If the water is low enough you can walk along the creek bed for most of the way, allowing better views of the gorge, but be prepared for muddy patches. Late in the dry season the shallow waterholes are densely populated by freshwater crocodiles. Although generally harmless, swimming is not advised when there are several in the one area.

Aboriginal history
The Bunaba people are the traditional custodians of Windjana Gorge. Carpenters Gap, in Windjana NP was the site where 40,000 year old stone tools have been found. Rock paintings in the gorge were done in the Windjana style. Many stories relate to features of the landscape.

The Ngigina people also lived in the Kimberley region, home to the famous Miriwun Shelters, situated above the Ord River flood plains. This place, where the Ngarinyin would camp and cook, contain the Wandjina rock paintings, some of the most spectacular rock art sites in the country.

THE PILBARA

KARIJINI NATIONAL PARK
This park provides an ideal opportunity to discover the barren beauty of outback Western Australia. In the Hamersley Ranges there are a number of

KARIJINI NATIONAL PARK

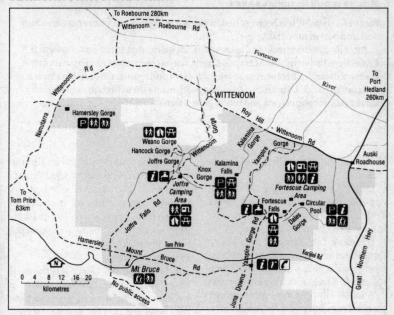

gorges, walks and campsites for you to explore and enjoy. Come prepared to stay a few days and immerse yourself in a pleasurable wilderness environment.

Location and access

Follow the Great Northern Highway south of Port Hedland for 261km to Auski Roadhouse. Alternatively, turn off the North West Coastal Hwy 14km east of Rowbourne and follow the scenic trip through Millstream-Chichester NP, along the Roebourne-Wittenoom Rd. It is sealed in sections although it can get corrugated during busy times. A slightly shorter way is along the Hamersley Iron Access Rd, which leaves the North-West Coastal Hwy 3km west of Karratha. To use this well-graded dirt road you must contact the tourist bureau in Karratha (phone: (08) 9144 4600) to obtain a Hamersley Iron permit. It is free of charge. Road conditions should always be checked prior to undertaking this trip as conditions can change rapidly, with tracts of dry roads followed by sections of boggy mud. Check road conditions with the Karratha tourist bureau or a road conditions hotline (phone: (08) 9143 6464).

Camping and facilities

Hamersley Gorge is 53km from Wittenoom. There are no camping facilities provided by CALM but beside the road, before the national park boundary, there are cleared areas where people camp. This is pastoral lease, so ensure that you leave no trace of your visit and this arrangement should continue.

Weano Gorge campsite, located near Weano Gorge Trail, has pit toilets, gas

> **MINING IN OUR NATIONAL PARKS**
>
> Part of Karijini NP has been excised to allow mining to occur in an area previously declared part of the park.
>
> After long consultation and assessment, including that of the Environmental Protection Authority, the Marandoo mine site has been allowed to operate in this corridor of land. There are many arguments for and against the decision to mine in national parks. Often individual cases will dictate the actual costs and benefits for the current population and future generations.

barbecues and a few tables, and is quite pleasant.

Joffre Gorge campsite is located opposite the turn-off to Joffre Gorge. Toilets and gas barbecues are provided in a relatively barren site.

Fortescue Falls camping area has recently been upgraded and is probably the most popular site, with regulated camping areas, toilet blocks and gas barbecues.

A seasonally operated visitor centre is planned to be built near Fortescue Falls.

The camp fees are $5 for two people plus $3 for an extra adult or $1 for each child. You can pay at self-registration stations. Drinking water is available from a tap near the turn-off to Joffre Gorge and near the turn-off to Fortescue Falls. No fires are allowed within the park boundaries due to the lack of wood available.

Walks and attractions

There are a great number of walks and sights in this park; I have included those I feel are most interesting. The national park brochure, available in the park, categorises all the walks in levels of difficulty.

There are lookouts at almost all of the gorges, which require only a short walk to reach.

Heed the warning signs at each gorge as there are real dangers. On average, one person each year is killed in the region. Slippery rocks on steep climbs are the main cause. If you're not confident about your ability to undertake these climbs, don't do them.

HAMERSLEY GORGE

For me, Hamersley Gorge was the most visually fascinating. Layers of rock have buckled over millions of years, so now they bend and curve in dramatic waves. From the car-park, walk down a steep path to a swimming hole edged by the layered rock. A route leads upstream for 500m to a fern-lined grotto. The route is of moderate difficulty and is marked by piled stones.

MT BRUCE

A steep crumbly climb (2km rtn–mod) leads to a magnificent view of the park, as well as providing a vista of the controversial Marandoo Mine.

The Marandoo View Walk (500m rtn–easy) leaves from the carpark and leads to a vantage point overlooking the Marandoo Mine operations. Continue further up the mountain on the Honey Hakea Track (4.5km rtn–mod). It is a steep, crumbly climb to views of Mt Bruce, Chinamen's Hut and the mountain ranges in the north.

The Mt Bruce Summit Route (9.5km rtn–hard) is a challenging trek and should be undertaken in the early morning. The summit route is a continuation of the Honey Hakea Track.

Handrail Pool Track

From the Weano car-park, walk down the steps and turn right. The walk involves wading through icy pools, along narrow ledges and through deep, water-worn rock alleys. At the end of the walk you climb down a rock ledge to a large pool, using thick, knotted rope. The deep-red corridors and still rock pools make this one of the most memorable places in the park (600m rtn–mod).

Hancock Gorge

This track also begins at the Weano car-park and leads down to the base of the gorge, which you can explore yourself (1.5km rtn–easy/mod).

Knox Gorge

Follow the steep path to the bottom of the gorge, where you can walk beside a tranquil, green pool for a short distance (2km rtn–mod).

Joffre Falls

Signs guide you from the car-park to the track leading down the gorge. Once at the base you can walk and wade some of the way, but further down you will have to swim or, if you are equipped with a lilo or tube, paddle along the gorge (3km rtn–mod/hard).

Kalamina Gorge

This gorge has a good swimming hole which is easily accessible for everyone. A short walk leads from the car-park. From here you can also walk to the Rock Arch Pool (3km rtn–easy).

Fortescue Falls

These permanent falls run down a natural staircase to a pleasant swimming hole in Dales Gorge (1km rtn–mod). From here you can walk downstream to Circular Pool (2km rtn–mod) or upstream to Fern Pool. Ensure you take care not to disturb the delicate, ferny environment.

Yampire Gorge

There is an asbestos warning for this area. Use recycle on your car air-conditioning, wind up the windows and avoid breathing dust. 4WD only.

Aboriginal history

Hamersley Range is the traditional land of the Banyjima, Kurrama and Yinhawangha who resided in various sections of the park. They called the range *Mallumallu*. The range is rich in habitation sites. Karijini Park Council is made up of members of the Banyjima, Kurrama and Yinhawangha people.

Mt Bruce is called *Bunurrunha* by Aboriginal people. Rock art sites exist in the park. The two most accessible sites are at Dales Gorge and Kalamina Gorge. Aboriginal cultural displays and information about art sites can be found at the Karijini Visitor Centre, Banyjima Drive, open in summer from 1pm — 3pm, Friday through to Tuesday. The centre is closed Wednesday and Thursday.

MILLSTREAM-CHICHESTER NATIONAL PARK

The attractions within this park are best visited on the way, or way back, from Karijini NP. It is a long detour from the coast highway for them alone, however. Crossing Pool and Deep Reach Pool provide excellent swimming and a comfortable place to spend a couple of days.

Location and access

From Karratha to the Millstream Homestead Visitor Centre and nearby campsites, via the company road (you

MILLSTREAM – CHICHESTER NATIONAL PARK

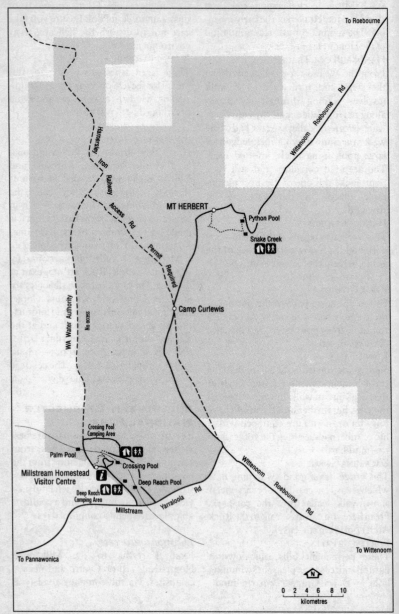

will need a permit), is 190km. An alternative route is along the Wittenoom-Roebourne Rd which leaves the North-West Coastal Hwy 27km east of Roebourne. The Snake Creek campsite and Python Pool are approximately 60km south of the highway.

Camping and facilities

The Crossing Pool campsite may be accessed by the Millstream-Yarraloola Rd and Snappy Gum Drive. Pit toilets, gas barbecues, fireplaces, tables and firewood are supplied. Deep Reach Pool campsite, a few kilometres before the visitor centre, has similar facilities. The Snake Creek campsite, in the Chichester section of the park, has a pit toilet.

Camping costs $5 for two people plus $3 for an extra adult or $1 for each child. The park entry is $5 per car.

Walks and attractions

MILLSTREAM HOMESTEAD

Millstream Homestead was built in 1914 as a homestead then operated as a tavern between 1975 and 1986. It has since been restored as a visitor centre, with displays dedicated to the Yinjibarndi people, early settlers and the surrounding environment.

CHINDERWARRINER POOL

A short walk from the homestead leads to the best-known feature in the park: a lily-covered pool surrounded by date palms and cadjeput, creating an oasis in a barren landscape.

MURLUNMUNJURNA TRACK

A walking track links Crossing Pool to Millstream Homestead Visitor Centre (6.8km o/w–easy). Try to arrange a vehicle pick-up at the other end.

CHICHESTER RANGE CAMEL TRAIL

This walk, best started from Mt Herbert, retraces a historic camel route to Python Pool (8km o/w–easy/mod). If you don't want to undertake the entire walk, you can go to McKenzie Spring (4.5km rtn–easy) and still appreciate the rocky terrain. The first part of the trail from the Python Pool is also worth doing for the good views.

Aboriginal history

The Yindjibarndi tribe led a nomadic life in the territory between Hamersley Range and the Chichester escarpment. Millstream was known as Ngarrari, which they believe was formed by the great water snake, Barrimindi, who lives beneath the Fortescue River. Barrimindi is the protector of the permanent waterholes along the river and has a strong spiritual significance today. Ngarrari was an important meeting place. Visitors would camp by the Chinderwarriner Pool, where fish and edible plant roots could be enjoyed. The Murlanmunjurna Track (see Walks and Attractions for details) is a self-guiding interpretive walk providing details about plant use.

CAPE RANGE NATIONAL PARK

If travelling from the north, Cape Range provides a refreshing change from 'croc' or 'stinger' infested waters, and from the inland gorges characteristic of the 'top end' parks. The scenery in the park includes turquoise coastal waters and the dramatic ridges of the Cape Range. The park joins Ningaloo Marine Park, where snorkellers are treated to a thriving sea-life only metres from shore.

Location and access

The park is located on the western side of the North West Cape, some 360km north of Carnarvon. All the camping areas are off the road which continues around the coast from Exmouth (pronounced X-mth). A track between Coral Bay and Yardie Creek (at the southern end of the park) means you can

CAPE RANGE NATIONAL PARK

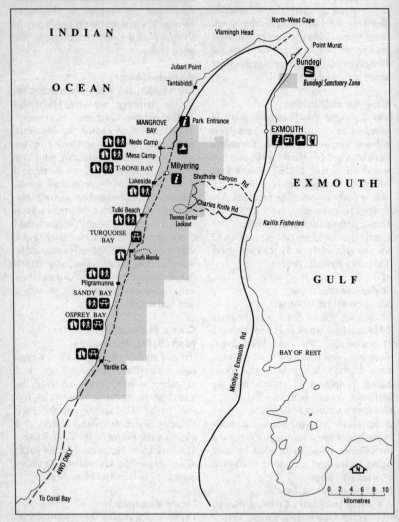

travel up via the coast from Coral Bay. There is little fresh water along this route and a 4WD is needed to cross Yardie Creek. You should check beforehand as it may be impassable.

If you are coming from the north, the Burkett Rd can save you a large detour. It is 81km of partially sealed road, easily traversed in 2WD. Those with caravans need to check conditions, particularly after rain when the surface may become slippery.

Camping and facilities

There are seventeen campsites dotted along the coastline in the park. Most have sealed vault toilets and all cost $5 per site for two people, plus $3 for an extra adult or $1 for each child. Park entry fee is $5 per car.

Longer term passes are available on request. Drinking water is not available in the park, so it is advisable to fill up in Exmouth. A limited supply of bore water is available from a tap near the Ned's Camp turn off. Camp fires are not permitted in the park in an effort to protect the fragile vegetation.

Walks and attractions

The most popular park activities are snorkelling, fishing and walking. Remember these are special conservation parks — nothing may be removed from marine park sanctuary areas, and fishing regulations may vary from other locations. The best time to visit is from March to September.

Milyering Visitor Information Centre is located 11km inside the northern boundary of the park. The centre provides extensive information on Cape Range National Park and Ningaloo Marine Park. Excellent visual displays, videos, library, brochures, souvenirs and drinks are available.

MANDU MANDU GORGE ROUTE

The first half of the route takes you along the northern rim of an interesting gorge carved by an ancient river. Return the same way or by the floor of the gorge (3km–2hrs rtn). Walking trail markers assist visitors along its length. A brochure on the park walking trails is available at the Milyering Visitor Information Centre.

BADJIRRAJIRRA ROUTE

Follow the Badjirrajirra route from the Thomas Carter lookout to the top of Shothole Canyon. From here negotiate the trail down to the carpark with care. This route is approximately 4km and will take you just over an hour.

Should you desire you can take the longer circuit route that returns to Thomas Carter lookout. The trail is clearly marked and skirts along the lip of a number of gorges. Approximately 9km, it will take you around 2.5 hours. The trail provides scenic views of Exmouth Gulf from several vantage points. The trail is rugged underfoot so wear sturdy boots and carry drinking water.

YARDIE CREEK TRACK

Extends 1km from the carpark along the edge of a colourful limestone gorge. Easy initially then slightly more diffiicult over the last section — 1hr rtn. This is the habitat for the rare Black Flanked Rock Wallaby. Visitors are asked to respect their seclusion.

Aboriginal history

A shell necklace, dated to 30,000 years, was found in the Mandu Mandu rockshelter, along with other occupational debris.

ON THE WAY

Located 154km south of Exmouth is Coral Bay, an ideal place to explore Ningaloo Marine Park. Snorkelling is easy, as you need only swim 20m from the shore to be surrounded by colourful, darting fish. Camping, fuel and supplies are available from the two caravan parks by the beach.

A few kilometres south of the Blowholes, about 80km north of Carnarvon, is an old seaside village, Point Quobba Coastal Reserve, which is fascinating to visit. It features several rustic tin sheds, mostly made by locals, near a nice beach. Camping costs $1 per person, which you can deposit in an honesty box on the way in. The Shire

> **DUGONG**
>
> These unusual sea-faring mammals make their home in the sub-tropical waters of Shark Bay. They look like a cross between a whale and a porpoise. Dugongs live in the warmer waters around the Australian coast north of Shark Bay on the west coast and north of Hervey Bay on the east coast. They do exist in other places in the world but Australian waters support the largest remaining populations.
>
> Seagrass is the main food for dugongs, making the fields in Shark Bay a popular spot. Reproduction is not frequent; females can breed after 10 years of age and gestation takes about 12 months. The calf often stays with the mother for over a year.
>
> Dugongs may live up to 60 or 70 years. Death from poachers and fish nets keeps the species at vulnerable levels as the number of young is not maintaining the population.

of Carnarvon is responsible for the area and provides toilets, rubbish bins and fireplaces for campers. You need to bring your own firewood.

66 kilometres north from the Blowholes will take you to Red Bluff Camp, an off-beat place with a unique atmosphere. It is a popular spot for surfies, but anyone can camp there ($2.50 per person). Beach shacks, called 'humpies', dot the hillside. Ask if there are any vacant, as you can stay in them for $3.50 per person. Use your speedometer to guide you there, as no signs exist. From the T-intersection near the Blowholes, it is 56km to where you turn off the main road. You will go over the '30 Mile Grid', 1km before the turn-off. On the way, or way back, it is worth taking a look at the *Korean Sta* shipwreck. This large bulk carrier was tossed against the treacherous coast by Cyclone Herbie in 1988.

The eastern side of the Kennedy Ranges, 250km from Carnarvon, is an ideal place to stop if you are heading toward Mt Augustus NP. The turn-off to Gascoyne Junction is approximately 5km north of Carnarvon. The recreation areas in the national park are about 50km north of Gascoyne Junction. There are toilets and one camping site.

The three car-park areas are reached by turning left from the main road and travelling 10km to a four-way intersection. Straight ahead leads to the central car-park and the camping area. The other two are reached by taking the left road for 1.5km or the right road for 2km. A map can be obtained from the shire office in Gascoyne Junction.

Aboriginal history
Kennedy Range was the boundary between the territories of the Malguru and the Maya tribes. The large area of land stretching east from the park to the Gascoyne and Lyons Rivers was home to the Malguru. The area west of the park to Carnarvon, belonged to the Maya. The semi-precious chert rock found in the range provided materials for stone tools. Kennedy Range contains a Thalu site, a place where a ceremony is held to draw upon spiritual forces to increase the abundance of a natural resource.

THE GASCOYNE

MT AUGUSTUS (BURRINGURRAH) NATIONAL PARK

Although a long way inland, this park has a lot to offer. There are many long and short walks to explore the world's largest rock, twice the size of Ayers Rock.

Location and access
The most common route is via Gascoyne Junction, past the Kennedy Ranges, then east to the park (470km from Carnarvon). The road is mostly gravel, so conditions should be checked after rain. Call (08) 9943 0988 for road conditions.

Camping and facilities
Privately run camping grounds exist at Cobra Homestead, 45km before the park, or at Mt Augustus Caravan Park (phone: (08) 9943 0527), near the rock. Camping costs $9 per person per night; a powered site is $11 per person.

Walks and attractions
There are several walking tracks leading to magnificent views and Aboriginal art sites. The Summit Trail (12km rtn–mod/hard–7 hrs) is a strenuous walk to the top. To reach good views with less effort I recommend Edney's Trail (6km rtn–easy/mod–2 hrs). Information on the walks is available from the caravan parks. Best time to visit is August and September when the wildflowers colour the landscape.

Aboriginal history
The Wadjari people occupied this area. They called Mt Augustus *Burringurrah*. The natural springs along the base of Mt Augustus were an important resource to Aboriginal people, particularly in times of drought. Mt Augustus features many rock-engraving sites.

Mundee Mundee is a 200 metre walk departing from the carpark, clearly sign-posted off the circuit drive. You can see engravings of bustard tracks, kangaroos and emus in three cave-like overhangs. According to Aboriginal beliefs a dreaming spirit did these engravings with his fingers when the rock was still soft.

At Beedobondu (Flintstone), also sign-posted off the circuit drive, you can follow the creek bed for 250 metres until you reach Flintstone Rock. Carefully crawl under the huge flat rock to see the engravings.

At Ooramboo, a short walk of 150m leads to more engravings. 100m further along this track is the Edney Spring permanent soak.

FRANCOIS PERON NATIONAL PARK

Camping within this park is limited to 4WD vehicles only. Conventional vehicles can reach the day-use area at Peron Homestead. Local tour operators offer various day and overnight trips into the park.

Location and access
The road into the park turns off the Monkey Mia Rd 4km from Denham. Peron Homestead, 10km along this road, can be reached by conventional vehicles. The Big Lagoon campsite can be accessed by the road which veers to the left from the homestead. The road to the right leads north to Cape Peron and the other camping areas. Care must be taken when crossing the 'birridas' (salt pans), as they can be like quicksand to vehicles. Staying on designated tracks ensures safety. For a map of the area collect a park brochure from the CALM office in either Denham or Monkey Mia.

Camping and facilities

The northern campsites include Herald Bight, on the eastern side of the peninsula, and South Gregories, Gregories and Bottle Bay, on the western side past the three-ways junction. Fees can be paid at the park entrance. Toilets and gas barbecues are provided at most sites. No drinking water is provided and you must take out all your rubbish.

Walks and attractions

The hot tub near Peron Homestead is a tank filled with hot artesian water. It is very relaxing in the cool of the evening. Take a walk on the Station Life Walk Trail for an insight into the workings of a sheep station.

Cape Peron, at the tip of the Peninsula, provides a spectacular lookout. Swimming, fishing and boating are popular activities in this park.

Aboriginal history

The Malkana people occupied the area around what is now Denham and the Francois Peron NP. Remnants of Aboriginal fish traps can be viewed along the Boolbardi walk which follows the coast from Denham to the Town Bluff.

MONKEY MIA RESERVE

Monkey Mia, arguably one of Western Australia's best-known attractions, is the place to see wild bottlenose dolphins which visit daily to greet onlookers and accept offerings of fish. CALM and the Shire of Shark Bay regulate the shoreline where the dolphins usually gather from about 8am to 1pm. Monkey Mia access costs $7 per person per day or $8.50 per person for a fortnight pass. CALM passes apply.

Monkey Mia Reserve is located 23km from Denham and camping is available at the Monkey Mia Dolphin Resort (phone: (08) 9948 1320).

Shark Bay, a World Heritage area, is also home to a large population of dugongs. The lush fields of seagrass support an estimated herd of 10,000.

Hamelin Pool Marine Nature Reserve, another Shark Bay attraction, is 27km from the North West Coastal Hwy. It is home to rare stromatolites — living organisms representing the Earth's earliest life forms, sustained by the highly saline water in the bay. A 200m boardwalk allows visitors to observe stromatolites without damaging them. A 1.5km walking trail highlights other features of the area including a working shell block quarry. Signs on the way direct you to the visitor site and the Hamelin Pool Telegraph Station (a private historic and commercial venture).

THE MIDWEST

KALBARRI NATIONAL PARK

Kalbarri is a varied park which features wildflowers, gorge scenery and coastal views. If you are travelling north, the gorges here are a good introduction to the magnificent ones ahead. For those heading south, some of the gorge lookouts might seem a trifle ordinary. However, the coastal views are very spectacular.

Location and access

The road to Kalbarri starts from the North-West Coastal Hwy 132km south of the Billabong Roadhouse or 49km north of Northhampton. The well-graded dirt roads to the river gorges rarely become impassable and roads to the coastal lookouts are sealed.

Camping and facilities

No camping is allowed in the park, but several good caravan parks are located in Kalbarri township, by the coast. Picnic

WESTERN AUSTRALIA

KALBARRI NATIONAL PARK

> **MARRON**
>
> These freshwater crustaceans (similar to yabbies and crayfish) can be found throughout the south-west. Regulations for minimum size, bag limits and restricted season (usually from January to February — see the Fisheries Department or CALM for season details as they may vary from season to season) exist to sustain numbers of the species for years to come. Visit a national park office or fisheries department to obtain a licence and legal guidelines for catching them.

facilities, including gas stoves, are located at the Loop car-park. To visit the Loop and Z Bend you must pay $5 per vehicle.

Walks and attractions

Hawks Head and Ross Graham Lookout are 4km and 2km respectively from the Ajana-Kalbarri Rd.

The Z Bend, 25km from the Ajana-Kalbarri Rd, has a lookout and 500m track to the river bed.

The Loop Walk (8km circuit–mod/hard) is an interesting walk past Nature's Window, along the east gorge rim then down to the river edge. Small rock piles direct you for the first section until you reach the river. You can walk in the eroded passages alongside the water or on the ledge above. The incredible colouring of the rocks in this section is a feature of the walk. Follow the river back to Nature's Window. The national park sign says to allow six hours to complete the walk, but don't be put off — we did it in a comfortable three hours. Most people just walk the 200m to Nature's Window.

The road leading south from Kalbarri takes you to coastal walks and lookouts in the park. These are Red Bluff Lookout, Mushroom Rock, Rainbow Valley, Pot Alley, Eagle Gorge, Shellhouse Grandstand, Island Rock and the Natural Bridge. Visitor fees apply.

ON THE WAY

Between Kalbarri NP and Perth there are several national parks which mainly preserve the wildflowers in the area (including many rare or unique species).

Two of the more popular ones are Mt Lesueur, 40km inland from Jurien, and Stockyard Gully, east of Leeman. Both are accessible only by 4WD. To reach these parks, turn off the Brand Hwy at Eneabba. No camping is allowed in the parks. Lake Indoon, 12km from Eneabba, has a campsite managed by Carnamah Shire Council, costing $7 per vehicle overnight.

NAMBUNG NATIONAL PARK

The famous Pinnacles Desert is in this park, 245km north of Perth. From the Brand Hwy take the Cervantes turn-off and follow Cervantes Rd almost to the township. Turn left at the sign-post to the Pinnacles and follow this road 16km to the desert. An entrance fee of $5 per vehicle is charged to tour around the dramatic scenery.

Picnic and barbecue facilities are available along the coast but no camping is allowed. More information is available from the gate keeper at the entrance to the Pinnacles, or from the ranger office located in the light industrial area of Cervantes (phone: (08) 9652 7043).

Aboriginal history

At the time of European contact, the Wajuk and Yuat tribes of the Nyoongar group frequented the coastal areas during the summer months. *Nambung* is an Aboriginal word meaning 'crooked' or 'winding', referring to the river from which the park drew its name. The caves which occur between Yanchep and Jurien, are significant to Aboriginal people. The mythical Wagyl serpent is believed to use the blowholes, pools and underground caverns to travel to the sea.

SWAN REGION

AVON VALLEY NATIONAL PARK
This park, only 70km from Perth, has some great camping spots. It is better to visit in the cooler months because in summer it is quite hot and dry.

Location and access
If coming from the north you need to go to Toodyay (turn-off at Gingin if travelling on the Brand Hwy) and travel south-west on the Toodyay Rd for about 20km to the sign-posted turn-off into Morangup Rd. From the city, head north on the Great Northern Hwy and turn right into Toodyay Rd then left into Morangup Rd. Follow the signs to veer left into Quarry Rd. Further along you will reach a fork in the road which indicates 'Bald Hill' to the left and 'River' to the right. Valley campsite can be reached by following the road to the river. Homestead, Drummonds and Bald Hill campsites are reached along the left road. The last 12km into the park is unsealed and can be rough — watch for oncoming vehicles. The roads to Drummond and Valley campsites can be narrow and winding and not suitable for caravans and heavy trailers.

Camping and facilities
All camping is $10 per site and firewood is provided.

Valley campsite has about seven sites, fireplaces, two undercover shelters, tables and toilets. Homestead campsite, the first on the track to Bald Hill, has water available, undercover shelters and toilets. Drummond campsite is a remote spot with toilets and fireplaces provided.

Bald Hill has toilets, water, tables, fireplaces and great views.

Walks and attractions
A riverside walk leaves from the Valley picnic area, at the end of Forty-One Mile Rd. You can follow the fire access trail in the park but contact the ranger beforehand and always carry water. A trail leads from Valley campsite to the river. Be careful as you cross the train lines, as trains give no warning of their approach.

WALYUNGA NATIONAL PARK
This day-use park, featuring many walks, is a little easier to reach than Avon Valley. Access to the park is via the Great Northern Hwy, 40km from Perth (a $9 vehicle entrance fee applies).

The Swan River, which runs through the park, becomes a raging torrent in winter and is home to the well-known Avon Descent — a white-water competition held on the first weekend in August.

Camping is allowed but you must call to notify the ranger beforehand (phone: (08) 9571 1371). A camp fee is charged.

Walking trails leave from the car-park and picnic areas.

The Echidna Trail (10.6km loop– easy/mod) provides several vantage points to survey the Swan River and Avon Valley.

Syd's Rapids (5.2km rtn–easy) walk follows the Swan River, allowing you to appreciate the foliage and wildlife in the area.

Other walks are listed on the information board.

AVON VALLEY AND WALYUNGA NATIONAL PARKS

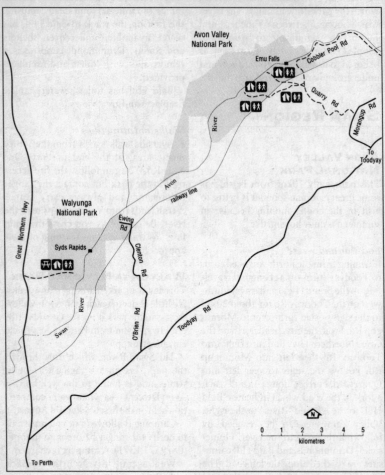

Aboriginal history

The Wajuk Nyoongar occupied this area, which has one of the largest known Aboriginal campsites around Perth. The Walyunga Heritage Trail (1.2km rtn 45 mins) links Walyunga Pool and Boogarup Pool. It is sign-posted with information about Aboriginal myths and traditional lifestyles. The Nyoongar people believe that the Rainbow Serpent, Waugul, travelled along the river and left stones for making tools.

ON THE WAY

Several parks exist on the outskirts of metropolitan Perth, such as John Forrest, Serpentine and Yanchep National Parks. Most are for day use only and function as recreation areas for people living in the city. For information on where they are and what they feature, contact the Swan Regional Office (ph: (08) 9390 5977).

LANE POOLE RESERVE

This reserve, declared to preserve northern jarrah forest, is a pleasant area featuring splendid native forests, several camping areas, paths and swimming holes.

Location and access

From Dwellingup, 100km south of Perth, take the Pinjarra-Williams Rd toward Boddington. Less than one kilometre out of town, turn right at the sign-post indicating Nanga Mill. Follow Nanga Rd to reach the camping sites. Watch the tight, unexpected corners and sign-posts along the way. Past Nanga Bridge is unsealed but well graded except for a few corrugated sections. Easily passable by conventional vehicles and caravans.

Camping and facilities

Camping fees apply in all camping areas.

BADEN POWELL

This large shady site is set among pine trees. Turn left off Nanga Rd just before Nanga Bridge. There are toilets, tables and fireplaces in the day-use and camping sections.

CHARLIE'S FLAT

This camping area, located on a one-way road off River Rd, has individual forest sites with tables, fireplaces and toilets.

TONY'S BEND

Similar layout and facilities to Charlie's Flat.

YARRAGIL

Further along this road is Yarragil, a small quiet spot next to the river; same facilities as Charlie's Flat.

NANGA MILL

This large site, located on the western side of the Murray River, is set among tall pine trees. Remains from the old sawmill, which burnt down in 1961, can be found in this area. There are toilets, tables, fireplaces and fresh water available.

NANGA TOWNSITE

This spot is recommended for group camping. There are toilets, tables and fireplaces.

THE STRINGERS

Not far from Nanga Mill, this campsite is set in native forests a short walk from the river. There are three or four large sites with fireplaces, tables and toilets.

Walks and attractions

ISLAND POOL

Island Pool is a nice spot to swim and is accessible from both sides of the river. Picnic facilities are on the eastern side of the river, just past Charlie's Flat.

KING JARRAH TRACK

The walk (18km loop–easy/mod) begins at the Nanga Mill site across the road. The first part is steep, leading to the top of the escarpment through the marri and jarrah forests. The return journey is along the banks of the Murray River.

SCARP LOOKOUT AND SCARP POOL

These worthwhile day-trip areas can be reached by taking the Pinjarra-Williams Rd, toward Pinjarra, 6km to the Scarp Rd turn-off. It is a 6km unpaved road to the lookout then another 2km to the Scarp Pool.

YALGORUP NATIONAL PARK

The park is located on the ocean side of the Old Coast Rd, south of Mandurah. Turn into Preston Beach Rd, which leads to Martins Tank campgound. There are fireplaces, water and toilets provided. The area is popular for swimming, fishing and exploring coastal terrain.

Aboriginal history

Yalgorup is derived from two Aboriginal words, *Yalgor*, meaning 'swamp or lake' and *Up* a suffix meaning 'place'.

LANE POOLE RESERVE

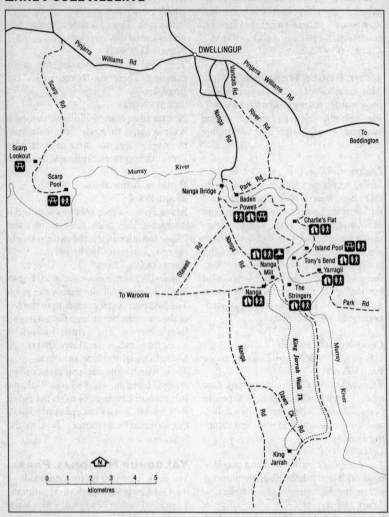

CENTRAL FOREST

🚙 ON THE WAY
By taking the Nanga Rd south past Lane Poole Reserve you can find your way to Hoffman Mill, on the banks of the Harvey River. A camping area is provided and several easy walks begin from the site. The camping fee is $5 per site for 2 people then $3 per extra person — children $1 per night.

THE WELLINGTON FOREST

A pleasant camping and swimming area can be found 30km west of Collie. Take the Wellington Dam Rd turn-off, 18km from Collie. Turn down River Rd and drive another 5km to reach Honeymoon Pool campsite. The road is unpaved, at times corrugated, but easily accessible by conventional vehicles. People towing caravans should proceed along River Rd with caution.

One kilometre further is the Ferns day-use area next to a large pool and rapids, which flow all year. If you have some form of floating equipment, such as a lilo or tube, you can drift back to Honeymoon Pool.

Follow the signs to Potters Gorge, on the edge of the Wellington Dam, or drive down Lennard Scenic Rd, which also links up with Honeymoon Pool.

LEEUWIN-NATURALISTE NATIONAL PARK

This park consists of most coastal areas between Cape Naturaliste, north of Yallingup, and Cape Leeuwin, near Augusta. The area is often referred to as the Limestone Coast, due to the sculpted cliffs which can be seen from several vantage points in the park. Because the park is so extensive, I have listed the features you will encounter in the context of travelling north to south from Cape Naturaliste to Cape Leeuwin.

CAPE NATURALISTE

It is 12km from Dunsborough to the lighthouse, along Cape Naturaliste Rd. From Bunker Bay you can undertake the 3.1km walk to the Cape.

Beautiful swimming beaches, with white sand and clear water, can be found on the northern side of the peninsula. For a scenic stopover, Sugarloaf Rock, on the southern coastline before the lighthouse, is a jagged rock formation with a small cove next to it.

INJIDUP

Eight kilometres south of Yallingup along the Caves Rd is an easy-to-miss sign for Wyadup Rd, which leads to Injidup picnic area. The beach is close, but to reach it involves a steep descent and then there's the breathless struggle back up.

'Tourist Caves' have stairs, handrails, lighting and guided tours. These include Lake Cave, Mammoth Cave, Yallingup Cave and Jewel Cave. For detailed information on caves, visit the CALM office in Margaret River or the Margaret River Tourist Information Centre.

ELLENSBROOK

Ellensbrook Homestead is within the park but managed by the National Trust. It is one of the earliest houses in the area and has been tastefully restored. There is a short walk from the car-park to Meekadarribee Waterfall. The waterfall is spring-fed and at its best on a hot summer day. Access is restricted to an elevated boardwalk, as the moss-covered ground is very fragile.

CONTO'S FIELD

Turn off the Caves Rd toward Lake Cave and continue along Conto Rd for 4km to reach Conto's Field camping area. There are 29 sites, which are busy over the summer holidays, but quieten down once school resumes. Sealed vault toilets, tables, fireplaces and water are provided.

A short drive leads to Conto Springs, where you can swim, fish and explore the rocky coastline.

BORANUP CAMPGROUND

Boranup Drive, a picturesque forest track, provides an alternative to Caves Rd, although it is unsealed and a bit rough at times. The Boranup campsite can be reached by following this road for nearly its full length, or by starting the Boranup Drive at the southern end, off Caves Rd, for 1km. Firewood, fireplaces, tables and toilets are provided in this 'Sherwood Forest' setting.

LEEUWIN-NATURALISTE NATIONAL PARK – NORTHERN END

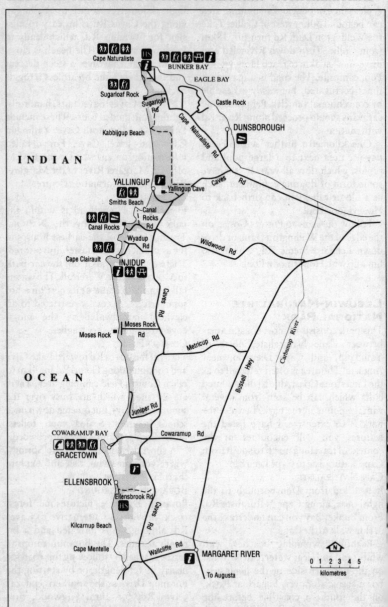

SOUTHERN FOREST

HAMELIN BAY
You can stay at a caravan park in this pleasant coastal area overlooking near-by Hamelin Island. This park is operated under lease from CALM. Peak season is busy and you may need to book. Fishing and swimming are popular activities.

SOUTHERN FOREST

BLACKWOOD RIVER FOREST
The tranquil jarrah and marri forests east of Margaret River provide scenic drives and a few camping spots you may wish to use. Camping fees apply.

SUE'S BRIDGE
Turn north off the Brockman Hwy, 40km from the Bussel Hwy or 46km west of Nannup. Ten kilometres along the unpaved road is Sue's Bridge campsite. Fireplaces, toilets and tables are provided. Bring your own drinking water.

WRIGHTS BRIDGE
The Blackwood River Scenic Drive links Nannup and Balingup. From Nannup it is 10km to Revelly Bridge picnic spot. Further along in the Bowalup Nature

Reserve, you will find the Wrights Bridge day-use area. Several sites, situated near the tree-lined Blackwood River, have fireplaces and tables.

BRIDGETOWN JARRAH PARK

Bridgetown Jarrah Park, 20km from Bridgetown going toward Nannup, is a good day-use park with picnic facilities and information about marked walking trails.

KARRI FOREST

There are several sites around the Manjimup and Pemberton areas which allow you to appreciate the beauty of this sprawling forest. Below are some of my favourites.

KING JARRAH

This huge jarrah tree, over 6 metres in girth, is just north of Manjimup along the Perup Rd.

100 YEAR FOREST

The 100 Year Forest is ten kilometres north of Pemberton along Eastbourne Rd, then 2km along an unsealed road. The Wheatfield Walk is 300m and the Lookout Loop is one kilometre; both are easy and leave from the picnic area.

GLOUCESTER TREE

Three kilometres out of Pemberton is a challenging climb to an old fire lookout, 64m above ground, nestled around the trunk of a huge karri. Few can avoid shaky legs on the return journey.

RAINBOW TRAIL

A pleasant drive leaves Pemberton, just west of the township. The 12.5km loop track follows a forest-lined drive to Big Brook Dam, Big Brook Aboretum and several nice picnic areas.

BEEDELUP NATIONAL PARK

This park off the Vasse Hwy, 20km west of Pemberton, has a spectacular waterfall. The falls are only a short walk from the car-park and flow all year.

WARREN NATIONAL PARK

You will find Warren NP an impressive place to visit and appreciate karri forests, up to 400 years old. Picnic and camping spots hug the Warren River in a peaceful environment.

Location and access

Head 7km south from Pemberton on the Northcliffe-Pemberton Rd, to the turn-off onto the Old Vasse Rd. Six kilometres along turn left into Heartbreak Trail which continues along Maiden Bush Trail to return to Old Vasse Rd. The drive itself is thrilling — a rollercoaster through nature. The roads are suitable for conventional vehicles, but caravans are not permitted. Only after heavy rains are the roads closed.

Camping and facilities

There are three camping areas of similar size and charm located next to the Warren River, about 2km apart. All have toilets and fireplaces. At the time of printing no fees were charged.

Walks and attractions

Canoeing, fishing and swimming are the most popular activities in the park. Short walk trails leave from the campsites.

D'ENTRECASTEAUX NATIONAL PARK

After camping and walking through the magnificent forests around Pemberton you may like the contrast of D'Entrecasteaux NP, on the coast.

Location and access

The main area accessible by conventional vehicle is Windy Harbour, 33km south of Northcliffe, along Windy Harbour Rd. An unsealed road veers to the left, 8km south of Northcliffe, leading to Broke Inlet.

The rough road to Mandalay Beach leaves the South Western Hwy 8km west of Walpole. All other areas, including Lake Jasper, Fish Creek, Calcup Hill, Jasper, Gardner, Yeagarup and Warren Beaches, require 4WD, as the roads are sandy.

Camping and facilities
Camping is allowed through most of the park, but you must carry out all rubbish and bury human waste 100 metres away from any watercourse.

Toilets, fireplaces and tables are provided at Crystal Springs (8km west of Walpole), Donnelly Boat Landing (off the Vasse Hwy between Pemberton and Nannup) and Lake Jasper (4WD only).

A shire caravan park is located at Windy Harbour.

Walks and attractions
Swimming and fishing are popular activities in the park. The rocky headland at Windy Harbour is a perfect spot to explore.

SHANNON NATIONAL PARK

The South Western Hwy dissects this park, 53km south of Manjimup. A road on the eastern side of the highway takes you to the camping ground and another road, 100m from that turn-off, leads to the Shannon Dam, information shelter and walking trails.

Camping and facilities
The large camping area, with several fireplaces, has two small wooden huts available for use. There is an amenities block with showers, the water for which you heat yourself using the wood-fuelled heating system. A fee of $5 is charged, payable at the self-registration booth.

Walks and attractions
The Rocks Walk Trail (5.5km loop–easy) can be started at the information shelter, or at the dam (accessible by vehicles). The distance given is taken from the shelter, so it is shorter from the dam. The Shannon Dam Trail (3.5km rtn–easy) is suitable for wheelchairs for the first 1.5km from the information shelter. It is a pleasant walk along the Shannon River surrounded by marri and karri trees.

MT FRANKLAND NATIONAL PARK

This isolated forest corner provides an enchanting night stay. A steep climb in the crisp morning is rewarded by splendid views of the area.

Location and access
Take the sign-posted road north of Walpole. It is 29km to the campsite, with the last 12km unsealed. Alternatively you can turn east off the South Western Hwy 35km from Walpole. This route leads past Fernhook Falls (detailed below).

Camping and facilities
There is only a small area available for camping. A charming hut, originally used by the towermen, is provided for use. No fee was applicable at the time of printing.

Walks and attractions
The Summit Trail (1.2km rtn–mod/hard) leaves the car-park along the closed off road and rises gradually to the steps, where the steep climb to the summit begins. You will appreciate a drink once you reach the top, so take one along.

The Rockwood Walk Trail, sign-posted as 'Walk Trail 1.5km', follows the base of the huge granite dome of Mt Frankland. The track winds through moss-covered rocks and cool forest. Views over the surrounding area can be appreciated from the board walk just before the two trails meet, 100m from the campsite.

ON THE WAY

Fernhook Falls, mentioned above, has two huts (for visitors to keep warm on chilly nights), fireplaces, tables, toilets and 10 campsites. The area can be reached by Beardmore Rd, which leaves the South Western Hwy 35km from Walpole; or by taking the road north of Walpole toward Mt Frankland and turning left at the four-way intersection. A camp fee is payable at the site.

Centre Road campsite is off the South Western Hwy, 19km west from Walpole or 26km south of Beardmore Rd. There is one hut, fireplaces and a small area for tents. It is near the banks of Deep River and is surrounded by tall forests.

There is a donation box for you to contribute to the upkeep of facilities.

There are many other sites managed by CALM in the state forest areas around Walpole. See the CALM district office, on the main road through Walpole, for more details.

WALPOLE-NORNALUP NATIONAL PARK

This park ranges from majestic forest to extensive waterways, providing activities such as fishing, bushwalking and scenic drives.

Location and access

Most of the camping and attractions are within a 20km radius of Walpole township.

Crystal Springs campsite (part of D'Entrecasteaux NP) is 8km west of Walpole, just off the highway, behind the ranger's residence. The road to the site is sign-posted Mandalay Beach.

Banksia camp, 3km west of Mandalay Beach (4WD only), is 11km from the highway, 3km of which is for 4WD only.

Rest Point, a popular fishing spot, is a few kilometres from Walpole along Rest Point Rd.

Coalmine Beach, south of Walpole, is another popular area to stay and explore. Turn off the South Coast Hwy 2km east of Walpole.

The Valley of the Giants is clearly sign-posted from the South Coast Hwy, 14km east of Walpole. For a longer drive you can follow the Valley of the Giants Rd, which turns off the highway at Bow Bridge Roadhouse.

Camping and facilities

Crystal Springs campsites are reached by a short, sandy road and are nestled amongst tea-trees. Fireplaces, pit toilets and tables are provided. Pay the fee of $10 per site at the ranger's house, next to the highway.

Rest Point has a caravan park situated next to the picturesque inlet. The fee is $18 per 2 adults and $4 per child for an unpowered site (phone: (08) 9840 1032).

There is a privately managed caravan park at Coalmine Beach, within the Walpole-Nornalup NP. Sites cost $10 unpowered or $11 powered (phone: (08) 9840 1026). Booking is advised in peak times (summer holidays and long weekends).

Walks and attractions

The Knoll Scenic Drive leads from Coalmine Beach to picnic spots and walking tracks. White-topped posts indicate the start of the short trails, which form an 'H'-shape path through damp forests and coastal terrain.

Sandy Beach to Rest Point Walk Track follows the scenic foreshore of Nornalup Inlet — linking the popular day-use area at Sandy Beach (swimming and fishing) with the Rest Point area.

WESTERN AUSTRALIA

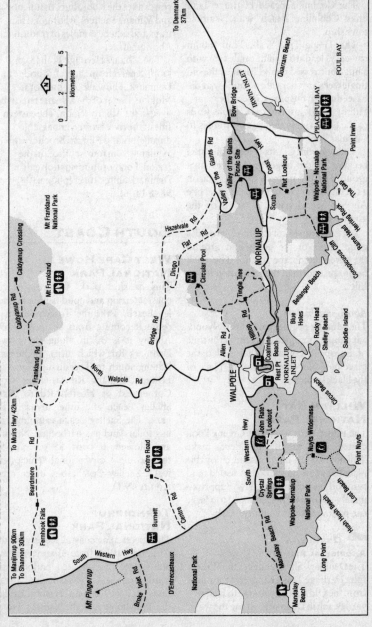

The Coalmine Beach Heritage Trail links Coalmine Beach with Walpole township.

The Tingle Tree Walk Trail (800m rtn–easy) leads to a giant tingle tree with a huge buttressed trunk. Most of the old tingle trees are charred and hollow at the base due to bushfires over the years. Hilltop Road, just east of Walpole, leads to the giant tingle tree and continues to Circular Pool.

Valley of the Giants is a famous area because of the huge tingle trees in a group. The 400-metre walk takes you on a circuit journey where you may feel like Alice in Wonderland, dwarfed by the grand trees.

Mt Pingerup (8km rtn–mod) provides good views of the coast and around the forest landscape inland. The walk begins just north of the turn-off to Broke Inlet.

Aboriginal history
The Minang people, part of the Nyoongar people, occupied this area at the time of European contact. They called the place *Nor-Nor-Nup*, meaning 'place of the black snake'.

WILLIAM BAY NATIONAL PARK

The transparent waters of Greens Pool, dotted with granite boulders, make William Bay an unusual and enjoyable place to swim and snorkel. A sealed road turns off the South Coast Hwy (approximately 14km west of Denmark) to a large car-park with toilet facilities nearby.

ON THE WAY
ABORIGINAL HISTORY
The Denmark Shire manages the Wilson Inlet Heritage Trail (12km rtn) running from the Old Railway Bridge to Rudgyard Beach in Denmark. Along the way you can see the Koorabup, Bandicoot and Minang Shelters, Aboriginal fish traps and other examples of traditional Aboriginal life.

The Mokare Heritage Trail (3km loop) departs from the traffic bridge in Denmark. The walk commemorates Mokare, leader of the Minang tribe who lived in the Albany region. The eastern side of the river is often impassable during July and August. Brochures are available from tourist offices in the region. For more information call Denmark Shire offices (phone: (08) 9848 1106).

SOUTH COAST

WEST CAPE HOWE NATIONAL PARK

This seaside park features rugged coastal terrain and good fishing at Shelley Beach. Take the Torbay alternate route if coming from Walpole. From Albany it is 30km along the Lower Denmark Rd, which turns off the road leading south to Torndirrup. Turn off Lower Denmark Rd at either Cosy Corner Rd or Horton Rd to reach Shelley Beach and other areas of the park. The Shelley Beach camping area has toilets and gas barbecues. No fires are allowed. It costs $5 per site for two people. Conventional vehicles can reach Shelley Beach, but other areas require 4WD.

TORNDIRRUP NATIONAL PARK

The spectacular coastal scenery of this park, only 10km from Albany, makes it one of the most visited parks in the south-west. Sealed roads lead to attractions such as The Gap, Natural Bridge, the Blowholes and the Salmon Holes.

TORNDIRRUP NATIONAL PARK

No camping is allowed. There is a private caravan park at the end of Frenchman Bay Rd (the main road through the park). It costs $15.40 unpowered, $17.60 powered per site for two people (phone: (08) 9844 4015).

Most of the attractions are only a short walk from the car-park areas. A long hike to Bald Head (10km rtn–mod–6 hrs) leaves from the Isthmus Hill car-park and passes over Isthmus and Flinders Peninsula.

Aboriginal history

Torndirrup is the name of the Aboriginal clan who lived on the peninsula and to the west of Albany. The Nyoongar people needed to construct bark-covered huts due to the cold winters. They also made buka (cloaks) made from three or more female kangaroo skins treated and sewn together with sinew and worn with the fur on the inside.

PORONGURUP NATIONAL PARK

If you're heading north from Albany, the forest-covered slopes of the Porongurup Range are a good introduction to the Stirling Range.

Location and access

From Albany you can travel north on the Chester Pass Rd, 40km to the Mt Barker-Porongurup Rd. Alternatively you can head toward Mt Barker on the Albany Hwy then turn right just before Narrikup at the sign indicating Porongurup. Turn left into Woodlands Rd, which is unpaved and leads to the scenic drive from where you can see the Stirling Range in the distance.

The Tree-in-the-Rock picnic area, in the heart of the park, is 1.5km along a sealed road from the Mt Barker-Porongurup Rd.

Camping and facilities

No camping is allowed in the park. There are camping and caravan facilities opposite the main road into the park.

The Tree-in-the-Rock picnic area has tables, toilets and gas barbecues in a bush setting.

Walks and attractions

The popular Devils Slide Walk (5km rtn–easy/mod) follows the Wansbrough Walk for 2km, leaving from the Tree-in-the-Rock, then turns to the right. Marmabup Rock is 500m past the Devils Slide. To make a loop journey, you can return via Nancy Peak and Hayward Peak, which is a steep trail if started from the Pass, on Wandsborough Walk.

The information board at the picnic area has more details.

The Castle Rock Walk (3km rtn–easy) leaves from another picnic area a short distance from the Mt Barker-Porongurup Rd (turn off 2km from Chester Pass Rd). Castle Rock is an impressive sheer block of granite. The huge sphere-shaped Balancing Rock nearby is also interesting.

The Wandsborough Walk (4km o/w) and the Millinup Pass (3.3km o/w) cross the range, linking Mt Barker-Porongurup Rd and Millinup Rd.

The wildflowers are best from October to December.

STIRLING RANGE NATIONAL PARK

This park has a myriad traversing trails for you to enjoy the native flora and fauna of this beautiful area. So be prepared for breathless climbs and breathtaking views.

Location and access

If coming from Perth, travel through Broome Hill then turn toward Gnowangerup, Borden and Amelup.

WESTERN AUSTRALIA

PORONGURUP NATIONAL PARK

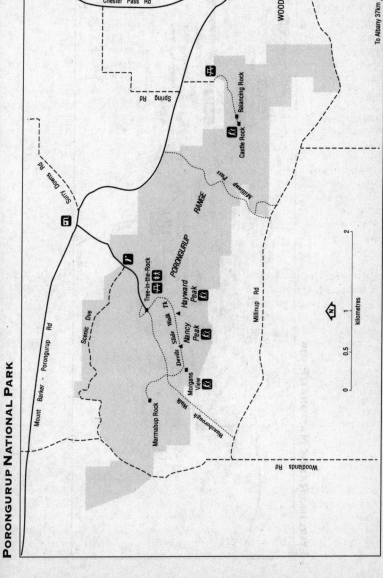

CAMPING AND TRAMPING

STIRLING RANGE NATIONAL PARK

> **DIEBACK**
>
> The plant disease Dieback is killing many plants in Australia, particularly in the south-west region. It is caused by a fungus which lives in the soil and can be easily spread by walkers and vehicles.
>
> Unfortunately, a large part of the Stirling Range has been closed off to the public in a bid to retard the spread of the disease. The soil fungus came from the tropics last century, but was not identified until the 1960s, when it had already spread beyond easy control. Until an effective method to combat the disease is found, then areas must be restricted to save the bush.
>
> This is a classic example of the dilemma faced by national park authorities, who must achieve a balance between the conservation needs of the park and the demands of the touring public.

Eight kilometres past Amelup Roadhouse is the turn-off to Bluff Knoll (the most popular feature of the park). From Albany travel 60km north along the Chester Pass Rd, which passes through the park.

Camping and facilities

The only camping area in the park is at Moingup Springs, off Chester Pass Rd. Tables and toilets are provided; $5 per site for two people. No fires are allowed — gas barbecues are provided.

The ranger station, where you can get information and register for long walks, is nearby.

A private caravan park (with a swimming pool) is opposite the access road to Bluff Knoll, to the north of the park. It is $9 each for unpowered sites (phone: (08) 9827 9229).

Walks and attractions

BLUFF KNOLL

The consistently steep climb to the summit (6.2km rtn–mod–3 hrs) requires a good degree of fitness. The satisfaction of climbing the second-highest peak in WA is rewarding enough, regardless of the magnificent 360° view.

TOOLBRUNUP PEAK

A more difficult walk is Toolbrunup Peak (1025m). The 2km climb to the peak is steep and slippery in the last half. It requires sturdy footwear and a good degree of fitness and skill.

MT HASSELL

A popular walk is to the summit of Mt Hassell (4km rtn–mod). The start of the walk is 4km along the Stirling Range Drive, from a car-park off the road.

TALYUBERUP PEAK

This (3km rtn–mod) and Mt Hassell are often recommended for family hikes, as they are fairly even and safe. The walk begins 24km along the Stirling Range Drive.

Check information boards and pamphlets for other walks.

Aboriginal history

The Stirling Range is part of the territory of the Qaaniyan and Koreng people. The range was known as Koi Kyeunu-ruff and the face-shaped rocks of Bluff Knoll earned the name *Pualaar Miial*, meaning 'hill of many faces'. The mists which are often hanging around the bluff are believed to be the only visible form of a spirit called *Noatch*, meaning 'dead body' or 'corpse'. Conical huts were built for shelter from the wet weather. They were made from a collection of sticks placed in the ground and bent to form a cone. Leafy branches, paperbark and rushes were then threaded through the sticks to make a wall.

The Stirling Range is believed to be a place for regenerating spiritual power.

FITZGERALD RIVER NATIONAL PARK

Many of the good spots in this park are accessible by 4WD only. As a significant wilderness area, there is good scope for those willing to explore the area by foot. The spots around Hopetoun are good if you are making only a brief visit to the park.

Location and access

The south-west part of the park can be reached by travelling along Pabelup Drive (turn off the South Coast Hwy 21km east of Jerramungup). This road leads to Point Ann and West Mt Barren. Information and the ranger's residence are located at the turn-off.

The Hopetoun area can be reached by turning off the highway at West River Rd (43km west of Ravensthorpe), which becomes Hamersley Drive. This road was quite corrugated on our visit. To the east and south of this road there is a mountain range and to the west the breakaway country of the Hammersley River and mountains. Probably the most comfortable way to reach attractions in the park is by detouring from Ravensthorpe and following the sealed road to Hopetoun. From there it is only a short drive to the camping area and walks.

Camping and facilities

Four Mile campsite, 200m from the beach, has a few tables, a toilet and a gas barbecue. Carry your own drinking water. Head west from Hopetoun and it is sign-posted from the ranger station. Camping is available at St Marys Inlet, 2km east of the Point Ann day use area. Tables, toilets and gas barbecues are provided. This location is accessible by conventional vehicle. Camping costs $10 per site for two people plus the $9 park entry fee per car. No fires are allowed.

Other bush camping areas are scattered through the park. Inquire at the ranger station (phone: (08) 9835 5043), or information boards.

Walks and attractions

East Mt Barren Walk (4km rtn–mod/hard–2 hrs) is a steep walk leading to impressive coastal views. The walk begins a short drive from Four Mile campsite.

West Mt Barren (3km rtn–mod/hard–2 hrs) is another steep climb and provides views of the southern section of the park.

Mt Maxwell Lookout is an easy 100m walk to good views. It begins from the information board, just off the Pabelup Loop Drive.

Aboriginal history

The Mongup, Quaalup, Bremer Bay and Corackerup clans of the Nyoongar people occupied this area. Many artefact scatters indicate heavy use of the region.

STOKES NATIONAL PARK

Stokes Inlet is a good stopover, where you will find pleasant camping areas and surrounds. Turn off the highway 107km from Ravensthorpe or 80km west of Esperance. The gravel road into the park is only 5km long and in good condition. The two campsites edging the inlet have toilets, tables, fireplaces and firewood. The camp fee is $10 for two people, plus the park entry fee of $9 per car.

A coastal trail follows the inlet and there is a wide variety of birdlife to watch.

WESTERN AUSTRALIA

FITZGERALD RIVER NATIONAL PARK

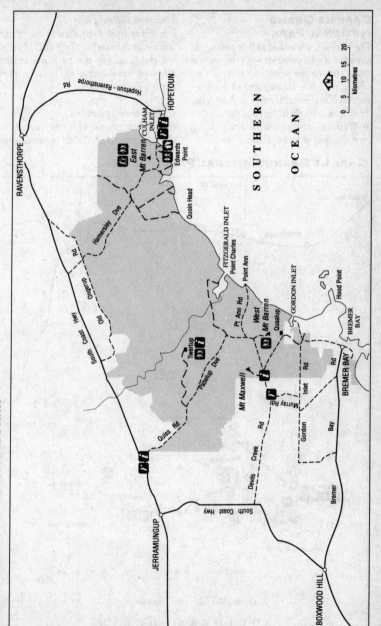

CAPE LE GRAND NATIONAL PARK

The beaches, with sand as fine and white as caster sugar, contrast with the surreal aqua-blue of the water. Granite slopes edging the coves create some of the most spectacular coastal scenery in Australia. This park is likely to be your first or last in Western Australia; it makes a fitting introduction or farewell to the State.

Location and access
It is 50km from Esperance to the ranger station at the start of the park. Most of the roads within the park are sealed, allowing easy access all year. A park entry fee of $5 applies.

Camping and facilities
Lucky Bay campsite (furthermost from the ranger station) has several sites,

CAPE LE GRAND NATIONAL PARK

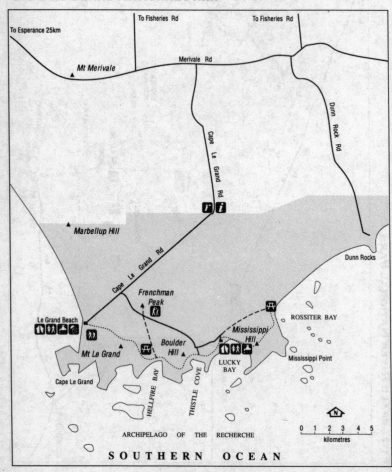

including a designated caravan area. The sites have septic toilets, solar showers, water, tables and fireplaces. Firewood is scarce so bring your own or use a gas cooker.

Le Grand Beach campsite, on the western side of the cape, has similar facilities.

Camping fee is $10 for two.

Walks and attractions

An excellent walk to appreciate most of the features of the park is the 15km (o/w) coastal track which goes from Le Grand Beach, via Hellfire Bay, to Rossiter Bay.

You can undertake separate sections, such as Lucky Bay to Rossiter Bay (5km–easy/mod) or the more difficult sections from Le Grand Beach to Hellfire Bay and Hellfire Bay to Thistle Cove.

Frenchman Peak is yet another scenic ascent. This walk (3km rtn) follows a path on the eastern slope to reach the summit and fine views. Please remember that short cuts are dangerous and can cause damage to the environment.

CAPE ARID NATIONAL PARK

The attractions at this park are similar to those at Cape Le Grand NP, but it is far more remote.

Location and access

You will need to make quite a detour, unless you are willing to take the long rough track which runs between Balladonia and Cape Arid (seek advice from the ranger at Cape Arid or Cape Le Grand, or from the Balladonia Roadhouse), as the park is 120km east of Esperance. To reach the Thomas River area, drive west along Merivale Rd or Fisheries Rd (which run parallel) to Tagon Rd, where you drive south-east to the camping area. Collect a map from the Cape Le Grand park office or once you arrive at Thomas River.

Camping and facilities

Camping areas are at Thomas River and Seal Creek. Both have pit toilets, fireplaces and tables. No drinking water is available in the park.

Walks and attractions

Tagon Trail (7km rtn–easy/mod) links Thomas River to Tagon Harbour and passes good coastal scenery.

Other walking trails in the park are detailed on the information board and brochure at Thomas River.

ON THE WAY

Most of the roadhouses dotted along the Eyre Hwy have large open areas for campers to use. For example Balladonia Roadhouse, 200km east of Norseman, charges $8 per night and has showers, a cafeteria and a bar. Expect inflated fuel prices between Norseman (WA) and Ceduna (SA).

There are two other national park regions in WA, the Goldfields and the Wheatbelt, containing such features as Wave Rock. These regions are not discussed here, but if you want to find out about them, contact the centres listed at the back of this book (Information and booking centres).

SOUTH AUSTRALIA

1. Nullarbor NP, see p248
2. Coffin Bay NP, see p249
3. Lincoln NP, see p250
4. Dutchmans Stern CP, see p250
5. Flinders Ranges NP, see p251
6. Gammon Ranges NP, see p252
7. Witjira NP, see p254
8. Mt Remarkable NP, see p255
9. Innes NP, see p256
10. Flinders Chase NP, see p258
11. Deep Creek CP, see p259
12. Newland Head CP, see p260
13. Murray River NP, see p261
14. Coorong NP, see p261
15. Little Dip CP, see p262
16. Beachport CP, see p262
17. Canunda NP, see p263
18. Bool Lagoon GR, see p264
19. Naracoorte Caves CP, see p264
20. Tantanoola Caves CP, see p264

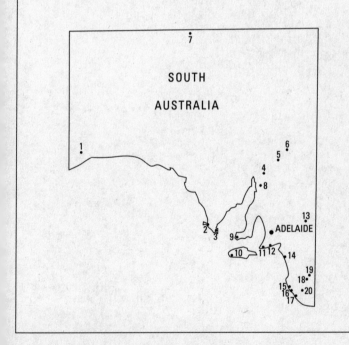

NOTE: Look through the chapter to the On the Way sections to see additional places to camp or visit.

NATIONAL PARKS SERVICE

The Department of Environment and Heritage (DEH) controls the parks in South Australia. (It was previously known as the Department of Environment and Natural Resources (DENR).)

CONTACT

THE ENVIRONMENT SHOP
(08) 8204 1910
77 GRENFELL STREET
ADELAIDE

ENVIRONMENTSHOP@ENVIRONMENT.SA.GOV.AU
WWW.ENVIRONMENT.SA.GOV.AU

REGIONAL RESERVES

Several areas in SA are classed as regional reserves (e.g. Innamincka Regional Reserve). This means they are multiple-use parks, administered and managed by the *National Park Act* but allowing for mining, pastoralism, tourism and conservation, which are regarded as land uses of equal standing.

You can purchase the Parks Vehicle Pass that allows you unlimited access to parks where a vehicle entry fee applies. This covers the camping fee if staying for less than 5 nights in any one location. Most travellers will get the best value from the Four Week Holiday Parks Pass for $18. Annual Regional Parks Passes are $120 or $170 with the desert parks included.

ABORIGINAL HISTORY

At the time of invasion an estimated 15,000 people lived in 43 tribal groups in South Australia. The Ngarrindjeri in the south-east, the Pitjantjatjara in the north and the Kaurna in the central region are the three main cultural linguistic groups in the state.

Many Adelaide-based indigenous people refer to themselves as *Nunga*, meaning 'the people'.

Tandanya National Aboriginal Cultural Institute, cnr Grenfell and Hutt Streets, has exhibitions, basket-weaving workshops and a resource shop. *Tandanya* means 'place of the red kangaroo'. The South Australian Museum in Adelaide has the largest collection of Indigenous artefacts in the country.

DESERT PARKS PASS

The landscape north of the Gammon Ranges is very dry, arid, sparsely populated and potentially dangerous if you're not well equipped. Exploration in the Simpson Desert, Witjira National Park, Innamincka Regional Reserve or Lake Eyre National Park require extensive equipment, experience and group travel with three or more vehicles.

To ensure people travel safely, the DEH legally requires you to purchase the Desert Parks Pass ($80 per vehicle) which includes maps, information and camp fees for most places north of the Flinders Ranges.

PUB PATRON GUIDE

Butcher	200ml
Schooner	285ml
Pint	425ml

Far West

Nullarbor National Park

Although this park has significant conservation value, to the passing visitor it has limited options for recreation, unless you are equipped and ready to explore.

Perhaps the most spectacular scenery, to be found without too much effort, is the Bunda Cliffs. Several roads lead off the Eyre Hwy, where you can drive in and walk to the edge of the cliffs. One of the best views is at Head of the Bight on Yalata Aboriginal land, 110km from the Western Australian border. Between June and October this spot is sure to yield views of Southern Right Whales which gather off the coast. Entry permits to this site are available from nearby roadhouses.

Aboriginal history

The Wirangu people from this area called the plains *Bunda Bunda*. Deep caves and caverns below the Nullabour Plains were occupied by Aboriginal people as long as 34,000 years ago. Rock art has been discovered in the caves.

On the way

Wittelbee Conservation Park and Laura Bay Conservation Park, only a short distance from Ceduna, are two coastal parks good for camping, swimming or just relaxing on the beach. Take the unpaved road south-east of Ceduna. Camping fees ($6 per car) can be paid at the DEH office in Ceduna or at the travel centre in Ceduna.

Point Labatt Conservation Park is

Coffin Bay National Park

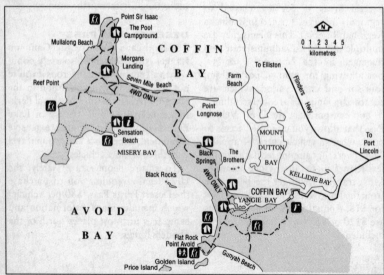

an ideal spot to view a special colony of Australian sea lions, which is the only breeding colony on mainland Australia. Binoculars or a zoom lens will enhance your visit. The park is well sign-posted, 51km south of Streaky Bay.

EYRE PENINSULA

COFFIN BAY NATIONAL PARK

This park is predominantly a coastal park with rugged cliff scenery. Con-ventional vehicles can reach Yangie Bay and Point Avoid. The road is unsuitable for cara-vans. Swimming and fishing are popular in some spots. To really explore and enjoy the features of this park a 4WD vehicle is needed.

Location and access
Coffin Bay township is 15km from the Flinders Hwy; the ranger station is a further 1km. Point Avoid is 18km from the ranger station and Yangie Bay is 15km. The road past the station is rough and winding.

Camping and facilities
Little is provided for visitors. Camping is allowed at Yangie Bay, where there is rough ground interspersed with coastal heath. Other camping areas are designated 4WD access only.

Walks and attractions
Point Avoid is a limestone headland overlooking reefs and an island. Marine life can often be seen from the point.

LINCOLN NATIONAL PARK

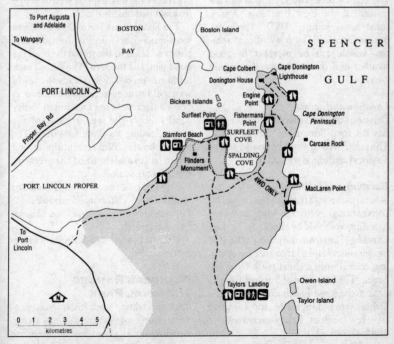

Short walks start from Yangie Bay (see information board near campsite).

Aboriginal history

The Nawu tribe occupied the south and western side of the Eyre Peninsula (including Coffin Bay). The area provided plentiful food resources including kangaroos and emus. Fire was used for hunting smaller mammals, such as wallabies and kangaroo rats, forcing them to flee from the scrub. Nondo beans, from the coastal wattle, were harvested and pigface fruit was another abundant food source. Aboriginal fish traps can be seen at a location 6km north-west of Coffin Bay, on the Horse Peninsula.

LINCOLN NATIONAL PARK

This coastal park is quite popular and is a feature of the Eyre Peninsula. Again, some areas require 4WD. There are beaches accessible by conventional vehicles which can be pleasant in good weather and there are several camping areas.

Location and access

Drive out of Port Lincoln, along Proper Bay Rd, for 10km, to the park entrance. The main road through the park, and to Taylors Landing, is well graded.

Camping and facilities

Several camping areas can be reached by conventional vehicles and caravans (conditions should be checked). Taylors Landing (7km from the main park road) has pit toilets and a large area for camping, and is only a short walk from the beach. The campsite at Surfleet Cove is near a sheltered beach and has toilets. Other areas designated for camping have few facilities. Take your own water and fuel cookers.

Walks and attractions

Stamford Hill is worth climbing to see the Flinders Monument and contemplate the vista of Port Lincoln and surrounds. Swimming is popular, but care should be taken in the open sea.

FAR NORTH

DUTCHMANS STERN CONSERVATION PARK

The Dutchmans Stern Conservation Park, 10km north of Quorn, in the southern Flinders Ranges, includes jagged cliff faces and deep, red gorges which are the home of the elusive yellow-footed rock wallaby.

From Quorn, take the Buckaringa Rd for 6.5km then turn west at the sign and travel for 3km. There are marked walking tracks for day trips as well as scope for extended bushwalks.

The Dutchmans Stern Trail (10.5km loop–mod–5 hrs) begins from the car-park and leads to the top of the bluff for good views of the area. The Weir Track (3km rtn–mod–2.5 hrs) leads to the old weir, below the eastern face of the range. For a longer walk the Dutchman Valley Trail follows the western side of the range, leading to three lookouts. The first lookout is 5km return, the second 10km return and the third 18km return, from the car-park.

Topographic maps are advised for longer trips. Camping is allowed for bushwalkers only — there is no vehicle-based camping.

Call (08) 8634 7068 for further information.

FLINDERS RANGES NATIONAL PARK

This sprawling, spectacular park provides ample opportunity for walking, camping and photography. Immerse

FLINDERS RANGES NATIONAL PARK

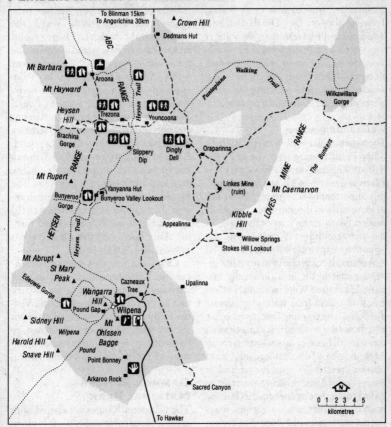

yourself in its timeless environment — in my view it is South Australia's best park. Reaching the rim of Wilpena Pound, after a long uphill climb, was one of the most satisfying moments of our entire trip.

Location and access

Turn off the Princes Hwy 7km southeast of Port Augusta. From there it is 100km north-east to Hawker and another 55km to Wilpena.

The post office in Hawker houses the national park office, so drop in for some advice when you're posting some letters.

From Wilpena, graded dirt tracks lead up into the park. It is 23km north to Bunyeroo Gorge and a further 10km to Brachina Gorge.

Camping and facilities

The caravan park and large campground at Wilpena is privately run. The charge is $17 for two in an unpowered site (phone: (08) 8648 0004). Fuel and supplies are available.

Camping in other areas of the park is

$3 per site for up to five people. Very few facilities are provided. Aroona Ruins, Trezona, Slippery Dip, Dingly Dell and Youncoona all have toilets. Aroona is the only place with drinking water available. There are many pleasant areas along the creek bed in Brachina Gorge which can be used for camping. Bins usually indicate places you can camp.

Walks and attractions

The most popular walk in the park is to St Mary Peak, to gaze over the dramatic sight of Wilpena Pound. The loop track is 17km and may take 8 hours to complete. It is important to take ample water. Try to leave early in the morning. The information board at the start of the walk, in the campground at Wilpena, lists the options for exploring Wilpena Pound.

Arkaroo Rock is one of many Aboriginal art sites in the area. From the carpark, 15km from Wilpena along Hawker Rd, it is a 3km (rtn) walk of moderate difficulty. The paintings are in red ochre and show emu and bird tracks, circles and the curved lines of a snake or serpent. According to Aboriginal legend, a giant serpent created Wilpena Pound and St Mary Peak. After drinking water from Lake Frome, the serpent edged its bulging body back to the Gammon Ranges, shaping the waterholes of Arkaroola Creek at his resting points.

Another good walk, beyond the northern border of the park, is from Angorichina to Blinman Pool. It is 12km return, and takes about 2.5 hours to reach the swimming spot at the end.

If you're up that way, the township of Blinman is a charming historic settlement to the north of the park. Food and fuel are available.

Aboriginal history

The Wailpi, Pangkala, Jadliaura and Kuyani tribes, of the Adnyamathanha lived in and around the Flinders Ranges. *Adnyamathanha* means 'hill or rock people'. The totem for the area is the bustard (wild turkey). Ochre found around Parachilna was traded to places as far as south Queensland. The ochre was highly sought after due to its shiny appearance when applied to the body. Aboriginal people call Wilpena Pound *Ikara*. The dramatic formation relates to creation stories about two giant serpents whose bodies form the walls of the pound. Arkaroo Rock, 16km south of Wilpena Pound, is a rock shelter featuring many paintings using red and yellow ochre. The Sacred Canyon site has over 100 engravings. Turn off the Hawker–Blinman Rd 1km north of the Wilpena Pound turn-off. After heavy rain the 14km track is only usable by 4WD vehicles.

Chambers Gorge is another significant art site featuring galleries of rock carvings. Display boards at the carpark and leaflets at the Wilpena Pound Visitor Centre provide information about the art sites. The gorge is reached by following a 10km rough road which turns off the Balcanoona-Blinman Rd.

GAMMON RANGES NATIONAL PARK

The Gammon Ranges are dotted with great spots to camp and walk. It is a long drive either directly from the Flinders Ranges or east from Leigh Creek, so you would need to plan on staying for a few days. The direct road leading north-east from the Flinders Ranges is rough in places but passable by conventional vehicles for most of the year. To check current road conditions call the Northern Road Conditions Hotline (phone: 1300 361 033), or ask at the park office in Hawker.

Arkaroola Village, to the north-east of the park, has supplies, fuel, a caravan park and information (phone:

COMMERCIALISATION OF PARKS

In 1989 the South Australian Government agreed to allow a $50 million tourist resort to be built within the Flinders Ranges National Park. In December 1988 a protest rally on the steps of Parliament House attracted a crowd of 2,500 protesters. The main concern about the decision was the precedent it will set for development in national parks. Regional concerns, such as the effects on water supply and endangered species, were highlighted to the government. A private company planned to build the resort 3km north-east of the entrance to Wilpena Pound. The government is currently renegotiating this option.

(08) 8648 4848). Camping costs $11 per site per night.

Camping areas are at Balcanoona Station, Arcoona Creek and Italowie Gorge. Permits to camp and advice on where to stay can be obtained from the rangers at Balcanoona Station (phone: (08) 8648 4829).

Aboriginal history

Tribes of the Adnyamathanha people lived in the Gammon Ranges and the traditional custodians are active in the care of the park. The Adnyamathanha call the ranges *Arrkunha*, meaning 'place of red ochre'. The permanent springs within the Gammon and Flinders Ranges areas were critical in times of drought. As well as a water source they were also a lure for game. As a result the springs are significant culturally and spiritually, with several waterholes representing resting places for creation beings. The last circumcision

GAMMON RANGES NATIONAL PARK

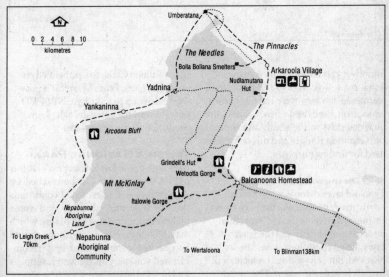

Mt Remarkable National Park

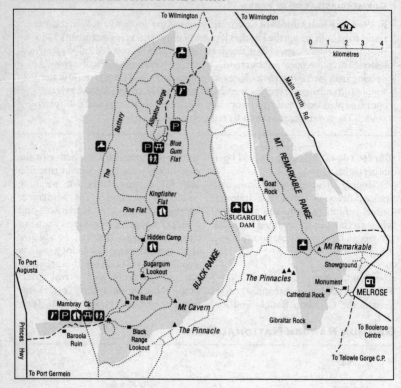

initiation ceremony of an Adnyamathanha man was in 1948. Major food sources in the area were red kangaroos, emus, fruit, seeds and yams. Large ochre quarries exist to the south and west of the Gammon Ranges and this ochre was used for trading purposes.

ON THE WAY
To avoid large detours when heading north, many people take the back roads through Marree, William Creek, then west to Coober Pedy and the Stuart Hwy. Road conditions should be checked, but conventional vehicles will usually be able to make it. The stretch from William Creek to Coober Pedy is sandy in places. From Marree it is possible to drive up to Lake Eyre NP (4WD only) to view the extensive salt plains. Again, check if access is safe.

WITJIRA NATIONAL PARK
Although classed as a desert park, this is one of the few that can be reached by conventional vehicles. Road conditions can be very unpredictable and some places require crossing salt plains, which may be boggy. Road conditions should be checked carefully and it is recommended you carry ample water, supplies and first aid gear.

The feature of the park is Dalhousie Springs, a large spring-fed pool of warm, thermal waters. Mt Dare Homestead, 50km from the springs, has camping, fuel, food and minor vehicle repair facilities.

You can reach the Springs and Dalhousie Ruins by travelling about 170km north from Oodnadatta or east from Kulgera (NT), through Finke. Advice should be sought before travelling to this park, especially in a conventional vehicle. It is a remote area and conditions can be life-threatening. A detailed map of the area is included in your Desert Parks Pass Information Pack, which you are required to purchase before exploring this park. DEH is negotiating with the traditional owners of Witjira for a joint management arrangement.

Aboriginal history
The Lower Southern Arrernte and Wangkangurru people occupied the area covered by Witjira NP. Aboriginal people called the main spring at Dalhousie *Irrwanyere*, meaning 'healing water'. The Irrwanyere Aboriginal Corporation now jointly manages the park with the DEH. Witjira refers to *Melaleuca glomerata*, the paperbark tree that surrounds many of the Dalhousie springs.

NORTH

MT REMARKABLE NATIONAL PARK
The three access points to this park are a considerable distance apart, making it difficult to visit each section. However, it is an attractive, forested area with good bushwalking opportunities.

Location and access
Alligator Gorge, Mambray Creek and Melrose are the access points to the park. Turn off Main North Rd a short distance south of Wilmington to reach Alligator Gorge (12km). Turn off Princes Hwy, 45km north of Port Pirie, to the camping area at Mambray Creek (4km). The roads to both these places are unsealed for the last part and tend to become slippery after heavy rain.

The Mt Remarkable summit walk leaves near Melrose, on the eastern side of the park. If you want to camp in this park you are better off taking the Princes Hwy rather than the inland route through Melrose and Wilmington.

Camping and facilities
A large campsite at Mambray Creek has modern flush toilets, fireplaces, gas barbecues and running water, and can cater for many campers. Booking is required for Easter and long weekends, as the site is very popular.

The Alligator Gorge section has picnic facilities and toilets. Bush camping spots in the park are reached by foot only and are closed during the fire-danger season (usually 1 November to 15 April).

Walks and attractions
From the Alligator Gorge parking area you can walk down some steep steps to explore along the floor of the gorge. The path to the right (upstream) leads into an area known as the Terraces and is scattered with interesting rocks, rippled like sand. At times the rock pools may be deep enough for a chilly dip.

From the base of the steps, the track to the left (downstream) leads you through a narrow and spectacular part of Alligator Gorge, known as the Narrows. When the water is low enough you can continue through this gorge to reach Blue Gum Flat, then back up to the car-park on a loop track 2km long.

From the gorge car-park, an easy walk to the Blue Gum Flat picnic area begins near the toilet block. This spot, which can also be reached by vehicle, has gas barbecues, toilets, tables and water.

A fee of $3 per vehicle is charged to enter the Alligator Gorge area. You can self-register at the information board near the park office.

The walk to Mt Remarkable Summit (8km rtn–mod–4 hrs) begins just north of Melrose township. It is a steep walk rewarded by excellent views over the valleys and gorges, and the rich farming land which fringes the park.

From the Mambray Creek campsite you can embark on a few good walks. The Mount Cavern Trail (11km rtn–mod–5 hrs) leaves from the picnic area and crosses the Black Range to reach the summit of Mt Cavern. For a less strenuous walk, the Sugar Gum Lookout Trail (8km rtn–easy/mod –3 hrs) follows the valley for most of the way until a short, steep path to the lookout. The Hidden Gorge Trail (15km rtn–easy/mod–6 hrs) takes you along narrow valleys and gorges, deep into the park, and returns along the high Battery Ridge, offering spectactular views of Spencer Gulf.

Longer walks generally require topographical maps and should be discussed with the ranger beforehand.

Aboriginal history

The Nukunu people lived in and around Mt Remarkable. 20 campsites have been recorded. The Mt Brown bushwalk, in Mt Brown Conservation Park, departs from Waukerie Falls, south of Quorn. The 16km loop trail has interpretive signs about Nukunu culture.

ON THE WAY

Telowie Gorge Conservation Park is a pleasant, low-key spot in which to walk. To reach the park from the north, turn off the road which links Port Germein and Murray Town. You can take the tourist drive south of Melrose to join this enjoyable drive. The turn-off is difficult to identify as there is no sign. It veers off the road just near a small creek, 9km from Port Germein and 17km from the Main North Rd turn-off. This dirt road continues along parallel with the conspicuous Morgan-Whyalla Pipeline, until a sign-posted turn-off toward the park. From the south, travel to Napperby, from where the road is sign-posted north to the park.

A 1.5km entrance road leads you to the start of the Nakura Walking Trail, an easy and enjoyable 20-minute walk alongside a bubbling creek (depending on the rainfall) which leads to a semi-permanent rock pool. If you approach quietly you may see some yellow-footed rock wallabies sunning themselves on high rocky ledges.

YORKE PENINSULA

INNES NATIONAL PARK

This park, at the tip of the Yorke Peninsula, is a popular place to relax in a coastal setting. There are several places to camp, bushwalk, swim, fish and surf.

Location and access

The park is 300km from Adelaide. Several roads branch down the peninsula, allowing you to explore the countryside. Once you reach Warooka it is 55km along a sealed road to Stenhouse Bay, where supplies, fuel, a public telephone and the ranger station are located. You can drive as far as Browns Beach on the unsealed road along the coast, before turning back to leave the park.

Innes National Park

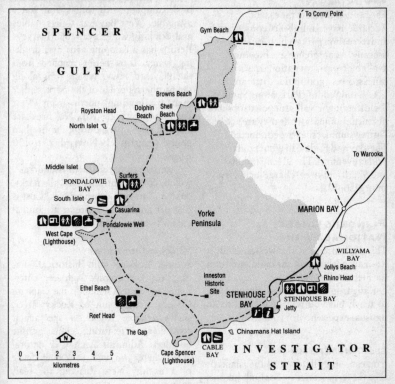

Camping and facilities

Camping is allowed at Jollys Beach, Stenhouse Bay, Cable Bay, Casuarina, Surfers, Shell Beach, Browns Beach and Gym Beach. Pondalowie Well is the main campground, with toilets and solar showers. Most of the other campsites are primitive. The map indicates which have toilets and open-air showers available. A $3 entrance fee is charged to all visitors. The camping fee is either $3 or $6 per night (depending on the site) for up to five people.

Walks and attractions

The park caters predominantly for water-based activities. You can walk to Gym Beach from the road leading to Browns Beach — 8km return and quite sandy. You can also walk from Dolphin Beach to Royston Head (4km rtn–mod). The short walk to the West Cape Lighthouse begins from the West Cape Rd car-park, before Pondalowie Well.

There is an abundance of wildlife and flora to be seen in this park.

Aboriginal history

The Narangga occupied most of the Yorke Peninsula. The Warri clan lived in what is now Innes NP. Creation stories of dreamtime figure Bulgawan relate to formations near Pondalowie Bay.

On the way

The Lofty Ranges, to the east of Adelaide, have a number of conservation and recreation parks which are for day use only. A comprehensive brochure, available from most national park offices, gives a good guide to the areas.

Cleland Wildlife Park, along Summit Rd, offers night walks for you to observe nocturnal animals while they are active. During summer they are conducted on Tuesday and Friday; in winter only Friday evenings. The $16.50 (adults) and $7.50 (children) charge includes a smorgasbord meal.

FLINDERS CHASE NATIONAL PARK

This park occupies the western end of Kangaroo Island, off the mainland from the Fleurieu Peninsula.

Kangaroo Island is an expensive place to reach but you will be treated to an unusual experience for your trouble.

Location and access

You can either fly/drive to the island or take the ferry service on SeaLink (phone: 13 13 01). The fare for two adults and a vehicle is $256 return from Cape Jervis.

The park pass for Kangaroo Island is $30 per adult, $80 family. Once on the island you can travel along the Playford Hwy or the South Coast Hwy to reach Rocky River, where the ranger station and main campsite are located. From there, minor roads lead to other attractions generally accessible by conventional vehicles. Check conditions with the ranger first.

Camping and facilities

The campground at Rocky River has showers, toilets, tables, barbecues and a public telephone. Snake Lagoon campsite, 8km from Rocky River, has bush camping with toilets and water available. West Bay has toilets, tables and drinking water available. Harveys Return has a camping area and drinking water. It is better reached from the Playford Hwy, which runs along the northern border of the park, rather than by heading north from West Bay along Shackle Rd. No fires are allowed in the park during the fire-ban period (usually 1 November to 30 April).

Visitors can purchase an Island Pass, which covers entrance to all parks, guided tours and camping fees. Cost is $15 per adult — enquire at a national park office for further details.

Walks and attractions

Several lookouts and historical sites can keep the average sightseer entertained for quite a while. In the Cape du Couedic area, south of Rocky River, is Remarkable Rocks, a spectacular coastal spot featuring giant granite boulders. Admirals Arch is a natural arch where you will to see evidence of a healthy New Zealand fur seals colony.

From Snake Lagoon a 1.5km walk leads to a small waterfall at the mouth of the Rocky River. Between Snake Lagoon and West Bay you can walk along the banks of the Breakneck River for 3km until it reaches the sea. Return along the same track.

Sandy Creek also has a walking track along its bank (3km rtn). Both lead to picturesque, sandy beaches which are enclosed by cliffs.

The Ravine des Casoars Walk (7km rtn–mod) leads to a secluded beach, from south of Cape Borda off the West Bay Rd. A steep descent on rough limestone makes the walk quite difficult in places.

Harveys Return, off the Playford Hwy, involves another steep descent along a cliff face. The old flying fox track makes this climb to the historic cove a little easier.

At Cape Borda, at the northern tip of the park, there are lighthouse tours for those who are interested in the historical significance of the place.

Aboriginal history
Archaeological evidence shows that occupation of Kangaroo Island is likely to have ended when the last ice age separated the island from the mainland, 10,000 years ago. The Ngarrindjeri and Kaurna people had the last connections with Kangaroo Island. Many occupation sites have been found, particularly around Murray Lagoon and other freshwater sources. Mainland Aborigines refer to Kangaroo Island as *Kart*, meaning 'island of the dead'. An interpretive display can be viewed in the Rocky River national park office.

ON THE WAY
Cape Gantheaume Conservation Park, along the south-coast region of Kangaroo Island, has camping and attractions at Murrays Lagoon and D'Estrees Bay. Several other areas on the island have walks and attractions. Check with the ranger for details and a guide. Seal Bay Conservation Park, located next to Cape Gantheaume Conservation Park, is home to several hundred Australian sea lions.

FLEURIEU PENINSULA

DEEP CREEK CONSERVATION PARK
One of the best places to stay on the peninsula is 13km south of Delamere. There are five lush campsites which are particularly good in summer, as they don't dry up as much as other places in the area. Most of the campsites have been recently enhanced with toilets and cleared camping areas. Turn south-east from Delamere and follow the signs to the camping areas. Trig campground has 25 sheltered sites with toilets, rainwater and picnic facilities. The Stringybark campsite has 15 sheltered sites with hot showers, toilets and drinking water. Cobbler Hill and Tapanappa have no basic facilities and some are located with superb views. Eaglewater Hole campground is on the Heysen Trail and is accessible to backpackers only. Rainwater is available at this site. Trig, Tapanappa and Cobbler Hill Campgrounds, all with toilet facilities, cost $5 per vehicle per night. Stringybark Campground, with toilets and hot showers, is $12 per vehicle per night. Eagle Waterhole costs $3 per person per night. Three holiday cabins are also available for hire.

The Deep Creek Cove Trail (6km rtn–easy/mod–2.5 hrs) departs from the Trig Campground and leads to a small cove at the mouth of the creek and provides good views over the sea and coastal terrain.

The Deep Creek Waterfall Trail (3.5km rtn–mod/hard–2 hrs), part of the Heysen Trail, is another walk which leaves from the Trig campground. It can also be started from Tapanappa lookout (same distance). Both walks meet at a pleasant waterfall which runs year round.

Information boards are located throughout the park and at the Park Headquarters.

Aboriginal history
The Kaurna and Ramindjeri people lived in the Deep Creek area. Places of

DEEP CREEK CONSERVATION PARK

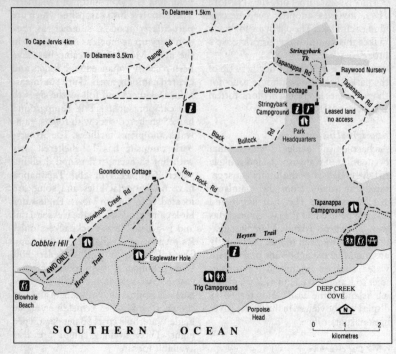

spiritual significance in the park relate to creation stories and dreamtime hero Ngurunderi.

NEWLAND HEAD CONSERVATION PARK

This camping area is situated 12km south-west of Victor Harbor. Take the Range Rd heading to Cape Jervis then follow the signs to Waitpinga Beach. A campground with toilets, gas cooking facilities and rainwater is located behind the sheltering sand dunes at Waitpinga Beach. Cost is $2 per night, payable to the patrolling ranger or the national park office in Victor Harbor. A pleasant walk to the lagoon at dusk (3km o/w–easy) will be rewarded by the sight of an abundance of birds and other wildlife drinking at the waterhole.

The beach is famous for salmon fishing and surfing, although care is needed in the water due to the rips along the coast. A pleasant walk follows the Heysen Trail along the cliff tops, offering superb coastal views before heading inland into regenerating coastal heaths and mallee (13km rtn–easy/mod–3.5 to 4 hrs). Spring time is a showcase of wildflowers on this walk.

There are great places to camp in the charming seaside township of Victor Harbor. An unpowered site at Victor Harbor Caravan Park is $9 (powered $11) (phone: (08) 8552 1142). An extra fee of $2 is charged at peak times.

Aboriginal history

The people of the Ngarrindjeri Nation occupied this area and many sites in the park relate to the Ngarrindjeri Dreaming. Waitpinga Beach was named after the Aboriginal word *Waitpiunga*, meaning 'windy place'.

THE MURRAYLANDS

MURRAY RIVER NATIONAL PARK

If you intend crossing directly between Adelaide and Mildura then this park, just south of the Sturt Hwy, makes a good stopping point. The park has three sections: Katarapko Creek, Lyrup Flats and Bulyong Island. Signs on the Highway near Berri will direct you to camp sites situated along the Murray River and connecting creeks. Camping fees are $2 per adult per night and 50¢ per child or concession per night.

Fishing, canoeing and swimming are popular recreations whilst camping. Birdwatchers will find the wetland environment very rewarding, particularly at dawn and dusk. There also many opportunities for bushwalking on the floodplain. The Kai Kai Nature Trail provides the opportunity to learn more about the surrounds of Katarapko Creek while enjoying an easy walk, and, for the canoers, a self-guided canoe trail is offered at Loch Luna Game Reserve.

Other parks and reserves on and away from the river also exist in this area. More information can be obtained from the Murraylands Regional Office (ph: (08) 8585 2111).

Aboriginal history

The Meru people lived in the Murray River region now covered by the national park. The Meru are part of the wider collection of about 18 tribes who refer to themselves as the Ngarrindjeri. Scarred trees are the most obvious signs of occupation. The scars are caused from bark being removed from trees to make shields, canoes, and carry dishes.

SOUTHEAST

COORONG NATIONAL PARK

This thin strip of coastal park stretches between the Murray Mouth almost to Kingston, South-East. The activities are mainly water-based (fishing, swimming), four-wheel driving or lazing in the sun.

Location and access

The Princes Hwy runs next to the park for most of its length. Dirt roads provide an alternate route along the way. If you're coming from Victor Harbor, an interesting short cut to the park is through Strathalbyn, then Wellington. The enjoyable ferry crossing at Wellington is free and operates every day.

From there you join the Princes Hwy and drive another 44km to Meningie where the park headquarters are located, opposite the Lions Park.

Many of the dirt tracks which lead to camp spots are passable by conventional vehicles. Several tracks in the park are for 4WD only, particularly those to the beach.

Camping and facilities

There are designated camping areas in the park. Ensure you adopt minimal-impact camping practices so that the secluded little spot you found will remain the same for others. Few facilities are provided and camping fees are $3 for up to five people. No open fires are allowed during fire danger season. Fresh water and supplies are available from Salt Creek, 60km south-east of Meningie.

Walks and attractions

This park is a popular fishing spot and there are many water ways for you to explore if you have a boat or canoe. Bird watching and beachcombing are also good activities for this area.

The Lakes Nature Trail (3km–rtn –easy) leaves from the carpark, 2km from the Salt Creek entrance. This self-guided trail provides numbered posts to identify vegetation along the way. Visit the Chinaman's Well to discover some local history from the Gold Rush days and the establishment of stock, mail and communication routes. Turn off the Princes Hwy 16km south of Salt Creek and travel 1.3km along the unsealed access road.

Contact the Meningie office for information on self-guided walking trails (phone: (08) 8575 1200).

Aboriginal history

The Ngarrindjeri Nation, consisting of 22 clans, occupied this part of SA. The Tanganekald clan lived in what is now Coorong NP. At the time of European settlement they numbered 600, occupying an area of 2,000 square km of coastline. Coorong is derived from the Aboriginal word *Karangk* meaning 'long neck', referring to Younghusband Peninsula. The Tanganekald clan lived in villages and made basketware, nets and skin cloaks, which were traded for spears, stone tools and ochre.

LITTLE DIP CONSERVATION PARK

To reach Little Dip CP take the Nora Creina Tourist Drive, south of Robe. This road is the main 2WD thoroughfare; most other tracks, which go to the beach and along the dunes, are for 4WD only. There are several quaint little camping areas which are pleasant places to stay for the night. They have a few facilities and are $3 per site. The sites are only a short drive from the Nora Creina Dve and are well signposted.

BEACHPORT CONSERVATION PARK

The tourist drive continues along to the small township of Beachport. If you drive 2km out of town (in a north-west direction) you will reach this small park where you can find basic campsites and an interesting walk around Wooley Lake, at the start of the park. Campsites are located on the edge of Lake George, which is good for swimming. Camping costs $2 per person.

Aboriginal history

People of the Boandik Nation occupied the territory from Glenelg River and the Grampians in Victoria, along the coast to Kingston, and inland to Naracoorte. They are famous for basket weaving and wood carving. *Boandik* means 'people of the reed.' They travelled inland during the winter months to escape the strong winds. Shell middens can be seen along the coast to the north of Beachport, the largest being at Three Miles Rock and Big Midden. The Boandik Cultural Centre, McCourt Street, Beachport (phone: (08) 8735 8208), open 10am–3pm daily, has a collection of Aboriginal heritage on display.

The Boandik population was decimated between 1840 and 1870. It is believed the last Boandik man died in 1904. His name was Lanky Kana and a memorial for him can be found in the Beachport cemetery.

CANUNDA NATIONAL PARK

This large coastal park, south-west of Millicent, has limited access for conventional vehicles.

CANUNDA NATIONAL PARK

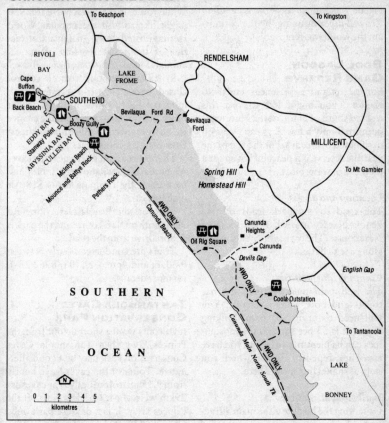

The Southend part of the park is 5km off the Princes Hwy and has an interesting walk near Cape Buffon. The camping sites near Boozy Gully are accessible by conventional vehicles. There are pit toilets and the camp fee is $3 per site. The other area you can reach is 14km south-west of Millicent, called Oil Rig Square.

Swimming is dangerous along the main beach area, but the secluded bay near Cape Buffon is safe.

Aboriginal history

People of the Drualat language group, part of the Boandik Nation, spent the summer months along the coast in what is now Canunda NP. They lived in temporary dwellings and gathered fruit and berries such as coastal berry bush, kangaroo apple and banksia honey cones. They also lived on a diet of crayfish and shellfish. During the winter they moved inland to more permanent structures and men hunted possums, wallabies, wombats and emus. Lake Frome was known as *Wringen warnap Kroand-umer* meaning 'by the cormorant the wood was removed'.

BOOL LAGOON GAME RESERVE

For a wetland experience similar to Kakadu, you might like to visit this reserve south of Naracoorte. Hunting is permitted only a few days each year on designated open days. For the rest of the year the reserve is a peaceful haven for a plethora of waterbirds.

Location and access
The road to the park leads off the Penola-Naracoorte Rd, 17km south of Naracoorte. The park is only 8km away, along a sealed road.

Camping and facilities
The well-maintained camping area has toilets and bore water available. You will need to bring you own drinking water. It is $3 per site and the mosquitoes can be plentiful, so ensure you have a net and repellent. Watch where you step, as snakes live around here.

Walks and attractions
Observing the birdlife is the main attraction. Early morning and evenings become a chorus of bird-calls.

The Gunawar Walk (45 mins–easy) is a boardwalk to Hacks Island which provides a useful viewing platform to see the many species of frogs, insects, reptiles and birds fossicking around in the reedy marshes.

The Tea-tree Boardwalk (90 mins–easy) serves a similar purpose, this time leading into the lagoon where the nests and larger birds are common.

NARACOORTE CAVES PARK

While you're in the Naracoorte area you might like to visit the popular World Heritage listed caves. An unusual attraction is the fossil remains of extinct animals found in the Victoria fossil cave.

In 1995 a unique remote control closed circuit television system with infra-red lighting was installed in Bat Cave, providing visitors with the chance to observe bats in Australia's largest Bent Wing breeding cave.

There is a camping area near the caves which has toilets, showers, tables and barbecues; the camping fee is $18 per night per car.

Turn off the Penola-Naracoorte Rd 9km south of Naracoorte and the park is a short drive from the road.

Tours are conducted hourly between 9.30am and 4pm. Call (08) 8762 2340 for more details.

TANTANOOLA CAVES CONSERVATION PARK

If you only want a short detour from the Princes Hwy then Tantanoola Caves Conservation Park may be a good alternative. Tours of the caves leave hourly from 9.15am to 4pm daily. The caves are 29km west of Mt Gambier, just off the Princes Hwy. It is a day-use park only. Call (08) 8734 4153 for details.

TASMANIA

1. Mt William NP, see p268
2. St Helens RA, see p269
3. Douglas Apsley NP, see p271
4. Freycinet NP, see p271
5. Maria Island NP, see p274
6. Coal Mines HS, see p275
7. Lime Bay NR, see p275
8. Port Arthur HS, see p275
9. Tasman NP, see p275
10. Remarkable Cave, see p276
11. Richmond Gaol HS, see p277
12. Bruny Island Reserves, see p277
13. Hartz Mountain NP, see p278
14. Hastings Cave and Thermal Springs SR, see p279
15. Mt Field NP, see p280
16. South West NP, see p281
17. Cradle Mt-Lake St Clair NP, see p282
18. Franklin-Gordon Wild Rivers NP, see p284
19. Walls of Jerusalem NP, see p285
20. Arthur-Pieman PA, see p286
21. Rocky Cape NP, see p286
22. Narawntapu NP, see p286

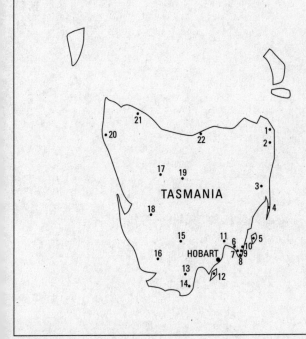

NOTE: Look through the chapter to the On the Way sections to see additional places to camp or visit.

NATIONAL PARKS SERVICE
Tasmanian national parks are managed by the Parks and Wildlife Service, Department of Primary Industries, Water and Environment.

CONTACT
INFORMATION LINE 1300 368 550
PARKSENQUIRIES@DPIWE.TAS.GOV.AU
WWW.DPIWE.TAS.GOV.AU

PARK-ENTRY FEE
A 24 hour vehicle pass is available for $10 or $3.50 per person. The Holiday Pass allows unlimited access to parks for 2 months. The $33 Holiday Pass covers all parks. Additional savings are available through annual passes for $46.20 per vehicle.

These passes allow entry to all 15 parks but does not usually cover camping and guided cave tour fees. All revenue raised from park entry fees is returned to Tasmania's parks for the improvement of visitor services and facilities.

ABORIGINAL HISTORY
Nine Aboriginal nations (language groups) occupied Tasmania before the British set up a colony on the island in 1803. The Tasmanian Aborigines were quite different from their northern neighbours, with their stature being notably smaller and their hair more curly.

Boomerangs, spear throwers and stone spear points were never produced here. The Tasmanian Aborigines did develop a distinctive watercraft; models can be viewed in the Tasmanian Museum and Art Gallery in Hobart.

Aboriginal tribes fought against the settlers for decades until the governor of the colony employed George Augustus Robinson to remove all remaining Aboriginal people and put them in a concentration camp called Wybalenna, on Flinders Island. The rounding up of people started in 1830 and was concluded in 1834. In all, George Robinson sent 220 people to Wybalenna, where most of them perished. Another group of 47 people were sent to Oyster Cove, 40km south of Hobart, where they also died. Trugganini, being the last of that small group of people, died in 1876 in Hobart.

EATING OUT
If you plan on dining out you might be wise to ensure you order before 8pm as most restaurant and pub kitchens close at that time.

MONEY
Don't rely on EFTPOS for getting fuel or cash. Establishments with this facility are sometimes hard to find, particularly in the west.

TRAVEL TIMES
If you look on maps or publications on Tasmania you will find times, rather than distances, are shown between towns. This is due to the generally winding roads. The time it takes to get from one place to another is more accurate, as speeds are restricted by the road conditions.

MAPS
For brochures and topographic maps the best place to visit is Tasmap. They have offices in Henty House, 1 Civic Square, Launceston, and in the Lands Building, 134 Macquarie Street, Hobart.

PUB PATRONS GUIDE
POT OR 10OZ   285ML

NORTHEAST

ON THE WAY
Launceston is a historic city with an impressive nature reserve within its boundaries. Cataract Gorge, near Kings Bridge, has walking trails and is particularly scenic in winter when it is in flood. From the city centre head along York St then turn right into Bourke St (past the turn-off onto the West Tamar Hwy).

Two kilometres from Lilydale, a township 25km north-east of Launceston, are the Lilydale Falls — a good spot to camp the night. Stop at the corner store in Lilydale to get a key for the showers and to pay the $3 camping fee (plus $5 key deposit). The camping area is just off the highway and has an undercover picnic area with barbecues, and ample grassy area for camping. There is a pleasant walk into lush rainforest for views of two small, but charming, waterfalls.

ON THE WAY
ABORIGINAL HISTORY
The Ben Lomond tribe occupied the region in and around the Ben Lomond National Park. They called themselves the Plangamairenaa. Occupation sites show that people chose campsites that were gently sloping and north-facing. People of the Ben Lomond tribe travelled to the coast via the South Esk and Georges Rivers.

MT WILLIAM NATIONAL PARK
This park in the north-east corner of Tasmania is a comfortable coastal area but may not be worth the detour if you're in a hurry and want to see and do more than just relax and enjoy the tranquil setting.

There is an abundance of birds and other wildlife, as well as long, empty beaches.

Location and access
The park is sign-posted from Gladstone, 16km away. The road is unsealed in parts but accessible by conventional vehicles.

Camping and facilities
Forester Kangaroo Drive leads to the four pleasant camping areas at Stumpys Bay. Each has facilities such as pit toilets, tables and fireplaces. Firewood is available from the ranger's house, as you enter the park. A donation box is provided for campers who use the wood. Bore water is available, but bring your own drinking water.

Camping is also permitted at Musselroe Top Camp — continue along the main road into the park instead of veering right toward Stumpys Bay. Deep Creek, in the southern part of the park, also has facilities for campers. The park-use fee applies.

Walks and attractions
Like many coastal parks, the best way to enjoy this park is to go out and explore it yourself. Mt William has a short walk to the summit from the car-park. It is an easy, well-graded track which provides widespread views. On a clear day you may see the Furneaux group of islands where the Strzelecki NP is located. You can fly to the island or get there by boat; camping is available for self-sufficient walkers.

Mt William National Park

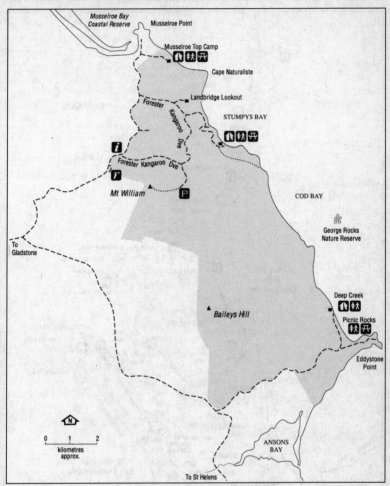

The Eddystone Point Lighthouse is an attractive landmark worth visiting.

One of the faunal features of the park is the forester kangaroo, the largest marsupial in Tasmania. Its numbers have diminished due to pastoral use, and the park was primarily set up to protect the species.

ON THE WAY

You can travel south to St Helens from Mt William National Park without returning to Gladstone and back to the Tasman Hwy. The road is unsealed but not bad. If you camp at Deep Creek, in the southern part of the park, this option is definitely worth considering.

St Helens Lands Recreation Area

If you are taking the Tasman Hwy between Scottsdale and St Helens, a worthwhile stop-off is to see the 110-metre St Columba Falls, 11km from Pyengana. Turn off 26km west of St Helens and travel 13km to the falls along a partly sealed road. An easy walk leads to the spectacular moss-clad falls.

From St Helens you have many opportunities to find good coastal camping spots. Bay of Fires Coastal Reserve — to the north along Binalong Bay Rd, then Old Gardens Rd (unsealed) — has several camping spots (Cosy Corner being one of the most popular). The sand along Binalong Bay is incredibly white. Aboriginal middens are dotted along the beaches.

Humbug Point State Recreation Area, at the end of Binalong Bay Rd, has sheltered sites and a walking trail at Skeleton Rock.

St Helens Point State Recreation Area can be reached by driving south of St Helens and turning left toward Akaroa and continuing to the camping area.

The camping is basic with public toilets in some places. For more information call Parks and Wildlife (ph: (03) 6376 1550).

Aboriginal history

The Pinterrairaa clan lived in this area. Captain Tobias Furneaux named the Bay of Fires after seeing many campfires as he sailed along the coast in 1773. Explorers noted how Aborigines would pick the banksia flowers and suck water and nectar from them. Stone arrangements can be viewed by walking south from Policemans Point for 2.5km. The arrangements are on a grass-covered ridge above Pebbly Beach. The arrangements consist of about 93 flat stones extending along a distance of 56 metres.

SOUTHEAST

DOUGLAS APSLEY NATIONAL PARK

At this stage Douglas Apsley is mainly a conservation area. However, it is well worth a visit to see the gorge, have a swim and go on an interesting walk.

Location and access

Turn off the Tasman Hwy 3km north of Bicheno. It is 7km to the car-park on a partly unsealed road. A 15-minute walk leads to the waterhole and lookouts.

Camping and facilities

Camping is allowed in the park, although there are no designated spots. You must camp at least 50 metres from Apsley waterhole and adopt minimal impact camping methods. There is no vehicle-based camping.

An undercover picnic area, toilet and information board are provided near the waterhole.

Walks and attractions

The Ridge Track (2km o/w–mod–1 hr) leads from the waterhole to Apsley Gorge. If the water is low and conditions are dry, you can make a circuit track by following the river bed either there or back. This route requires agile rock-hopping and will take about 2 hours one way.

Apsley waterhole is a wonderful swimming hole in the warm weather.

FREYCINET NATIONAL PARK

One of the finest parks in Tasmania. Freycinet can offer clear days, excellent walks and unforgettable scenery. The granite peaks of The Hazards, filling the landscape with their majestic presence, remind me of The Remarkables, near Queenstown in New Zealand.

The park has the added advantages of

Freycinet National Park

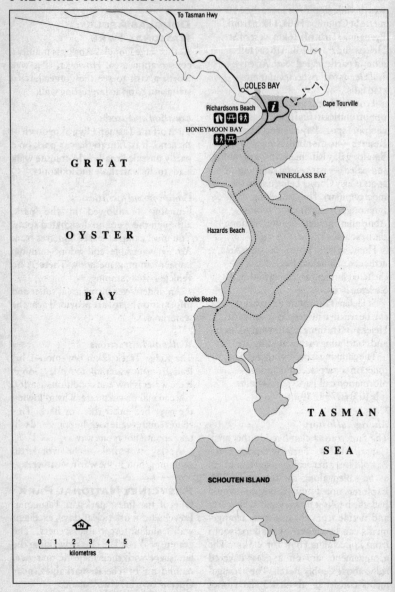

easy access, good camping and a nearby township if you don't quite want to get away from it all.

Location and access
Turn off the Tasman Hwy 11km south-west of Bicheno, or 32km north-east of Swansea. It is 31km south to the township of Coles Bay, then another kilometre to the park and the national park camping area. Within the park there are roads leading to various vantage points and beaches. The 8km drive up to Cape Tourville is steep and a bit rough but is still passable by conventional vehicles. It is worth the bumps for a great view of the coastline.

Camping and facilities
The vehicle based camping areas are not far inside the park boundary. On your left is the entrance station, where you can pay the park entrance fees and self-register for a site or pay both at the reception desk. Powered and unpowered sites, flush toilets, fireplaces, and fresh water are provided. There are no hot showers. Firewood is limited so collect your own before entering the park. This is a pleasant area with skilful brushtail possums who try to steal your food.

Picnic areas and toilets are provided at Honeymoon Bay and Ranger Creek.

Booking a site is necessary for Easter and the summer holidays (December to March).

Bushfires have been a problem in the area so please use fireplaces provided. Overnight walkers are required to use fuel stoves for cooking.

If you want to camp somewhere a little more low-key, camping is allowed at Friendly Beaches. The turn-off to the site is 12km from the Tasman Hwy or 19km north of Coles Bay. A 7km unsealed road leads to the beach. There is a basic camping area with no drinking water.

Walks and attractions
Most walks depart from the car-park a few kilometres past the entrance station. You should fill in the walker registration form before you go and remember to sign-off on your return.

One of the most popular walks, and rightly so, is to Wineglass Bay. A short, steep climb leads to views of the bay: a vivid white arch, curved around clear turquoise waters.

We did the Wineglass Bay–Hazards Beach Circuit (10km–mod–4 hrs), which is long but easy and enjoyable. The hardest section is the steep climb to the lookout where you can see Wineglass Bay, Hazards Beach, Promise Bay, Refuge Island and south along the peninsula to Mt Freycinet and Mt Graham. The walk then descends to the beach. The Isthmus Track, which follows the circuit, veers off just before the beach at Wineglass Bay. This is an easy, flat section which emerges onto Hazards Beach. Turn right and follow the beach to the end where sign-posts direct you back onto the track. The rest of the path follows the coastline back to the car-park.

There is a day-walk pamphlet, available from the self-registration station, which shows the several other walks in the park.

Overnight hikes are very popular.

The coastal area between Richardsons Beach (where the main camping area is located) and Honeymoon Bay can be explored on foot. Pink granite outcrops near the water create rock pools and crevices, into which small sea creatures scuttle and hide.

Aboriginal history
The Paradarermaa Nation (Oyster Bay) occupied the south-east of Tasmania. The Toorenamairremenaa, of the Oyster Bay Nation, lived around

Freycinet. Oyster shells dominate the middens. Some accessible middens are situated at the northern end of Hazards Beach, and can be reached by the Wine Glass Bay–Hazards Beach Circuit (see Walks and attractions for details).

MARIA ISLAND NATIONAL PARK

Maria Island (pronounced Ma-rye-a), 15km off the east coast of Tasmania, cannot be visited with a vehicle. If you can be self-sufficient on foot you should be rewarded with a fascinating visit. The only vehicle on the island is that of the ranger, so you will find a solitude not granted in other places frequented by tourists.

Location and access

The Maria Island Ferry Service leaves from the East Coast Resort. Ferries depart at 10.30am, 1pm and 3.30pm during summer. For more information ring 0418 136 862.

Camping and facilities

The ferry lands at Darlington, where you will find toilets, a public telephone, historical buildings, information and the main camping area. There is drinking water available at Darlington and other small camping areas on the island.

Walks and attractions

Many scenic attractions can be found on the island, including limestone and sandstone cliffs, sculpted with exquisite detail by wind and waves. Several old ruins from convict days were abandoned in 1852.

Aboriginal history

The Tyredemaa people, a clan of the Oyster Bay Nation, lived on Maria Island for most of the year and travelled to the mainland during the winter months. They called the island *Toarra-Marra-Monah*. The 15km journey across the Mercury Passage was done in canoes made from bundles of reed, stringybark or paperbark tightly bound together. Lachland Island provided a midway stopping point. Huts were built on the island and the dead were buried there. Ochre was one of the resources to be found on the western coastline, around Bloodstone Point.

ON THE WAY

To avoid a large detour between Orford and the Tasman Peninsula you might like to take the very scenic Wielangta Road Forest Drive. The unsealed road begins 5km south of Orford and passes the Thumbs Lookout and picnic area, and through Sandspit Forest Reserve before linking up with the main highway, just west of the small township of Copping.

The Thumbs Track (2hr rtn–mod) begins 500m from the Thumbs Lookout. The Rainforest Loop Walk (20 mins–easy) begins a short distance from the Sandspit Forest Reserve picnic area.

Not far from the road leading south to Port Arthur are some sights you may be interested in visiting. As you arrive at Eaglehawk Neck you will see a signpost to the Tessellated Pavement — a flat outcrop near the sea which has eroded into even squares like a tiled floor.

Further along there is a turn-off to Tasman Arch. Follow this sealed road to see the Blowhole or veer off to the right to reach the Tasman Arch and Devils Kitchen.

A walk leads from the Devils Kitchen to Waterfall Bay (3km rtn–easy–1 hr) passing Patersons Arch on the way.

A 10km track leads from Waterfall

Bay to Fortesque (see Tasman National Park for details).

COAL MINES HISTORICAL SITE

Port Arthur is such a phenomenally popular tourist destination that most people channel in and out of the peninsula without exploring this glorious region further. The Coal Mines Historical Site offers an opportunity to do this and provides you with a low-key bush camping site.

Just south of Taranna, turn right toward Saltwater River and Nubeena. Keep following the signs to Saltwater River and the site is only a few kilometres past the township. The Plunkett Point camping area has pit toilets, tables and fireplaces. There is no drinking water available. Camping fee is $3.30 per adult or $8.25 per family; payment is by self-registration.

Nearby are the underground prisons used for convicts who were working on the mine. Information on the history of the area is available there.

LIME BAY NATURE RESERVE

Further past Plunkett Point is Lime Bay, where you will find a basic camping area dotted by she-oaks. From here you can take an easy walk to Lagoon Bay (5km rtn) for views of Slopen Island. Lime Bay is home to the endangered Hairstreak Butterfly.

Access is by dirt road, but is good all year. Fees and facilities are the same as Plunkett Point.

TASMAN NATIONAL PARK

Another low-key spot to explore is Fortescue Bay in Tasman National Park. Turn off 4km south of Taranna then follow the road 12km to the camping area. Water is available and there are tables, toilets, fireplaces, firewood for sale and cold showers. Adults $5.50 per night and families $11.

The Cape Huay Track (8.6km rtn–mod–4 hrs) leads to an impressive view over the Lanterns, the Candlestick and Mitre Rock. This is an excellent walk revealing the striking coastline of the area.

If you want a more challenging walk you might like to seek out some local advice on how to reach Mt Fortescue, as the track is rough and some skill is needed to reach the summit, for a wholescale view of the area.

The Tasman Trail (10km o/w–mod–6 to 8 hrs), which links Waterfall Bay to Fortescue Bay, is one of Tasmania's best coastal walks. If you want a day walk from Fortescue Bay then just walk to Bivouac Bay (4km rtn–easy/mod).

For more information on the park, contact Parks and Wildlife (03) 6250 2433.

PORT ARTHUR HISTORIC SITE

Probably the most famous and visited place in Tasmania. The well-managed settlement has a great deal of information about white settlement here. The buildings are outstanding attractions themselves. The sandstone walls contrast with the neat lawns and gardens, making the place look more like an English manor than an ex-prison.

Location and access

Port Arthur is in the centre of the Tasman Peninsula, 90km from Hobart. Sealed roads lead to the park and you are unlikely to get lost trying to find it.

Camping and facilities

Picnic facilities and a kiosk are located within the site, but no camping is allowed.

The nearest caravan park is at Garden Point, 2km north of Port Arthur (phone:

TASMAN NATIONAL PARK

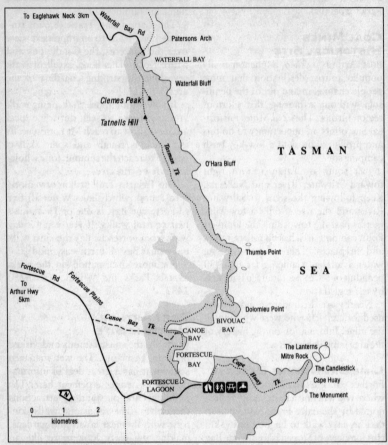

(03) 6250 2340). The fee is $15 for an unpowered site (plus a couple of dollars for the coin-operated showers).

Walks and attractions

It is $22 per adult (children $10, family $48) to enter Port Arthur Historic Site and wander through all the buildings (open from 9am to 5pm daily). Once inside you can take the ferry across to the Isle of the Dead (burial place for many of the settlement's residents). In the evening you may like to return to watch *For the Term of his Natural Life* which was filmed in the settlement (7.30pm, $5). Visitors can take a 'Ghost Tour' through some of the buildings. The film and ghost tour run every night except Christmas and New Year's Eve.

REMARKABLE CAVE

A short distance past Port Arthur is the turn-off to Remarkable Cave. Follow this road 5km to the car-park. Walk down some steps to a tunnel-like cave which leads to the open sea. When the tide is low enough you can walk part the way into the cave, where you may notice the entrance at the other end appears similar in shape to Tasmania.

RICHMOND GAOL HISTORICAL SITE

The township of Richmond is a quaint historic village only 29km from Hobart. The old gaol ($2 entry) is a digestible dose of history. I thoroughly enjoyed wandering through the old prison and being locked into one of the solitary confinement cells (serving a maximum term of 5 minutes). It is a short walk from the main street, behind the current police station.

While you're in Richmond be sure to have a look at the bridge at the end of the main street.

SOUTHWEST

 ON THE WAY

Hobart is a beautiful city to explore. Try to see the Salamanca market on Saturday, with its colourful display of craft stalls, food and buskers.

A good day trip from the city is to Mt Wellington, 20km away. Follow the Huon Hwy to Ferntree, then veer right into Pinnacle Rd.

BRUNY ISLAND RESERVES

This island playground has many attractions to make the vehicular crossing worthwhile. As well as the coastal features of the island there are some good walks into rainforest and onto hilly ranges.

Location and access

To cross to the island from the mainland, travel 30km south of Hobart to the township of Kettering. There are regular ferry crossings which take 15 minutes one way and cost $21 return per vehicle and pedestrians are free. Call (03) 6273 6725 for times. Most areas are accessible by conventional vehicles all year. Once you arrive, obtain a detailed map of the island from the information centre.

Camping and facilities

There are camping areas provided at Neck Beach, Cloudy Bay and Jetty Beach, all with toilets, tables and fireplaces. Bring your own firewood and drinking water to these sites. No fees are charged as yet. Enquiries can be directed to the ranger (phone: (03) 6293 1408).

There are supplies, fuel and telephones available on the island. Police and the medical centre are at Alonnah.

Walks and attractions

Bruny Island Neck Game Reserve, in North Bruny, features fairy penguin and muttonbird rookeries. When the birds are nesting you can see them returning to their burrows at dusk. The penguins nest between September and February and the muttonbirds from September to April. During these times drive carefully across the Neck (the narrow stretch of land between the islands) and if you are going to observe them, don't wear bright clothing.

You can also take a few marked walks to Cape Queen Elizabeth and Moorina Bay or up to Church Hill.

Once through the Neck there are good opportunities for swimming at Neck Beach or Adventure Bay.

From the south end of Adventure Bay you can embark on the Penguin Island Walk (3km rtn–easy–1.5 hrs). The walk leads to Grassy Point from where — at low tide — you can cross to Penguin Island.

Further south, Fluted Cape State

Reserve has a 2.5-hour circuit track which is steep and rugged in places.

Just inland from Adventure Bay is Waterfall Creek State Reserve. A good walk leads through tree ferns and stringybark forests to the Mavista Falls. The track can be wet at times, but the return walk should take about one hour to complete.

At the southern tip of the island is Labillardiere State Reserve. Jetty Beach camping area is a perfect spot to stay overnight before embarking early on the 7-hour circuit walk around the peninsula.

Aboriginal history

The Nuenonne clan, of the South East Tribe, occupied Bruny Island. They called the island *Lunnawannalonna*. Alonnah and Lunawanna are two place names coming from the Aboriginal name. Stone arrangements are situated along the coastline of the park. Nuenonne was the birthplace of Truganini.

HARTZ MOUNTAIN NATIONAL PARK

There are several rugged alpine walks at Hartz Mountain but no formal camping area. On a clear day the walks can be pleasant and scenic.

This is a good place to visit on the way down to Hastings Caves or just for the drive through the splendid apple-growing region of Tasmania on the way.

Location and access

From Geeveston, 68km south-west of Hobart, it is 22km to Waratah Lookout, mostly unsealed. Drive through Geeveston and west along the Arve Rd. The road is well graded and used by log trucks. Only after snow is the road impassable.

Camping and facilities

There are no camping facilities in Hartz Mountain NP. The Tahune Forest Reserve, managed by the Forestry Commission, has a pleasant camping and picnic area nearby. There are tables, fireplaces and toilets. Follow the Arve River Rd past Arve River crossing and continue straight ahead, instead of turning left toward Hartz Mountain.

At Arve River Crossing, 11km from Geeveston, on the way toward Hartz Mountain, is a pleasant picnic area. It is a large, grassy spot by the river with several picnic tables, wood and three fireplaces. A 10-minute forest walk begins at the picnic area.

Further up the mountain, at Waratah Lookout, is a picnic shelter and toilets.

Walks and attractions

A short walk leads to Waratah Lookout, where you can look over rolling forested slopes with an unusual sprinkling of stark white trees, casualties of the 1967 bushfires. Two kilometres along the road is the start of the Arve River Falls Walk (2km rtn–easy/mod–30 mins).

At the end of the vehicular road is an information board on the walks and a walker registration book. There are day walks to Hartz Peak, Hartz Lake and Mt Snowy, or shorter walks to Lake Osborne and Lake Esperance.

Walks to Waratah Lookout, Arve Falls and Lake Osborne are high-grade, dry shoe standard, with viewing platforms at Waratah Lookout and Arve Falls.

This is alpine country and usually wet underfoot. Be prepared for rapid changes in weather.

Aboriginal history

The Mallukaadee people belonged to the South East group whose territory ranged from the Huon Valley to Bruny Island and New Norfolk. The Mallukaadee occupied the Huon area and travelled to the coast for shellfish and muttonbirds, and travelled inland for plant foods and wallabies.

HASTINGS CAVE AND THERMAL SPRINGS STATE RESERVES

Having some bubbling thermal springs near a sparkling cave certainly offers a treat for the senses. Submerge yourself in the still coolness of the Newdegate Cave (constant 9°C) then shed your woollens and soak in the therapeutic 28°C of the springs.

Location and access
Travel south past Dover to Southport where you drive west to the reserves. Access is good all year and the route is well signed.

Camping and facilities
There are no facilities near the caves or thermal springs. However, 25km further south there are camping sites in the Cockle Creek and Recherche Bay state recreation areas.

Otherwise there are caravan parks in Dover and Southport.

Toilets and change rooms are near the thermal pool. Picnic shelters, tables, fireplaces and electric barbecues are also provided.

Walks and attractions
The 45 minute Newdegate Cave tours

TAHUNE FOREST RESERVE

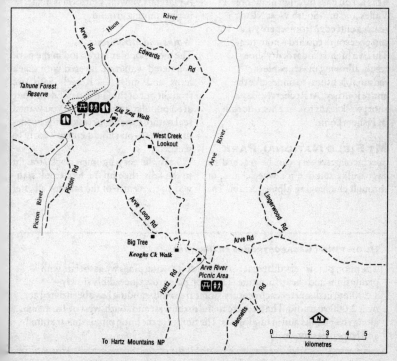

leave at 11am, 12pm, 1pm, 2pm, and 3pm in off-peak and additional tours at 11am, 4pm and 5pm during peak times. Tour price is $14.50 per adult, $7.25 children or $36.25 for families. There is a short nature walk nearby.

A dip in the thermal pool costs $2.50 for adults or $1.50 for children (families $6). From the pool you may like to undertake the Fernglade Walk (10 mins) or the Hot Springs Walk (30 mins). For more information call the park office (phone: (03) 6298 3209).

ON THE WAY

Cockle Creek and Recherche Bay, mentioned above, have camping facilities and access to walks.

From Cockle Creek you can walk to South Cape Bay (16km rtn–mod–4 hrs). You pass through Blow-hole Valley and into South West NP to reach a cliff edge from where you can peer south toward Antarctica. This is a high-standard, dry shoe track, allowing most people of reasonable fitness to undertake the entire journey. At Recherche Bay a short walk leads to some historic ruin at Fishers Point.

MT FIELD NATIONAL PARK

Spectacular scenery can be reached by easy walks suitable for wheelchairs, or through challenging alpine terrain. The park is a gem for its easy access and great scope for adventure.

Location and access

From Hobart travel along the A10 to New Norfolk and continue to Bushy Park then to the township of National Park. Cross over the railway line before the town to reach the camping ground and the ranger station.

The 16km drive from here to Lake Dobson is steep, and slippery after rain.

Camping and facilities

An excellent camping ground is located to your left as you drive into the park. There are hot showers, laundry facilities and a public phone. Fees are $6 per adult. Information (ph: (03) 6288 1526). Toilets and shelter are at Lake Dobson. A platypus viewing platform is adjacent to the camping ground.

Walks and attractions

The most popular attraction in the park is a tiered waterfall, layered with green ferns and moss — Russell Falls are straight out of the Garden of Eden. They are a popular attraction so if you want a real nature experience (minus the hordes of tourists) you should embark early to see them.

Take the easy bitumen track straight to the falls, then up the fern trunk stairway to the centre of the falls for a better

---

HUON PINE (*LAGAROSTROBOS FRANKLINII*)

The huon pine is very different from the fast-growing pines we associate with plantations and cheap furniture. The huon pine grows incredibly slowly — 1,200mm in diameter each century. Some trees still standing have been dated at over 2,000 years old. The trees are found in the west and south-west of Tasmania, along river banks and in rainforests. The timber of the huon pine is fine-textured and has a pleasant smell.

view of the top section. Quite a steep track leads to the top of the falls and you can return via a circuit track to the carpark. Otherwise you may continue to see Lady Barren Falls and the Tall Trees Walk, all well sign-posted and easy to follow. The Tall Trees Walk (750m–easy–30 mins) can be started 1.5km from Russell Falls along the road leading to Lake Dobson.

The other main walking area — a world away from the protected chambers of the rainforest walks — is Lake Dobson, in the alpine region. With its dramatic glacial landforms, it is one of few places providing easy access to a truly wilderness experience.

The Tarn Shelf Walk (mod/hard–6 hr circuit) is one of the most popular walks. Midway around the walk is the Twilight Tarn Hut, used by skiers and skaters since early this century. There is memorabilia posted within the hut.

An easier walk is to Pandani Grove (1.5km rtn–easy–1 hr), which leads to views of the lake.

Before deciding what walk to do, stop at the information office for details of all the walks and obtain some detailed maps. In the alpine region temperatures change dramatically and you should be well prepared. During winter Mt Field is a popular skiing area.

Aboriginal history

The Pangerninghe clan, of the Lairmairrmenaa language group (Big River Tribe), are believed to have occupied the areas around Mt Field National Park. Artefact finds and scatters have been found inside the park. Evidence of occupation found in caves near the Florentine River shows people were there over 30,000 years ago. White settlers reported large numbers of Aboriginal people around the Russell Falls area.

ON THE WAY

Tree ferns crowd around Marriotts Falls. Turn right off the road to Maydena, 6.5km west of the town of National Park. The walk to these falls (2.5km rtn–easy–1 hr) is unlikely to be as crowded as the one to Russell Falls.

SOUTHWEST NATIONAL PARK

This World Heritage wilderness area is mainly used by overnight hikers who are well prepared for sudden weather changes and several days of self-sufficient walking. For a vehicle-based traveller, Strathgordon and Scotts Peak Dam provide a reasonable glimpse of this remarkable country.

Location and access

Continue west along the Gordon River Rd through Maydena and the gatehouse where the park entry fee is payable and you can obtain a map of the area.

The unsealed road to Scotts Peak Dam begins 31km past Maydena. Otherwise you can continue a further 43km to Strathgordon.

Camping and facilities

If you take my recommendation and head south to Scotts Peak Dam you will find a very pleasant camping spot at the Huon Camping Area. It is a grassy place set amongst green forest. There are compost toilets, tables, fireplaces, firewood and tank waters in this sheltered area.

If you continue along the sealed road toward Strathgordon there is the Wedge River camping and picnic area at the foot of the dramatic Sentinel Range. It has toilets and an undercover picnic area with tables. While it is not ideal for tents, as the ground is pebbly and hard, it is a large, protected area just off the road to Strathgordon.

Ted's Beach, 10km further, is an exposed spot overlooking Lake Pedder. There are tables and electric barbecues.

Camping within the park is covered by the entrance fee.

Walks and attractions

The Creepy Crawly Nature Trail (15 mins–easy) is a self-guiding rain-forest walk starting from Scotts Peak Rd, not far from the intersection with Gordon River Rd. In the Scotts Peak area you can walk to Lake Judd and Mt Anne, both moderate day walks or combine the tracks into a three-day circuit walk (hard).

There is good trout fishing in Lake Pedder. The season is from early August to late April.

Aboriginal history

People of the Toogee Nation lived in this area. Red hand stencil paintings have been found in caves and some have been dated to 10,000 years making them some of the oldest art works in the world. At the time of colonisation there were two Aboriginal groups living along the rugged coast. Dome-shaped huts were built from thatched grass and sticks, lined with bark or feathers. The last Aboriginal people living in this area were rounded up in 1833 and taken to Flinders Island.

WEST

CRADLE MOUNTAIN–LAKE ST CLAIR NATIONAL PARK

LAKE ST CLAIR SECTION

Probably less known and visited than Cradle Mountain, the Lake St Clair section of the park has much to offer the visitor. The lake itself is the deepest in Australia and looks like a mist-covered moor in the cool mornings.

Location and access

Travel along the Lyell Hwy to Derwent Bridge, where you can turn toward Cynthia Bay at the sign-post and drive 5.5km along a sealed road. Roads in the area may be occasionally blocked by snow during winter.

Camping and facilities

There is a large forested area where the campsites are scattered. Pay the camp fee at the kiosk and they will direct you where to set up camp. Fees are $8 per site for two (unpowered) and $10 for a powered site. There are hot showers, toilets and laundry facilities. For inquiries regarding booking call the kiosk (phone: (03) 6289 1137).

Walks and attractions

There is ample information on the walks, including specific pamphlets, available from the ranger station (near the kiosk).

There are several day walks of varied length and difficulty, as well as overnight walks for the well equipped.

Ask at the kiosk about ferry rides, to combine walking with cruising the tranquil waters of Lake St Clair. For example, the boat trip to Narcissus Bay can be combined with a walk along the Narcissus River (2km rtn–easy), passing a picturesque suspension bridge along the way.

The Mt Rufus circuit is a popular walk for the fit and agile. It is a 6–7 hour walk and requires a good degree of fitness. For those a little less energetic, the Shadow Lake Walk is 3–4 hours return. The first part of the walk is uphill, so take time to catch your breath and you'll make it.

It is in your own interest to register

your name when going on a walk, so while you're at the ranger station getting some information, jot down your plans and don't forget to deregister on your return.

The road from the Lake St Clair section to the Cradle Mountain section of this national park passes the Franklin-Gordon Wild Rivers NP, so you will probably find yourself stopping there on the way (see entry following).

CRADLE MOUNTAIN SECTION

This remarkable wilderness area has made Cradle Mountain an up-market world-class destination with easy access and excellent facilities. For the average 'camper and tramper' the place has much to offer.

Location and access

The Cradle Mountain Link Rd turns off the Murchison Hwy 40km north of Tullah; continue another 40km to the turn-off into the park. The road is sealed to Cradle Mountain Lodge and the park visitor centre (4km). The camping facilities are on the right-hand side, before Cradle Mountain Lodge.

Most people drive a further 7km along the Lake Dove Rd to the magnificent vista of Lake Dove and the craggy mountain surrounds. This road is unsealed but not too bad.

Camping and facilities

The camping ground has excellent facilities, including two large indoor shelters for cooking, socialising and keeping warm on cold evenings. These recreation rooms have open fireplaces (wood supplied), picnic tables, sinks and hot plates. There are modern amenities blocks with hot showers. Camping is $8 per person in an unpowered site. For bookings call (03) 6492 1395.

Walks and attractions

There is an excellent visitor centre, with displays and details of walks, located on the main road through the park.

Many day walks can be undertaken from the car-park at the edge of Lake Dove.

The Truganini Track is a good, easy walk along the eastern shore of Lake Dove. From the car-park take the path to the left leading to Suicide Rock, where Truganini starts. The walk passes through rainforest and along quartzite beaches, taking about two hours return.

A new track has been built linking Truganini track to the Ballroom Forest. This high-quality track takes about two hours to complete and is good in all weathers. It features local heathland, quartzite pebble beaches, ancient temperate rainforests, a 300-metre waterfall and superb views of Cradle Mt.

Marions Lookout Walk (2 hrs rtn–mod/hard) is a good walk to undertake if you are short on time and high on energy. Follow the signs along the lake edge and then up a steep gradient to the peak where you can overlook Little Horn and Weindorfers Tower and the suspended Lake Wilks. To make a circuit track, return by the track looking down into Crater Lake, and via Wombat Pool and Thrush Forest (sign-posted 'To car-park').

Most walks in this area are well signposted. But, to be safe, fill in your details at the walker registration booth in the car-park.

Aboriginal history

The Larmairremenaa people, of the Big River Tribe, occupied this area. They called the lake *Leeawuleena*, meaning 'sleeping water'. The one hour long Larmairremener tableti cultural walk departs from the visitor centre at Lake St Clair.

> **DAMMING THE FRANKLIN**
>
> In the 1980s the Tasmanian Government planned to dam the Gordon River beyond Butler Island, thereby flooding the Franklin River and its rich banks. A massive protest ensued which few Australians will forget — 1,200 people were arrested between December 1982 and March 1983. In the federal election of 1983 the damming of the Franklin was one of the major policy issues. The case went to the High Court, which prohibited the damming, and World Heritage classification of the area soon followed.

FRANKLIN–GORDON WILD RIVERS NATIONAL PARK

The most spectacular wilderness area protected in this park is most commonly appreciated from the cruises which regularly venture along the Lower Gordon River. A few opportunities to walk within the park begin from the Lyell Hwy between Queenstown and Derwent Bridge.

Location and access

From Queenstown continue 36km along the Lyell Hwy to Strahan, a well-equipped tourist town.

Muttonbird rookeries are along a road just north of Strahan, sign-posted to Ocean Beach. This 6km road is unsealed and a little rough in places.

Camping and facilities

There are caravan parks in Strahan and Queenstown. For bush camping you can stop at the small Collingwood River camping site, which is just off the Lyell Hwy about 30km east of Queenstown. Tables, toilets and fireplaces are provided. It is also a good place to stop for a picnic.

A very basic camping spot near Strahan may be found at Macquarie Heads, 12km from town. Head toward Ocean Beach and turn left at the aerodrome. A rough, unsealed road leads to the campground.

Walks and attractions

A picnic area next to the bridge over the Franklin River is 2.5km west of Derwent

FRANKLIN – GORDON WILD RIVERS NATIONAL PARK

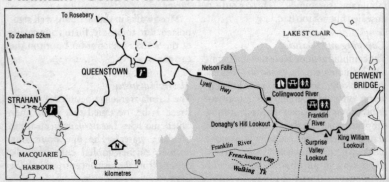

Bridge. There are toilets nearby and a short riverine rainforest walk follows the river upstream (unmarked).

Three kilometres further is the start of the Frenchman's Cap Trail, which takes experienced hikers four to five days to complete. You might like to walk the first 15 minutes to the aerial cable-way which walkers use to cross the Franklin.

Donaghys Hill Wilderness Lookout Walk begins a few kilometres further. Park your car in the cleared area and walk along the old road to the start of the trail. It is an easy 40-minute return walk and provides views over the Franklin River Valley and Frenchman's Cap.

Collingwood River is the next stopping point where you can picnic, camp or take a short walk to the Alma River Crossing.

Nelson Falls is a popular walk which begins 4km west of Victoria Pass. It is an easy 10-minute walk through temperate rainforest, ending at the gushing, moss-covered falls.

Once in Strahan the cruise boat operators are easy to find. There are half-day and full-day cruises and many other opportunities, limited only by the depth of your wallet. January and February are busy months in this area so if you intend visiting, make sure you book ahead for accommodation and cruises. The Strahan Visitor Centre may provide a valuable insight into the history of the area. An entrance fee is charged and the centre is located along the main road through Strahan (near the cruise boat operators).

From October to April the muttonbirds swarm the Ocean Beach area to breed. There is a lookout and viewing platform and the best time to observe them is from dusk to dawn.

Aboriginal history
It is likely the Mimegin and Lowrenee people of the Toogee nation (language group) lived in this area. Kutakina Cave, situated deep in the heart of this park, is one of the most significant archaelogical sites in Australia. *Kutakina* means 'spirit'. Radiocarbon dating shows the caves were used from 20,000 years ago until 14,000 years ago, when they were apparently abandoned. This area is very remote and can be accessed only by white water rafting or long distance hiking. European explorers found Aboriginal huts near where the highway crosses the Franklin River.

NORTHWEST

WALLS OF JERUSALEM NATIONAL PARK

To reach this rugged park, turn off the Bass Hwy at Deloraine toward Mole Creek. Travel along Mersey Forest Rd (unsealed). This park is mostly used by rock climbers and overnight walkers. To reach the rocky amphitheatre, at the heart of Walls of Jerusalem, you will need to stay overnight.

Aboriginal history
People of the Lairmemenairrmenaa Nation — possibly the Luggamairenernapairaa clan or a clan from the Tommaginnee–Pallitoree — lived in this area. Hand stencils have been found in caves at Kuti Kina, Ballawinne, Parmerpar Meethana and Wargata Mina. Occupational debris in these caves show use over 35,000 years ago. Several sites have been returned to Aboriginal people of Tasmania in recognition of the significance of these sites.

ARTHUR-PIEMAN PROTECTED AREA

To really detour from the tourist circuit you may like to venture into the north-west corner to Arthur River. Head south of Marrawah until you reach the unsealed section. About 8km further is a small sign directing you to the camping area. Basic camping facilities such as toilets, tables, fireplaces and tap water are provided. The nearby river is not bad for a chilly dip.

Aboriginal history

The North West Tribe occupied most of the west coast as far south as Macquarie Harbour. This tribe consisted of nine or ten clans. Of these clans the Peerapper, Tarkinener and Manegin led a semi-permanent existence along the coast in the Arthur Pieman area, with huts being constructed at West Point and other places. The tribes would have moved inland during certain periods of the year to find seasonally available food resources.

Resistance to white settlement was strong, however, in 1834 George Augustus Robinson removed the last officially recognised Aborigines of the North-West Tribe from their land. Many significant sites exist in the Arthur–Pieman Protected Area.

ROCKY CAPE NATIONAL PARK

This is a day-use park only, where you may undertake some interesting walks overlooking the strewn headlands. If you're feeling energetic, the walk to Sisters Beach is a six-hour return trip.

Another feature of the park is North Cave — a significant Aboriginal site — which is located to the right of the lighthouse where the road ends.

Aboriginal history

The Tommaginnee people of the North West Tribe occupied the area as far south as Macquarie River. They called the Rocky Cape area *Tang Dim Mer*. Caves along the coastline contain a rich collection of occupation deposits that make it one of the most significant archaeological sites in Australia. Debris from past use make it possible to trace the habits of early inhabitants, including the change in tool use, from bone tools to stone tools, and also the alleged removal of fish from the diet, while increasing the intake of seals. There are some sites accessible to visitors and featuring interpretive signs. North and South Caves can be accessed by turning right off the Rocky Cape Rd at the Rocky Cape Roadhouse. Both walks are 20min return. The South Cave walk begins at Burgess Cove and North Cave walk is sign-posted from along the road to the lighthouse.

NARAWNTAPU NATIONAL PARK

This park is a low-key coastal park which may be a good spot to stay before leaving for the 'mainland', as it is about 45km from Devonport.

Location and access

Turn off Frankford Rd just east of the Franklin River. Most of the 15km to the park is unsealed.

Camping and facilities

There are four different sites you can choose from, each with toilets, tables, fireplaces and firewood (although stock may be low so ensure you have fuel for your cooker just in case). The fee is $4.40 for adults ($11 per family) per night. Drinking water is available from Springlawn and Griffiths Point campsites.

NARAWNTAPU NATIONAL PARK

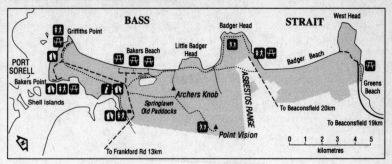

Walks and attractions
As you arrive in the park there is an information centre which has details of the walks. The beach between Bakers Point and Griffiths Point is particularly beautiful at sunset.

The park is a haven for wildlife and you are sure to be pestered by wallabies and other wildlife around your campsite.

Aboriginal history
The Narawntapu area was most likely shared between the Punnilapannaa and the Panninaa peoples even though they were from two totally different clan groups. The ranges may even have represented a boundary between the two groups.

Information and Booking Centres

This list of contact addresses and phone numbers is by no means complete because there is such a large number of work centres and ranger stations situated near the national and state parks. These will help you if you want to book in advance or, if you're in the area and need information about road conditions, campsite availability or any other assistance, you'll be able to contact the caretakers of the various parks. Some of the centres are not, strictly speaking, information centres so it may be difficult to speak directly to the ranger.

Offices move and phone numbers change, so if you find you can't get through to a centre, contact the regional office.

The addresses follow the regional order in each state and territory.

Victoria

All centres to be addressed as Parks Victoria; ph: 13 1963

South-West and Coast

South-West Area Office
Cnr Mair and Doveton Streets
Ballarat 3350
(03) 5333 6782

Forest Road
C/– Post Office
Nelson 3292
(03) 8738 4051

8–12 Julia Street
PO Box 471
Portland 3305
(03) 5523 3232

Mt Eccles NP
Mt Eccles Road
Macarthur 3286
(03) 5576 1014

214 Koroit Street
Warrnambool 3280
(03) 5562 4577

Halls Gap Visitors Centre
Grampians Road
Halls Gap 3381
(03) 5356 4381

Zumstein Recreation Area
Mt Victory Road
Horsham 3401
(03) 5383 6242

Morris Street
Port Campbell 3269
(03) 5598 6492

Cnr Cartwright and Nelson Streets
PO Box 63
Apollo Bay 3233
(03) 5237 6889

86 Polwarth Road
Lorne 3232
(03) 5289 1732

Glenelg Highway
Scarsdale 3351
(03) 5342 8503

THE MALLEE

North-West Area Office
Cnr Hargreaves and Mundy Streets
Bendigo 3550
(03) 5444 6666

6 Victoria Street
Nhill 3418
(03) 5391 1275

253 Eleventh Street
Mildura 3500
(03) 5022 3000

Wyperfeld NP
RMP 1465
Yaapeet 3424
(03) 5095 7221

Pickering Street
Ouyen 3490
(03) 5092 1322

Pink Lakes
C/- Post Office
Underbool 3509
(03) 5094 6267

Hattah/Kulkyne NP
RSD Hattah 3501
(03) 5029 3253

AROUND MELBOURNE

Metropolitan Regional Office
205 Thomas Street
Dandenong 3175
(03) 9706 7000

The Complex
Main Street
Bacchus Marsh 3340
(03) 5367 2922

Nepean Highway
Dromana 3936
(03) 5987 2755

You Yangs Recreation Park
Branch Road
Lara 3212
(03) 5282 3356

Kinglake NP
National Park Road
Pheasant Creek 3757
(03) 5786 5351

NORTH-EAST AND ALPS

57 Bridge Street
Benalla 3672
(03) 5761 1611

46 Aitken Street
Alexandra 3714
(03) 5772 1633

58 Lyell Street
Marysville 3779
(03) 5963 3306

Fraser NP
(03) 5772 1293

Mt Buffalo
Park Road
Mt Buffalo Chalet 3745
(03) 5756 2328

46 Bakers Gully Road
Bright 3741
(03) 5755 1577

1 McKoy Street
Wodonga 3690
(03) 6055 6111

43 Hunter Street
Mansfield 3722
(03) 5775 2788

Day Avenue
Omeo 3898
(03) 5159 1231

163 Welsford Street
Shepparton 3630
(03) 5831 1777

225 Pakenham Street
Echuca 3625
(03) 5882 4493

Jamieson Road
Eildon 3713
(03) 5772 1293

Main Street
Bendoc 3888
(03) 6458 1456

Corryong Office
8 Jardine Street
PO Box 71
Corryong 3707
(03) 6076 1655

**GIPPSLAND AND
THE FAR EAST**
71 Hotham Street
Traralgon 3844
(03) 5172 2111

Wilsons Promontory NP
Tidal River 3960
(03) 5680 9555

Tarra Bulga NP
Balook Road
Yarram 3971
(03) 5196 6127

Morwell NP
(03) 5122 1478

Thomson Valley Road
Parkers Corner 3825
(03) 5165 3204

18 Dixon Street
Stratford 3862
(03) 5145 6581

The Lakes Park Office
(03) 5146 0278

52 McLean Street
Maffra 3860
(03) 5147 1081

1 Lacey Street
Sale 3850
(03) 5144 3048

Lind Avenue
Dargo 3862
(03) 5140 1243

Gippsland Lakes
Loch Sport 3851
(03) 5146 0278

7 Service Street
Bairnsdale 3875
(03) 5152 0400

Orbost
Rainforest Centre
(03) 5161 1375

Buchan Caves
Buchan 3885
(03) 5155 9264

Princes Highway
PO Box 60
Cann River 3889
(03) 5158 6351

Australian Capital Territory

Centres to be addressed as ACT Parks and Conservation Service. Environment Information Centre ph: (02) 6207 9777.

Namadgi NP
GPO Box 158
Canberra 2601
(02) 6237 5222

Tidbinbilla Nature Reserve
PO Box 1065
Tuggeranong 2901
(02) 6237 5120

New South Wales

All centres to be addressed as New South Wales National Parks and Wildlife Service; ph: 1300 361 967.

*Those centres marked with an asterisk are open 7 days.

Alpine

Sawpit Creek
(Private Mail Bag)
via Cooma 2630
(02) 6456 1700

PO Box 19
Khancoban 2647
(02) 6476 9373

74–8 Capper Street
Tumut 2720
(02) 6047 0264

South-East

Merimbula
(02) 6495 5000

36 Princes Highway
PO Box 282
Narooma 2546
(02) 4476 2888

24 Berry Street
PO Box 707
Nowra 2541
(02) 4423 9800

Minnamurra Rainforest Centre*
Minnamurra Falls Road
via Jamberoo 2533
(02) 4236 0469

Fitzroy Falls Visitor Centre*
Nowra Road
Fitzroy Falls 2577
(02) 4887 7270

Central

Cadmans Cottage*
110 George Street
The Rocks
Sydney 2000
(02) 9253 4600

Royal NP
Audley
PO Box 44
Sutherland 2232
(02) 9542 0666

Botany Bay NP
Captain Cook's Landing Place
Kurnell 2231
(02) 9668 9111

La Perouse Museum
Anzac Parade
La Perouse 2036
(02) 9311 3379

Sydney Harbour NP
Greycliffe House
Nielson Park
Vaucluse 2030
PO Box 461
Rose Bay 2029
(02) 9337 5355

Blue Mountains Heritage Centre*
Govett's Leap Road
PO Box 43
Blackheath 2785
(02) 4787 8877

Bruce Road
PO Box 6
Glenbrook 2773
(02) 4739 2950

Hartley Historic Site
Hartley 2790
(02) 6355 2117

38 Ross Street
PO Box 330
Oberon 2787
(02) 6336 1972

370 Windsor Road
PO Box 198
Richmond 2753
(02) 4588 5247

Bobbin Head
via Turramurra 2074
(02) 9472 8949

Kalkari Visitors Centre*
(02) 9457 9853

Alan Morris
Suites 36–8
207 Albany Street
PO Box 1393
Gosford South 2250
(02) 4324 4911

Lot 5 Bourke Street
PO Box 270
Raymond Terrace 2324
(02) 4987 3108

160 Bridge Street
PO Box 351
Muswellbrook 2333
(02) 6543 3533

Shop 4, 79 Church Street
Mudgee 2850
(02) 6372 7199

Putty Road
Bulga 2330
(02) 6574 5275

Macquarie Nature Reserve
Lord Street
PO Box 61
Port Macquarie 2444
(02) 6584 2203

NEW ENGLAND AND ESCARPMENT FORESTS
87 Faulkner Street
PO Box 402
Armidale 2350
(02) 6776 4260

404 Grey Street
PO Box 281
Glen Innes 2370
(02) 6732 5133

NORTH COAST AND HINTERLAND
Dorrigo Rainforest Centre*
Cnr Dome Road and Lyrebird Lane
PO Box 170
Dorrigo 2453
(02) 6657 2309

Suite 9, Colonial Arcade
75 Main Street
PO Box 91
Alstonville 2477
(02) 6627 0200

50 Victoria Street
Grafton
(02) 6641 1500

WEST
105 Banna Avenue
PO Box 1049
Griffith 2680
(02) 6966 8100

154 Russell Street
Bathurst 2795
(02) 6331 9777

19 Barton Street
PO Box 453
Cobar 2835
(02) 6836 2692

56 Cassilis Street
PO Box 39
Coonabarabran 2357
(02) 6842 1311

Warrumbungle Visitors Centre*
(02) 6825 4364

165 Maitland Street
PO Box 72
Narrabri 2390
(02) 6792 4724

FAR WEST
Shop 8, Buronga Shopping Centre
PO Box 318
Buronga 2648
(02) 5021 8900

Briscoe Street
c/– Post Office
Tibooburra 2880
(02) 8091 3308

21 Mitchell Street
PO Box 18
Bourke 2840
(02) 6872 2744

PO Box 459
5 Oxide Street
Broken Hill 2880
(02) 8088 5933

Centre to be addressed as Australian Nature Conservation Agency

Park Headquarters
Booderee National Park
Village Road
Jervis Bay 2540
(02) 4443 0977

QUEENSLAND
All centres to be addressed as Queensland Department of Environment. Natural Queensland Information Centre ph: (07) 3227 8197.

SOUTH-WEST
158 Hume St
Toowoomba 4352
(07) 4639 4599

Girraween
via Ballandean 4382
(07) 4684 5157

Main Range
Cunninghams Gap
MS 394
Warwick 4370
(07) 4666 1133

Crows Nest/Ravensbourne
PO Box 68
Crows Nest 4355
(07) 4698 1296

Information and Booking Centres

Bunya Mountains
MS 501
via Dalby 4405
(07) 4668 3127

Cania Gorge
PO Box 226
via Monto 4630
(07) 4167 8162

Carnarvon
Carnarvon Gorge section
via Rolleston 4702
(07) 4984 4505

Mt Moffatt section
via Mitchell 4465
(07) 4626 3581

Blackdown Tableland
via Dingo 4702
(07) 4986 1964

SOUTH-EAST

Naturally Queensland Information Centre
160 Ann Street
Brisbane 4000
(07) 3227 8197

Burleigh Heads Information Centre
Gold Coast Highway
PO Box 612
Burleigh Heads 4220
(07) 4535 3032

Springbrook
via Mudgeeraba 4215
(07) 4533 5147

Natural Bridge
via Nerang 4211
(07) 4533 6156

Lamington
Binna Burra section
Beechmont
via Nerang 4211
(07) 4533 3584

Lamington
Green Mountains section
via Cunungra 4275
(07) 4544 0634

Tamborine Mountain
Knoll Road
North Tamborine 4272
(07) 4545 1171

Mt Glorious
C/– Post Office
Mt Nebo 4520
(07) 3289 0200

Glass House Mountains
Roys Road
Beerwah 4519
(07) 5494 6630

Kondalilla/Mapleton Falls
3 Kondalilla Falls Road
Flaxton
via Nambour 4560
(07) 5445 7301

Sunshine Coast District Centre
9 Golf Street
Maroochydore 4558
PO Box 168
Cotton Tree 4558
(07) 5443 8944

Noosa Heads NP
Park Road
Noosa Heads 4567
(07) 5447 3243

Cooloola
Freshwater 4870
(07) 5449 7959

Sir Thomas Hiley Visitors Centre
(07) 5449 7364

Elanda
MS 1537
Tewantin 4565
(07) 5485 3245

Bruce Highway
Monkland 4570
PO Box 697
Gympie 4570
(07) 5482 4189

Rainbow Beach Road
PO Box 30
Rainbow Beach 4851
(07) 5486 3160

CENTRAL COAST
Cnr Norman and Yeppoon Roads
Rockhampton 4700
PO Box 3130
Rockhampton Shopping Fair 4701
(07) 4936 0511

Fraser Island
Eurong
(07) 4127 9128
Emergencies Only
(07) 4127 9222
Central Station
(07) 4127 9191
Waddy Point
(07) 4127 9190
Dundubara
(07) 4127 9138
Ungowa
(07) 4127 9113
(07) 4127 9124
Dilli Village
(07) 4127 9130

Woodgate
PO Box 167
Woodgate 4660
(07) 4126 8810

Mon Repos
PO Box 1735
Bundaberg 4670
(07) 4159 2628

Cnr Wharf and Richmond Streets
PO Box 101
Maryborough 4650
(07) 4123 7711

Cnr Goondoon and Tank Streets
PO Box 506
Gladstone 4680
(07) 4976 0738

NORTH
Eungella
C/– Post Office
Dalrymple Heights 4757
(07) 4958 4552

Ross Courtenay
River and Wood Streets
PO Box 623
Mackay 4740
(07) 4951 8788

Cape Hillsborough NP
MS 895
Seaforth 4741
(07) 4959 0410

Whitsunday Information Centre
Cnr Shute Harbour and Mandalay
Roads
PO Box 332
Airlie Beach 4802
(07) 4946 7022

Information and Booking Centres

Bowling Green Bay/ Mt Elliot
PO Box 1954
Townsville 4810
(07) 4778 8203

Northern Regional Centre
PO Box 5391
Townsville Mail Centre
Qld 4810
(07) 4722 5211

Magnetic Island
23 Hurst Street
Picnic Bay 4816
(07) 4778 5378

Mt Spec (Crystal Creek)
Main Street
CMB 16
Paluma 4816
(07) 4770 8526

11/213 Lannercost Street
PO Box 1293
Ingham 4850
(07) 4776 1700

FAR NORTH
Far North Regional Centre
10–12 McLeod St
PO Box 2066
Cairns 4870
(07) 4052 3096

Rainforest and Reef Centre
Bruce Highway
PO Box 74
Cardwell 4816
(07) 4066 8601

Edmund Kennedy
via Cardwell 4816
(07) 4066 8850

1st floor, Rising Sun Arcade
27–9 Owen Street
PO Box 44
Innisfail 4860
(07) 4061 4291

Wooroonooran
Palmerston
PO Box 800
Innisfail 4860
(07) 4064 5115

Garners Beach Road
PO Box 89
Mission Beach 4854
(07) 4068 7183

Department of Primary Industry
83 Main St
Atherton
PO Box 210
Qld 4883
(07) 4091 1844

Barron Gorge/Davies Creek
1 Moffat Street
Cairns 4870
(07) 4053 4310

Shop 6, Mt Demi Plaza
Johnston Road
PO Box 251
Mossman 4873
(07) 4098 2188

Cape Tribulation
PMB 10
PS 2041
Mossman 4873
(07) 4098 0052

Coleman Close
C/– Post Office
Coen 4871
(07) 4060 1137

Lakefield
PMB 29
Cairns Mail Centre 4871
(07) 4060 3271

New Laura
PMB 79
Cairns Mail Centre 4871
(07) 4060 3260

Bizant
PMB 30
Cairns Mail Centre 4871
(07) 4060 3258

Rokeby
PMB 28
Cairns Mail Centre 4871
(07) 4060 3256

Iron Range
King Park
Lockhart River 4871
(07) 4060 7170

Jardine River/Heathlands
PMB 76
Cairns Mail Centre 4871
(07) 4060 3241

Queensland Herbarium Office
28 Peters Street
PO Box 1054
Mareeba 4880
(07) 4092 1555

Lake Eacham
McLeish Road
PO Box 21
Yungaburra 4871
(07) 4095 3768

Cnr Cathedral and Queen Streets
PO Box 38
Chillagoe 4871
(07) 4094 7163

INLAND
42–6 Hodgkinsons Street
PO Box 1017
Charters Towers 4820
(07) 4787 3388

Cnr Hilary and Butler Streets
PO Box 2316
Mt Isa 4825
(07) 4743 2055

Lawn Hill
PMB 12
MS 1463
Mt Isa 4825
(07) 4748 5572

Park Street
PO Box 149
Charleville 4470
(07) 4654 1255

Currawinya
PMB 25
via Cunnamulla 4490
(07) 4655 4001

Hospital Road
PO Box 906
Emerald 4720
(07) 4682 4555

Cnr Miller and Bonner Streets
PO Box 175
Taroom 4420
(07) 4627 3358

Plover Street
PO Box 202
Longreach 4730
(07) 4658 1761

NORTHERN TERRITORY

Centres to be addressed as Parks and Wildlife Commission of the Northern Territory

THE CENTRE
Sth Stuart Highway
PO Box 2130
Alice Springs 0871
(08) 8951 8211

KATHERINE REGION
Giles Street
PO Box 344
Katherine 0851
(08) 8973 8888

THE TOP END
Gaymark Building
Frances Mall
PO Box 496
Palmerston 0831
(08) 8989 4555

Centres to be addressed as Australian Nature Conservation Agency

Park Headquarters
Kakadu National Park
Kakadu Highway
PO Box 71
via Jabiru 0886
(08) 8979 9101

Rangers Station
Uluru National Park
PO Box 119
via Yulara 0872
(08) 8956 2299

WESTERN AUSTRALIA

All centres to be addressed as Department of Conservation and Land Management; ph: (08) 9334 0333

THE KIMBERLEY
Messmate Way
PO Box 942
Kununurra 6743
(08) 9168 0200

Herbert Street
PO Box 65
Broome 6725
(08) 9192 1036

THE PILBARA
SGIO Building
Welcome Road
PO Box 835
Karratha 6714
(08) 9186 8288

THE GASCOYNE
Lot 391 Thew Street
PO Box 201
Exmouth 6707
(08) 9949 1676

Small Boat Harbour
PO Box 500
Carnarvon 6701
(08) 9941 1801

Knight Terrace
Denham 6537
(08) 9948 1208

THE MIDWEST
Main Roads Department Building
PO Box 328
Moora 6510
(08) 9651 1424

SWAN REGION
Swan Regional Office
3044 Albany Highway
Kelmscott 6111
(08) 9390 5977

Banksiadale Road
Dwellingup 6213
(08) 9538 1001

Mundaring Weir Road
Mundaring 6073
(08) 9295 1955

George Street
Jarrahdale 6203
(08) 9525 5004

5 Dundebar Road
Wanneroo 6065
(08) 9405 1222

CENTRAL FOREST
Central Forest Regional Office
North Boyanup Road
Bunbury 6230
(08) 9725 4300

14 Queen Street
Busselton 6280
(08) 9752 1255

147 Wittenoom Street
Collie 6225
(08) 9734 1533

64 Weir Road
Harvey 6220
(08) 9729 1104

South Western Highway
Kirup 6251
(08) 9731 6232

Warren Road
Nannup 6275
(08) 9756 1101

Bussell Highway
Margaret River 6285
(08) 9757 2322

SOUTHERN FOREST
Southern Forest Regional Office
Brain Street
Manjimup 6258
(08) 9771 1988

Kennedy Street
PO Box 20
Pemberton 6260
(08) 9776 1107

South Western Highway
Walpole 6398
(08) 9840 1027

SOUTH COAST
Albany Regional Office
120 Albany Highway
Albany 6330
(08) 9842 4500

92 Dempster Street
PO Box 234
Esperance 6450
(08) 9071 3733

GOLDFIELDS
Hannan Street
PO Box 366
Kalgoorlie 6430
(08) 9021 2677

WHEATBELT
7 Wald Street
PO Box 100
Narrogin 6312
(08) 9881 1444

56 Clive Street
PO Box 811
Katanning 6317
(08) 9821 1296

104c Barrack Street
PO Box 332
Merredin 6415
(08) 9041 2488

SOUTH AUSTRALIA
All centres to be addressed as Department of Environment and Heritage; ph: (08) 8204 1910

FAR WEST
11 McKenzie Street
PO Box 569
Ceduna 5690
(08) 8625 3144

EYRE PENINSULA
75 Liverpool Street
PO Box 866
Port Lincoln 5606
(08) 8688 3177

FAR NORTH
Post Office Building
60 Elder Terrace
Hawker 5434
(08) 8648 4244

NORTH
9 Mackay Street
PO Box 78
Port Augusta 5700
(08) 8648 5310

YORKE PENINSULA
Innes NP
CMB
Stenhouse Bay 5577
(08) 8854 4040

FLEURIEU PENINSULA
PO Box 721
57 Ocean Street
Victor Harbor 5211
(08) 8552 3677

Kangaroo Island
37 Dauncey Street
PO Box 39
Kingscote 5223
(08) 8482 2381

THE MURRAYLANDS
28 Vauthan Terrace
PO Box 231
Berri 5343
(08) 8585 2111

SOUTH-EAST
11 Helen Street
PO Box 1046
Mt Gambier 5290
(08) 8735 1177

TASMANIA
All centres to be addressed as Parks and Wildlife Service Tasmania; ph: 1300 358 550

NORTH-EAST
Mount William
PO Box 1
Gladstone 7264
(03) 6357 2108

Flinders Island
PO Box 47
Whitemark 7255
(03) 6359 2217

St Helens
C/– Council Chambers
St Helens 7216
(03) 6376 1550

Douglas Apsley
122 Tasman Highway
Bicheno 7215
(03) 6375 1236

Freycinet
C/– Post Office
Bicheno 7215
(03) 6257 0107

SOUTH-EAST
Surf Road
Seven Mile Beach TAS 7170
GPO Box 44A
Hobart 7001
(03) 6233 8011

Maria Island
Maria Island National Park
via Triabunna 7190
(03) 6257 1420

Tasman
RMB 922
Taranna 7180
(03) 6250 3497

Bruny Island
Lunawanna
Bruny Island 7161
(03) 6293 1408

Esperance
Station Road
Dover 7116
(03) 6298 1577

SOUTH-WEST
Mount Field/South-West
PO Box 41
Westerway 7140
(03) 6288 1149

Liawenee
Liawenee 7030
(03) 6259 8148

WEST
Strahan
PO Box 62
Strahan 7468
(03) 6471 7122

Queenstown
PO Box 21
Queenstown 7467
(03) 6471 2511

Lake St Clair
Derwent Bridge 7140
(03) 6289 1172

Cradle Mountain
PO Box 20
Sheffield 7306
(03) 6492 1133

NORTH-WEST
Arthur River
C/– Post Office
Marrawah 7330
(03) 6457 1225

Stanley
PO Box 75
Rocky Cape 7331
(03) 6458 1415

Barrington
PO Box 101
Sheffield 7306
(03) 6491 1301

Mersey
PO Box 153
Devonport 7310
(03) 6428 6277

Mole Creek
C/– Post Office
Mole Creek 7304
(03) 6463 5182

DIARY OF EVENTS AND HOLIDAYS

Every year, various festivals and other events are held in each state. You might want to attend some of these, so the following list is provided to help you plan your holiday. Contact the state tourist bureau, or the local tourist information centre for festival particulars.

VICTORIA

JANUARY	Anglesea	New Year's Day River Regatta
	Cobram	Peaches and Cream Festival (biennial—odd years)
	Corryong	Nariel Creek Folk Festival
	Lorne	Pier to Pub Swim Classic
	Metung	Regatta
	Orbost	Snowy River Country Music Festival
	Woodend	Hanging Rock Picnic Races
FEBRUARY	Melbourne	Chinese New Year
	St Kilda	St Kilda Festival
	Warrnambool	Wunta Festival
	Buninyong	Buninyong Gold King Festival
MARCH	Bairnsdale	Riviera Festival
	Ballarat	Begonia Festival
	Branxholme	Bush Wackers Carnival
	Bundoora	National Folk Festival
	Camperdown	Leura Festival
	Corryong	High Country Festival
	Koo-wee-rup	Potato Festival
	Korumburra	Korumburra Karmai Festival
	Latrobe Valley	Latrobe Valley Festival
	Longford	Gippsland Vintage Tractor Rally
	Melbourne	Moomba
		Comedy Festival
		International Dragon Boat Festival
	Milawa	Wine and Trout Festival
	Mildura	Great Mildura Paddleboat Festival
	Port Fairy	Folk Festival
	Warrandyte	Warrandyte Festival
EASTER	Beechworth	Golden Horseshoe Festival
	Dargo	Walnut Festival
	Halls Gap	Grampians Easter Arts and Craft Exhibition

	Mallacoota	Easter Carnival
	Myrtleford	Tobacco, Hops and Timber Festival
	Stawell	Stawell Gift
	Torquay	Bell's Beach Surfing Carnival
	Warracknabeal	Wheatlands – Warracknabeal Easter Festival
APRIL	Bright	Autumn Festival
	Montrose	Montrose Festival
MAY	Lakes Entrance	Kinkuna Festival
	Swan Hill	Kuwayung Festival
JUNE	Ballarat	Kite Festival
	Numurkah	Octoberfest
	Rutherglen	Winery Walkabout
JULY	Daylesford	Mid-Winter Festival
	Swan Hill	Italian Festival and Fireworks
	Hamilton	Wool Heritage Week
	Leongatha	Daffodil Festival
SEPTEMBER	Airey's Inlet	Angair Festival
	Kyneton	Daffodil and Arts Festival
	Maryborough	Golden Wattle Festival
	Melbourne	Melbourne International Festival of the Arts
		Fringe Festival
		Spring Racing Carnival
	Nhill	Little Desert Wildflower Exhibition
	Silvan	Tulip Festival — Tesselaars Tulip Farm
OCTOBER	Avoca	Avoca Wool and Wine Festival
	Carlton	Lygon Street Festa
	Echuca	Echuca–Moama Rich River Festival
	Ferntree Gully	Stringy-Bark Festival
	Maffra	Mardi Gras and Agricultural Show
	Mansfield	Mountain Country Festival
	Myrtleford	Ovens and King International Festival
	Warburton	Orchid Festival
NOVEMBER	Benalla	Rose Festival
	Castlemaine	Castlemaine State Festival
	Maldon	Maldon Folk Festival
	Mandurang	Arts and Orchid Festival
	Melbourne	Melbourne Cup
	Mt Macedon	Mt Macedon Festival
	Wangaratta	Festival of Jazz
	Yarrawonga	Great Inland Boat and Water Show

DIARY OF EVENTS AND HOLIDAYS

DECEMBER	Daylesford	Highland Gathering
	Melbourne	Melbourne to Hobart Yacht Race
	Portland	Summer Festival

AUSTRALIAN CAPITAL TERRITORY

MARCH	Canberra	Canberra Festival
SEPTEMBER–OCTOBER		Floriade Spring Festival

NEW SOUTH WALES

JANUARY	Deniliquin	Sun Festival
	Tamworth	Australasian Country Music Festival
FEBRUARY	Wagga Wagga	World Championship Gumi Race
MARCH	Carcoar	Lachlan Valley Festival of International Understanding
	Cowra	Festival of Lachlan Valley
	Griffith	The Food and Wine Festival
	Tenterfield	Highland Gathering
EASTER	Byron Bay	Blues Festival
	Leeton	Sunwhite Rice Festival (biennial – even years)
	Wollongong	Easter Jazz Festival
APRIL	Albury	Heritage Festival
	Alstonville	Tibouchina Festival
	Deniliquin	Jazz Festival
	Penrith	Penrith River Festival
	Ulladulla	Blessing of the Fleet Festival
	Wee Waa	Cotton Festival
MAY	Tumut	Festival of the Falling Leaf
JULY	Ballina	Winter Sun Carnival
	Lismore	Highland Gathering
AUGUST	Bellingen	Jazz Festival
	Murwillumbah	Tweed Banana Festival
SEPTEMBER	Bowral	Tulip Time Festival
	Broken Hill	Carnivale
	Coffs Harbour	Coffs Harbour City Festival
	Forster	The Great Lakes Oyster Festival
	Lightning Ridge	Opal Festival
	Nambucca Heads	Back to Bowra Celebrations
	Narrabri	Narrabri Festival
	Parramatta	The Wistaria Garden Festival
	Walcha	Spring Arts Festival
OCTOBER	Batlow	Apple Blossom Festival
	Bellingen	Folk Festival
	Cowra	Sakura Matsuri and Cherry

		Blossom Festival
	Gilgandra	Coo-wee Festival
	Leura	Gardens Spring Festival
	Lismore	Art and Craft Expo
	Mandurang	Arts and Orchid Festival
	Manly	Jazz Festival
	Narrandera	Narrandera Treemendous Festival
	Wollongong	Put into Port Festival
NOVEMBER	Blackheath	Rhododendron Festival
	Cessnock	Greta Silky Oak Festival
	Glen Innes	Land of the Beardies Festival
	Grafton	Jacaranda Festival
	Penrith	Penrith City Jazz Band Festival
	Shoalhaven	Shoalhaven Spring Festival
	Yass	Yass Festival
DECEMBER	Glen Innes	Dundee Bushman's Carnival
	Parkes	Christmas Festival
	Sydney	Start of the Sydney to Hobart Yacht Race, Boxing Day

QUEENSLAND

JANUARY	Maleny	Maleny Folk Festival
EASTER	Warwick	Rock-Swap Festival
APRIL	Brisbane	Comedy Bonanza
MAY	St George	The Cotton Carnival
JUNE	Charters Towers	The Goldfields Festival
	Laura	Laura Aboriginal Festival
AUGUST	Cairns	Festival of the People of Australia
SEPTEMBER	Atherton	Maize Festival
	Birdsville	Birdsville Race Meeting
	Brisbane	Warana Festival
	Bundaberg	Bundaberg Harvest Festival
	Cunnamulla	World Lizard Racing Championship
	Herberton	The Tin Festival
OCTOBER	Cairns	Fun in the Sun Festival

NORTHERN TERRITORY

JANUARY	Darwin	Australia Day Giant Pool Party and Official Flag-Raising Ceremony
	Alice Springs	Australia Day Giant Pool Party and Official Flag-Raising Ceremony
	Katherine	Australia Day Giant Pool Party and Official Flag-Raising Ceremony
APRIL	Tennant Creek	Lions Goldrush Festival
MAY	Alice Springs	Bangtail Muster
		Lions Fosters Camel Cup

DIARY OF EVENTS AND HOLIDAYS

		Food and Wine Festival
	Darwin	North Australian Eisteddfod
JUNE	Katherine	Barunga Sport and Cultural Festival
JULY	Darwin	Nortrek Corroboree
AUGUST	Daly River	Merrepen Arts Festival
NOVEMBER	Darwin	Mango Harvest Festival

WESTERN AUSTRALIA

JANUARY	Busselton	Festival of Busselton
FEBRUARY	Perth	Festival of Perth
MARCH	Pemberton	Karri Karnival
	Toodyay	Moondyne Festival
EASTER	Northcliffe	Forest Festival
MAY	Carnarvon	Carnarvon Tropical Festival
JUNE	Toodyay	Western Australia Folk Federation Annual Festival, Queens Birthday
JULY	Derby	Boab Festival
	Wyndham	Top of the West Festival
AUGUST	Broome	Shinju Matsuri (Festival of the Pearl)
	Pingelly	Tulip and Art Festival
SEPTEMBER	Broome	Kimberley Aboriginal Music and Cultural Festival
	Geraldton	Sunshine Festival
	Koorda	Corn Dolly Festival
	Ravensthorpe	Wildflower Exhibition
OCTOBER	Manjimup	Timber Festival
	Margaret River	Spring Festival
NOVEMBER	Broome	Mango Festival
	Narrogin	Music Festival
DECEMBER	Derby	Boxing Day Sports
	Rockingham	Cockburn Sound Regatta

SOUTH AUSTRALIA

JANUARY	Hahndorf	Schuetzenfest
	Penneshaw	New Year's Day Carnival
	Port Augusta	Australia Day Festival
	Port Germein	Festival of the Crab
	Port Lincoln	Tunarama Festival
FEBRUARY	Coonawarra	Grape Zenolian Festival (biennial— odd years)
	Mount Compass	Compass Cup— cow race
MARCH	Adelaide	Festival of the Arts (biennial -even years)
	Port Augusta	Head of the Gulph Festival

	Port Pirie	International Food Fair
EASTER	Angaston	Barossa Valley Vintage Festival (biennial — odd years)
	Coober Pedy	Opal and Outback Festival
	Lyndoch	Barossa Valley Vintage Festival (biennial — odd years)
	Nuriootpa	Barossa Valley Vintage Festival (biennial — odd years)
	Oakbank	Oakbank Easter Racing Carnival
APRIL	Laura	Folk Fair
MAY	Clare	Wine and Food Festival, Adelaide Cup Day
	Melrose	The Mountain Fun Festival
	Moonta	Cornish Festival (biennial — odd years)
JUNE	Barmera	Country and Western Festival
JULY	Willunga	Almond Blossom Festival
OCTOBER	Andamooka Opal Fields	Opal Festival
	Burra	Copper Festival (biennial — even years)
	Goolwa	Folk and Steam Festival
	McLaren Vale	Annual Wine Bushing Festival
NOVEMBER	Adelaide	Formula One Grand Prix
	Hahndorf	Blumenfest — Festival of Flowers

TASMANIA

JANUARY	Hobart	Finish of the Sydney to Hobart Yacht Race, New Year's Day
	Launceston	Burnie New Year's Day Carnival
FEBRUARY	Hobart	Royal Hobart Regatta
	Evandale	Evandale Village Fair — Penny Farthing Race
SEPTEMBER	Devonport	Mersey Valley Music Festival
	Stanley	Circular Head Art Festival
OCTOBER	Hobart	Salamanca Arts Festival
DECEMBER	Ulverstone	Fiesta and Potato Festival

INDEX

NOTES:

Page numbers for maps are shown in **bold type**.

Names of locations beginning with 'Cape', 'Lake', 'Mt', 'Point' and 'Port' are indexed under 'C', 'L', 'M', 'P' and 'P', not under the initial letter of the second word.

Locations named after people are indexed under the first name, not the surname; i.e. Edmund Kennedy NP (Qld) appears under 'E', not 'K'.

National parks, state forests, reserves, etc. appearing on maps, whether or not they are mentioned in the title of the map, are also included in the index.

ABBREVIATIONS USED IN INDEX:

AR – Alpine Reserve
CoP – Conservation Park
CoR – Conservation Reserve
CP – Coastal Park
CR – Coastal Reserve
EP – Environmental Park
FlR – Flora Reserve
FP – Forest Park
FR – Forest Reserve
GR – Game Reserve
HR – Historical Reserve
HRA – Historic Recreation Area
HS – Historical Site
MNP – Marine Nature Park
MP – Marine Park
NaP – Nature Park
NP – National Park
NR – Nature Reserve
PA – Protected Area
RA – Recreation Area
RP – Regional Park
SF – State Forest
SP – State Park

SR – State Reserve
SRA – State Recreation Area
WHR – World Heritage Region
WP – Wildlife Park

Alfred NP (Vic), 52
Alice Springs Telegraph Station HR (NT), 182
Alpine NP (Vic), 34–7, **35**
   Bogong High Plains area, 34–6
   Cobberas-Tingaringy area, 37
   Wonnangatta-Moroka area, 36–7
Amaroo FlR (NSW), **112**
Arakoon SRA (NSW), **97**
Arltunga HR (NT), 184–5
Arthur-Pieman PA (Tas), 286
Atherton Tableland (Qld), **167**, 167–8
Auburn River NP (Qld), 137
Avon Valley NP (WA), 223, **224**
Ayers Rock (Kata Tjuta NP) (NT), **187**, 187–9

Bald Rock NP (NSW), 105, **130**
Barren Grounds NR (NSW), **73**, **74**, 76
Barrington Tops NP (NSW), **92**, 92–4
Baw Baw AR (Vic), **44**
Baw Baw NP (Vic), 42, **44**
Bay of Fires CR (Tas), **270**
Beachport CoP (SA), 262
Beedelup NP (WA), **229**, 230
Bellingen Island Flora and Fauna Reserve (NSW), 105–6
Ben Boyd NP (NSW), **64**, 64–5
Berry Springs NaP (NT), 200
Big Scrub FlR (NSW), **112**
Black Ash NR (NSW), **73**
Black Scrub FlR (NSW), **112**
Blackall Ranges (Qld), **148**
Blackdown Tableland NP (Qld), 140, **141**
Blackwood River Forest (WA), 229–30
Blue Mountains NP (NSW), 79–80, **87**
Booderee NP (NSW), 70–1
Boogarem Falls FlR (NSW), **112**
Bool Lagoon GR (SA), 264
Booloumba Creek SF (Qld), 149
Booloumba Creek SFP (Qld), 148
Boomerang Falls FlR (NSW), **112**
Boondelbah Island NR (NSW), **90**
Boonoo Boonoo NP (NSW), 104–5, **130**
Boorganna NR (NSW), 96
Booti Booti NP (NSW), 91
Border Ranges NP (NSW), **112**, 113–15, **114**

INDEX

Botany Bay NP (NSW), 78
Bouddi NP (NSW), 83–4
Bournda NP (NSW), 65
Bowling Green Bay (Mt Elliot) NP (Qld), 158
Brisbane FP (Qld), 145–6, **146**
Brisbane Ranges NP (Vic), 21, **22**
Brisbane Water NP (NSW), 82–3, **83**, **87**
Broadwater NP (NSW), 110–11
Bruny Island Reserves (Tas), 277–8
Budderoo NP (NSW), **73**, **74**, 75–6
Bundjalung NP (NSW), 108–10, **109**
Bungle Bungle (Purnululu) NP (WA), 206–7
Bungonia SRA (NSW), **72**
Bunya Mountains NP (Qld), **134**, 134–5
Burringbar SF (NSW), **112**
Burringurrah (Mt Augustus) NP (WA), 219
Burrowa-Pine Mountain NP (Vic), 37, **38**
Burrum Coast NP (Qld)
　Kinkuna section, 154–5
　Woodgate section, 154
Butterfly Gorge NP (NT), **191**, 192

Camooweal Caves NP (Qld), **173**, 174–5
Cania Gorge NP (Qld), **136**, 137
Canunda NP (SA), **263**, 262–4
Cape Arid NP (WA), 243
Cape Gantheaume CoP (SA), 259
Cape Hillsborough NP (Qld), 156–7
Cape Le Grand NP (WA), **242**, 242–3
Cape Range NP (WA), 215–18, **216**
Carnarvon NP (Qld), **138**, 138–40
Cathedral Range SP (Vic), 26–8, **27**
Cathedral Rock NP (NSW), **97**, 100–1
Cattai NP (NSW), 86
Cecil Hoskins NR (NSW), **73**
Cedar Creek NP (Qld), **144**
Chambers Pillar HR (NT), 185
Charlie Moreland SF (Qld), 149
Charlie Moreland SFP (Qld), **148**
Chillagoe/Mungana Caves NP (Qld), 169–71, **170**
Cleland WP (SA), 258
Coal Mines HS (Tas), 275
Cocoparra NP (NSW), 115–16, **117**
Coffin Bay NP (SA), **248**, 249–50

Conimbla NP (NSW), 118
Conway NP (Qld), 157–8
Coorong NP (SA), 261–2
Cooturandee NR (NSW), 120
Cradle Mountain-Lake St Clair NP (Tas)
    Cradle Mountain section, 283
    Lake St Clair section, 282–3
Crater Lakes NP (Qld)
    Lake Barrine section, 169
    Lake Eacham section, 169
Croajingolong NP (Vic), 51–3, **52**
Crowdy Bay NP (NSW), 94–6

Daintree NP (Qld), 165–7, **166**
    Cape Tribulation section, 165–7
Danbulla Forest Drive (Qld), 168–9
Dandenong Ranges NP (Vic), **23**, 23–4
Davies Creek NP (Qld), 168
Deep Creek CoP (SA), 259–60, **260**
Deepwater NP (Qld), 155
D'Entrecasteaux NP (WA), **229**, 230–1, **233**
Deua NP (NSW), 67–9, **68**
Devils Glen NR (NSW), **73**
Devils Marbles Reserve (NT), 179–80
Dharug NP (NSW), 86–9, **87**, **88**
Discovery Bay CP (Vic), **4**, 5–7, **6**
Dorrigo NP (NSW), **97**, 106–7
Douglas Apsley NP (Tas), 271
Douglas Hot Springs NaP (NT), **191**, 191–2
Douglas HS (NT), **191**
Dutchmans Stern CoP (SA), 250

Edmund Kennedy NP (Qld), 162
Eildon SP (Vic), 28–31, **29**
Elsey NP (NT), 189
Emily NaP (NT), 182–3
Errinundra NP (Vic), **49**, 49–50
Esmerelda HS (NT), **191**
Eungella NP (Qld), 155–6
Eurimbula NP (Qld), 155
Ewaninga Rock Carvings CoR (NT), 185
Expedition NP (Qld), **138**

Finke Gorge NP (NT), **180**, 182
Fitzgerald River NP (WA), 240, **241**

Flinders Chase NP (SA), 258–9
Flinders Ranges NP (SA), **251**, 250–2
40 Mile Scrub NP (Qld), 171
Forty Spur FlR (NSW), **112**
Francois Peron NP (WA), 219–20
Franklin-Gordon Wild Rivers NP (Tas), **284**, 284–5
Franklin Park (Macrozamia Grove NP) (Qld), **144**
Fraser Island RA (Qld), 152–4
Fraser NP (Vic), 28, **29**
Freycinet NP (Tas), 271–4, **272**

Gammon Ranges NP (SA), 252–4, **253**
Geikie Gorge NP (WA), **208**, 209
George Rocks NR (Tas), **269**
Gibraltar Range NP (NSW), 102–3
Gippsland Lakes CP (Vic), 45
Girraween NP (Qld), **130**, 130–1
Glass House Mountains NP (Qld), 146–8, **147**
Goldfields NP (WA), 243
Goldsborough Valley SF (Qld), **164**, 164–5
Goomburra SF (Qld), **132**
Goonengerry SF (NSW), **112**
Goulburn River NP (NSW), 84–5, **85**
Grampians NP (Vic), **9**, 10–12
Great Sandy NP (Qld), 149–52
  Cooloola section, **151**
  southern end, **150**
Gregory NP (NT), 192–3, **193**
Gurig NP (NT), 199–200
Guy Fawkes River NP (NSW), **101**, 101–2
Gwongorella NP (Qld), **142**

Hartz Mountain NP (Tas), 278–9
Hastings Cave and Thermal Springs SR (Tas), 279–80
Hat Head NP (NSW), 96, 97
Hattah-Kulkyne NP (Vic), 19–21, **20**
Henbury Meteorites CoR (NT), 185
Hidden Valley (Mirima) NP (WA), 206
Hill End HS (NSW), 118–19
Howard Springs NaP (NT), 200

Inner Pocket NR (NSW), **112**
Innes NP (SA), 256–8, **257**
Inneston HS (SA), **257**
Ironbark Grove FR (NSW), **112**
Isla Gorge NP (Qld), 137

Jessie Gaps NaP (NT), 182–3
Joalah NP (Qld), **144**
John Forrest NP (WA), 224
John Gould NR (NSW), **90**
Jourama Falls NP (Qld), 161–2

Kakadu NP (NT), 195–9, **196**
Kalbarri NP (WA), 220–2, **221**
Kanangra-Boyd NP (NSW), 80, **87**
Karijini NP (WA), 210–13, **211**
Karri Forest (WA), 230
Kata Tjuta NP (NT), **187**, 187–9
Katherine Gorge NP (NT), 190
Katherine Gorge (NT), 189
Keep River NP (NT), 193–5, **194**
Kinchega NP (NSW), 123–5, **124**
Kinglake NP (Vic), 24–5, **25**
The Knoll NP (Qld), **144**
Kondalilla NP (Qld), **148**, 148
Kosciusko NP (NSW), **56**, **62**, 63
Ku-Ring-Gai Chase NP (NSW), 80–2, **81**, 87

Lake Albacutya RP (Vic), **16**
Lake Barrine NP (Qld), **167**
Lake Eacham NP (Qld), **167**
Lake Eyre NP (SA), 254
The Lakes NP (Vic), 45, **46**
Lamington NP (Qld), 143–5
Lane Poole Reserve (WA), 225, **226**
Laura Bay CoP (SA), 248
Lawn Hill NP (Qld), 173, 173–4
Leeuwin-Naturaliste NP (WA), 227–9, **228**
Lime Bay NR (Tas), 275
Limeburners Creek NR (NSW), **97**
Limpinwood NR (NSW), **112**
Lincoln NP (SA), **249**, 250
Lind NP (Vic), 50
Litchfield NP (NT), 200–1, **201**
Little Broughton Island NR (NSW), **90**
Little Desert NP (Vic), **14**, 15–16
Little Dip CoP (SA), 262
Lower Glenelg NP (Vic), 3–5, **4**, **6**
Lumholz NP (Qld), 161

MacDonald NP (Qld), 144
Macquarie Pass NP (NSW), **73**, 77
Macrozamia Grove NP (Franklin Park) (Qld), **144**
Magnetic Island NP (Qld), 158–9
Main Range NP (Qld), 131–2, **132**
Mapleton Falls NP (Qld), 148, **148**
Maria Island NP (Tas), 274–5
Marramarra NP (NSW), 85
Mebbin Lagoons FlR (NSW), **112**
Mebbin SF (NSW), **112**
Melba Gully SP (Vic), **12**
Millstream-Chichester NP (WA), 213–15, **214**
Millstream Falls NP (Qld), 171
Mimosa Rocks NP (NSW), 65–6, **66**
Minyon Falls FlR (NSW), **112**
Mirima NP (WA), 206
Mitchell River NP (Vic), 42–4
Mon Repos CoP (Qld), 155
Monkey Mia Reserve (WA), 220
Mootwingee NP (NSW), 120, 125–6
Mornington Peninsula NP (Vic), 24
Morton NP (NSW), 72, 72–5, **73**
Morwell NP (Vic), 42, **43**
Mt Arapiles-Tooan SP (Vic), **14**, 17
Mt Augustus (Burringurrah) NP (WA), 219
Mt Barney NP (Qld), 133, **133**
Mt Brown CoP (SA), 256
Mt Buffalo NP (Vic), 31–4, **33**
Mt Eccles NP (Vic), 7–10, **8**
Mt Field NP (Tas), 280–1
Mt Frankland NP (WA), 231–2, **233**
Mt Grenfell HS (NSW), 121
Mt Hyland NR (NSW), **101**
Mt Hypipamee NP (Qld), **167**, 169
Mt Kaputar NP (NSW), 120–1, **122**
Mt Remarkable NP (SA), **254**, 255–6
Mt Richmond NP (Vic), **6**, 7
Mt Samaria SP (Vic), 31, **32**
Mt Spec NP (Qld), 159–61, **160**
Mt Warning NP (NSW), **112**, 113
Mt William NP (Tas), 268–71, **269**
Munghom Gap NR (NSW), **85**
Mungo NP (NSW), 121–3
Murramarang NP (NSW), **69**, 69–70

Murray-Kulkyne RP (Vic), **20**
Murray River NP (SA), 261
Murray-Sunset NP (Vic), 18–19, **19**
Musselroe Bay CR (Tas), **269**
Mutton Bird Island NR (NSW), **97**
Myall Lakes NP (NSW), **90**, 90–1

Namadgi NP (ACT), 55–7, **56**
Nambung NP (WA), 222–3
Naracoorte Caves Park (SA), 264
Narawntapu NP (Tas), 286–7, **287**
Natural Arch NP (Qld), **142**
N'Dhala Gorge NaP (NT), 184
New England NP (NSW), **97**, 99–100
Newland Head CoP (SA), 260–1
Nightcap NP (NSW), 111–12, **112**
Ningaloo MP (WA), 217
Nitmiluk NP (NT), 189
Noosa NP (Qld), 149, **150**
Nullarbor NP (SA), 248–9
Nullum SF (NSW), **112**
Numinbah SF (Qld), **142**

Olgas (NT), **187**, 187–9
Organ Pipes NP (Vic), 21–3
Otway NP (Vic), **12**, 13–15
Oxley Wild Rivers NP (NSW), **97**, 98–9

Palm Grove NP (Qld), **144**
Panorama Point NP (Qld), **144**
Parnella CR (Tas), **270**
Parr SRA (NSW), **88**
Point Labatt CoP (SA), 249
Point Quobba CR (WA), 217
Porcupine Gorge NP (Qld), 163, 171–3, **172**
Porongurup NP (WA), 236, **237**
Port Arthur HS (Tas), 275
Port Campbell NP (Vic), **11**, 12–13
Purnululu (Bungle Bungle) NP (WA), 206–7

Queen Mary Falls NP (Qld), 131

Rainbow Valley CoR (NT), 185
Red Rocks NR (NSW), **73**
Remarkable Cave (Tas), 276–7
Richmond Gaol HS (Tas), 277

Roadway NR (NSW), **73**
Robertson NR (NSW), **73**
Rocky Cape NP (Tas), 286
Royal NP (NSW), **76**, 77–8, **87**

St Helens Lands RA (Tas), **269**
St Helens Point SRA (Tas), **270**
Seal Bay CoP (SA), 259
Seal Rocks NR (NSW), **90**
Serpentine NP (WA), 224
Seven Mile Beach NP (NSW), 71
Shady Camp Reserve (NT), 199
Shannon NP (WA), **229**, 231
Snowy River NP (Vic), 45–9, **47**
Southwest NP (Tas), 281–2
Springbrook NP (Qld), 140–3, **142**
Stirling Range NP (WA), 236–40, **238**
Stokes NP (WA), 240
Sturt NP (NSW), 126
Sundown NP (Qld), **130**, 131
Sydenham Inlet–Cape Conran CR (Vic), 50–1
Sydney Harbour NP (NSW), 78–9

Tabletop HS (NT), **191**
Tahune FR (Tas), **279**
Tamborine Mountain NP (Qld), **144**, 145
Tantanoola Caves CoP (SA), 264
Tarra-Bulga NP (Vic), 40–1, **41**
Tasman NP (Tas), 275, **276**
Telowie Gorge CoP (SA), 256
Thirlmere Lakes NP (NSW), 77
Throsby Park HS (NSW), **73**
Tidbinbilla NR (ACT), **56**, 57
Tomaree NP (NSW), 90
Torndirrup NP (WA), 234–6, **235**
Trephina Gorge NaP (NT), **183**, 183–4
Tunnel Creek NP (WA), **208**, 209

Uluru-Kata Tjuta NP (NT), **187**, 187–9
Umbrawarra Gorge NP (NT), 191
Undara Volcanic NP (Qld), 171
Upper Big River Valley SF (Vic), **26**
Upper Goulburn HRA (Vic), 29–31, **30**

Wadbilliga NP (NSW), **67**, 67
Walls of Jerusalem NP (Tas), 285

Walpole-Nornalup NP (WA), 232–4, **233**
Walyunga NP (WA), 223–4, **224**
Warrabah NP (NSW), 120
Warren NP, (WA), **229**, 230
Warrie NP (Qld), **142**
Warrumbungle NP (NSW), 119–20
Washpool NP (NSW), 103–4, **104**
Watarrka NP (NT), 186–7
Weddin Mountains NP (NSW), 116–18, **118**
Wellington Forest (WA), 227
Werrikimbe NP (NSW), 94, **97**, 97–8
West Cape Howe NP (WA), 234
West MacDonnells NP (NT), **180**, 180–2, 186
Wheatbelt NP (WA), 243
Whian Whian SF (NSW), 111, **112**
Wildman Reserve (NT), 199
Willandra NP (NSW), 123
William Bay NP (WA), 234
Wilsons Promontory NP (Vic), 38–40, 39
Windjana Gorge NP (WA), **208**, 210
Witches Falls NP (Qld), **144**
Witjira NP (SA), 254–5
Wittelbee CoP (SA), 248
Woko Bay NP (NSW), **95**
Woko NP (NSW), 94
Wolfe Creek Meteorite Crater NP (WA), 207–9
Wollemi NP (NSW), 86, **87**
Wooroonooran NP (Qld)
 Bellingen Ker section, 163–4
 Palmerston section, 162–4, **163**
Wyperfeld NP (Vic), **16**, 17–18
Wyrrabalong NP (NSW), 84

Yalgorup NP (WA), 225
Yauchep NP (WA), 224
Yengo NP (NSW), **88**, 89–90
Yuraygir NP (NSW), 107–8, **108**

Available from Random House Australia

Priceless – The Vanishing Beauty of a Fragile Planet
Bradley Trevor Grieve with images by Mitsuaki Iwago

The world is as delicate and as complicated as a spider's web. If you touch one thread, you send shudders running through all the other threads. We are not just touching the web, we are tearing great holes in it. GERALD DURRELL

Most people know of numerous exotic animals, from dinosaurs to dodoes, that no longer exist. But international bestselling author Bradley Trevor Grieve (BTG) would like everyone to discover the extraordinary creatures that can still be saved from extinction – and then do something about it.

With a simple, poetic narrative that is inspiring and at times even amusing, accompanied by stunning photographs of gorillas, humpback whales, tigers, koalas, king birds of paradise and more, BTG and renowned wildlife photographer Mitsuaki Iwago showcase the earth's magnificent and diverse animal inventory. They highlight species that once were plentiful, but now are scarce – some that are tragically close to extinction – and point out the specific dangers these animals face and the fate we all share with them.

Priceless is a must-have book for animal lovers and fans of Bradley Trevor Grieve, along with everyone interested in premium wildlife photography, the environment, biodiversity and indeed, all life on earth.

Also by Bradley Trevor Grieve: *The Blue Day Book, The Blue Day Journal, Dear Mum, Looking for Mr Right* and *The Meaning of Life.*

Available from Random House Australia

The Tree in Changing Light
Roger McDonald

The Tree in Changing Light is the moving and personal statement of a writer about his relationship with the land, with language, with memory and with Australia's cultural and literary heritage.

Roger McDonald meditates on our unique landscape and its rich tapestry of native and introduced trees, which 'give language to our existence'. His most intimate and personal book to date, it also celebrates country men like his grandfather Chester Bucknall, a forester and pine-planter, of whom he writes, 'I believe him to have been a dreamer about trees.'

Here too are historical vignettes of a landscape husbanded for many centuries by Aborigines, yet swiftly and irrevocably changed by European settlement; encounters with poets and painters inspired by trees; tales of ordinary people for whom trees are talismanic; and interwoven throughout are autobiographical sketches, slices of family history and episodes from Roger McDonald's own life as a writer and sometime planter of trees. An unusual and beautiful book by the internationally acclaimed, bestselling author of *Mr Darwin's Shooter*.

'... distinguished by a delicacy of evocation, by an expert manipulation of tone and by obvious passion for the subject ... It reveals an unusual facet of a gifted writer's sensibility.'
ANDREW REIMER, *SYDNEY MORNING HERALD*.